KT-172-262

# THE ARDEN SHAKESPEARE

**GENERAL EDITORS:**
**RICHARD PROUDFOOT, ANN THOMPSON**
**and DAVID SCOTT KASTAN**

## THE SECOND PART OF
## KING HENRY IV

# THE ARDEN SHAKESPEARE

All's Well That Ends Well: edited by G. K. Hunter
Antony and Cleopatra: edited by John Wilders*
As You Like It: edited by Agnes Latham
The Comedy of Errors: edited by R. A. Foakes
Coriolanus: edited by Philip Brockbank
Cymbeline: edited by J. M. Nosworthy
Hamlet: edited by Harold Jenkins
Julius Caesar: edited by T. S. Dorsch
King Henry IV, Parts 1 & 2: edited by A. R. Humphreys
King Henry V: edited by T. W. Craik*
King Henry VI, Parts 1, 2 & 3: edited by A. S. Cairncross
King Henry VIII: edited by R. A. Foakes
King John: edited by E. A. J. Honigmann
King Lear: edited by Kenneth Muir
King Richard II: edited by Peter Ure
King Richard III: edited by Antony Hammond
Love's Labour's Lost: edited by Richard David
Macbeth: edited by Kenneth Muir
Measure for Measure: edited by J. W. Lever
The Merchant of Venice: edited by John Russell Brown
The Merry Wives of Windsor: edited by H. J. Oliver
A Midsummer Night's Dream: edited by Harold F. Brooks
Much Ado About Nothing: edited by A. R. Humphreys
Othello: edited by M. R. Ridley
Pericles: edited by F. D. Hoeniger
The Poems: edited by F. T. Prince
Romeo and Juliet: edited by Brian Gibbons
The Taming of the Shrew: edited by Brian Morris
The Tempest: edited by Frank Kermode
Timon of Athens: edited by H. J. Oliver
Titus Andronicus: edited by Jonathan Bate*
Troilus and Cressida: edited by K. J. Palmer
Twelfth Night: edited by J. M. Lothian and T. W. Craik
The Two Gentlemen of Verona: edited by Clifford Leech
The Winter's Tale: edited by J. H. P. Pafford

\* Third Series

THE ARDEN EDITION OF THE
WORKS OF WILLIAM SHAKESPEARE

# THE SECOND PART OF
# KING HENRY IV

Edited by
A. R. HUMPHREYS

LONDON and NEW YORK

The general editors of the Arden Shakespeare have been

*First Series*
W. J. Craig (1899–1906) and R. H. Case (1909–44)

*Second Series*
Una Ellis-Fermor (1946–58), Harold F. Brooks (1952–82),
Harold Jenkins (1958–82) and Brian Morris (1975–82)

*Third Series*
Richard Proudfoot, Ann Thompson and David Scott Kastan

This edition of *King Henry IV, Part II*, by A. R. Humphreys,
first published in 1966 by
Methuen & Co. Ltd
Reprinted 1966

First published as a University Paperback in 1967
Reprinted seven times

Reprinted 1988, 1989, 1991, 1993, 1994, 1996
by Routledge
11 New Fetter Lane, London EC4P 4EE
29 West 35th Street, New York, NY 10001

Editorial matter © 1966 Methuen & Co. Ltd

ISBN (hardback) 0 415 02721 7
ISBN (paperback) 0 415 02688 1

Printed in England by Clays Ltd, St Ives plc

For Louis and Frances Wright,
and Christopher

... Though the Fox and subtill Alchimist,
Long intermitted could not quite be mist,
Though these have sham'd all the Ancients, and might raise
Their Authours merit with a crowne of Bayes,
Yet these sometimes, even at a friends desire
Acted, have scarce defrai'd the Seacoale fire
And doore-keepers: when let but *Falstaffe* come,
*Hall, Poines*, the rest you scarce shall have a roome
All is so pester'd.

> Leonard Digges, *Vpon Master William Shakespeare*, prefacing Shakespeare's *Poems*, 1640

It is not very grateful to consider how little the succession of editors has added to this authour's power of pleasing. He was read, admired, studied, and imitated, while he was yet deformed with all the improprieties which ignorance and neglect could accumulate upon him; while the reading was not yet rectified, nor his allusions understood; yet then did Dryden pronounce, that Shakespeare was the man who, of all modern and perhaps ancient poets, had the largest and most comprehensive soul.

> Samuel Johnson, Preface to *The Plays of William Shakespeare*, 1765

Him we may profess rather to feel than to understand; and it is safer to say, on many occasions, that we are possessed by him, than that we possess him. And no wonder;—He scatters the seeds of things, the principles of character and action, with so cunning a hand yet with so careless an air, and, master of our feelings, submits himself so little to our judgment, that everything seems superior. . . . We see these Characters act from the mingled motives of passion, reason, interest, habit, and complection, in all their proportions, when they are supposed to know it not themselves; and we are made to acknowledge that their actions and sentiments are, from these motives, the necessary result.

> Maurice Morgann, *Essay on the Dramatic Character of Sir John Falstaff*, 1777

# CONTENTS

# PREFACE

FOR this edition I have drawn on the wealth of illustration provided by the original Arden editor, R. P. Cowl, though with many omissions and additions. Otherwise I have not based my work on his. I have greatly profited from Matthias A. Shaaber's New Variorum edition, from the commentaries of Johnson, Maurice Morgann, H. N. Hudson, and Geoffrey Bullough (in *Narrative and Dramatic Sources of Shakespeare*, vol. iv), and from E. M. W. Tillyard's *Shakespeare's History Plays*, J. Dover Wilson's edition and *The Fortunes of Falstaff*, D. A. Traversi's *Shakespeare from Richard II to Henry V*, and L. C. Knights's *Some Shakespearean Themes*. The General Editors, Dr Harold F. Brooks and Professor Harold Jenkins, have surpassed all that might be hoped for; their aid has throughout been unstinted and stimulating. Mr John Adair, Dr T. W. Craik, Professor Charlton Hinman, Professor J. C. Maxwell, Mr Dipak Nandy, Dr Hereward T. Price, Dr and Mrs Peter Russell, Professor Eugene Waith, and Mr E. R. Wood have thrown light on particular points; I thank them all warmly. Miss Caroline Herbert (Mrs David Palframan) has typed her way valiantly through many pages of difficult draft. My wife, by diligently revising the commentary and amplifying the notes, has eased my work and made it the more pleasurable. She and I owe more than we can say to the administrators of the Folger Shakespeare Library, whose generosity allowed us two busy and happy periods in Washington. The delights of that noble institution go far beyond the extraordinary research facilities it provides. Its director, Dr Louis B. Wright, and Mrs Wright, and the members of its staff, in particular Dr Giles Dawson, Miss Dorothy Mason, Dr James McManaway, and Miss Eleanor Pitcher, extended to us a most heart-warming friendship. That my own university released me to go there, and my colleagues shouldered extra burdens to let me do so, is not the least of my themes of gratitude. And finally, I must salute the exemplary care with which The Broadwater Press set up so exacting a text, and the intelligent attentiveness to the proofs shown by Miss Magdalen Newland Smith.

*The University, Leicester.*          A. R. HUMPHREYS
*April 1965*

# INTRODUCTION

The text is based on the first issue of the Quarto of 1600, amplified to the extent of Act III, scene i, by the second issue, and by the recovery from the Folio of certain passages not in the Quarto (cf. p. lxx). The Folio text, though inferior to the Quarto, is of sufficient authority to warrant the adoption of some of its readings. The introduction surveys the main considerations relevant to the study of the play, and the footnotes deal, it is hoped, with most of the matters which need elucidating.

## I. PUBLICATION

In 1600 the booksellers Andrew Wise and William Aspley acquired the copy of *2 Henry IV*, presumably by purchase from the Lord Chamberlain's company of players who had owned it. It was entered to them in *The Stationers' Register* as follows:

23 Augusti [1600]

Andrewe Wyse   Entred for their copies vnder the handes of the
William Aspley   wardens Two bookes. the one called *Muche a*
             *Doo about nothinge.* Thother *the second parte of the*
             *history of kinge HENRY the iiii$^{th}$ with the humours of*
             *Sir IOHN FFALLSTAFF:* Wrytten by master
             Shakespere.                xij$^{d}$ [1]

The sale may have taken place partly because on 22 June the Privy Council had restricted stage performances to two a week,[2] and so disposed the players to redress their losses by publication, and partly because the company feared piratical printing.[3] The Quarto came out in an issue (Qa) which lacks the first scene of Act III. The title-page reads:

1. *Op. cit.*, ed. E. Arber, 1875, III. 170.
2. *Acts of the Privy Council, A.D. 1599–1600*, New ser., xxx, 1905, pp. 395–8.
3. Cf. A. W. Pollard, *Sh.'s Fight with the Pirates*, 1921, p. 49. On 4 August 1600, the Lord Chamberlain's Men entered *As You Like It, Henry V*, and *Much Ado* on *SR* to be 'stayed' from publication, yet *Henry V* was printed piratically by Thomas Millington and John Busby. This, Pollard suggests, may have hastened the sale to reputable book-sellers of *Much Ado* and of *2 Henry IV* along with it.

THE / Second part of Henrie / the fourth, continuing to his death, / *and coronation of Henrie* / the fift. / With the humours of sir Iohn Fal- / *staffe, and swaggering* / Pistoll. / *As it hath been sundrie times publikely* / acted by the right honourable, the Lord / Chamberlaine his seruants. / *Written by William Shakespeare.* / LONDON / Printed by V.S. [Valentine Sims] for Andrew Wise, and / William Aspley. / 1600.

The missing scene was first published in the second issue (Qb).[1] An appreciable time may have elapsed between the two issues, for copies of both survive in considerable (and almost equal) numbers—ten of the first and eleven of the second.[2] A good many of Qa were perhaps bound up before the defect was remedied, and Qb not put out until these had been sold off.

No other printing took place until that in the First Folio in 1623. Here the play appears under the title:

The Second Part of Henry the Fourth, / Containing his Death: and the Coronation / of King Henry the Fift.

Why was no Quarto reprint needed? *1 Henry IV* was so popular that two editions were called for in the year it was published (1598), and five more before the Folio (1599, 1604, 1608, 1613, 1622). It has been argued that political censorship may have prevented any reprint of *2 Henry IV*, since all references to Richard II were left out of Qa and the appearance of this risky topic in Qb might result in a total ban.[3] Yet this is not wholly convincing.

1. The issues are distinguished as Qa and Qb but these symbols indicate texts which are identical save in the portion where the addition of new material resulted in differences. Qb consists of the sheets of Qa modified by the inclusion of the new scene and the consequent resetting of adjacent parts of II. iv and III. ii (II. iv. 338–87; III. ii. 1–103 'young'). The compositor, Dr Charlton Hinman tells me, was the same for both issues, and a comparison of the overlapping portions of II. iv and III. ii in each issue throws an interesting light on his practices. In the 165 lines reset, besides making 165 variants in accidentals he introduced seven material changes—four additions, two omissions, and one transposition. This freehandedness in setting from print indicates that the Quarto would be even less a scrupulous rendering of its MS, even had this always made easy reading—which, being 'foul papers', it would not have done. The Quarto, then, though it remains the prime authority, need not receive unquestioned faith.

2. H. C. Bartlett and A. W. Pollard, *Census of Sh.'s Plays in Quarto, 1594–1709*, rev. edn, 1939, pp. 30–2.

3. L. L. Schucking, in *TLS*, 25 Sept. 1930, p. 752; A. Hart, *Sh. and the Homilies*, 1934, pp. 154–218; Wilson, N.C.S., p. 120. The trouble over Sir John Hayward's *Life of Henrie IIII* (1599) may be relevant. This came out, with preface addressed to Essex, shortly before Essex left for Ireland in March 1599. When Essex was disgraced over the Irish campaign, Hayward was involved also, for he had written of Richard and *his* Irish campaign, and of his deposition (the offensive nature of which to Queen Elizabeth had already caused the deposition scene to be omitted from the Quartos of *Richard II*). Hayward and his printer were

The message of Act III, scene i, should have been welcome to any censor; far from recommending usurpation it shows the usurper miserable. Even if one assumes a high level of censorial stupidity the fact remains that *1 Henry IV*, which refers often enough to Richard's overthrow, went on being reprinted, that *Richard II* itself was reissued in 1608 and 1615, and that the 1608 reprint actually includes, for the first time, the abdication scene. An embargo on *2 Henry IV* would hardly be maintained in such circumstances.[1]

Why there is only one Quarto may never be known. But two suggestions may be offered. First, commercial shrewdness may have prompted an unusually large printing. *1 Henry IV* had run to three editions in 1598–9 alone. Here, in 1600, was a companion play with more 'humours of sir Iohn Falstaffe' and, moreover, with such swaggerings of Pistol as to call for notice on the title-page. Such a play should sell as well as the three editions of Part 1 combined. A mere fragment remains of the first Quarto of *1 Henry IV*, and only three and ten copies respectively of the next two Quartos, but no fewer than twenty-one copies are known of *2 Henry IV*.[2] Second, what is unusual is rather *1 Henry IV*'s plethora of reprints than *2 Henry IV*'s dearth. Of the thirty-six Folio plays, eighteen are published there for the first time, including some of the finest.[3] Of *Love's Labour's Lost*, *Much Ado*, and *Othello* there is one quarto only.[4] Of *The Merchant of Venice* and *A Midsummer Night's Dream* the single editions of 1600 sufficed until 1619. Perhaps, then, one need not look beyond the accidents of commerce,

imprisoned and tried, and Sir Edward Coke urged it against Hayward that he had revived a 200-year-old story to apply it to the present, so that a monarch was shown misgoverning, the Council corrupt, parasitism rampant, the Commons oppressed, and the Irish expedition mismanaged.

1. In the original Arden edition (pp. xi–xiv) R. P. Cowl suggested that a passage in Jonson's *Poetaster* (the 'apologeticall Dialogue', ll. 40–8; H. & S., IV. 318) echoed a speech by the Archbishop omitted from Q and extant only in F. This might come, Cowl thought, from some non-extant Q which had restored the speech. But the resemblances are too slight to support the theory.

2. Charlton Hinman points out that from 1587 to 1635 the Stationers' Company put a maximum of 1,500 copies to be printed from the same setting of type, except after special licence (*Printing & Proof-Reading of the First Folio*, 1963, I. 39). No signs of a special licence are known for *2 Henry IV*. But how rigorous the order was is hard to say.

3. *Tempest, Two Gentlemen, Measure for Measure, Comedy of Errors, As You Like It, Taming of the Shrew, All's Well, Twelfth Night, Winter's Tale, John, 1 Henry VI, Henry VIII, Coriolanus, Timon, Julius Caesar, Macbeth, Antony, Cymbeline.*

4. I.e. before the First Folio. The *Othello* was as late as 1622. Of *Love's Labour's Lost* there may have been a 'bad' Q preceding the 'good' one of 1598; A. W. Pollard, *Sh. Folios and Quartos*, 1909, p. 70.

whether in the printing of a large edition, or the strange hap-
hazardness of output, or both, to explain the single Quarto of
2 *Henry IV*.

## 2. DATE

To date the play within a few months is difficult. By 1599 Jonson could refer to it familiarly in *Every Man Out Of His Humour*: to
Saviolina's question, 'What's hee, gentle Monsieur BRISKE? not
that gentleman?', Fastidius answers, 'no ladie, this is a kinsman to
iustice *Silence*' (v. ii. 20–2; H. & S., iii. 567). *Henry V*, to which the
Epilogue of 2 *Henry IV* in its revised form looks forward, was probably started in the spring of 1599; the unrevised Epilogue for
2 *Henry IV*'s original performances precedes the revised by some
unknown interval. 2 *Henry IV* would be finished, then, certainly
before the end of 1598, perhaps well before.[1]

Working the other way, one notes the influence of Daniel's
*Ciuile Wars* (1595; see below, p. xxxiii), and possible echoes of cur-
rently read books which, however, are no closer than Daniel and
do not narrow the limits of time.[2] Muhammad III succeeded to
the Turkish Sultanate in late January 1596, and murdered his
brothers: this prompted the allusion at v. ii. 48, though Shakespeare used not Muhammad's name but that of his predecessor
Murad (Amurath) III, who likewise had killed his brothers

1. J. W. Lever, 'Three Notes on Sh.'s Plants', *RES*, New ser., iii, 1952, pp. 117–
29, suggests, as the germ of the forked-radish-and-mandrake jest, a passage of
Gerard's *Herball* given below in the note on iii. ii. 305–6. The *Herball* was entered
on *SR* on 6 June 1597. But it includes prefatory Latin verses dated December
1597 and Gerard's own address to his readers of the same month, so it cannot
have appeared until well into 1598—it is a large work. If the *Herball* came out in
the late spring or summer of 1598, and if Falstaff's joke derives from it, Shakespeare must have lighted upon it with surprising promptness. If there is a connection, it may rather have been through conversation. The two men are not
known to have met, but in 1597 Shakespeare was living in Silver Street, Holborn,
near Gerard's well-known botanical garden. He may, indeed, have known something of the *Herball* while it was being compiled. But the connection is not certain.
Though his passage and Gerard's look similar, both writers mention root-
carving and mandrakes as common tavern-drinkers' jests, and they may both be
commenting independently on a familiar diversion. Gerard in fact, though
nearest to Shakespeare in some details, is not the first to write of the mandrake
in these terms. William Turner's *Herbal* (1568) has a woodcut of the mandrake
with a tuft of leaves and entwined root, like the human body from the waist down.
It comments, 'The rootes whiche are conterfited & made like little puppettes &
mammettes . . . are nothyng elles but folishe feined trifles & not naturall. For they
are so trymmed of crafty theues to mocke the poore people withall' (Pt ii, 45ᵛ–
46ʳ). So a connection between Shakespeare and Gerard is less demonstrable than
at first appears.

2. See notes on iii. ii. 253–5, 260–4, 264–6; iv. iii. 94–100.

(in 1574), and whose name was a byword for tyranny. This item might be expected to reach London in February–March 1596.

Can any light on dating be derived from the revision of the Epilogue? The original form of the Epilogue was presumably the first paragraph only of the existing three. Shakespeare, as the author, apparently spoke it, and offered 2 *Henry IV* as amends for some earlier play. As revised for later occasions the Epilogue presumably contained parts but not all of the first paragraph, together with the second and third; it was spoken by a dancer (doubtless one of the boys), and it presumably had no reference to the late 'displeasing play'. As the existing third paragraph shows, it not only promised that Sir John would appear in France but apologized to the shade of Sir John Oldcastle, whose name Shakespeare originally used for the 'old lad of the castle', later re-christened Falstaff, when the family of Brooke (Lords Cobham and descendants of Oldcastle) objected. Finally, the editor of the play for the Folio removed the prayer for the Queen to the end.[1]

From this may be deduced the following probabilities: (*a*) that the original Epilogue reflected no Oldcastle fuss; (*b*) that it must have been delivered, or at least written, before the fuss broke out, or at least before it proved so serious as to require an apology; (*c*) that, had only Part 1 been finished at that stage, any apology would have been affixed to that, rather than left to a successor. Now the Oldcastle fuss occurred some time between the early performances of *1 Henry IV* in the 1596–7 season (with the Oldcastle nomenclature) and the *SR* entry of *1 Henry IV* on 25 February 1598, where the fat knight is named Falstaff.

This pushes back the composition of *2 Henry IV* into 1597. The assumption that it followed *1 Henry IV* closely is supported by traces of the old nomenclature. The Quarto (printed from Shakespeare's 'foul papers') has the speech-prefix '*Old.*' at I. ii. 119, and the entry-direction '*sir Iohn Russel*' at the head of II. ii (changed to '*Bardolfe*' in the Folio). A 'Rossill' appears together with a 'Haruey' in both Quarto and Folio of *1 Henry IV*, at a point where editors since Theobald print 'Peto' and 'Bardolph' (*1H4*, I. ii. 182). The Quartos of *1 Henry IV* also print '*Ross.*' as a speech-prefix (II. iv. 193, 195, 199), where the Folio and most editors read '*Gad[s].*'. An original Russell has therefore been renamed Bardolph, Peto, and Gadshill by different editors in different places, but that is of

1. The first paragraph is given in this edition as in the Quarto, ending with the prayer for the Queen.

less moment than the survival of his name, and Oldcastle's, into Part 2.[1] The names are strong presumptive evidence that Shakespeare had got at least into Act II of Part 2 before rechristening his characters. Even if '*Old.*' were a slip, prompted by the fat knight's familiarity, such a relapse is unlikely with a minor character. It seems likely, therefore, that when the Brookes protested (that is, as the New Arden Part 1 introduction argues, very early in 1597), either all or part of Part 2 was written.[2]

Against this it can be argued that no edition of *1 Henry IV* before the Folio specifies it as a first part. But Shakespeare may have written his title before deciding that the *Henry IV* material would fall into two parts: the *Stationers' Register* and Quarto title-page would follow suit. Such things were often neglected: the 1599 edition of Part 1, though claiming to be '*Newly corrected*', failed to distinguish itself as Part 1, though Part 2 already existed.[3] No more conclusive is the mention of '*Henry the 4*' in Francis Meres's *Palladis Tamia* (*SR*, 7 September 1598) as proving Shakespeare 'most excellent . . . for Tragedy'. Meres may have known of only one part, even though two surely existed by late 1598; or he may have considered the Henry IV theme as one subject; or indeed, since he is thinking of 'Tragedy', he may have in mind rather the dark tone of Part 2 than the bright tone of Part 1. In any case, his list of authors and plays is suspiciously symmetrical; nor does it include all Shakespeare's plays up to 1598.[4] It cannot be taken as evidence that Part 2 was not yet current.

1. That Russel in Part 2 is the Rossill or Ross. of Part 1 has been disputed, but on what reasonable grounds it is hard to see.

2. Joseph Ritson (cf. Steevens-Reed, *Shakespeare*, 1793, viii. 595) argued that 'Oldcastle' would fit the six lines in Part 2 where 'Falstaff' occurs in verse if the lines were slightly adjusted; in *Some Problems of Sh.'s 'Henry the Fourth'* (1924) A. E. Morgan offered what he surmised to have been the 'Oldcastle' versions. But the argument that 'Oldcastle' would fit the lines if the lines would fit 'Oldcastle' is not helpful. No instance is as convincing as 'Away, good Ned, Falstaff sweats to death' (*1H4*, II. ii. 115) which occurs in a decasyllabic context (though QqF print it as prose), and would likewise be decasyllabic if the name were 'Oldcastle'.

3. Elizabethan registrations and publication often ignore such details. Thomas Heywood's *If You Know Not Me* (1605) did not specify its first part as such, either in *SR* or the title-page, though Part 2, registered two months later, must almost certainly have existed. His *Iron Age* was published in two parts simultaneously in 1632 and the first part's Epilogue refers to 'our second part': yet the first-part title-page makes no mention of it as Part 1. As for *1 Henry IV*, no reference to it as a first part seems to occur before a *SR* entry of 25 June 1603, when '*HENRY the 4 the firste part*' was among five books transferred from Andrew Wise to Mathew Law (*SR*, iii. 98).

4. Cf. D. C. Allen, *Francis Meres's Treatise 'Poetrie'*, 1933, pp. 9–60; William Green, *Shakespeare's 'Merry Wives of Windsor'*, 1962, pp. 209–13.

The timing speculatively offered in the New Arden *1 Henry IV*
is perhaps the best one can do with the available evidence. It is as
follows: that Oldcastle–Harvey–Russell versions of the *Henry IV*
plays were seen in the winter season of 1596–7; that the Brookes
protested about the disgrace ot Oldcastle; that the plays would
then be withdrawn for revision; that about April 1597 Shakespeare was hurriedly called on for a comedy on the fat knight
(tactfully renamed), to celebrate the election of new Knights of
the Garter (who included Lord Hunsdon, the patron of Shakespeare's company); that he revamped a lost source-play as *The
Merry Wives*; that when the theatres reopened after being closed
from July to October 1597, as punishment for the performance of
Jonson and Nashe's 'very seditious and sclanderous' *Isle of Dogs*,[1]
the *Henry IV* plays would return to the stage for the winter of
1597–8 (with the offending names suitably changed), and that
*1 Henry IV* was printed early in 1598 to publicize the alterations.[2]
The epilogue to *2 Henry IV* in its original form apparently contained no apology about Oldcastle and presumably antedated the
protests; but Shakespeare doubtless came to feel that amends
should be made, and some time before he began *Henry V* in the
spring of 1599 he was moved not only to promise a further instalment of Falstaff but also to redeem Oldcastle's injured fame.[3]

1. Privy Council Minutes of 28 July, 15 August 1597; Chambers, *El. St.*, iii.
454, iv. 322–3. During the interdict the Lord Chamberlain's Men travelled. They
are recorded at Rye, Dover, and Bristol; *ibid.*, ii. 196.

2. Harvey and Russell were names of high families, which might not appre-
ciate their bestowal on low comics.

3. A scheme offering an interesting variation on this was put forward by
Henry N. Paul (*1 Henry IV*, New Var., p. 355). It holds that the composition of
*The Merry Wives*, about April 1597, interrupted that of *2 Henry IV* approximately
after the end of Act III, the first three acts having been written with the original
names, but the Brookes' protests resulted in alterations when Shakespeare
resumed work. If this interruption did take place, and if something in the *Merry
Wives*' source-play caused Shakespeare to associate the victimized Shallow with
Gloucestershire, one would have the explanation of why in *2 Henry IV* Shallow's
habitat appears to change from Lincolnshire to Gloucestershire (cf. Appendix
IV). But there is no point in basing a solution on the merest guess-work. Hotson's
case for dating *The Merry Wives* in April 1597 is most thoroughly examined and
strongly supported by William Green in *Shakespeare's 'Merry Wives of Windsor'*,
1962. A suggestion possibly relevant to the dating of *The Merry Wives* is made by
Roy F. Montgomery ('A Fair House Built on Another Man's Ground', *Sh.Q.*, v,
1954, pp. 206–7). At *Wiv.*, II. ii. 223–6, Ford likens his love to 'a fair house built
on another man's ground; so that I have lost my edifice by mistaking the place
where I erected it'. In April 1597, the lease of Burbage's theatre in Shoreditch
expired and Giles Alleyn, the landlord, declined to renew it. The building was
forfeit unless removed by the expiry date. The matter caused a wrangle for more
than a year; then the company found a new site and paid a contractor to convey
the theatre away. The removal took place hurriedly on 28 December 1598,

### 3. THE EXTENT OF REVISION

Discussion about revision in the *Henry IV* plays can be set forth as it concerns the names, and the general form and content.

#### (i) *Changes of Names*

That some of the comic characters originally had other names has been mentioned already. *The Famous Victories of Henry the Fifth* gave Shakespeare the name of Sir John Oldcastle, though not of Harvey or Russell for Sir John's cronies. These three names would be changed as a consequence of the offence given, though Ned Poins may survive from some original since in *The Famous Victories* a Ned is the Prince's particular friend.

The renaming of Oldcastle as Falstaff removed a cause of complaint but only at the cost of colossal injustice. The historical Sir John Fastolf (1378–1459), like the historical Oldcastle,[1] was one of Henry V's generals, and he fought well at Agincourt. At the battle of Patay (1429), however, his manœuvres failed and the English hero Sir John Talbot was captured by the enemy. Fastolf was exonerated, but sixteenth-century chroniclers derived from Monstrelet's *Chroniques* the mistaken idea that he was deprived of the Garter for cowardice, and he appears in this light in *1 Henry VI* (IV. iv. 33–43), transliterated as 'Falstaffe'. When, therefore, Oldcastle was to be let off, Fastolf–Falstaff was revived from *1 Henry VI* to step into the vacancy.

The old name, however, survived long in memory. In the anonymous *Meeting of Gallants at an Ordinarie* (1604), the Host is 'a madde round knaue, and a merrie one too: and if you chaunce to talke of fatte *Sir Iohn Old-castle*, he wil tell you, he was his great Grandfather, and not much vnlike him in Paunch' (sig. B4). Nathan Field's *Amends for Ladies* (c. 1610–11) inquires

> Did you never see
> The Play, where the fat Knight hight *Old-castle*,
> Did tell you truly what this honor was?[2]

---

when Alleyn was away: the rebuilt playhouse was called The Globe. *The Merry Wives*' remark might have been suggested by this situation—the building was not actually 'lost' but about April 1597 would certainly appear so.

1. Sir John Oldcastle (c. 1378–1417), High Sheriff of Herefordshire, became Lord Cobham by marriage in 1409. He was 'highly in the king's favour', 'a valiant capteine' in the French wars (Hol., iii. 62) but he was later condemned for Wycliffite heresy and on Christmas Day 1417 was hanged and burnt. His conflicting reputations, as hero and coward, are surveyed in the New Arden *1 Henry IV*, pp. xxxix–xl.

2. IV. iii. 23–5; Nathan Field, *Plays*, ed. W. Peery, 1950, p. 216.

In *A Wandering-Jew, Telling Fortunes to Englishmen* (anon., c. 1628, printed 1640), the glutton declares that '*Sir Iohn Old-castle* was my greatgrandfathers fathers Uncle' (*SAB*, i. 446). And the *Henry IV* pair (or one of them) was sometimes called *Sir John Falstaff* and apparently *Sir John Oldcastle* also, as late as 1651.[1]

During the next few decades the historical Oldcastle was repeatedly vindicated by writers distressed at his involvement in the Boar's-Head goings-on. Of these it may suffice to quote those of Thomas Fuller, in his *Church History* (1655) and *Worthies of England* (1662)[2]: Fuller's reference to 'malicious Papists' in the following passage reflects the fact that, Oldcastle being a martyred Lollard, the view of him transmitted by fifteenth-century orthodoxy was strongly hostile.[3] Against both Papists and poets, Fuller is ardent to defend the proto-Protestant:

> *Stage-Poets* have themselves been very *bold* with, and others very *merry* at, the Memory of S$^r$ *John Oldcastle*, whom they have fancied a *boon Companion*, a *jovial Royster*, and yet a *Coward* to boot, contrary to the credit of all Chronicles, owning him a *Martial man* of merit. The best is, S$^r$ *John Falstaffe*, hath relieved the Memory of S$^r$ *John Oldcastle*, and of late is substituted *Buffoone* in his place, but it matters as little what *petulant Poets*, as what *malicious Papists* have written against him.[4]

When the *Worthies of England* arrives at Norfolk in its enumeration of notables it is concerned to vindicate Fastolf also, as well as Oldcastle:

> JOHN FASTOLFE Knight, was a native of this County. . . To avouch him by many arguments valiant, is to maintain that the sun is bright, though since the *Stage* hath been over bold with his memory, making him a *Thrasonical Puff*, and emblem of *Mock-valour.*
>
> True it is, Sir *John Oldcastle* did first bear the brunt of the one, being made the *make-sport* in all plays for a *coward*. It is easily known out of what *purse* this black *peny* came. The *Papists* railing on him for a *Heretick*, and therefore he must also be a *coward*, though indeed he was a *man* of *arms*, *every inch of him*, and as valiant as any in his age.
>
> Now as I am glad that Sir *John Oldcastle* is *put out*, so I am sorry that Sir *John Fastolfe* is *put in*, to relieve his memory in this base

1. Chambers, *W. Sh.*, i. 382, ii. 322, 353. There was, of course, the rival Sir John Oldcastle play by Drayton, Munday, Hathaway, and Wilson, but the instances Chambers cites are probably not references to this.

2. Other vindications are given in Chambers, *W. Sh.*, ii. 241–2, and in the New Arden *1 Henry IV*, p. xvii.

3. See the New Arden *1 Henry IV*, pp. xxxix–xl.

4. *Church History*, 1655, Bk IV, XV Cent., 168.

service, to be the *anvil* for every *dull wit* to strike upon. Nor is our Comedian excusable, by some alteration of his name, writing him Sir *John Falstafe*, . . . seeing the *vicinity* of sounds intrench on the memory of *that worthy Knight*, and few do heed the *inconsiderable difference* in spelling of their name.[1]

Seldom can a dramatist's indiscretion have provoked such long-lived concern. It is tantalizing to hear these reverberations but to know so little of what really happened, and who made the noise, and when, and what exactly Shakespeare did, and why the flurry lasted so long in memory.

## (ii) *Further Revisions?*

Some scholars, particularly Professors A. E. Morgan and Dover Wilson, have held that *Henry IV* originally differed much from the extant plays, that the comedy was briefer and written in comic verse (like that of the Nurse in *Romeo and Juliet* or Robert Faulconbridge in *King John*), and that (according to Morgan) the history was longer and was later cut to make room for more comedy. Dover Wilson also thinks that the comedy was expanded, but, believing that a single play grew into two, he need not seek signs of cutting elsewhere, though he sees signs of re-working.[2]

But the alleged evidence is unconvincing. The argument for cuts depends on the existence in both parts of characters with little or nothing to do,[3] and of supposedly curtailed lines. Yet mutes are common in Shakespeare, and the Quarto text, being from 'foul papers', is the very place one would expect to find entries never followed up. Nothing can be deduced from this save that Shakespeare summoned up more characters than he actually needed to use.[4] The 'curtailed' lines afford no more substantial evidence, and no significance can be attached to the brief phrases the Folio

1. *Worthies of England*, 1662, ii. 253.

2. A. E. Morgan, *Some Problems of Sh.'s 'Henry the Fourth'*, 1924; J. Dover Wilson, 'The Origins and Development of Sh.'s *Henry IV*', in *The Library*, 4th ser., xxvi, 1945.

3. In *2 Henry IV* these are the Umfrevile to whom Q refers (I. i. 34) and gives one line (I. i. 161; F leaves the reference but cuts the line); Lord Fauconbridge (Q I. iii, S.D.); Bardolfe (Q IV. i, S.D.; he is mute throughout the scene); Kent (Q IV. iv, S.D.); and Blunt, who says nothing, though he is introduced (Q III. i. 31, V. ii. 42, S.D.s) and is addressed by Prince John (IV. iii. 73).

4. Umfrevile's appearance in Q is accounted for differently. He seems once to have played a part but to have had it switched to Lord Bardolph. Faulty revision would explain his line at I. i. 161 (in Q; not in F), and the fact that Travers, riding for news of Shrewsbury, is turned back by Umfrevile bearing 'joyful tidings', whereas the bearer of these to Warkworth proves to be Lord Bardolph, who has outridden Travers to arrive first (I. i. 30–6).

adds, though Morgan thinks they are meant to patch over cuts.[1]

The evidence offered to support the alleged original comic-verse Oldcastle part consists of supposed 'fossils', decasyllables interpreted as survivals of metre in the prose. According to Morgan, the Lord Chief Justice's entry at II. i. 59 is, for instance, 'the signal for verse', and so, after intervening prose, is Gower's at II. i. 131. These lines are held to reveal a verse-form of the scene later mostly overwritten with prose. Yet it is natural that the Lord Chief Justice, representing authority, should speak some verse, though to do so consistently throughout the comic exchanges would be unfitting. Hal's part likewise is said to show 'fairly copious' verse-relics, especially in II. iv. But except when the tone turns serious (as at II. iv. 352–63), there are really no signs of metre; and that at serious moments he should turn to verse simply shows that different purposes need different media. It is true that in IV. iii Falstaff exchanges with Prince John some stumbling decasyllables (ll. 79–81); but this indicates no more than that Shakespeare's pen was not always sure whether its master was in a verse-mood or a prose-mood. Such vacillating passages are rare, and offer no proper basis for a theory of revision.[2]

## 4. THE RELATIONSHIP TO '1 HENRY IV'

Discussions of how Part 2 relates to Part 1 go back over two centuries. In his *Critical Observations on Shakespeare* (1746) John Upton observed that

> these plays are independent each of the other. . . . To call [them], *first and second parts*, is as injurious to the author-character of Shakespeare as it would be to Sophocles, to call his two plays on Oedipus, *first and second parts of King Oedipus*.

To this, Johnson firmly rejoined in his edition

> Mr *Upton* thinks these two plays improperly called the *first* and *second parts* of *Henry* the *fourth* . . . [yet they] will appear to every reader, who shall peruse them without ambition of critical dis-

---

1. See collations at IV. ii. 117; IV. iv. 52, 120, 132; and IV. v. 49, for the sort of 'patching' on which the theory depends.

2. Discussing the revision-theory, E. K. Chambers comments, 'I do not think that these rhythms have any such significance. They are a constant feature of Shakespeare's prose. . . The number might be much increased if, with Professor A. E. Morgan, one took into account not only regular decasyllabic rhythms but others which could be carried as such in a blank verse passage by substituting a verse intonation for a prose one and allowing for trisyllabic feet. These however when they come in a prose passage do not really read as anything but prose' (*W. Sh.*, 1930, i. 233).

coveries, to be so connected that the second is merely a sequel to the first; to be two only because they are too long to be one.

Capell went further and asserted that 'both these plays appear to have been plan'd at the same time, and with great judgment' (*Notes and Various Readings*, 1779).

Yet argument has continued. Was Part 2 foreseen, and planned as a separate part, when Part 1 was started? Or was it 'an unpremeditated addition caused by the enormous effectiveness of the by-figure of Falstaff',[1] a 'hastily-written encore'?[2] Did Shakespeare originally intend a single play but change his plan as his material proved too ample?[3] Did he, even, originally manage his story in a single play, which grew into two upon revision?[4] Are we or are we not to say that *Henry IV*, as Hudibras says of Man,

> Is of two equal Parts compact,
> In Shape and Symmetry exact,
> Of which the Left and Female Side
> Is to the Manly Right a Bride,
> Both join'd together with such Art
> That nothing else but Death can part?

Elizabethan two- or three-part plays show such a variety of procedures as to leave Shakespeare free to do whatever he thought fit. Yet already the tripartite *Henry VI* (whether wholly his or not) had shown how a powerful imagination could direct a continuous, if not tightly-wrought, sequence—Professor Peter Alexander justly describes the whole scheme as evincing 'Shakespeare's accustomed ease and certainty of design'.[5] No one can actually know what Shakespeare had in mind as he began *Henry IV*. But nothing the stage had to show need actually have deterred him from thinking, from the beginning, of two parts rather than one.[6]

1. C. F. Tucker Brooke, *Tudor Drama*, 1911, p. 333.

2. A. Attwater, in *Companion to Sh. Studies*, ed. G. B. Harrison and H. Granville Barker, 1934, p. 229.

3. This position is argued by Harold Jenkins in *The Structural Problem in Sh.'s 'Henry the Fourth'*, with an illuminating survey of views on the plays' relationship, pp. 2–5; see below, p. xxv–xxvii.

4. J. Dover Wilson, in 'The Origins and Development of Sh.'s *Henry IV*' (*The Library*, 4th ser., xxvi, 1945), suggested that after the Oldcastle fuss Shakespeare so revised and developed his supposed original single play that 'in the end Falstaff, grown out of all compass, needed a double drama to contain him'. But for this the evidence is insufficient and (insofar as it depends—as it largely does—on 'fossil' verses) quite unconvincing; see above, pp. xx–xxi.

5. *Sh.'s 'Henry VI' and 'Richard III'*, 1929, p. 205.

6. A second part was sometimes an afterthought, as *2 Tamburlaine*'s prologue admits was the case with that play. Some second parts followed long after the first and were doubtless not foreseen; for instance, Chapman's *Revenge of Bussy* (? late 1610–early 1611, as against *Bussy*, 1604: cf. *Tragedies of Chapman*, ed. T. M.

As, having finished *Richard II*, he turned to the consequences of the usurpation described by the chronicles and prophesied in that play by the Bishop of Carlisle, the following points would present themselves:

(*a*) that Richard's deposition and murder are crime and sacrilege;

(*b*) that the people themselves, having connived at Richard's overthrow, deserve a long period of trouble;

(*c*) that Bolingbroke is to suffer an unquiet time, weariness, and remorse, before his death;

(*d*) that in the popular memory Shrewsbury is to be a major conflict, a great crisis[1];

(*e*) but that further troubles are to follow, including the final insurgence of the Percy family;

(*f*) and that true rule will return spectacularly when Bolingbroke's son, transformed as if by miracle, becomes the hero-king.

These *donnés*, expressed alike in scholarly chronicles and popular traditions, were the expected shape and tone of Henry IV's reign.

---

Parrott, 1910, p. 571), and perhaps Heywood's *Fair Maid of the West*, of which Part 2 (though the preface links it with Part 1) may have been twenty years later (cf. A. M. Clark, *Thomas Heywood*, 1931, p. 110). Sometimes, though two parts were written fairly close together, nothing more than casual sequence is apparent; in this category fall the three *Parnassus* plays, Heywood's *If You Know Not Me*, Dekker and Middleton's *Honest Whore*, and Marston's *Antonio* pair. Sometimes, as with *If You Know Not Me*, *The Honest Whore*, and Heywood's *Iron Age*, neither *SR* entry (if there is one—none exists for *The Iron Age*) nor first title-page mentions Part 1, though when the parts of *The Iron Age* were published together Part 2 was so described. Some plays, however, have an action such as to suggest that the first half was not meant to complete the story. The two parts of Heywood's *Edward IV*, though largely disjunct, carry Jane Shore's story to what seems a necessary end; Part 1 does not compel one to read Part 2, but a sequel relating Jane's fate seems desirable. Heywood's *Iron Age*, episodic cycle though it is (like its precursors *The Golden Age*, *The Silver Age*, and *The Brazen Age*), has a first part ending in Thersites' epilogue about 'our second part', and it makes some show of carrying through the Trojan-War story to the deaths of Agamemnon and Clytemnestra. Munday's *Downfall of Robert Earle of Huntingdon* and Munday and Chettle's *Death of Robert Earle of Huntingdon* (noted by Henslowe as 'the firste parte of Robyne Hoode' and 'the second parte of the downefall of earlle Huntyngton surnamed Roben Hoode') were written almost simultaneously, as Henslowe's payments show (*Henslowe's Diary*, ed. W. W. Greg, i. 83, 84). The *Downfall* ends with an address announcing the subjects of the *Death*, as the *Death* begins by recapitulating the conclusion of the *Downfall*. Many other plays planned or executed in more than one part are recorded but not extant. Clearly there was much variety of practice in respect of sequels.

1. Gregory's *Chronicle* calls it 'one of the wyrste bataylys that evyr came to Inglonde, and vnkyndest, for there was the fadyr a-yenst the sone and the sone a-yenst the fadyr, and brother and cosyn a-yenste eche othyr' (ed. Wm Gairdner, Camden Soc., New ser., 17, 1876, pp. 103–4). The *Brut* comments in almost identical terms (EETS, Orig. ser., 136, p. 549). Carlisle foresees that 'tumultuous wars / Shall kin with kin and kind with kind confound' (*R2*, IV. i. 140–1).

But did Shakespeare, perhaps, mean to stop with Hotspur's defeat? This is most unlikely. In Part 1, five scenes point significantly towards events after Shrewsbury:

(a) In I. ii Falstaff repeatedly asks Hal what will happen 'when thou art king'. Hal answers cryptically, but clearly time will show. Hal's soliloquy in that scene promises that idleness will not always be upheld and that he will shine forth unclouded (this, though Shrewsbury is an earnest of it, must point to the coronation);

(b) In II. iv the theme of banishment is sounded. 'Banish plump Jack, and banish all the world', Falstaff says, as a pure hypothesis: 'I do, I will,' Hal replies, though no one pays any attention;

(c) in IV. iv the Archbishop, fearing Hotspur's defeat, prepares further hostilities by writing to his friends, including Scroop and Mowbray (neither at Shrewsbury, but Mowbray to be a leading rebel in Part 2);

(d) in V. v the King is equally anticipating further action. He sends Westmoreland and Prince John 'To meet Northumberland and the prelate Scroop', while he and Hal go off against Glendower;

(e) and, not least, in V. iv, there are aspects of Prince John and Falstaff which call for further treatment. Presumably Prince John figures at Shrewsbury (unhistorically—he was only thirteen) because, like the Archbishop, he is to appear in a later action and so has already engaged Shakespeare's interest. John, not his elder brother Thomas of Clarence, must be chosen because of his later Gaultree eminence; Gaultree is already foreseen, and Shakespeare is unobtrusively preparing both leaders there, the Prince and the Archbishop. As for Falstaff, this is the scene where, after Hotspur's death, he follows 'for reward'. He is at the height of his prospects, favoured as never before, with Hal countenancing the most preposterous of his japes, and the looked-for retribution is still not in sight. Clearly, both serious and comic themes require further stages of the action.

Those critics who consider Part 2 as an 'unpremeditated addition', therefore, are going against the evidence. They have on their side the fact that Shrewsbury is a wonderful climax and Part 1 superbly handled, and acceptable in itself. But of course no play patently dependent on another would satisfy its customers; historical dramas must be dramatically complete, even though history itself is incomplete. Shrewsbury is an interim triumph, but the stress of the whole story requires an end beyond Shrewsbury. No matter where Shakespeare looked in the chronicles he would find that the expected counterpart to the overthrow of Richard II was the unquiet time of Henry IV—that was what the reign of Henry meant. And Falstaff must curve downwards to his doom. So the heroics and gaiety of Part 1 must yield to the darker history and more ominous comedy of Part 2. Part 2 is the necessary complement of Hal's evolution, and Henry's, and Falstaff's.

But given that Shakespeare did not mean to stop at Shrewsbury, did he originally expect to comprise the whole reign in one play? Or did he from the beginning intend two? Professor Harold Jenkins has argued persuasively that he started with the idea of a single play but found himself compelled to change his scheme by the plenitude of his material.[1] The twin-themes of Hal's emergence into heroic splendour and of the scapegraces' rejection are announced together in Hal's soliloquy (*1H4*, I. ii. 219 ff.). For three acts Shakespeare develops these together, in Hal's hints that retribution will befall Falstaff, and in the great interview between Hal and Henry which is the 'nodal point' of Part 1. The intention, Professor Jenkins suggests, was perhaps that Shrewsbury should be followed (as in Daniel) by a drastic foreshortening of King Henry's latter years[2] and by his death and Hal's coronation, with the rejection of Falstaff. But by Act IV so much material has presented itself that 'any thought of crowding into the two-hour traffic of the play the deaths of the old king and the coronation of the new has by now been relinquished, and instead the battle of Shrewsbury is being built up into a grand finale in its own right'. The 'revised' plan, Professor Jenkins concludes, is superbly handled, the excitement is intense, Shrewsbury 'brings each man to a destiny we perceive to be appropriate', and Shakespeare is free to continue or not as he sees fit, doubtless fully intending to do so unless unforeseen circumstances intervene. This view, indeed, allows for one of the forces most evident in the composition of these plays, that of organic evolution. It offers a way round the dilemma of planned-interdependence versus unpremeditated-addition (both of which raise problems), while facing us with the paradox (the truth of which we can admit) that '*Henry IV* is both one play and two . . . the two parts are complementary, they are also independent and even incompatible.'[3]

1. *The Structural Problem in Sh.'s 'Henry the Fourth'*, 1956.

2. Daniel, it may be noted, however, though compressing his story after Shrewsbury, has before Shrewsbury referred to Northumberland's rising as part of the 'Nemesis' afflicting Henry.

3. *Op. cit.*, p. 26.

The argument is presented most thoughtfully, lucidly, and persuasively. To that part of it which argues for the paradox of simultaneous independence and interdependence of the two parts there can be nothing but assent—each play requires the other, yet each stands on its own. As for the problem by which Hal, redeemed in Part 1, is unredeemed again in Part 2, with no one showing any cognizance of the excellence he so eminently displayed at Shrewsbury —that problem is beautifully dealt with by the observation that 'there is a type of hero whose adventures always can recur', that 'in folk-lore, though not in history, you can be at the same point twice'. Prince Hal is a folk-lore hero, as well as a historical person. His glory at the end of Part 1, and his ignominy in the early scenes of Part 2, are not a matter of reform and relapse, the purely naturalistic process Johnson pointed towards in saying, 'The trifler is roused into a hero, and the hero reposes again in the trifler. This character is great, original, and just.' No: Shakespeare's psychology with Hal is not wholly naturalistic, any more than it is when he gives him the apparently cynical but in reality merely expository soliloquy in Part 1, I. ii. Naturalistically, Hal would not, after redeeming himself at Shrewsbury, be thought of by almost everybody as a wastrel, his merits unrecognized. But symbolically, demonstratively, or parabolically he may be shown going through two quite separate moral evolutions which the play's chronology presents as successive but which in fact are in parallel. 'In the two parts of *Henry IV* there are not two princely reformations but two versions of a single reformation. And they are mutually exclusive,' Professor Jenkins excellently says. Had Shakespeare been writing a modern sophisticated morality based, say, on Dunne's theory of Serial Time, he might have back-tracked his whole action to show the second redemption as co-existent with the first. But he is writing an Elizabethan history with sequential chronology. So he simply assumes that there is no problem; Part 1 showed Hal's accession to Chivalry, Part 2 will show his accession to Good Rule, the two requisites for a king. And no spectator will ask too many questions.

The other part of Professor Jenkins's argument, that up to some point in Act IV of Part 1 Shakespeare intended only a single play, is harder to accept. There is, of course, no inherent unlikelihood in the idea that he may at first have hoped to reach the coronation-and-rejection in one play; he doubtless did not write 'The First Part' in his title, otherwise this would appear in the Quarto. And Professor Jenkins argues shrewdly for signs of a close linkage originally intended between the dooms of Hotspur and of Falstaff.

Yet it is not easy to accept the idea that Shakespeare's plan changed so much, and so late as the end of Act III. Such a change would surely produce more dislocation or disproportion than Part I shows: and actually the historical action develops, as Professor Jenkins says, 'with a fine structural proportion throughout'. Besides this, there is such fullness of invention in the whole treatment that from quite early on one would not expect the story to get farther than Shrewsbury—it looks like being Hotspur's play and bound to culminate in Hotspur's battle. A quick post-Shrewsbury passage to Henry's death would moreover forfeit one of the main elements in all the chronicles of his reign—that it was full of retributive worry and wearisome turmoil. Henry's guilt needs longer expiation than a Shrewsbury triumph and a quick death would admit of. Furthermore, though Hal certainly gives Falstaff hints of doom, the play does nothing to bring those hints *near*; they seem to relate—as Professor Jenkins recognizes—to a distant unspecified future before which there is ample scope for fleeting the time carelessly. The touches in Hal's fencing with Falstaff do not seem serious (e.g. *1H4*, I. ii, and II. iv. 508–9, 542); Hal's manner is one of rich, even affectionate, appreciation, as though age could not wither nor custom stale his old acquaintance's infinite variety. How could the rejection follow soon upon this? Half-way through Part I (the end of II. iv), where Professor Jenkins thinks the Hotspur and Falstaff plots show 'every sign of moving towards their crisis together', Hal is promising an 'honourable' place to Peto and undertaking to procure Falstaff a charge of foot, clearly still ready for reckless jesting with him. In other words, the whole pace, fashioning, and conception of Part I, whatever the initial intention, rule out the possibility of disposing of both Hotspur and Falstaff within the one play, and they do this, one would think, almost from the beginning. It seems better to assume that at the outset, or at least very soon after, Shakespeare envisaged two plays, both of which would deal with the traditional story of the Wild Prince reformed, but one of which would aim at Shrewsbury and Valour, the other at Westminster and Justice.

This assumption finds support in the sources. These take the material in different ways and at different speeds. The historical detail is mainly Holinshed's. The spirit—the valiancy of Part I, the gravity of Part 2—is Daniel's. The comedy is from *The Famous Victories* (or some original of this), based on Stow (to whom Shakespeare also goes direct). These sources have very different curves of events and combining them is tricky. In the historical interpretation Daniel is Shakespeare's controlling genius. Daniel's major climax is at Shrewsbury, with a valiant Prince encountering (and by implication slaying) Hotspur—one might indeed say that Daniel gave Shakespeare the historical form of Part I ready-made, a complete drama to his hand, culminating in the battle. But of course a play on Hal must include the Wild-Prince comedy, with Hal redeemed from low life to high. In terms of the Daniel version of things, the redemption must take place at Shrewsbury, since that is where Hal is Daniel's hero. So *The Famous Victories'* comedy plus Daniel's Shrewsbury climax (plus facts from Holinshed) almost inescapably creates the shape of Part I and produces the first redemption, in terms of Valour.

But assuming, as is surely certain, that Shakespeare meant to follow through to Henry's death, his main source after Shrewsbury must be Holinshed, since Daniel is short of material. Holinshed's story is a long series of struggles and revolts, ranged round the prophecy *Stirps Persitina periet confusa ruina*. With this it mixes the discord between Henry and Hal, the reconciliation, the crown-on-the-pillow, and Henry's death-bed confession to the now-trusted Prince. Daniel contributes the sombre spirit, Stow perhaps the stress on justice. But Holinshed gives the narrative form, of Percy turbulence and princely reformation (as Daniel had done that of Part I), with *The Famous Victories* bringing in the fall of the scape-graces on Hal's coronation. Really, the practical answer to the question why Hal is redeemed in both plays is that Daniel shows him so in Chivalry at Shrewsbury, and Holinshed so in Good Rule at Westminster. And Shakespeare follows each in succession.

The conclusion, then, is that Shakespeare seemingly intended two plays from the outset, or very near it; that Daniel shaped the one play for him and Holinshed the other; that the Wild-Prince traditions required Hal to spend most of each play in disgrace but that Daniel's account showed him as heroic at Shrewsbury and Holinshed's as kingly at his accession; that while naturalistically speaking these twin-redemptions are an incoherence, dramatically and by folk-tale or morality canons they are acceptable; and finally that, though one must reject the idea that the two parts reveal an embracing ten-act-cycle form (as contended by Dover Wilson and Dr Tillyard), yet despite their ability to stand each on its own they belong powerfully together in tracing the fortunes of Henry, Hal, the Percys, and Falstaff.

## 5. THE MAIN SOURCES[1]

As was observed in the introduction to Part 1 (New Arden),

Literary sources are, rightly speaking, the whole relevant contents of the writer's mind as he composes, and no account of
them can be complete. To specify the *Henry IV* plays' 'sources'
is to run the risk of seeming too narrow, of circumscribing works
that so generously embrace Elizabethan life and thought as to be
an individual's expression of a whole nationhood.

The same point needs making here. There are evident direct and
immediate sources in chronicles and plays (including recapitula-
tions of *Richard II*). There are indirect sources conveyed through
the direct ones and showing how widely current was the matter of
Hal's redemption—fifteenth-century stories carried forward by the
chronicles of Gregory, Fabyan, Hall, and others, and by additions
to Tito Livio's *Vita Henrici Quinti* which transmit some of the most
interesting episodes of Hal's youth.[2] These stories form the central
current of the historical or pseudo-historical tradition, broad in its
flow, and, as it approaches the moment of Hal's coronation, strong
with dramatic expectancy. But the central current is not the whole
of the river. Contributory eddies and flows join in—Biblical and
theological echoes, travesties of military, medical, and psychological theories, reflections of current satire on country justices and
corrupt soldiers, ballads and songs, proverbs and tags, sidelights on
life and work, revelry and street brawls, parodies of dramatic fustian and morality-play idiom; and behind all this the tradition that
history inculcates the importance of national unity and strong rule.
All this is expressed in the play by an imaginative mind of unique
brilliance, using as its resources of expression the English language
in its most exuberant phase of development. To borrow again from
the introduction to Part 1,

The true 'sources' are a whole national life, thought, and language as felt by a great poet; they far outrange any mere inter-
leaving (as some critics have thought) of perfunctory history and
vivid comedy or (as others have thought) of purposeful history
and irrelevant (though welcome) comedy. Both history and
comedy combine in surpassingly rich interrelationships, whose
'source' is Shakespeare's myriad-mindedness. . . To list a few
documents is therefore to give no adequate account of the
materials. Yet Shakespeare's indebtednesses are great, and the

1. The commentary on the sources, and indeed on the whole play, in Geoffrey
Bullough's *Narrative and Dramatic Sources of Sh.*, vol. iv, 1962, is so strikingly good
that it is a pleasure to call attention to it.

2. For the additions to Tito Livio see below, pp. xxxvii–xxxviii.

more his identifiable sources are studied the more evident does it
become that his structural power in uniting diverse materials is
as extraordinary as his psychological, moral, or poetic power.

### (i) Raphael Holinshed: 'Chronicles of England' (2nd edn, 1587)[1]

More fully here than in Part 1 Shakespeare depends on Holinshed rather than on Daniel, for Daniel devotes a mere stanza to
Henry's 'intricate turmoiles, and sorrowes deepe' after Shrewsbury (but without any specific events), and then puts him upon his
death-bed. The coalescence in Part 1 whereby Daniel's spirit and
tone colour Holinshed's facts, however, finds its parallel here in the
darker and graver mood. Holinshed is followed faithfully, though
with constructive selection, condensation, and rearrangement of
events; these are necessary since the historical material relevant to
Part 2 occupies in Holinshed five times as much space as that for
Part 1, with haphazard forays against Scots, Welsh, and French
(cf. I. iii. 70–85), and Parliamentary affairs. These items are too
formless to be used directly, though references to them create the
play's sense of disturbance at home and abroad[2] and elements of it
are concentrated, though not very specifically, in the Archbishop's
complaints of repressive government. The heart of the rebels'
grievances, according to the Archbishop, is 'feare of the king, to
whom he could have no free access'—this is reflected at IV. i. 73–9.
Holinshed's vagueness about the rebels' motives is rather concealed
in the play by the poetic force of the speeches Shakespeare devises
—by Northumberland's violence, the Archbishop's rich passion
of good intentions, Lord Bardolph's practical energy, Hastings's
briskness, and so forth. These individualizing qualities Shakespeare
elicits from slight hints in Holinshed—the Archbishop's authority
from a short reference to 'the grauitie of his age, his integritie of
life, and incomparable learning, with the reuerend aspect of his
amiable personage', Mowbray's caution from six words in paren-
thesis—'the archbishop ... gaue credit to the earle [Westmoreland]
and persuaded the earle marshall (against his will as it were) to go
with him.' Such fruitful germinations from small seeds are characteristically and beautifully Shakespearean.

1. The 1587 edition has the word 'pickthanks' (cf. Appendix I, p. 199) which
Shakespeare picked up in *1 Henry IV*, III. ii. 25; that of 1577 does not. References
are to the 6-volume reprint of 1807–8.

2. A proposed taxation of the clergy, mooted by the Commons in an anti-
clerical mood in 1410 (Hol., iii. 48, 65), is not mentioned in *2 Henry IV* but is the
subject with which *Henry V* opens; cf. *H5*, I. i. 1–20. The references to grievances
in *2 Henry IV* are mostly of a general kind—e.g. I. i. 207–8; I. iii. 87 ff.; IV. i. 54 ff.,
168 ff.; IV. ii. 32 ff., 113–14. This vagueness corresponds on the whole with
Holinshed.

Shakespeare's adjustments are equally significant.

(a) He makes Hal accompany the King against the Welsh after Shrewsbury (*1H4*, v. v. 39–40; *2H4*, I. iii. 83, II. iv. 290). Holinshed refers to campaigns which Henry plans or executes but he does not say that Hal participates. Shakespeare doubtless feels that, since Prince John is to command at Gaultree (and indeed is sent, unhistorically, from Shrewsbury with Westmoreland against the northern rebels), Hal needs to compete in military reputation.

(b) Important condensations take place over the rebellions. The Archbishop's is, in Shakespeare, in train even before Shrewsbury (*1H4*, IV. iv): Holinshed puts it two years later (1405). In Holinshed, Northumberland separately threatens danger immediately after Shrewsbury, though he withdraws, and then plots with the Archbishop in 1405 and finally rises in 1408. These three movements of revolt Shakespeare virtually combines; the first two become a single post-Shrewsbury threat by Northumberland and the Archbishop, and Westmoreland and John go straight from Shrewsbury to Gaultree to meet it (*1H4*, v. v. 35–8).[1] Gaultree (1405) and Bramham (1408) are announced almost together, and immediately afterwards the King is fatally stricken, though historically this happened five years later. These changes concentrate the play both in itself and in its relationships with Part 1.

(c) A comparably powerful unification occurs over the King's illness. This, probably through Daniel's influence, is much predated. Holinshed first mentions it in 1412, and the fatal apoplexy strikes only in March 1413. Indeed, in Holinshed the King is a vigorous leader for ten years after Shrewsbury—the fact that not he but his commanders crush the rebellions of 1405 and 1408 is merely because they arrive first. In the play he is afflicted almost immediately after Shrewsbury and he ails throughout. As in Daniel, melancholy and wasting disease colour the whole period of the action.

(d) The development of Northumberland both adds to and subtracts from Holinshed. Holinshed presents him as an indecisive trouble-maker who, detained from Shrewsbury by sickness, thereafter advances powerfully against Henry's forces but retreats when opposed. He then shares in plans for the Archbishop's revolt, though the Archbishop moves too quickly for him actually to support it. Finally he fights bravely at Bramham Moor. His presentation in Shakespeare is more damaging. He is 'crafty-sick' (Induction, 37), whereas none of the sources blames his absence from

1. In Holinshed, not Prince John but Sir Robert Waterton accompanies Westmoreland. But Shakespeare treats this rising and Gaultree (where John was present) as one.

Shrewsbury on craft. This must be a sign of Shakespeare's pre-judice, for he is not actually presented, either here or in Part 1, as *wilfully* ailing. Shakespeare perhaps conceived a dislike of him for acting as Bolingbroke's jackal against Richard II; or he may have observed the sinister traits attributed to Northumberland in the *Myrroure for Magistrates*.[1] At any rate, Northumberland's absence from Shrewsbury looks like treachery even if it is not, as Worcester remarks (*1H4*, IV. i. 62–5). In Part 2 he again abandons his allies, this time inexcusably, whereas in Holinshed the fault is the Arch-bishop's precipitancy and Northumberland flees only when all is already lost. Finally, the play allows him no valour in his death. One must agree that 'Shakespeare has formed his Northumberland in a narrow mould, chiefly, it seems, by sharpening and intensifying the selfish traits that he finds in Holinshed's character'.[2]

(*e*) The Gaultree negotiations are in Holinshed handled entirely by Westmoreland, who is responsible for the trickery, though in an alternative account Prince John receives the rebels' submission as his father's representative. Neither version shows John in the dis-agreeable light of the play. In 'this same young sober-blooded boy' Shakespeare stresses the 'cold blood' of the Bolingbrokian line against which the more generous Hal is set.

(*f*) Finally, Shakespeare handles the reconciliations differently. Holinshed and *The Famous Victories* provide a single one between King and Prince, at which Hal arrives curiously dressed (cf. Ap-pendix I, p. 198), humiliates himself, and offers the King his dag-ger. Shakespeare has his first reconciliation in Part 1, without the strange apparel and the melodramatics. In Part 2 he develops the crown-on-the-pillow incident and thereby has a father-and-son crisis in each play. This is (as far as each play separately goes) good drama. But is it bad management? Not seriously so; Henry recog-nizes Hal's military gifts in Part 2, since he takes him on his Welsh campaign, and he speaks not unappreciatively of him in IV. iv. 20–48. It is only when, dying, he hears that Hal still meets 'Poins, and other his continual followers', and when the taking of the crown shocks him (as well it might) that he ignores the hopes Part 1 has aroused and despairs of Hal.

In all these details, Shakespeare's dramatizing gift is clear. The result is less shapely than Part 1 because the events are scrappier.

1. See below, p. xxxvii. Professor Dover Wilson holds that among the sources of *Richard II* was Jean Créton's verse *Histoire du Roy d'Angleterre*, in which Richard is likened to Christ and Northumberland to Judas. Whether Shakespeare in fact knew Créton is uncertain, but Hall, Stow, Holinshed, and Daniel did.

2. Sarah Dodson, 'The Northumberland of Shakespeare and Holinshed', *Univ. Texas Studies in English*, 1939, p. 85.

But the degree of improvement over Holinshed's formless and prosaic narrative is hardly less striking than it was in the earlier play.

(ii) *Samuel Daniel: 'The First Fowre Bookes of the Ciuile Wars Between the Two Houses of Lancaster and Yorke'* (*1595*)

Daniel's influence, as has been said, is rather on tone and attitude than on facts, but since the tone and attitude centre upon the King, a king with 'the makings of a tragic hero',[1] they control the emotional timbre of the play. Writing in verse, he achieves a higher potency of feeling, and his simple outlines and clear treatment bring his effects movingly home.

(*a*) He deeply affects the way Shakespeare treats Henry's culpability. Our judgment on this must depend on our knowledge of Henry's relations with Richard II, and these Daniel surveys much more lucidly than does Holinshed. At first, Richard's licentiousness is stressed, and as a result Bolingbroke laments the nation's calamities (*C.W.*, i. 61). Hereupon Mowbray traduces him to Richard and sets the quarrel abroach. Bolingbroke is banished and the populace is desolate.[2] Daniel insists on Richard's flagrant misrule and on the almost inevitable trend of events which occasions his downfall. Almost without his will Bolingbroke is carried to usurpation and power—ambition is his tragic flaw, but this less by plan than by fatalism; he is the servant rather than the master of his fate. All this in Daniel is the basis of Henry's claim in the play that he came to power unintentionally (*2H4*, iii. i. 72–4):

> Though then, God knows, I had no such intent
> But that necessity so bow'd the state
> That I and greatness were compell'd to kiss.

Henry is to be believed here; both the earnestness of his whole speech and the tenor of Daniel vouch for this.

Yet about Henry's motives Daniel, like Holinshed and Shakespeare, is somewhat ambiguous. As well as 'forward ambition' (*C.W.*, ii. 99) he attributes to him 'craft' (ii. 83), 'pride' (ii. 66), exultation at displacing Richard (ii. 69), 'colours of deceit' (iii. 2), and the instigation of Richard's murder. Henry, therefore, though an opportunist rather than a plotter like Richard III, bears a deserved weight of guilt, and this is felt with sombre emotion in Daniel's pages as in Shakespeare's.

(*b*) All but one of Daniel's post-Shrewsbury stanzas are con-

1. O. Elton, 'Style in Shakespeare', *Proc. Brit. Acad.*, 1936, p. 85.
2. Daniel's lines on popular partisanship and fickleness seem echoed by the Archbishop (cf. *2H4*, I. iii. 91–3 and below, pp. 204–8, stanzas i. 70–1, ii. 13–16).

cerned with the King's death-bed. Though lacking in events, however, this account (so different from Holinshed's) becomes in spirit Shakespeare's. In the play, Henry is not even seen until Act III; then the forceful monarch of Part I appears harassed, mournfully reflective, sleepless, and ill. Even earlier, even before we have heard that he and Hal are campaigning against the Welsh (I. iii. 83), Falstaff declares him to have fallen into a 'lethargy [which] hath it original from much grief, from study, and perturbation of the brain' (I. ii. 110 ff.). Hal and Poins speak of him as gravely ailing (II. ii. 39 ff.). After Act III, scene i, he is not seen again until Act IV, scene iv, when, though he proposes a crusade, he needs 'a little personal strength'. In the next scene he is dying. At times he talks of the kingdom's troubles, and he shows a firm sense of the practical (III. i; IV. iv–v); thereby he gives an impression (as in Daniel he does not) of having for a long though unspecified time been grappling with dangerous affairs (IV. v. 190–212). Yet all we actually see is the ailing, afflicted monarch of Daniel.

(c) As in Part I, Daniel sounds the theme of nemesis for Henry's usurpation. Though he ignores the risings after Shrewsbury he foretells Northumberland's when, absent from Shrewsbury, Northumberland is described as being

> yet reseru'd, though after quit for this,
> Another tempest on thy [Henry's] head to raise,
> As if still wrong-revenging *Nemesis*
> Did meane t'afflict all thy continuall dayes.
>
> (*C.W.*, iii. 98)

One major difference between Daniel and Shakespeare should be noted, however. In Daniel the King strives, fleetingly, to salve his conscience by giving the crown up 'to whom it seem'd to appertaine'—presumably to Lord Mortimer (*C.W.*, iii. 122). In the play, Henry's concern is just the contrary—it is the thought that the crown, so dearly won, may be forfeited through Hal's wildness. The crown, it is true, has been 'troublesome', a source of guilt; almost Henry's last words are 'How I came by the crown, O God forgive'. Yet he immediately follows this with 'And grant it may with thee in true peace live', and he gives Hal cogent advice about safeguarding it. This advice owes much to Daniel; the Machiavellian scheme of promoting foreign wars to avert faction at home is much nearer to Daniel than to Holinshed (*C.W.*, iii. 127–9). But Shakespeare will not have Daniel's impulse of resignation. He sacrifices thereby an element of remorseful emotion. But he preserves the King's unwavering tenacity of power.

(iii) *John Stow: 'The Chronicles of England'* (*1580*): *'The Annales of England'* (*1592*)

Stow's *Annales* overlap and resemble his *Chronicles* and also the 1587 edition of Holinshed (which he helped to compile and which Shakespeare used). Many of the play's details, therefore, cannot be assigned without cavil to one rather than another of these works; yet some do seem to originate with Stow rather than Holinshed. The title of 'Duke of Lancaster' for Prince John may do so (cf. I. iii. 82 and note); and the Archbishop's reference to a 'schedule' of grievances (IV. i. 168) doubtless echoes Stow's 'scedule' (*Chron.*, p. 563; *Annales*, p. 529) rather than Holinshed's 'scroll' (Hol., iii. 37). Further, Stow's image of the heart and members of the body may have prompted Falstaff at IV. iii. 109–10 (cf. Appendix I, p. 217).

More importantly, Stow seems to be the source for (*a*) the Lord Chief Justice's prominence, (*b*) the tenor of the dying King's advice, and possibly (*c*) touches in Hal's accession-speech.

(*a*) Following Elyot's *Gouernour* closely, Stow tells with impressive solemnity the story of Hal's threatening the Lord Chief Justice, and records the Justice's grave counsels to the heir of the crown (cf. Appendix I, p. 218). The importance given to his role may have been Shakespeare's lead for the key-position he holds in the play.

(*b*) Holinshed treats the death-bed advice briefly, but Stow dwells at length on Henry's 'diuerse notable doctrines'. The earnest religious tone he attributes to Henry is indeed more striking than the practical realism of the corresponding speech in the play (IV. v. 181–219), but though Shakespeare alters the tone Stow probably was the inspirer of Henry's 'very latest counsel', and doubtless gave something also to the new King's solemn manner as he addresses his brothers and the Lord Chief Justice, vowing to cherish his realm under impartial law. In Stow, the dying King urges three themes: strict maintenance of justice to all; attention to subjects' weal; and gratitude to God, 'since all commeth onely of the goodnesse of the Lord'. These three Shakespeare would seem to have marked. The first forms the whole moral theme of the play, by which Hal, who once defied the Lord Chief Justice, accepts him as mentor; the second is reflected in Hal's resolve to govern with 'limbs of noble counsel' in 'our high court of parliament'. And the third may well have been in Shakespeare's mind as he wrote *Henry V*; Henry IV's words, and Stow's comment (cf. below, pp. 217, 220), seem to sound the religious note of that play, though admittedly Holinshed has it too.

(*c*) In Stow, the new King prays that his accession shall be conditional on God's favour, and that he may die rather than reign if God does not approve him. This sounds like the germ of v. ii. 143–5:

> And, God consigning to my good intents,
> No prince nor peer shall have just cause to say,
> God shorten Harry's happy life one day!

Holinshed makes clear the new King's religious devotion but has nothing quite corresponding to these lines.

### (iv) *Sir Thomas Elyot: 'The Gouernour'* (*1531*)

Evidence that Shakespeare knew Elyot's work, and drew upon it, accumulates.[1] Elyot is the earliest known source for the story that Prince Henry invaded the court of the King's Bench and threatened the Lord Chief Justice (*Gov.*, ii. vi). Whether Shakespeare drew on *The Gouernour* for Hal's words in the play as he recalls his father's comment on the affair (v. ii. 108–12) it is hard to say, since Elyot is reproduced in Stow almost verbatim for the whole incident. Shakespeare's debt to Stow for other material being demonstrable, it may well be that here too he took Stow's account, rather than seeking it (in all but identical form) in the earlier work. However, since the words Shakespeare recasts are in fact Elyot's—whether directly or *via* Stow—Elyot's account is given in Appendix I, p. 220.

### (v) *'A Myrroure for Magistrates'* (*1559*)

It seems likely that Shakespeare drew some details from this much-respected collection of stories about men in power.[2] Stow and Holinshed make no mention of Prince Hal's campaigning in Wales (*1H4*, v. v. 39; *2H4*, I. iii. 83; II. iv. 290). Hall does (cf. below, p. 233), and it might be thought that Shakespeare found the point there. But the *Myrroure* has it also, in the tale of Owen Glendower whence Shakespeare drew some details for Part I:

> When Henry king the victory had wunne,
> Destroyed the Percies, put their power to flyght,
> He did appoynt prince Henry his eldest sunne
> With all his power to meete me [Owen] if he might.[3]

1. See Harold F. Brooks, 'Shakespeare and *The Gouernour*', *Sh.Q.*, xiv, 1963, pp. 195–9.

2. Signs that in *1 Henry IV* (as in *Richard II*) Shakespeare borrowed from the *Myrroure* are discussed in the New Arden edn, p. xxxvii.

3. *Op. cit.*, ed. L. B. Campbell, 1938, p. 138. Actually, no source specifically sends the King to Wales at this point, though Holinshed describes an ineffective campaign later; cf. *2H4*, I. ii. 102–3.

Since in Part I apparent borrowings from Hall seem more likely to come from the *Myrroure* (itself based upon Hall, Fabyan, and others), this is probably the case here. Shakespeare's harsh reading of Northumberland may owe something to the *Myrroure* too, for Northumberland there, though having good grounds for grievance, embodies 'couetise ioynt with contumacy' such as 'Doth cause all mischief in mens hartes to brede'.[1] Slighter possibilities of influence are that in three successive stories the *Myrroure* gives the falls of Glendower (with Hotspur), Northumberland (with the Archbishop), and Richard Earl of Cambridge (the rebel of *Henry V*). This last, though 'not very notable', is included as ending the successive conflicts between the Mortimer and Bolingbroke lines, and the three successive stories may have helped to shape Shakespeare's choice of successive subversions in the series from *I Henry IV* to *Henry V*.

### (vi) *The 'Wild Prince Hal' Stories*[2]

Stories of Henry V's madcap youth go back to his own lifetime. In 1418 Thomas of Walsingham records his sudden reformation on succeeding to the crown[3]; the virtually 'official' *Vita Henrici Quinti* (c. 1437) by Tito Livio admits his wildness; the popular *Brut* chronicle tells how, as Prince of Wales, 'he fylle & yntendyd gretly to ryot, and drew to wylde company; & dyuers Ientylmen and Ientylwommen folwyd his wylle', and how only three honest counsellors opposed him, whom 'he louyd aftyrward best, for þere good counsayle'.[4] Fabyan's *Chronicle* (1516; written before 1513) speaks of 'all vyce and insolency' (p. 577), until on his accession 'suddenly he became a newe man', banishing his mates ten miles upon pain of death (the first known mention of this threat). In 1513 an English translation of Tito Livio added extra material, of first-rate interest, from Enguerrand de Monstrelet's *Chroniques* (including the crown-on-the-pillow incident) and from the recollections of the fourth Earl of Ormonde (1392–1452), whom Henry knighted at Agincourt and whose information the translator derived probably from reports of some scholar whom Ormonde patronized. Thence, that is, directly from one who knew Henry well, comes the story that he would lie in ambush to rob his own receivers, that the

1. *Ed. cit.*, p. 137.

2. The first two paragraphs of this account are closely from the introduction to Part I, New Arden edition, as being relevant here too.

3. 'Mox ut initiatus est regni insulis repente mutatus est in virum alterum' (*Historia Anglicana*, ed. H. T. Riley, 1863, ii. 29).

4. *Op. cit.*, ed. F. W. D. Brie, EETS, Orig. ser., 136, ii. 594–5, and to similar effect p. 499.

King misliked 'the great recourse of people to him' and 'the acts of youth which he exercised more than meanly [i.e. immoderately]', that to make amends the Prince approached his father in fantastic garb, that when dying the King made him a speech of good counsel repenting the usurpation, to which the Prince proudly replied that he would maintain the succession, and that while loose in morals before his accession he thereupon became strictly continent.[1]

Though this translation was not printed until 1911, its MS form was influential since its stories appeared in Stow's *Chronicles* (1580) and *Annales* (1592), and some of them (though not the receiver-robbing) in Holinshed. Together with the famous anecdote that the Prince threatened or struck the Lord Chief Justice and was sent to prison they comprise the legend of the Wild Prince, the origins of which thus date from the fifteenth century and seem reasonably authentic.

The affair of the Lord Chief Justice is one of the most cherished of the legends. First extant in Elyot's *Gouernour* (1531),[2] it is given in Stow's *Annales* in words almost identical with Elyot's: both accounts describe the Prince as threatening the Justice (though not as striking him), being sent to prison, and losing his place as Privy Councillor. Robert Redmayne's *Vita Henrici Quinti* (c. 1540) refers to a blow with the fist, giving the forfeited Councillorship to Thomas of Clarence.[3] Hall and Holinshed make the same points. *The Famous Victories* has 'He giueth him a boxe on the eare', and this ear-boxing figured in Tarlton's play; Shakespeare adopts it,[4] and also the dismissal from the Council, which the *Famous Victories* does not mention. The Tudor chroniclers refer the dismissal to this assault, yet they hint also at the true reason, that the Prince was suspected of planning treachery. This suspicion is reflected in *1 Henry IV* when the King calls Hal 'my nearest and dearest enemy' (III. ii. 123) and when he finds his fears dispelled on the battlefield (v. iv. 47–51). It may be reflected too, though uncertainly, in *2 Henry IV* (IV. v. 74–9, 92–3, 104–8).

1. C. L. Kingsford, *The First English Life of Henry V*, 1911, pp. xxv–xxx.
2. It may descend from a non-extant London civic chronicle.
3. No contemporary report has been found of any committal of Prince Henry, but a similar incident occurred when Edward I banished 'filium suum primogenitum et carissimum Edwardum Principem Walliae' until he had made amends to a royal official for uttering in a quarrel at court 'quaedam verba grossa et acerba'; Boswell Stone, *Sh.'s Holinshed*, 1907, pp. 161–2, note.
4. *2H4*, I. ii. 193–5; less specific references at I. ii. 55–6, v. ii. 80. Other treatments before Shakespeare are in Angel Day's *English Secretarie*, 1586, pp. 80–1 (here the Prince 'strooke the Judge on the face', but no dismissal from the Council is recorded), and John Case's *Sphæra Ciuitatis*, 1588 (see notes below, on v. ii. 73 and 108–12).

No previous treatment of Henry IV's reign or Henry V's accession gives the Lord Chief Justice the prominence he has in Shakespeare, where Hal's conduct with him is made a central element on which to display the conversion to kingliness. The early scenes when he embodies order against anarchy are purely Shakespeare's own (I. ii, II. i). The position of royal mentor and 'father' conferred on him is likewise Shakespeare's; in the chroniclers the King commits himself to a 'vertuous Monke',[1] or to good counsellors.[2] In *The Famous Victories* Henry, about to depart for France, appoints his old opponent as guardian of the realm, but this is only a passing incident. That Shakespeare should give the Lord Chief Justice such pre-eminence and such a fatherly function, while never showing the assault on him (doubtless as too damaging to the Prince), is a mark of his instinct for moral structure.

As for the other Wild-Prince elements in the play, the submissive interview originates with Ormonde and occurs in Stow, Holinshed, and *The Famous Victories*. Shakespeare cuts out the unruly supporters, Hal's strange guise, and the offer of the dagger. Instead, there are the earnest private meetings with the King in both Parts. Traces of Hal's recklessness survive in his protraction of tavern life while King and country are ailing, and his over-brisk entry into Henry's bedchamber, but he is restive in the tavern and quickly sobered in the sickroom. And his alienation from Falstaff is increasingly evident.

As for the crown-on-the-pillow and Henry's dying counsel, these features need some comment. The first, originating in Monstrelet's *Chroniques*,[3] is repeated by the 1513 translator of Tito Livio and then by Hall and Holinshed (but not Stow), *The Famous Victories*, and Daniel. Shakespeare's version combines substance from Holinshed, *The Famous Victories*, and Daniel, with the grave earnestness of Stow's death-bed exhortations. Hall and Holinshed give almost identical brief factual accounts. *The Famous Victories* works the episode up crudely but not unmovingly and it gives in outline something like Shakespeare's treatment. In Daniel the elements are similar (the King reproaching the Prince for haste, and grieving at his own misdeeds), but the theme of remorse is developed and Henry counsels his son both to strengthen his weak title by good rule and to distract restive energies with a crusade. (There is in fact a strong practical bent in Daniel at this point, which the play re-

1. C. L. Kingsford, *The First English Life of Henry V*, 1911, p. 17.
2. *The Brut*, ed. F. W. D. Brie, EETS, Orig. ser., 136, pp. 594–5; and Holinshed, iii. 62—'He elected the best learned men in the lawes of this realme, to the offices of iustice'. Holinshed reproduces Hall almost verbatim; Hall, pp. 46–7.
3. Enguerrand de Monstrelet, *Chronicles*, tr. T. Johnes, 1809, i. 317, chap. ci.

flects.) Stow, though silent about the crown-and-pillow, fills the last scene of Henry's life with those 'notable doctrines' which enrich the emotion with which Shakespeare invests the scene. Four sources, then, combine without strain as Shakespeare handles the climax-scene between father and son.

### (vii) 'The Famous Victories of Henry the Fifth' (1594?–8)

The anonymous *Famous Victories* play, entered on *SR* by Thomas Creede on 14 May 1594, is not known in any edition until 1598, when Creede issued it as 'plaide by the Queenes Maiesties Players'. Its publication or republication was doubtless prompted by the appearance of *Henry IV*, though its appearance with 'Sir Iohn Old-castle' among the Prince's rapscallions is odd at the very time when both parts of *Henry IV* were briskly dissociating themselves from any stigma on that unfortunate nobleman.

It is in effect in two parts, though printed as one; the first deals with the Prince's pranks up to his accession and reform, and the second corresponds closely with the course of *Henry V* from the Archbishop's recommendation of war to the winning of victory. In this part comes also the new King's commendation of the Lord Chief Justice. Some low comedy characters (though not the first half's Oldcastle, Ned, and Tom) provide the comedy, such as it is, of the French campaign. It includes nothing on Henry IV's 'un-quiet time' save that Henry is sick unto death, remorseful, and grief-stricken at his son's misdeeds.[1] Shakespeare could find in it (or its presumed better original, since it is virtually unplayable) an outline of the youthful escapades but almost nothing on the penalties of usurpation and nothing at all on education for king-ship.

The play's resemblances to *2 Henry IV* are as follows. The Prince has three scapegrace cronies, Oldcastle, Tom, and Ned (this last his favourite, as Ned Poins is in the play). They are called, but do not act like, knights, a status perhaps reflected in the 'sir Iohn Russel' of Q's stage direction (II. ii. 1). The Prince frequents the 'old taverne in Eastcheape' and praises its hostess. The King laments his follies and intends to disinherit him. A thief named Cuthbert Cutter or Gadshill (from the scene of his exploits) is tried for assaulting a carrier and stealing 'a great rase of ginger' (cf. *1H4*, II. i. 27). With his cronies the Prince comes to the court and boxes the Judge on the ear, whereupon he is committed to the Fleet. Henry despairs, but, being mollified when the Prince repents,

1. The Prince is called 'Henry V' even while his father is alive, or else 'Harry', but never 'Hal'.

he prophesies (on what must be thought slender evidence) that his son will rule valiantly. Dying, he asks for music to lull him asleep, and dozes with the crown beside him. The Prince enters grieving, takes the crown, and has an interview with the King, who confesses 'how hardly I came by it'. The Prince undertakes to maintain it, and to strains of music the King dies. The Judge expects punishment while the madcaps look for advancement and Ned aspires to being Lord Chief Justice. Henry V enters to the sound of coronation trumpets, is hailed by Ned (not Oldcastle), and banishes his mates ten miles, though promising assistance if they amend. Later, after refuting the tennis-ball insult by the French ambassador, he commends the Lord Chief Justice and appoints him Regent during the French war; and as the war is prepared there is a farcical impressment.

The resemblances to Shakespeare are evident, and not all are paralleled in the chronicles. The King's passionate grief and despair are notable, for the chronicles merely speak of an estrangement arising from suspected treachery. The death-bed scene, above all, shows a kinship of conception and even of phrasing, though not of quality. A comparison of *The Famous Victories*, scene viii, and *2 Henry IV*, IV. v, will reveal many common details, not all by any means found in the chronicles—music soothing the King, the Prince weeping, the lords calling the King after his doze and missing the crown, and particulars of the Prince's answer (cf. IV. v. 138–76 and note).

Yet the resulting effects are wholly different. In *The Famous Victories*, besides being a hooligan, the Prince longs for his father's death. He promises to make Ned Lord Chief Justice, and he goes rowdily to court when the King is ill, 'to clap the Crowne on my head'. He gets drunk, brawls, is gaoled more than once, appears oddly dressed at the royal interview with a 'verie disordered companie', approaches the King with dagger drawn, and then suddenly and fulsomely repents. The other rowdies have no resemblance to Shakespeare's; Oldcastle is neither old, thirsty, witty, fat, jovial, untruthful, nor voluble. Not from *this* version of the play, it seems clear, could Shakespeare catch a glimmering of sweet Jack Falstaff, kind Jack Falstaff, true Jack Falstaff, valiant Jack Falstaff, old Jack Falstaff, or of 'that father ruffian, that vanity in years'. As for the Hostess and Doll, no such persons appear. Nor is there any sign of country life in Gloucestershire.

Shakespeare's version is immeasurably better. In *Richard II*, Hal's escapades are reported but never seen (*R2*, v. iii. 1–12). In *1 Henry IV* they are harmless. In *2 Henry IV* he is weary and grieved,

virtually separated from Falstaff, and wholehearted in the repara-
tion he makes the Lord Chief Justice. In material Shakespeare
owes his comic original much; in spirit he follows the sober Holinshed. In preserving so many Wild-Prince elements yet harmonizing
them to his own conception of Hal's evolution he showed the
mastery of his genius.

### (viii) *Other Prince Hal Plays?*

Since on the first entrance of Oldcastle–Falstaff in *1 Henry IV*
Shakespeare assumes the audience will recognize him without his
being named or prepared for, there was presumably some prior
treatment more adequate than *The Famous Victories* from which he
would be familiar: indeed, *The Famous Victories* is so poor that a
better original must surely be supposed for it.[1] There were certainly pre-Shakespearean Henry V plays. *1 Henry VI* is a sequel to
some account of Henry V's victories, and a passage from *Tarlton's
Jests* is relevant to *2 Henry IV*:

> At the [Red] Bull in Bishops-gate, was a play of Henry the
> fift, where in the judge was to take a box on the eare; and because
> he was absent that should take the blow, Tarlton himself, ever
> forward to please, tooke upon him to play the same judge, be-
> sides his owne part of the clowne.[2]

Since Tarlton died in 1588 it seems there was a Henry V play before that. Nashe's *Pierce Penilesse* (1592) calls up a scene like, though
not identical with, the end of *The Famous Victories*:

> What a glorious thing it is to have Henrie the fifth represented on
> the stage leading the French King prisoner and forcing both him
> and the Dolphin to swear fealty. (McKerrow, i. 213)

On 14 May 1594, Thomas Creede entered *The Famous Victories* on
*SR*. And Henslowe's *Diary* records *harey the v* as acted by the Lord
Admiral's Men on 28 November 1595 at the Rose. This was still
being played in July 1596; since it belonged to a rival company, it
is not likely to have been Shakespeare's source.

*The Famous Victories*, as has been seen, claims to have been played
by the Queen's Majesty's Players (the leading company of the
1580's, though declining thereafter). If so, that company must have
acted a better version, in which perhaps the Prince's pranks and a
more memorable Oldcastle featured. Yet if Oldcastle bore a part
in the original *Famous Victories* prominent enough to enable an

---

1. The problem of *The Famous Victories'* antecedents is discussed in the New
Arden edition of *1 Henry IV*, pp. xxxiv–xxxvi.
2. *Sh.'s Jest-Books*, ed. W. C. Hazlitt, 1864, ii. 218.

audience to recognize him without prompting in *Henry IV*, it is strange that the existing *Famous Victories* handles him so ineptly. Perhaps there was an intermediate working-up between the original *Famous Victories* and Shakespeare. The hypothesis speculatively offered in Part 1 (New Arden), and owing much to other scholars, may be the right way of covering the known facts. It is that

> the original *Famous Victories* was in two parts, boiled down into one for provincial performance by needy players and memorially corrupted in the process; that its first part was a fuller version than survives in *The Famous Victories* of Hal's pranks (referred to in *Tarlton's Jests*) . . . and its second part dealt with Henry V's French wars (referred to by Nashe); that the second part was perhaps re-done as *harey the v* and later drawn upon by Shakespeare (since *The Famous Victories* and *Henry V* are evidently related); and that the first was perhaps re-done in a non-extant version which so familiarized the Elizabethan audiences with Oldcastle that Shakespeare took their familiarity for granted.

## 6. THEMES AND THEIR TREATMENT

The New Variorum edition presents an interesting range of estimates of the plays, from H. N. Hudson's 'Everyone, upon reading these two dramas, must be sensible of a falling-off in the latter' (1852 edn, v. 294) to R. G. White's claim that 'it is unsurpassed in its combination of variety and perfection by any other production of his pen' (New Var., 565). Sometimes a view that Part 2 is inferior to Part 1 leads to, or derives from, the belief that it was unpremeditated. If, with Mr R. W. David, one thinks that it is a 'ramshackle rag-bag', with 'pot-boiler written all over it', one probably decides that it was an afterthought; if, on the other hand, one holds with the Cowden Clarkes that 'far from the falling-off observable in most sequel productions, this Second Part is nobly maintained at the high-level, table-land altitude' of the First, one may conclude, as they do, that it was composed 'while the writer's brain was still in the same exalted mood that produced his admirable First Part'.[1]

However that may be, Shakespeare shows every sign of strong interest, from the lines in which Rumour conjures up a nation in tumult, through the tragic urgency of Northumberland's and Morton's exchanges and the council of war, to the confrontation of the opponents. Henry appears late and infrequently, but there is a

---

1. R. W. David, 'Sh.'s Historical Plays—Epic or Drama?' in *Sh. Survey*, 6, 1953, p. 129; and C. and M. Cowden Clarke, 1865 edn, ii. 171.

moving power in his utterance. Falstaff lacks Hal, but his exchanges with the Lord Chief Justice, Mistress Quickly, and Shallow are boldly impudent. Shakespeare is extending his range in the
psychology of ambiguous motives and making that exploration of
the national life of which Eastcheap, in its new Hogarthian character, and Gloucestershire are the remarkable discoveries. Professor Clifford Leech has indicated in Part 2 a unity of more
thoughtful tone and inquiring implications than in Part 1.[1] The
morality-elements endemic in much of Part 1's idiom, as well as in
Hal's poise between opposed incentives, are here more deeply
realized; human life is, in general, more complicated and pre-
carious than the confident enjoyable matter it had been in Part 1.
More miscellaneous though it is, and less co-ordinated by a total
creative impulse, Part 2 is hardly less powerful as an act of the
imagination, with a vitality and indeed violence in its comedy, a
passion and thoughtfulness in its history, without which the canon
of the plays would be much the poorer. It is unified by the powerful
treatment of a nexus of themes.

## (i) *Richard and Henry*

The chronicles give a deeper sense of the ambiguities of the
Richard–Henry story than the play-reader may get, and these are
not extraneous to criticism of the plays since the Elizabethans took
this situation in the context of their knowledge. Richard is repeatedly made out a very bad king, by Walsingham, the *Brut* chronicle,
Froissart, Holinshed, Daniel, and others.[2] In particular, Richard's
murder of his uncle, Thomas of Woodstock, Duke of Gloucester,
the subject of a *Myrroure for Magistrates* story and the anonymous
play of *Woodstock*, was held a brutal crime. This is reflected in
*Richard II* through Gaunt, the Duchess of Gloucester, and York,
though eclipsed later on by the pathos of the fallen King. To the
Elizabethans, lamentable though an anointed monarch's overthrow might be, a kingdom's collapse was still worse. Professor
Irving Ribner has commented that

> the Elizabethans made much of the distinction between private
> and public virtues . . . [and] the public virtues which enable
> [Henry] to remedy the insufficiencies of Richard's reign are evi-
> dent from his first appearance . . . [Shakespeare] believed in the
> doctrine of degree, but he concluded that if the demands of the

1. 'The Unity of *2 Henry IV*' in *Sh. Survey*, 6, 1953, pp. 16–24.
2. E.g., Walsingham's *Historia Anglicana*, ed. H. T. Riley, 1863, ii. 156 ff.,
223 ff.; Froissart's *Chronicles*, ed. W. P. Ker, Tudor Translations, 1903, vi. 306;
*The Brut*, ed. F. W. D. Brie, EETS, Orig. ser., 136, ii. 356; Holinshed's *Chronicles*,
ii. 808; Daniel, *Ciuile Wars*, i. 58.

divinely sanctioned social hierarchy conflicted with the obvious good of England, the latter must take precedence. . . The test of a good king is his ability to maintain civil order.[1]

In *2 Henry IV* the King certainly suffers from remorse; he yearns for an expiatory crusade, he admits 'indirect crook'd ways', and he prays God for forgiveness, as his son prays on the eve of Agincourt that God will not visit upon him 'the fault / My father made in compassing the crown' (*H5*, IV. i. 310–11). Yet the sense behind the play, and in Henry's mind, is not one *primarily* of remorse afflicting him but of anxiety over political unrest. Henry's anguish has to do with his usurpation, but it centres mostly on Hal's wildness which threatens to lose the crown to rivals. Henry's worries are superimposed on a troubled conscience; yet one feels that if the worries would abate the conscience would settle itself too. The play is one of practical power, with Divine Right in a very minor place; the Archbishop may 'derive from heaven his quarrel and his cause', yet the one who scores a success which he ascribes to God is Prince John. As between Richard and Henry, the position the play expresses is that God approves the king whose rule best satisfies the needs of his subjects. That rule is Henry's.

## (ii) *Henry and Necessity*

How guilty nevertheless is Henry, how far the 'vile politician', how far the 'tragic hero'? The chroniclers make clear the drift of events by which Bolingbroke, having returned merely to remedy the withholding of his just rights, is swept into usurpation. 'The revolution of the times' makes human will uncertain, though not powerless (the actors are not puppets). Even the murder is virtually fated; while Richard lives and rebels rally round him, Bolingbroke cannot reign in quiet.

Behind the plays there are the potent symbols of the Wheel of Fortune and Mutability, factors of fatalism.[2] But in the foreground there is practical and secular Necessity, calling forth the will. The plays are not primarily religious parables of God's wrath for sin, or mythopoems of Mutability; they deal with men who elect to do what they deem necessary actions. The King acts so, but so also do the rebels—'Necessity' is their very natural plea.[3] Henry is 'guilty'

1. 'Political Problems of Sh.'s Lancastrian Tetralogy', *SP*, 1952, vol. 49, pp. 177, 184.

2. The Wheel of Fortune and its potency in the historical cycle are well discussed by Paul Reyher, *Les Idées dans l'Œuvre de Sh.*, 1947, and R. Chapman, 'The Wheel of Fortune', *RES*, New ser., i, 1950, pp. 1–7.

3. 'Necessity, in one form or another, is accepted by all the characters in the play, the young and successful to whom the future belongs not less than the old

of not resisting the events which bring him to power; yet he is justified in that he was 'compell'd' to act so. The retribution which falls upon him shows the same paradox; it certainly accords with the religious foresight of the Bishop of Carlisle in *Richard II*, yet it has much less a religious air (contrast with it the dooms of Richard III and Macbeth) than a purely secular one—the strain of maintaining a disputed authority. True, Henry V later makes all possible religious expiation—and this is genuine penitence, not the cynical insurance policy it would have been if, say, Richard III had done any such thing. But the mainspring is secular, practical, the ensuring of success; and guilt in a religious sense runs second to guilt against the codes of political order. And to this second guilt Henry can reply that he meant to bring political order, not to destroy it.[1]

## (iii) *Statecraft and Morality*

Yet to judge that the only criterion is success or failure, 'Is the King strong or weak?',[2] is too narrow. Success or failure is of course important to monarchs. But behind the success or failure some moral significance should be felt. Behind Henry's success, blemished though it is, there must be a larger welfare than the dynastic, and this must indeed be more than the mere national magnification of his personal success. It must be the whole welfare of the state, the great living order which is expressed here by those who oppose the Archbishop of York (IV. i. 32–52; IV. ii. 4–30) and in *Henry V* in the Archbishop of Canterbury's honey-bees speech (*H5*, I. ii. 183–213). Behind the rebels' failure there must likewise be some moral fitness; their lack of cohesion, their well-meant recklessness, would have augured ill for the nation had they won.

It seems possible, much though one would rather think otherwise, that Shakespeare saw moral fitness behind the Gaultree stratagem. But Gaultree deserves particular treatment, and this is furnished in Appendix V. The thought of it, however, leads towards some political assessments, for it is often cited as the crowning

---

and disillusioned elders'; D. A. Traversi, *Sh. from R2 to H5*, 1957, p. 136. See IV. i. 70 ff., 99 ff.; IV. ii. 30 ff.

1. In 'Sh.'s Politics', *Proc. Brit. Acad.*, 1957, p. 117, Professor L. C. Knights comments on 'the sombre demonstration in King Henry IV of what is involved in getting and keeping power', and points out a parallel of *realpolitik* when Henry faces the consequences of his ambition ('For all my reign hath been but as a scene / Acting that argument'; IV. v. 197–8) and when Marvell brings out the lesson of his *Horatian Ode*—'The same Arts that did gain / A Power must it maintain'.

2. J. F. Danby, *Sh.'s Doctrine of Nature*, 1949, p. 90.

evidence that the Bolingbrokes, father and sons, are a family of hypocrites, an interpretation put with some force by Professor Charlton:

> Though it may be largely hidden, the truth as Shakespeare grasped it [is] the sense that not only is politics a nasty business but that a repugnant unscrupulousness is an invaluable asset in the art of government. That is the burden of the English History plays, jubilant as they are in pride of country and race.[1]

*King John* had already pointed towards this reading of political behaviour, especially in Faulconbridge's satire on Commodity. *Henry IV* and *Henry V*, in Charlton's view, reveal 'a distinctly contemptuous view of statesmen and statecraft'.[2] Is this true?

Surely it is not. It ignores the complex purposes and moral insights of the plays and equates Shakespeare with the doctrinaire whose thought takes place in ready-made categories and jaunty generalizations. The whole moral sense of the *Henry IV*s is of the contrary kind, and in that lies its value.[3]

The theme is not the contemptibility of statesmen but Hal's emergence to good rule. Good rule is not the wielding of power but the fostering of the good life on a national scale. That is what a king is for. Henry V is not everybody's ideal monarch but the defences of him offered in, for instance, the New Cambridge and New Arden introductions to his play are truer to what Shakespeare gives us than are the famous denunciations of Hazlitt and Yeats.[4] In *2 Henry IV* an inherent pattern of moral choices is discernible, just as in *1 Henry IV* there is an instructive disposition of motives in Henry, Hotspur, and Falstaff, in relation to which Hal is subtly poised. The King here is less prominent than in Part 1 but he is anything but contemptible. The complexities of right and wrong in his usurpation continue in his exercise of power, and the responsibilities of rule, rendered harsh by his own acts, and his capacity for melancholy analysis, ally him with the flawed heroes of the tragedies.

Centring on the King are Prince John, Westmoreland, and the Lord Chief Justice: antithetical to his role as fount of authority, and akin in anarchic promotion of their own interests, are the rebels and Falstaff. The royal representatives exemplify Justice, which the Elizabethans enshrined among the highest virtues. It

---

1. H. B. Charlton, *Sh., Politics, and Politicians*, 1929, p. 18.        2. *Ibid.*, p. 13.

3. 'Fundamentally, [Shakespeare's realism] is a refusal to let the abstract and general obscure the personal and specific'; L. C. Knights, 'Sh.'s Politics', *Proc. Brit. Acad.*, 1957, p. 117.

4. See New Arden *Henry V*, pp. xlvi–l.

could have its Aristotelian excess, mean, and defect. John and Westmoreland represent its extreme, the justice which metes without mercy what each deserves; such justice is needed in statecraft but only in emergencies.[1] The regular mode should be justice tempered by mercy (which is in fact just what Falstaff finally receives), as Shakespeare had declared in defining a king's authority:

> His sceptre shows the force of temporal power,
> The attribute to awe and majesty,
> Wherein doth sit the dread and fear of kings;
> But mercy is above this sceptred sway,
> It is enthroned in the hearts of kings,
> It is an attribute to God himself;
> And earthly pow'r doth then show likest God's
> When mercy seasons justice.
>
> (*Merchant of Venice*, IV. i. 190–7)

If rigour is one extreme, anarchy (the defect of justice) is the other, adumbrated in Falstaff's prospects, trumpeted in his cry 'the laws of England are at my commandment', imminent in his promises to deliver Doll and to promote to 'what office thou wilt' that very Shallow whose foolishness, he thinks, will keep Hal laughing through the wearing out of six fashions. In the historical plot, the same defect of justice appears in the rebels. They have a motive, certainly, but not such as warrants the overthrow of a kingdom; their motive is Northumberland's strained destructive passion ('Let order die!') and the Archbishop's generous but vague sense of grievances.

If these, then, are divergent extremes from firm but merciful authority, the Lord Chief Justice embodies those qualities which Hal requires, good government in the microcosm of man and the macrocosm of the state. He is invulnerable to Falstaff; indeed, his rebuke, 'You speak as having power to do wrong', puts in eight words the danger in Falstaff's lack of scruple. He it is who is finally entrusted with the madcaps' subjection, and whom the new King accepts as 'father'. It is exactly in this respect, of enforcing the requirements and responsibilities of good rule, that Stow, reporting the dying King's injunctions, seems most to have affected the play.

Statesmen and statecraft are not, then, held to be by nature contemptible. Daily exigencies may tarnish the kingly function, as the burden of rule oppresses kings themselves, but on the earthly plane

---

1. Even in emergencies it is distasteful; a relevant comment is in *A Myrroure for Magistrates*, ed. Lily B. Campbell, 1938, p. 145:

> God hateth rigour though it furder right, . . .
> Who furdereth right is not therby excused,
> If through the same he do sum other wrong.

good statecraft is the highest of human exercises, that 'hard condition / Twin-born with greatness' in which men show likest gods when they rule with honour to their place and with the love of their subjects. The moral centre of the sequence from *Richard II* to *Henry V* is the nature and the gravity of rule. Shakespeare has made his plays most thoughtful enactments of the art of the possible.

### (iv) *Miscalculation*

One of the most evident themes is that of miscalculation. The play is introduced by Rumour, spirit of unrest and false knowledge. The chronicles say nothing about Northumberland's hearing deceptive reports from Shrewsbury, and Shakespeare's invention of Rumour is a pure imaginative device, to create the world of 'surmises, jealousies, conjectures'. On the serious level, most of the characters could cry out with the Archbishop, 'What trust is in these times?' or, with the King, 'how chance's mocks / And changes fill the cup of alteration / With divers liquors'. On the comic level, there is the vague belief that Falstaff performed valiantly at Shrewsbury; the Lord Chief Justice refers to it, warriors seek the hero out, Colevile surrenders without a blow (and is executed, a disturbing switch from histrionic farce to historic fact). Living on a false reputation, Falstaff himself hubristically miscalculates Hal. At the centre, of course, is Hal's intention to surprise everyone:

> So, when this loose behaviour I throw off,
> And pay the debt I never promised,
> By how much better than my word I am
> By so much shall I falsify men's hopes.
>
> (*1 Henry IV*, 1. ii. 232–5)

Optimistic and pessimistic, falsified hopes (i.e. expectations) spread throughout the play. Insofar as it concerns Hal himself, the dramatic expectancy lies in the anticipations of him so variously entertained by the King on the one hand, and Falstaff on the other. But there are other aspects of the same theme. The rebels' war-council is equally concerned with the unpredictable future; they are betrayed dangerously when Northumberland abandons them and disastrously when they miscalculate Prince John. To sum up, the rebels are tragically foiled of their expectations, Falstaff and Shallow comically foiled of theirs, and the King and Lord Chief Justice fortunately foiled of theirs. Only Hal, 'Machiavel of goodness', is not Time's or Fortune's fool.[1]

1. Chapter 1 of John Lawlor's *Tragic Sense in Sh.*, 1960, examines most interestingly the 'Appearance and Reality' theme in the *Henry IV*s which prompts so much miscalculation.

## (v) *Anarchy*

Other themes interplay in both serious and comic plots to give coherence. Anarchy threatens throughout. The rebels and Falstaff both prepare it; the King expects it on Hal's accession, and he anticipates disorder (IV. v) in terms which foreshadow Ulysses' speech on chaos in *Troilus and Cressida*. Northumberland's 'strained passion' rivals, briefly, the anarchic violences of Lear, Timon, and Macbeth. The Archbishop, though nobler in his impulses than Northumberland, proposes to throw England into the melting-pot of popular fickleness. For Falstaff, of course, the law of nature decrees that the old pike should snap up the young dace; he devours the rustic recruits and Shallow alike without the slightest semblance of exertion, and he prepares short shrift for the Lord Chief Justice and the laws of the land. A common courting of chaos moves rebels and Falstaff alike.

## (vi) *Age and Disease*

Northumberland and the King, the main participants in Richard's overthrow, are physically afflicted as well as morally blemished; Shallow and Silence are captivatingly senile; and 'in Falstaff the comedy of ageing flesh is grotesque as well as amusing'.[1] Not all the elders, certainly, are unsound; the Archbishop, though an unskilful leader, is a noble prelate, the 'opener and intelligencer' between God and man; and the Lord Chief Justice is worthy to be a king's guardian. Hal will surround himself with wise veterans, as *Henry V* shows him to have done—'The silver livery of advised age' was always a moving idea to Shakespeare. But the old blemished order must change; the new King must show himself part of the nation's healthy rather than its failing stock. Until he does so, however, age and disease affect the body politic; this theme is common to the King and Archbishop alike (III. i; IV. i). As for Falstaff, he turns diseases to commodity, and he flirts with Doll through a desire which has long outlived performance. He is far from senile, but the 'vanity in years' feels shadows of mortality. And he and the tavern-life centring upon him are now, as they were not in Part 1, too deeply blemished for a prince's health. He is master of his court, but of a court much grosser, less gay, and more salacious. The tavern-comedy is splendidly vivacious; the great Boar's-Head scene, the last gathering of the whole company at Eastcheap, is given with a creative enthusiasm which averts the censoriousness some critics have sought to pin upon Shakespeare. Still, wonderful though its reading of life, its themes of age and dis-

1. Clifford Leech, 'The Unity of *2 Henry IV*', in *Sh. Survey*, 6, 1953, p. 18.

ease link with those of the serious plot in a symbolic rendering of the state of England.

## (vii) *Life in Place and Time*

Of all the plays, this most richly draws the panorama of national life.[1] The troubled kingdom is evoked in many a speech from Rumour's onwards, and the contrasting ideal community is expounded by Westmoreland, Prince John, the Lord Chief Justice, and the new King himself.[2] There is varied and vigorous movement throughout the land. The military scenes show a nation swarming with the concerns of war; topographical and social references abound; messengers ride and armies march. Outside the history plot, Mistress Quickly seems the very embodiment of her Eastcheap neighbourhood, and Doll is as common as the St Albans road. Shallow, whose cousin is at Oxford, equally embodies Old England, recalling his days at Clement's Inn with little John Doit of Staffordshire and Will Squele a Cotsole man, when he took on Samson Stockfish behind Gray's Inn while Jack Falstaff, page to the Duke of Norfolk, was breaking Scoggin's head at the court gate. Bullocks are sold at Stamford, sacks lost at Hinckley fair; William Visor of Woncot needs help against Clement Perkes o'the Hill. The Gloucestershire scenes have been called a glorious irrelevance.[3] But are they? The hero of the history plays is the nation; the theme is the state of England. The idea that Eastcheap is an irrelevance has long been given up; so should any such idea about Gloucestershire, which is the rural counterpart of Eastcheap, allied with the rest of the play by its themes of justice and war working down to the common folk, and by its rendering of common life proceeding in quotidian tragi-comedy behind the self-importance of the great. 'In *Henry IV*, which is so much more than a political play, the public situation is defined and judged in terms of a richly human context in which Falstaff's ragged regiment and the Cotswold conscripts are an indispensable part.'[4] Eastcheap and Gloucestershire together present the heart-warming common stock of things. Mistress Quickly and Davy, as Dr Tillyard observes, are comforting assurances that 'civil war will yield, as the play's main theme, to England'.[5] And if the whole panorama is spread out,

1. There are some admirable pages on this in Tillyard, *Sh.'s History Plays*, 1943, pp. 300–4.
2. Cf. IV. i. 41–52; IV. ii. 4–22; V. ii. 75–101, 129–45.
3. R. W. David, 'Sh.'s Historical Plays', in *Sh. Survey*, 6, 1953, p. 137.
4. L. C. Knights, *Poetry, Politics, and the English Tradition*, 1954, p. 10.
5. Tillyard, p. 301. Tillyard cites Hardy's 'In Time of the Breaking of Nations' as akin in its contrast of transient events, however great, and country continuity. For another good comment by Tillyard see below, III. ii. Location, note.

from Pie Corner in Eastcheap to the Gloucestershire hade land to be sown with red wheat, from Poins's tennis-court to Northumberland's castle, if messengers devour the way, and Falstaff founders nine score and odd posts between the Boar's Head and Gaultree, the topography is a matter not merely of the passing moment but of a fully rendered local colour, of history seen in the events of men's lives.

Furthermore, the play embeds itself in a deep layer of time.[1] Time has two main aspects—the present as it presses towards the future, the past as it revives in the present. In the former aspect, it presses towards finality, precipitating the rebels' plans and the King's counter-plans. Hal feels himself much to blame, 'so idly to profane the present time'. The urgent observation of time which weighs upon men in high places is a major part of the play's stress, and even the life of the tavern, though trying to ignore it, is more under its sway than in Part I. Scarcely any play has so definite a *terminus ad quem*; for all parties 'the stream of time doth run' towards a conclusion. 'In the perfectness of time' Hal is to reign, and this event impends with fear in the mind of the court, glee in that of the tavern, and gravity in his own. Moreover, the present pressing towards the future is not only insistent, it is inexorable. It brings those revolutions of the times against which, for all his planning, man cannot secure himself. Even beyond 'the victorious acts of Henry the Fifth' there loom the further troubles foreseen by Northumberland and prophesied by Hastings (I. i. 153–60; IV. ii. 44–9). Above all, it brings age and death, and it is in deeply admitting this quality of time that the play takes on its sombre grandeur.

But the second aspect of time, the past revived in the present, is enrichingly evident also. The story of Shrewsbury is more than once recalled for continuity; Hotspur is movingly memorialized; Richard's fall is retold; the Coventry lists whence the whole division arose are vividly conjured up; and the dying King summarizes his whole reign as 'a scene / Acting that argument' of conflict.[2] The comic scenes also are as deeply involved in the past. The Hostess has known Falstaff these twenty-nine years, come peascod time; old Double is dead, beloved of yore by John a Gaunt, but Jane Nightwork still lives though it is fifty-five year since she had Robin Night-

1. Cf. B. T. Spencer, '2 *Henry IV* and the Theme of Time', in *Univ. Toronto Quarterly*, July 1944, p. 397.

2. When the whole historical sequence is over, the concluding speech in *Richard III* sums up the strife in which 'England hath long been mad, and scarr'd herself': it brings formally to an end the long internecine struggle the Bishop of Carlisle had forecast when Richard II was deposed.

work by old Nightwork. Falstaff remembers Shallow's Clement's Inn days, and Shallow Falstaff when he was a crack not thus high. Time, its pressure in the present and future, its legacies from the past, is integral to the play, but not time as mere linear flow, time rather (through expectation and reminiscence) becoming the broad and intimate picture of the nation, opening out into that larger 'revolution of the times' in which all things are subject to Mutability, and giving life its larger context.

Life is not thereby humiliated. No play gives a richer sense of its reality. War and government with their plans, tavern-life with its humours, age with its ailments, local affairs run by such as Masters Tisick, Shallow, and Silence—trades, sports, songs, and dissipations, all form the variety of the action. Play-tags, military terms, ballad-snatches, Biblical fragments, and Homily echoes jostle references to shopkeepers' satins, pewterers' hammers, brewers' buckets, the tilling of land, the skills of archery, and caliver-management. Slang and colloquialisms abound, the language of swaggerers, catchpoles, and whores. And what is seen and heard on the stage affects us as the mere observable portion of an inexhaustible circumambient life.

As for defining the Shakespearean view of life here, no interpretation in terms of Jonsonian or minatory morality ought to be offered. Rightly wishing to show Shakespeare's responsible sense of moral values, Professor L. C. Knights nevertheless went too far in setting him magisterially over his characters:

> No one has yet pointed out that drunkenness, lechery, and senile depravity (in II. iv, for example) are *not* treated by Shakespeare with 'good-natured tolerance'. Shakespeare's attitude towards his characters in *2 Henry IV* at times approaches the attitudes of Mr Eliot towards Doris, Wauchope, &c., in *Sweeney Agonistes*.[1]

This view needs amending, and indeed Professor Knights himself admirably amends it in a later essay.[2] But others have pressed it further, seeing in Falstaff, for instance, 'a disturbingly actual old man, an ugly *memento senescere*',[3] and in his light-of-love 'the dreadful Doll, harridan and whore'.[4] This takes one aback. True in a literal sense, such readings leave so much out. Responsible moral

1. 'Notes on Comedy', in *Determinations*, ed. F. R. Leavis, 1934, p. 131.

2. 'Time's Subjects: the Sonnets and *2 Henry IV*', in *Some Shn Themes*, 1959 one of the few first-rate discussions of the play.

3. R. W. David, 'Sh.'s History Plays', in *Sh. Survey*, 6, 1953, p. 138.

4. Wilson (*Fortunes*), p. 118. It should be made clear that Professor Dover Wilson's purpose, very rightly, is to justify Falstaff's rejection by desentimentalizing his situation, and that he does this admirably. So humane a critic does not on the whole forgo the charity of judgment which art allows.

standpoints great literature is expected to have, and the *Henry IV*s are both great literature and related to, though transformed from, the morality tradition. The problem is to get the morality substratum into balance with the whole, in a response combining both judgment and sympathy so as to be neither priggish nor sentimental. The morality substratum gives the elements of guilt oppressed by anxiety, hubris riding for a fall, youth choosing codes of conduct; but humanity itself gives that enriching cast of colour whereby a mortal destiny broods above the doomed rebels and the stricken King, the senile Justices, the tavern-revellers, and the not-invulnerable Falstaff. One of the best points Professor Knights makes is that, while Shakespeare is in the play deeply inquiring into the conditions of life and offering a troubled wisdom, he offers grounds for judgment yet not for overtly didactic stances:

> Not only is there the vigour of mind with which the political theme is grasped and presented, there is, in the Falstaff scenes, a familiar comic verve together with an outgoing sympathy— even, at times, liking—for what is so firmly judged . . . We know that we are dealing with a free mind—one that is neither driven by, nor bent on driving, an 'idea'; the sombre preoccupations are not obsessions.

## 7. FALSTAFF

Whence Falstaff acquired his qualities, other than through Shakespeare's inventive genius, has caused much debate. His historical original, Sir John Oldcastle (*c.* 1378–1417), Lord Cobham by marriage, was High Sheriff of Herefordshire, valiant in war, but early in Henry V's reign condemned as a Wycliffite, and, after escaping to Wales, captured and burnt at the stake. In the fifteenth century he was maligned by anti-Wycliffites, in whose eyes, as Bale reports, he was 'a myghtye mayntener of other heretyques, . . . chylde of iniquyte and darkenesse'.[1] His escape to Wales was taken as cowardly evasion of Henry's wars, his Lollardy as wickedness, and his friendship with the King as a matter of Henry's wild youth only, abruptly terminated when Henry reformed. In the sixteenth century, however, he emerged as a precursive martyr for the reformed faith. Bale treated him as 'the good lorde Cobham' and was followed by Hall and (almost verbatim) by Foxe in the *Actes and Monuments* (1563). Echoing Bale, Foxe calls him a 'constaunt seruant of the lorde and worthye knyght',[2] 'a principall fauourer,

1. John Bale, *Brefe Chronycle Concernynge . . . the blessed martyr of Christ syr Johan Oldecastell the Lorde Cobham*, 1544, fol. 38ᵛ.

2. John Foxe, *Actes and Monuments*, 1563, p. 263. The phrase is from Bale, *op. cit.*, fol. 15ʳ.

receiuer, and maintainer of . . . Lollards',[1] a Protestant hero, scholar, philosopher, man of virtue, and religious convert.[2] In this account the rejection took place not on Henry's accession but later, and not for wildness but for Wycliffite staunchness.[3] Bale also records a confession by Oldcastle that 'in my frayle youthe I offended the[e] (lorde) most greeuouslye in pryde, wrathe, and glottonye, in couetousnesse and in lechere'.[4]

The elements the historical Oldcastle shares with Falstaff are those rather of the hostile than the favourable tradition—fortunately so, since the disreputable 'martlemas' has been better worth having than any such 'valiant Martyr' and 'vertuous peere' as figures in the Munday–Hathaway–Wilson–Drayton play of *Sir John Oldcastle* (1599), drawn from Foxe. The Oldcastle of *The Famous Victories* has little that can be attributed to any source save that his disreputableness must derive from the hostile tradition. In the *Henry IV*s Falstaff is sanctimonious and given to Scriptural quotation; this may derive, impudently, from the 'vertuous' Lollard famous for theological disputation but more probably it is part of the whole irreverent fun Shakespeare has with his creation. Whence his age and obesity came into Shakespeare is uncertain.[5]

Falstaff, a modern critic observes, 'commits what Shelley was to call "the generous error", the error of those who try to live life by a vision of it, thus transforming the world about them and impressing upon it their own character. . . His vision of life takes over whenever he is on the stage'.[6] This is true of Part 1. But the situation in Part 2 is more complicated.

He starts promisingly. Shrewsbury has done him good. Shakespeare discreetly avoids the too-open question, 'What did the King and court *really* think he had done there?', though in fact Morton and Lady Percy know that Hal, not he, killed Hotspur. There is an undefined impression that 'he hath done good service'; he is sent 'with some charge' to Prince John, to whom in fact he dispatches a letter. His service at Shrewsbury, the Lord Chief Justice admits, 'hath a little gilded over' his Gad's Hill exploit (a very grudging admission if Falstaff were really supposed to have killed Hotspur). Shakespeare has it both ways—Falstaff has killed Hotspur, and is

1. Foxe, *op. cit.*, 1596 edn, i. 513.

2. 'His youthe was full of wanton wildenesse before he knew ye Scriptures' (Bale, *op. cit.*, fol. 4ʳ).

3. These contrasted versions are well set out in Wilhelm Baeske, 'Oldcastle–Falstaff in der engl. Literatur bis zu Sh.', *Palaestra*, vol. 50, 1905.

4. Bale, *op. cit.*, fol. 26ʳ⁻ᵛ.

5. His age may derive from popular traditions punning on his name; cf. *1H4*, I. ii. 47—'my old lad of the castle'; Baeske, *op. cit.*, p. 70.

6. Robert Langbaum, 'Character versus Actors in Sh.', *Sh. Q.*, viii, 1957, p. 66.

being rewarded; he has not killed Hotspur, and nobody is fool enough to say he has. But at least Falstaff is tolerably elevated, entering with sword and buckler borne by his page; he seeks two and twenty yards of satin for his short cloak and slops (a lavish supply even for a Falstaffian girth); he is impudent with the Lord Chief Justice; he 'holds his place' so as to exasperate the Prince and Poins; he is sought by a dozen captains; and he deals masterfully with the egregious Colevile.

Yet there is something ambiguous in all this. The insouciant mastery which floated him through Part 1 is not so certain. The Lord Chief Justice and Prince John, while not actually quashing him, show him as less than commanding. He cannot even best the Lord Chief Justice's servant. Since he thinks that the Prince is on his side, that the Lord Chief Justice is heading for disgrace, and that the laws of England are to be at his commandment, he is not perturbed. But the 'generous error' is in fact dangerous; Part 2 is a play in which men destroy themselves by delusions. There are hints often enough that Falstaff's 'vision' is blindness, the ground under his feet hollow. As late as the end of Act v, scene i, he expects to make Hal laugh heartily; as late as the end of Act v, scene iii, he 'know[s] the young King is sick for [him]'. This complacency is folly.

Shakespeare makes clear the Prince's separation from him. Almost as soon as Falstaff sets foot on the stage he is confronted not by Hal but by the Lord Chief Justice, to whom Hal is to entrust his own guidance and the enforcement of Falstaff's dismissal, and through whose agency the King has 'severed' Falstaff and Hal (I. ii. 202). But the severance is Hal's own, too; the rejection in effect takes place not as the play ends but as it begins. If made explicit at the outset it would seem too drastic after the high favour of Part 1, but it is already under way. Hal is kept out of sight until Act II, scene ii; then he enters not with Falstaff but with Poins, in a state of chrysalis-uneasiness over his misspent time. He meets Falstaff only in the latter part of Act II, and in no friendly spirit. Throughout, every remark he makes about Falstaff is derogatory; he addresses him only three civil words—'Falstaff, good night' (II. iv. 363)—the last time he speaks to him before the rejection scene. Ignorant of Falstaff's whereabouts, he must ask Poins whether the old boar feeds in the old frank. Neither he nor Poins knows who Doll Tearsheet is. And he dines not specifically with Falstaff but 'With Poins, and other his continual followers'. The spectators, like bystanders seeing most of the game, have every chance to read the danger signals, displayed in the relationships

between the Lord Chief Justice, Falstaff, and Hal, in the marked
coarseness of Boar's-Head life and indeed of Falstaff's witticisms,[1]
and in the imminent dangers of anarchy. But Falstaff sacrifices his
intelligence to his self-satisfaction; only when the blow falls does he
sense that anything has changed.[2]

In other respects he has lost little of his verve. His mind is still
able; he knowledgeably caricatures military theory and medical
science (III. ii. 253–66, IV. iii. 94–112); he is familiar with Galen,
the Bible, the Homilies, and literary fashions. His speech, if less
elegant than in Part 1, is not without virtuosity and Lylyan graces.[3]
His wit still flashes so comprehensively that a commentator pursu-
ing him with notes feels like a lepidopterist after not one butterfly
at a time but a host. Even so, his increasing coarseness is noticeable,
both in gross equivoques and in self-approval. Nor does he so
readily outshine others. The Lord Chief Justice holds his own; the
Hostess has most of the best things in II. i, and she, Doll, and Pistol
are the main comic forces in II. iv. Indeed, Falstaff's own humours
must divide the honours of the title-page with Pistol's swaggerings.
In Gloucestershire, his superiority of wit is not more remarkable
than Shallow's inferiority. He lacks Hal to bring him out. His mind
operates, then, less refreshingly than in Part 1, in ways touched
with the gross, the patronizing, even the sinister. Proximity to the
throne can be no place for him.

Still, one holds towards him a double attitude. Since he swindles
Mistress Quickly and Justice Shallow, treats Hal cavalierly, and
recruits his yokels for slaughter, he has been called 'the most piti-
less creature in the play'.[4] As another critic observes,

> he added hypocrisy to debauchery, cowardice and bragging
> impudence, and so, to accord with his profession of swash-
> buckler in chief, assumed a choler though he had it not.[5]

Yet the element of truth in these judgments does not reflect one's

1. In chronicle-tradition, while loose in morals before his accession Prince
Henry turned strictly continent on becoming king (C. L. Kingsford, *The First
English Life of Henry V*, 1911, p. xxx).

2. Bertrand Evans studies 'Shakespeare's devotion to a dramatic method that
gives the audience an advantage in awareness, and thus opens exploitable gaps
between audience and participants, and between participant and participant'
(*Sh.'s Comedies*, 1960, p. viii).

3. See I. ii. 5–30, note. C. L. Barber observes about the styles of Nashe and
Falstaff that both deal in conceits elaborated with 'consciously specious plau-
sibility', mock-heroic elevations, and formally marshalled argument (*Sh.'s
Festive Comedy*, 1959, p. 71).

4. J. F. Danby, *Sh.'s Doctrine of Nature*, 1949, p. 84.

5. J. W. Draper, *The Humors & Sh.'s Characters*, 1945, p. 38.

whole sense of what is going on. The moralistic strain of criticism which judges Falstaff's actions as if they were actions of real life is sounder than its opposite, which takes them in a gay separation from anything real, but it errs in neglecting the controlling context of tone and manner. Shakespeare has provided much besides mere judgment-by-the-letter-of-the-law. Realistically considered, of course, Falstaff's recruiting is disgraceful. Dramatically considered, however, its disgracefulness is relieved by the whole treatment, which invites enjoyment rather than indignation. One never supposes, somehow, that the recruits will come to harm. And in fact, since Falstaff arrives late at Gaultree, there is no harm for them to come to.[1] In real life, Falstaff's victims would suffer hardships and perhaps disaster: in the play, not only are they, like Falstaff himself, positively funny but they do not evidently suffer from their victimizing.

Yet, while keeping all this well within the sphere of the comic, the play does impose its responsible moral terms. One laughs at the comic aspect of Falstaff's misdeeds, but one is well aware that they disqualify him from a king's favour. He deteriorates not in artistic quality (not much, at any rate), but in the totality of qualities to be liked. One takes him in the tolerance of comedy when the results are comic; one condemns only when they threaten to be serious.

## 8. THE REJECTION

Playgoers have discussed Falstaff's dismissal for centuries. 'I don't know', Rowe commented in 1709, 'whether some People have not, in remembrance of the Diversion he had formerly afforded 'em, been sorry to see his friend *Hal* use him so scurvily.' Johnson rejoined that since Falstaff 'has nothing in him that can be esteemed, no great pain will be suffered from the reflection that he is compelled to live honestly'. Yet Hazlitt much preferred him to Hal, and Bradley, admitting that the rejection had to come, regretted that it was done in public, in a display of Bolingbrokian 'hardness and policy'. For Professor Danby, Hal is a 'makeshift ideal' for the theme of 'Commodity', a brilliant façade before a vacuity of true feeling; 'to pseudo-fellowship in Hal', he comments, 'must be added pseudo-morality'.[2]

1. In Part I, where Falstaff's 'ragamuffins' do reportedly come to harm, or at least are humorously and improbably said by Falstaff to be all dead except two, one never sets eyes on them. They exist, rather, as creatures of Falstaff's comic fantasy.

2. J. F. Danby, *Sh.'s Doctrine of Nature*, pp. 85–90.

Shakespeare's problem was not wholly tractable. The Wild-Prince stories presented a licentious ribald miraculously converted, which was material rather for a romance than a history. A Wild Prince, on the other hand, whom his fellow-nobles knew to be grooming himself for responsibility would contravene the chronicles and forfeit that dramatic emergence into virtue which was integral to the legend. Shakespeare effects a skilful compromise. Hal is reputedly dissolute but, as far as one sees him, harmless enough. He is aware of his destiny. While the crown is remote, and Falstaff's japes are innocuous, he enjoys the Boar's Head, though hinting that the revelry must end. As the accession grows nearer and Falstaff grosser, he avoids him. Three things make his course seem heartless in a way Shakespeare probably never intended: these are Hal's soliloquy (*1H4*, I. ii. 219 ff.), Warwick's declaration that Hal frequents the Boar's Head simply to recognize and disclaim vice (*2H4*, IV. iv. 67 ff.), and the rejection speech. But these three need taking with care. Hal's soliloquy is a morality-manifesto rather than heartless policy, Warwick is providing a gloss to console the dying King, and the rejection speech is official rather than personal, a required public demonstration. The general tenor of Hal's evolution deserves respect. In Act II, scene ii, he jests uneasily to distract himself from the misery of his father's illness, and Falstaff's presumption affronts him. After a brief and indeed disapproving intervention at the Boar's Head he recalls his responsibilities, though since the chronicles leave the suppression of the Archbishop entirely to Westmoreland and Prince John he does not appear at Gaultree (and thereby escapes odium). His bearing in the sick-room is admirable, and his address to the lords is honourable. The opposed evolutions of Falstaff and Hal, rightly observed, will dispel any notion that Falstaff is scurvily treated; only the most careless reading could take the rejection as a melodrama prepared by a calculating Prince against a hoodwinked crony. As for the publicity which Bradley regrets, Falstaff's hubris positively demands a public scene; he flaunts his way of life for all to see, and boasts that it will be the King's, too. The public disgrace is the appropriate nemesis, and the punishment is lenient—temporary committal to a prison reserved for important notables who fell out of favour, followed by a life 'very well provided for', ten miles from court. Falstaff's pride is hurt, his overweening confidence deflated. But the 'fracted and corroborate' heart reported in *Henry V* is an after-thought irrelevant to *Henry IV*, occasioned by the change of plan whereby Falstaff was dropped from *Henry V* and had to be disposed of. 'Dickens', Sir Alfred Duff Cooper suggests, would have settled Falstaff down with a pension in a country cottage, with honeysuckle round the door, and a hospitable inn hard by, where the old gentleman, grown quite respectable, would have recounted tales of the riotous past, to the wondering yokels, and where the King would have paid him an occasional visit. But Shakespeare did not live in a sentimental age.[1]

In fact, unsentimental though Falstaff's dismissal is, Shakespeare provided a future for him at the end of 2 *Henry IV* not far different from that thus humorously described—though no Shakespearean Falstaff, one hopes, would grow 'quite respectable', whatever a Dickensian one might do. The rejection, in short, is necessary, well-prepared, and executed without undue severity.

'And yet', Mr Dipak Nandy writes to me, 'might not something more be said? One asks why, despite all these considerations, one's feelings are nevertheless jarred. Why is there, in Morgann's terms, such a gap between one's understanding and one's impressions?' He makes three suggestions. First, the rejection dislocates not only Falstaff's self-esteem but our very 'taking' of him as a splendid performer in his own role. However reprehensible in real terms, he has appreciatively acted out the great enlargement of comedy, and 'the success of a role depends in large part on the acceptance of the role-player *as a role-player*.' Falstaff not only has been enjoyable, he has shown himself a virtuoso in relishing his part. 'I know thee not, old man' strips him bare of the gorgeous assumptions he has donned for our pleasure, and turns him into an aged cast-off: 'in rejection, the multitude of roles we call Falstaff seems to become suddenly humanized into a person; and this', Mr Nandy observes, 'I find pathetic'. Second, the terms of Henry's reproof—fool, jester, a dream he despises—though accurate in sense, destroy that balance of judgment so well held in Part 1, by which Falstaff is a rascal and yet contributes wisdom to a world of harsh purpose. They invite us to assume the same tone, to accuse ourselves in the same terms, as Henry uses; and this we are wholly unwilling to do. To do so would in some sense be treachery to ourselves. So strict a rejection of what has pleased us may be the tribute duty owes to responsibility; yet it impoverishes our sense of life. And third, though the rejection is inevitable, its very necessity marks a narrowing (not less regrettable because absolutely requisite) in Henry himself. 'Are we not', Mr Nandy writes, 'witnessing the disjunction between the King and the man that the histories stress as, at moments of crisis, their kings have to confront in their own souls the realization that they are

1. *Sergeant Shakespeare*, 1949, p. 85.

men no more? Is it not possible for the sentimentalists to argue that the sense of loss they feel at the rejection derives not only from the loss of Falstaff, not only from the decease of a human relationship, but also from the loss of something, some generosity perhaps (not in what he *does* to Falstaff, which is mild enough, but in what he *says*), in Henry himself, from the feeling that the transformation of Hal into Henry involves—and that "necessarily"—some sacrifice?'

This is said well; it reflects something of what we feel; and we cannot but regret that stroke which eclipses the gaiety of nations and impoverishes the public stock of harmless pleasure. Yet taking all in all—the seamier streaks, the dangerously predatory impulses, revealed in Falstaff, Hal's disciplining through grief, the noble idea of justice that dominates the accession, the need for unmistakable severance, and the comfortable leniency of the sentence—it is still possible to hold that Shakespeare *has* here achieved a balanced complexity of wisdom not inferior to that in Part 1, the acknowledgement of necessity with its double face of grief and consolation; that Hal has deepened, not narrowed; and that Falstaff (at a distance of ten miles) can fleet the time carelessly with his cronies, remedying the long consumption of his purse at the expense of the royal exchequer. His well-wishers need ask no more.

## 9. THE STYLE AND ITS FUNCTIONS

Those critics who have belittled Part 2 may be suspected of failing to respond to its vitality and maturity of style. Among the aspects of style may be reckoned the interplay of moods and tones. After the urgency of Rumour and the northern nobles, in strenuous verse and tragic tone, Falstaff's wit and foolery are lavish and expansive, quick as the preceding passions but quick with the virtuosity of ease and leisure, elegant wit-patterns contrasting with the thrusting roughness that has preceded them. The comedy of Master Dommelton's reported recalcitrance (which casts Falstaff into a self-appreciative performance of indignation) and of the fencing with the Lord Chief Justice exists in a world antithetical to Northumberland's. The council of war follows, a return to urgent high policy, and then one of Mistress Quickly's great scenes, comic at the most plebeian level so far met in either of the *Henry IV*s. The play extends its scenes and styles to make the widest exploration of the nation's life. London's alleyways in their uproarious disorder form their counterpart to the baronial disorder (and both levels of riot are fated to be quelled by complementary instruments of government, the King's generals, and the King's Justice). This scene (ii. i), in boisterous vernacular, forms an offset to the next, that of Hal and Poins at an uneasy loose end, fooling in a restless comedy, somewhat exasperated, somewhat bitter. Critics who think Part 2 to be merely marking time on Part 1 ignore the new elements, of which Hal's restive alienation from his old life is one. In sharp contrast, Lady Percy recreates Hotspur, as a reminder, after Hal's unrest, of what the model of chivalry had been.[1] Then follow in succession the tavern scene, as tellingly coarse as anything in Langland or Hogarth (yet done rather in Chaucer's spirit), an unblinkable indication that Hal must commit himself to a new life; and then the King's meditation on the revolving times and his own time in particular, a discourse poetically charged, wholly contrasting with Boar's-Head life, yet enrichingly juxtaposed with the plebeian state of those over whom, at the other end of the spectrum, kings rule; and then the switch from London, whether plebeian or courtly, to Gloucestershire, a part equally of the King's domain but complementary in spirit and idiom to the components which have gone before. To pursue the inter-relationships further would be superfluous save, perhaps, for indicating the striking force of the scene of Doll's arrest (v. iv), placed between the anarchistic hopes Falstaff has just voiced, and the regal authority Henry is just about to exert. This inter-inanimation of successive levels, speeds, manners, and languages of the play is the more important, dramatically, in that the narrative content is not greatly compelling. Much less than in Part 1, or *Richard II*, or *Julius Caesar*, or *Macbeth*, or *Othello*, does one ask, 'What happens next?', though one certainly asks, 'What happens at the coronation?' The play is narrative, certainly, but its dramatic interest is less in narration than in the varying paces, pressures, and qualities that make the living nation of men. It is in the manner of writing, the style or styles, that these reveal themselves.

The play has been thought deficient in 'poetry', by adherents of that 'lyric heresy' which Lascelles Abercrombie defined as 'the doctrine that poetry can only be lyrical; [that] even epics and dramas . . . can only justify themselves as poetry by their lyrical moments'.[2] This debilitating doctrine can be maintained only by those unwilling to recognize that 'poetry' co-exists with the whole expressive vitality of language. It is this fuller kind of poetry which

---

1. Hal, of course, must transcend Hotspur, since Hotspur's valour is anarchic. But at least he must have Hotspur's virtues (and has, in *Henry V*), of which Lady Percy's speech is a reminder.

2. *Theory of Poetry*, New York, 1926, p. 216.

*2 Henry IV* abundantly displays. Dr Tillyard gives the right lead:

> In *Henry IV* there is a variety of style, fully mastered, which is new in Shakespeare and which can hardly be matched even in his later work. This variety contrasts, and I believe was meant deliberately to contrast, with the comparative monotony of *Richard II*. . . . Taken together, the verse and prose of the play are a stylistic exhibition of the commonwealth.[1]

The style, in the first place, expresses great vivacity and manifold energies, observable from the start in the flexible rhetoric of Rumour, engaging the attention by functional changes of direction, rhythm, and stress, reflecting the speaker's heady character in the flux of metaphors, half-emerging and then swept out of sight by others:

> Upon my tongues continual slanders *ride*,
> The which in every language I pronounce,
> *Stuffing* the ears of men with false reports . . .
> Whiles the *big year*, *swoln* with some other grief,
> Is thought *with child* by the stern tyrant War,
> And no such matter? Rumour is a *pipe*
> *Blown* by surmises, jealousies, conjectures,
> And of so easy and so plain a *stop*
> That the *blunt monster with uncounted heads*,
> The *still-discordant wav'ring* multitude,
> Can *play* upon it.

This swift generation of metaphors can be studied in the figurative sequence of Morton's speech at I. i. 112–25. Here the firing and chilling of spirit, the tempering of metal, and the flight of missiles follow with the swiftest of transitions, so mercurially effected that the mind receives the impress of graphic suggestion without pausing to define the causes, the whole being kept in the plane of suggestiveness (rather than definition) by verbal legerity, almost legerdemain. Such language is vitally metaphorical: it conveys its effects effortlessly but it defies translation into prose. The King's speeches at IV. iv. 19–66 evolve with a similar velocity. Such metaphors wed thought and figure intimately—a notable instance occurs at IV. v. 98–100:

> Stay but a little, for my cloud of dignity
> Is held from falling with so weak a wind
> That it will quickly drop; my day is dim.

The King's supremacy, overshadowing rather than glorious (and imaged as a cloud), upheld only by his fading breath as a cloud's

1. Tillyard, pp. 295–6.

rain is by gently fluctuating air, will dissolve (a helpless and mournful yielding is appropriate to the King's despondency); his eyesight, life, and reign together are fading. Such is the characteristic metaphorical language of the play.

The style is cogent and picturesque, perpetually enlivened by physical realization. The times brawl, and war has a 'harsh and boist'rous tongue'. Northumberland's bosom 'burns with an incensed fire of injuries',[1] the rebels 'should not step too far / Till we had his assistance by the hand'. Hotspur's fascination is reflected in his admiring imitators—nothing could be more graphic than the lines in which Lady Percy evokes him (II. iii. 18–32), or those from Travers (I. i. 34–48). Animal imagery adds its quota of the spirited —the French and Welsh bay at Henry's heels; the populace is the common dog at its vomit:

> Contention, like a horse
> Full of high feeding, madly hath broke loose,
> And bears down all before him.    (I. i. 9–11)

> For the fifth Harry from curb'd licence plucks
> The muzzle of restraint, and the wild dog
> Shall flesh his tooth on every innocent.    (IV. v. 130–2)

Animal imagery is as effective in the comic prose, with Falstaff before his page like a sow that hath overwhelmed all her litter but one, Pistol not swaggering with a Barbary hen if her feathers turn back in any show of resistance, and Feeble as valiant as the wrathful dove or most magnanimous mouse.

This is, of course, not the mode of this play uniquely; it is Shakespeare's usual vivacity. But in this play of the insistently actual, as in Part I, its graphic force is accentuated to convey the characteristic spirit of its subjects. The body politic, with foul sin gathering head and breaking into corruption, is tragically turbulent (disease imagery figures notably among the physical realizations); tavern-life is comically gross and sensual, country life comically bucolic and practical.

The energy is capable of many modulations; it is the flexible instrument of the imagination. As Hazlitt remarks:

> The peculiarity and the excellence of Shakespeare's poetry is that it seems as if he made his imagination the handmaid of nature, and nature the plaything of his imagination. He appears to have been all the characters, and in all the situations he describes.[2]

1. The literal and figurative senses of 'incensed' are equally active; see I. iii. 14, note.

2. *Characters of Sh.'s Plays*, 'Henry IV'.

This operates stylistically. The energy can quieten into level exposition, as at the opening of IV. iv; it can rise into frenzy, in Northumberland (I. i. 136–60) and the King (IV. v. 92–137)—in these two
cases the heightening from normal tone into virtual hysteria is
wonderfully managed, the pulse and insistence rising by inner
pressure. And the energy can communicate subtle distinctions, as
in the differences between the Archbishop's speech at I. iii. 85–108
and Lady Percy's at II. iii. 9–45. Both are persuasive; both lead to
unsound counsel. But the differences in manner are worth noting.
Lady Percy, while deeply moved, is real and particular in evoking
Hotspur—this is speech we can trust—and if her counsel is falla-
cious the fault is not hers for offering it (since she is swayed by
pathetic emotion) but Northumberland's for accepting. The Archbishop's motives are noble. But his speech is florid and fulsome, the
rhetoric of illusion, and its graphic quality is the quality not of
realization but of prejudiced assumption. The rebels in both Parts
are recurrently at the mercy of their own eloquence—Hotspur,
Northumberland, the Archbishop.[1] In IV. i the Archbishop's reply
to Westmoreland is a cover-up for what is hardly, in any particular
terms, made out to be a case at all; the thought sequence reflects a
basic incoherence. This reveals itself in generalized metaphor, in
ambiguity (he is not a physician, yet he is [ll. 60, 63–6]), and in pro-
nouncements which never yield a graspable point ('Wherefore do
I this? so the question stands' . . . 'we are all diseas'd' . . . 'Hear me
more plainly' . . .). The only reason which emerges to explain the
revolt is that he cannot approach the King. Westmoreland, little as
one may like what he will shortly do, is much more in command of
his speech than the Archbishop or Mowbray, whose brilliant lines
on the Coventry lists end (as hot-headed partisanship is apt to end)
in guess-work (IV. i. 117–29), which Westmoreland authoritatively
answers.[2] Never previously had Shakespeare's style so translated
speakers' minds and moods, expressing them explicitly and impli-
citly also. There is magniloquence appropriate to high status in
lines like

1. Once or twice the King, so much in command of his language in Part 1, is
nearly its victim in Part 2—in his melancholy contemplation of futurity (III. i)
and his anticipation of Hal's reign (IV. v). But in these cases Warwick and Hal
pull him back. On the rebels' councils of war (I. iii; IV. i. 183–227), Hereward
T. Price observes, 'Shakespeare was fond of showing clever men arguing themselves into their own destruction. . . One of [his] favorite themes is the spectacle
of men too clever for their own good, too clever to be wise', and he cites also
*JC*, II. i. 10 ff., IV. iii. 196 ff. (*JEGP*, vol. 57, 1958, p. 807).

2. Westmoreland's authority is not merely his position as official spokesman
(which would be suspect); his statement is true to historical fact, as Holinshed
indicates (Hol., ii. 838, 843, 848–9).

So looks the strond whereon the imperious flood
Hath left a witness'd usurpation . . .

or

In cradle of the rude imperious surge.

There is an 'official' grandiloquence, for presenting the ideal order of the state (IV. i. 41–52; IV. ii. 4–22; V. ii. 129–45). There are, on the other hand, the uneasy stops and starts in the sick King's meditation (IV. v. 59–79), in which the irregularities convey his distraction and which seem like an early movement towards King Lear's broken rhythm.[1] There is also the measured, rational, and cogent manner of discourse in which the new King, his brothers, and the Lord Chief Justice confront each other (V. ii. 43–129).

The responsiveness of style in the prose is not less complete. Falstaff's cadenzas of wit have a sprightly elegance and pattern, and a quicksilver play of notion (I. ii. 5–48; III. ii. 295–327; IV. iii. 84–123; V. i. 59–82). The auditory expressiveness is impeccable in everything uttered by Falstaff, Mistress Quickly, Doll, or Shallow, by Bullcalf while dodging recruitment, or by Feeble while, with a volley of popular tags, accepting it. The vernacular is true throughout, generated by a speech-sense which, through the prose movement and texture, creates the living utterance. Among the novel exercises of this power are the Lord Chief Justice's authoritative wit and good sense, Shallow's babbling incoherence, Hal's disturbed play with Poins, and, above all, Doll's extraordinary force. Naturally alien to any elegances of style, she scolds her way through her ejaculatory violences, or coaxes by professional habit, and in either case one hears her very tones. In these and in other manners the prose corresponds even more fully than the verse can do to the range of life displayed.

The words have more complex things to do than they had in Part I where the characters, brilliantly though they are drawn, are simpler. Part I has nothing so ambivalent to convey as the King's trouble of mind, the Archbishop's high-minded fumbling, Northumberland's undependable vehemence, Falstaff's dangerous brilliance, Doll's violence and pathos, or Shallow's equal crassness and rustic sense (Shallow is, as Tillyard well observes, a good countryman,[2] and he does his best, such as it is, as farmer, host, and King's representative). These intermingled qualities, pointers to a developing subtlety in the reading of human nature, are conveyed in the manner of writing. 'The King's mutability speech', Professor Knights comments, 'is not just a bit of moralizing appropriate to a

---

1. Cf. *Lr*, IV. vi. 112–31, for example.          2. Tillyard, p. 302.

sick and disappointed man. . . It is an explicit formulation of feelings and attitudes deeply embedded in the play'.[1] Moreover, in the varying manners of the speech, in the play of idea and mood reflected in line-movement and syntax, are felt the form and pressure of Henry's inner conflicts—the yearning, the despondency, the moralizing, the recapitulation of the past, with the mind ferreting over the course of things and interjecting its self-justification.[2] The vehicle for the changing moods is changing expressiveness of tone and movement in the verse. This stylistic maturity and complexity, co-ordinated as it is with the deeper exploration now going on into the ambiguities of human nature, is recognized in one of the best comments on the play:

> Shakespeare . . . shows a further characteristic of great genius: he can feel for, can even invest with dignity, those representative human types who, in the complex play of attitudes that constitute his dramatic statement, are judged and found wanting. When Falstaff celebrates with Doll Tearsheet, at the Boar's Head Tavern, his departure for the wars (II. iv), there is nothing comic in the exhibition of senile lechery. Yet the tipsy Doll can move us with 'Come, I'll be friends with thee, Jack, thou art going to the wars, and whether I shall ever see thee again or no there is nobody cares'. And at the end of the scene Mistress Quickly too has her moment, when sentimentality itself is transformed simply by looking towards those human decencies and affections for which—the realities being absent—it must do duty:

>> Well, fare thee well. I have known thee these twenty-nine years, come peascod-time, but an honester and truer-hearted man—Well, fare thee well.

> There is nothing facile in Shakespeare's charity; it is simply that Shakespeare, like Chaucer, is not afraid of his spontaneous feelings, and his feelings are not—so to speak—afraid of each other . . .
> Shakespeare never explicitly points a moral; . . . [yet] it seems to me that what is coming into consciousness is nothing less than an awareness of how men make the world they inhabit, an understanding of the relation between what men are and the kind of perceptions they have about the nature of things. It is this growing awareness, linking the overt social criticism with the more deep-lying and pervasive concern with time's power, that explains our sense of fundamental issues coming to expression. It explains why the tone of 2 *Henry IV* is entirely different from the tone of detached observation of the earlier plays. . . . In tech-

1. L. C. Knights, *Some Shn Themes*, p. 57.
2. Similar fluctuations can be traced through IV. iv–v.

nique too we are beginning to find that more complete per-
meation of the material by the shaping imagination which dis-
tinguishes the plays that follow it from those that went before.
The words do not yet strike to unexpected depths (it is significant
that some of the most vividly realized scenes are in prose); but in
the manner of its working the play is nearer to *Macbeth* than to
*Richard III*; the imagery is organic to the whole, and the verse
and prose alike are beginning to promote that associative acti-
vity that [is] the distinguishing mark of great drama. It is this
imaginative wholeness that allows us to say that Shakespeare is
now wholly *within* his material.[1]

## 10. THE TEXT

### (i) *The Transmission of the Text*

Except insofar as it is defective, the 1600 Quarto is the primary
authority for the text, and its readings prevail over the Folio's
unless the latter are demonstrably better. It is, to quote Greg, 'the
typical example of a play set up from the author's original draft'.[2]
It preserves the interesting spelling of Silence as Scilens.[3] It shows
also the normal evidence of a script from the author's own hand,
the 'foul papers' characterized by marked variation in the forms of
speech-prefixes,[4] authorial descriptive details in stage-directions,[5]

1. L. C. Knights, *Some Shn Themes*, pp. 63–4.

2. W. W. Greg, *The Sh. First Folio*, 1955, p. 266.

3. The same spelling occurs in the presumed Shakespearean pages of *Sir Thomas More* (A. W. Pollard and others, *Sh.'s Hand in Sir Thomas More*, 1923, l. 50 of transcript following p. 229). It is not normal Elizabethan spelling (or at any rate not normal printing-house spelling), though as Mr John Crow observes (*TLS*, 28 Oct. 1955, p. 639) Marston's *Sophonisba* (1600) has 'scilence' (sig. D4ᵛ) and 'scilent' (sig. E3ʳ)—cf. Marston, *Plays*, ed. H. H. Wood, ii. 33, 37. The 'sc' is not uncommon, but the final -s for -ce is unusual, and 'the combination is, so far as is known, unparalleled outside Shakespeare' (W. W. Greg, *The Sh. First Folio*, 1955, p. 147, note). See collations at III. ii. 87, 205–6, 282–3, v. iii S.D., 4, 16, for a complete list of its occurrences in 2 *Henry IV*.

4. In I. i, Northumberland is *Earle* until his last speech, then *North*. In I. ii, Falstaff is *Iohn*, *sir Iohn*, *Falst*., and (once) *Old.*: his attendant is *Page* and *Boy*; the Lord Chief Justice is *Iustice* and *Lord* (or *Lo.*). In II. i, Gower is *Gower* and *Mess* [*enger*]. In II. iv, Mistress Quickly is *Quickly* (or *Qui.*) and *host.* (or *Ho.*); Doll Tearsheet is *Tere.*, *Teresh.*, *Doll* (or *Dol*), and *Dorothy* (or *Doro.*); Falstaff in the same scene is *sir Iohn* and *Falst.* (or *Fal.*). In III. ii, Shallow is *Shal.* (or *Sha.*) and (once) *Iust.* In IV. ii and IV. iii Lancaster is *Iohn* and *Prince* (or *Prin.*). In IV. iv, Gloucester is *Glo.* and *Hum.*; Clarence is *Clar.* (or *Cla.*) and *Tho.*; in IV. v, Hal is *Harry* and *Prince*. In v. iii, Falstaff is *Falst.* (or *Fal.*), *sir Iohn*, and *Iohn*. In v. iv, Doll is *Whoore*. And in v. v, Falstaff is *Falst.* (or *Fal.*) and *Iohn*, though within a few lines *Iohn* is used also for Lancaster. This list is not exhaustive.

5. E.g. Induction, *Enter Rumour painted full of Tongues*; I. ii, *Enter sir Iohn alone, with his page bearing his sword and buckler*; I. iii, *Thomas Mowbray* (*Earle Marshall*);

imprecision and inadequacy in entry-directions,[1] imperfect correspondence between these and speech-prefixes,[2] entries marked for characters who perform no function in the scene,[3] and possibly directions of a technical kind which show the dramatist thinking in stage terms.[4] These loose ends and informalities are the accepted signs of the writer's work-desk.

But the foul papers had been interfered with before they reached the press. Besides whatever circumstances caused the omission from Qa of Act III, scene i, there were eight considerable passages cut from the text and recoverable only from the Folio. The opinion once held,[5] that they reflect abridgements in a copy used for prompt-purposes, does not really meet the case. Not all the cuts can be attempts to shorten the play in production (cf. pp. lxx–lxxi). Moreover, Q shows no signs at all that its copy was affected by a prompt-book. It is defective in many details which a prompt-book would supply. No text would be practicable for prompt purposes if it did not excise unnecessary mute characters, imprecise directions, and markedly variant speech-prefixes of the kind so common in Q.

---

III. i, *Enter the King in his night-gowne alone*; IV. i, *Enter the Archbishop, Mowbray, Bardolfe, Hastings, within the forrest of Gaultree.*

1. E.g. II. i, *Enter Hostesse of the Tauerne, and an Officer or two*; II. i. 50, *Enter Lord chiefe iustice and his men*; II. ii, *Enter the Prince, Poynes, sir Iohn Russel, with other*; II. iv, *Enter a Drawer or two* (one of whom immediately speaks as *Francis*); III. ii, *Enter Bardolfe, and one with him*; IV. iii. 23, *Enter Iohn Westmerland, and the rest*; v. iv, *Enter Sincklo and three or foure officers*; v. v, *Enter strewers of rushes.* In III. i, the King, directed to *Enter . . . in his night-gowne alone*, immediately addresses an attendant. At II. iv. 18, Q has *Enter Will* (nowhere else referred to) but fails to make it apparent which, if any, of the drawers' speeches are meant for him.

2. E.g. at II. i. 132, Q reads *enter a messenger*, who is at once addressed as Gower; in II. iii, *the wife to Harry Percie* of the entry-direction speaks as *Kate*.

3. E.g. in I. iii, *Fauconbridge*; in II. ii, *sir Iohn Russel*; in III. i, *sir Iohn Blunt*; in IV. i, *Bardolfe*; in IV. iv, *Kent*; in v. ii, *Westmerland*; at v. ii. 42, *Blunt*. Surrey and Blunt are mute in III. i and IV. iii respectively but are referred to in the dialogue.

4. E.g. I. i, *Enter the Lord Bardolfe at one doore.* Such a direction is not necessarily authorial, since a prompter might add it, but along with so much other evidence in Q *2 Henry IV*, it looks like Shakespeare's.

5. E.g. by the Cambridge editors and by R. P. Cowl in the original Arden edition (p. x). Cowl comments, 'It is apparent that the Quarto version was derived from a theatre copy which had been cut, and negligently cut, for representation on the stage'. He admits, however, that some of the cuts leave the sense incomplete—and so, surely, would be unsatisfactory to the actors. He argues that 'the intrusion into the Quarto text, here and there, of what are evidently a prompter's notes, points to the conclusion that the original of the Quarto had been used as a prompt-copy'. The instances he had in mind (he specifies none) are perhaps such as *Enter the Lord Bardolfe at one doore* (I. i, S.D.), *Enter the King in his night-gowne alone* (III. i, S.D.), and *Iohn prickes him* (III. ii. 110). But in fact none of these looks like prompter's work, and none can outweigh the evidence that the original of Q could not have served as a prompt-book.

Moreover, Q needs many more entry- and exit-directions. Some of the missing ones Shakespeare may have neglected to write in because they are self-evident,[1] but a prompt-book would surely supply them. Others are not self-evident, and a prompt-book would need to insert them,[2] as it would need also to rectify misplaced directions[3] and inadequate indication of stage-effects.[4] It is clear that Shakespeare's MS was not used as the prompt-copy, and that the printer received it, apart from the cuts, in an interestingly original condition.

### (ii) The Cuts in the Quarto

Besides many apparently authentic words and short phrases which the Folio contains and the Quarto does not, and apart from the scene (III. i) not in Qa, eight passages occur only in the Folio. These are: (a) I. i. 166–79; (b) I. i. 189–209; (c) I. iii. 21–4; (d) I. iii. 36–55; (e) I. iii. 85–108; (f) II. iii. 23–45; (g) IV. i. 55–79; (h) IV. i. 103–39.

Of these, four may reflect an attempt to shorten the play for performance. Passage (a) is not needed for the action; (c) is unimportant; (d) is an expansion, the excision of which hardly harms the scene; and (f), though a moving recollection of Hotspur, holds the action up.

The four others, however, damage the coherence, balance, or

---

1. E.g. I. ii. 228, 244, 250 (scene-end); II. i. 190 (scene-end); II. iv. 366; III. i. 3; III. ii. 327 (scene-end); IV. ii. 71, 92, 96, 123 (scene-end); IV. iii. 25, 73, 83, 130 (scene-end); IV. v. 19, 240 (scene-end); V. i. 84 (scene-end); V. iv. 31 (scene-end); V. v. 4, 72, 109 (scene-end). In all these instances the required entrance or exit is indicated in the dialogue.

2. E.g. the porter's entrance and exit at I. i. 1 and 6; the entrance of the Lord Chief Justice's attendant with him at I. ii. 54; the group exit at II. i. 162; the drawer's, or drawers', exit at II. iv. 21 (except for Francis's); Bardolph's entry at II. iv. 107 (Q's *Bardolfes boy* is an error for *Bardolfe and his boy*; cf. collation); Pistol's exit at II. iv. 204; Bardolph's exit and entrance at II. iv. 204, 208, or again at 366; Bardolph and the rest's exeunt at II. iv. 378; the attendant's entrance in III. i; the recruits' entrance and exeunt in III. ii; Colevile's entrance in IV. iii; Blunt's entrance at IV. iii. 23; Warwick's re-entrance at IV. v. 224; Davy's exits at V. iii. 29 and 69; Bardolph's exit at V. iii. 128; Mistress Quickly's and Doll's entrance at V. iv; and the entrance of officers attending Prince John and the Lord Chief Justice at V. v. 90. The list is not exhaustive.

3. E.g. the direction at II. i. 162 comes in Q after 160; at II. iv. 18, Q's direction *Enter Will* (whomever it is meant for) is probably misplaced; at the opening of v. ii Q wrongly brings on Lancaster, Clarence, Gloucester, and Westmoreland, and then repeats the entry of the first three at line 13. Errors of misplacing may arise from some obscurity in the copy, or from the book-keeper's editorial tinkering, as duplications probably do also.

4. E.g. Q fails to provide for the knocking at II. iv. 365 and for the coronation shouts and trumpets (v. v. 39), as it fails also to introduce any ceremony at v. ii. 42, merely directing *Enter the Prince and Blunt*.

significance of their scenes, and all remove passages of political import. Without passage (*b*), Morton has two pointless lines and Northumberland answers, apropos nothing in particular, 'I knew of this before'. Without (*e*), the Archbishop, in a scene where he should stand out as leader, speaks only four lines at the beginning and a final one-line query (which the Folio shows to have been transferred from Mowbray). Without (*g*), his defence against Westmoreland is a flaccid ten lines devoid of serious content. Without (*h*), Westmoreland refers to 'digression from my purpose' (IV. i. 140) when no digression is apparent.

These lacunae may result from political censorship.[1] Passages innocent in 1597 would sound dangerous in 1600. By then, two dangers were at their climaxes—the Irish insurrection which Essex failed to crush in 1599, and Essex's own disaster. As Hart points out, 'early in 1600 Oviedo, a Franciscan monk, had come from Spain to Ireland with the title of Bishop of Dublin; in April he conferred with the native chieftains, gave them £6,000 in money, and promised them Spanish military aid'. A text which showed an archbishop rising against an established monarch, proclaiming the good of the nation, religiously blessing insurrection, and citing Richard II's death under Bolingbroke, might well seem an allegory for Oviedo and the Irish leaders fighting Elizabeth, and pleading the cause of Ireland and the Roman Church against the Queen under whom the symbol of their faith, Mary Queen of Scots, had been executed. The twin-crisis of Essex's rebellion, followed by his trial and death in 1600, might equally suggest censorship. Elizabeth curiously likened herself to Richard II and dreaded a similar fate, and Essex's supporters launched their uprising by commissioning a performance of *Richard II*. Allusions to Richard were highly dangerous.[2] Passage (*b*) tells how the Archbishop incites his allies with 'the blood / Of fair King Richard'; (*e*) is his lament for the popular fickleness which vacillated to and from Richard and Henry in turn; (*g*) shows him asserting that the country suffers 'a burning fever' like that from which 'Our late

---

1. Suggested by F. G. Fleay (*Wm Sh.*, 1886, p. 200), developed by L. L. Schücking (*TLS*, 25 Sept. 1930, p. 752) and elaborated by Alfred Hart (*Sh. and the Homilies*, 1934, pp. 179 ff.). W. W. Greg is sceptical, however (*The Sh. First Folio*, 1955, p. 274).

2. Sir John Hayward's *First Part of the Life and Raigne of Henrie IIII* (pub. January 1599), dedicated to Essex, was felt to be embarrassing by Essex himself, and the dedication was suppressed. Hayward was nevertheless tried during the panic caused by Essex's rising and though he disclaimed any covert allusions he was imprisoned. Fulke Greville burnt the MS of his tragedy on Cleopatra for fear it might be thought to allude to Essex.

King Richard being infected died', and that his enemies deny him all access to the King[1]; (*h*) recapitulates the Mowbray–Bolingbroke quarrel from which sprang the causes of Richard's downfall.

Censorship seems, then, a likely reason for the cuts. Every allusion to Richard II has gone from Qa, though Qb, issued somewhat later, includes the references contained in Act III, scene i. The Archbishop's part is reduced to insignificance, and his cause is given far less chance to justify itself than it has in F. Whoever made the cuts did so with a gross disregard of the dramatic niceties.[2] His only concern, it seems, was that two dangerous themes should 'Have their stings and teeth newly ta'en out'.

Two other omissions need a comment. These are the omission of IV. i. 93 and 95 from some copies of Q, and from F; and the omission of III. i from Qa. Lines IV. i. 93 and 95 were cut as Q was being printed: they were set up and then taken out, leaving the page two lines short in the corrected state. They do not seem objectionable: 93 is no more dangerous than 92, and indeed is the culmination of Westmoreland's reproof to the Archbishop; 95 is cryptic but not evidently offensive. It has been suggested that heavier cuts took place hereabouts (since ll. 94–6 are not an adequate rejoinder to Westmoreland, and 'any such redress' in l. 97 lacks a specific referent). But if so, it is odd that F, which restores the cuts at ll. 55–79 and 103–39, restores nothing here: the cryptic sense of ll. 93–7 is probably due to short-circuits in Shakespeare's ideas. A further suggestion, which has caused some editors to drop the lines, is that Shakespeare himself cancelled them, but imperfectly, so that the deletion escaped the eye of the compositor but not the proof-corrector; or that they were jottings he rejected. But there seems no reason why he should do this. The most interesting proposal to date is Dr Alice Walker's.[3] She suggests that Q's cut beginning 'O, my good Lord Mowbray' (l. 103) was actually marked to begin at l. 101, that the compositor erred, and when instructed to remove ll. 101–2 also he took out instead ll. 93 and 95, which begin with the same words. As Dr Walker points out, ll. 101–2 sound quite as dangerous as others excised from this scene; a censor might

1. This, Hart points out, was the purpose of Essex's rising, 'to force his way into the presence of the Queen' (*Sh. and the Homilies*, p. 209).

2. Someone tinkered a little with the cuts, fitting speech-prefixes to abbreviated speeches (I. iii. 56, IV. i. 140) and, more enterprisingly, making the Archbishop speak I. iii. 109 to compensate for the loss of I. iii. 85–108 and to enable him to show some small signs of leadership at the end of this scene as well as at the beginning.

3. *Textual Problems of the First Folio*, 1953, pp. 104–5.

leave to Mowbray his reference to 'the bruises of the days before' (l. 100) but cut that to current injustices shown to the King's opponents. The proof-corrector would content himself with marking the error for correction but would not bother to ascertain whether or not the 'correction' was accurately made.[1] From the erroneously 'corrected' Q the omission of ll. 93, 95, as well as the presence of ll. 101–2 could pass into F, whether directly from Q or *via* a transcript.[2]

On the last problem of omission, the absence of iii. i from Qa may have been accidental, or it may have been deliberate. That it was accidental was first suggested by J. P. Collier in his first edition of Shakespeare (1842, p. 339). A. W. Pollard, reckoning that Shakespeare normally wrote about 54 lines to a page, suggested that the scene's 108 lines might take up two sides of a single sheet and that if this sheet were mislaid its absence might go unobserved since the scene is not essential to the action.[3] That the omission was deliberate was suggested by Alfred Hart, who thought that since the scene does not appreciably contribute to the action it would undergo heavy cutting for stage-abridgement, and that if in addition the censor marked for omission the reflections on national disorder and the fate of Richard II the result would be too fragmentary for publication.[4]

On balance, the missing-leaf theory seems slightly the better. The problem is not very important, though some interesting consequences might depend upon the answer: Dover Wilson, for example, suggests that the script was submitted for censorship without this scene and that Qb's subsequent appearance with the unsubmitted material provoked a ban on republication—hence no further editions. But this is only conjecture, and the facts may never be known.[5]

(iii) *The Copy for the Folio*

'Of all Shakespearean texts this, together with *Othello*, seems to

---

1. At Q iii. ii. 326–7 proof-'correcting' introduced nonsense into an originally correct text (cf. collation): clearly little was done to check corrections. At iii. ii. 54, neither uncorrected nor corrected Q seems to give a satisfactory reading, for which one goes to F (cf. collation).

2. On the nature of F's copy, see below.

3. The supposedly Shakespearean three pages of *Sir Thomas More* have 45, 52, and 53 lines each (the first having also a spaced stage direction); A. W. Pollard, 'Variant Settings in *II Henry IV*', *TLS*, 21 Oct. 1920, p. 680.

4. *Sh. and the Homilies*, pp. 175 ff.

5. Greg points out several difficulties in both the whole 'censorship' theory of Q's cuts and in the idea that unauthorized insertion of iii. i in Qb caused a ban on republication (*The Sh. First Folio*, 1955, p. 274).

provide the most difficult problem about the nature of the printers' copy for the Folio.'[1] The intimidating announcement is justified: F's relationship to Q is a first-class puzzle. Was F printed from (a) a MS quite independent of Q (and if so, what kind of MS); or (b) from Q corrected by collation with a MS (and if so, what kind of MS); or (c) from a MS itself transcribed from Q but incorporating from some other source many details not in Q; or (d) from a MS transcribed jointly from Q and some other MS? These four possibilities provide the bones of contention. But first, F's main differences from Q need enumerating.

### (iv) *Comparison of the Quarto and Folio Texts*

The differences are as follows:

(a) Though lacking short passages found in Q, F restores the eight passages Q omits. For these passages it is therefore the substantive text. It includes also III. i, omitted from Qa.

(b) F varies from Q in many words and phrases, by insertions, omissions, transpositions, or alternatives. Some of its readings seem better than Q's. Some seem equally good, and only Q's generally superior authority causes their rejection. Most, however, are worse.

(c) F's punctuation is a thorough (sometimes excessive) revision and augmentation of Q's light and often inadequate stopping.[2]

(d) All but a few of the simplest stage-directions differ from Q's. Descriptive expansions are omitted,[3] as are several mute or supposedly mute characters.[4] Vague directions become specific.[5] Entry- and exit-directions correspond better with the action,[6] though with some anomalies,[7] and with omission of some necessary directions which Q contains.[8]

---

1. Fredson Bowers, *Studies in Sh.*, 1953, p. 25.

2. One feature is a strong penchant for unexpected hyphens—e.g. 'Worme-eaten-Hole' (Induc. 35), 'smooth-Comforts-false' (ibid., 40), 'Rascally-yea-forsooth-knaue' (I. ii. 35–6), 'hold-vp-head' (I. iii. 17), 'hooke-on, hooke-on' (II. i. 160), 'heart-deere-*Harry*' (II. iii. 12), 'Noble-Youth' (II. iii. 22), and so on.

3. Cf. collations at openings of Induction; I. i; I. ii; I. iii; II. i; III. i; IV. i.

4. Cf. collations at I. iii (opening); II. iv. 18–19; III. i. 31 S.D.; IV. i (opening); IV. iv (opening); V. ii. 42 S.D.

5. Cf. collations at II. i (opening); II. ii (opening); II. iv (opening); III. ii. 53 S.D.; IV. iii. 23 S.D. (*Enter . . . others*).

6. Cf. collations at I. i (opening); I. ii. 54 S.D.; II. iv. 107 S.D.; III. i (opening); III. ii (opening); III. ii. 327; IV. ii. 71, 92, 96, 123; IV. iii (opening), 73, 83, 130; V. iv (opening).

7. Cf. collations at openings of IV. i, V. i, V. ii, V. iii.

8. Cf. S.D. collations at I. iii. 110; II. i. 59, 162; II. ii. 65; II. iv. 348; III. ii. 214, 235; IV. i. 182.

(*e*) Characters are named in stage-directions and speech-prefixes more tersely, formally, and uniformly.[1]

(*f*) Act- and scene-divisions are inserted.[2]

(*g*) F shows signs of apparent stage practice. It omits Q's *Vmfr.* and his one line (I. i. 161), which modern editors give to Travers or Lord Bardolph. Shakespeare seemingly wrote Lord Bardolph's part originally for a Sir John Umfrevile (at I. i. 30–2 Lord Bardolph declares that he was Travers's informant about Shrewsbury, whereas at ll. 34–6 Travers, in no spirit of contradiction, says his news came from Sir John Umfrevile). He then failed to change the name in l. 161 (as well as in l. 34, where it does not matter), whereupon the actors, taking Umfrevile to be a minor character, probably saved a part by excising him. F's different arrangement of the drawers' speeches at II. iv. 1–21, with the deletion of one speech (ll. 13–14) and of Q's *Enter Will* (l. 18), may reflect stage practice. In III. ii, F brings the recruits on at the beginning, whereas Q apparently leaves them 'off', to appear individually (cf. Shallow's 'Let them appear as I call'; ll. 98–9). Most notably, F differs markedly in v. v. Not only does it reduce Q's three rush-strewers to two and curtail one speech (cf. l. 4) but it omits the coronation procession to the Abbey (l. 4, S.D.) and shows only the return (l. 40, S.D.). At v. i, in addition to Q's Shallow, Falstaff, and Bardolph, F brings on Silence, the Page, and Davy. The two latter are indeed shortly needed, but Silence lives up to his name by saying and doing nothing; he may be there merely because he and Shallow were considered inseparable on the stage. At v. v. 90, F marks no re-entry for Prince John and the Lord Chief Justice, and seems to imply that they remained on-stage, but this would surely be awkward and the omission is presumably an error.

(*h*) F's text has been zealously, though not completely, purged of profanity.[3] Some indecencies also have been excised, though many others remain.

1. Cf. collations at openings of II. i, II. ii, II. iii, III. ii, IV. iv. As against Q's variant forms of speech-prefixes (p. lxviii, fn. 4), F is markedly uniform. Northumberland is *Nor(th.)*, Falstaff is *Fal./Falst./Falstaffe*. His attendant is *Pag(e)*. The Lord Chief Justice is *(Ch.) Iu(st.)*; Mistress Quickly and Doll Tearsheet are *Host(esse)* and *Dol*. Shallow is *Shal(low)*. Lancaster is *Ioh(n)*. Gloucester is *Glo(u)*. Clarence is *Cla(r)*. Hal is *P. Hen./Pr./Prin(ce)*. But Gower remains, as in Q, either *Gow.* or *Mess.*

2. F calls the Induction *Actus Primus. Scœna Prima*, so the numbers of subsequent scenes of Act I are one higher than in editions from Pope's onwards. In Act IV, F marks only two scenes; *Scena Prima* includes the modern scenes i–iii, *Scena Secunda* the modern scenes iv–v. See Appendix VI.

3. With *Othello*, the *Henry IV*s are the most heavily expurgated of F's plays;

(*i*) A great number of Q's colloquialisms, archaisms, rusticisms, and apparent solecisms are turned into 'proper' forms. This is one of F's most remarkable features.[1]

Some of these changes could have been made on any kind of copy, with no aid but his own wits, by whoever prepared F's material; this applies to the changes under (*c*), (*d*) on the whole, (*e*), (*f*), and (*h*).[2] To some extent (*d*)'s changes, and more decidedly (*g*)'s, reflect stage management, and might arise from reference to a prompt-book—though at many other points the guidance of a prompt-book seems conspicuously lacking. The changes under (*a*) certainly require MS reference, as also do such under (*b*) as look like authentic readings not attainable by guess-work. Those under (*i*) are the most curious of all. Q is strikingly rich in colloquial speech-forms, and F refines almost all of them away. So methodical a revision was quite out of the province of F's compositors, however freehanded these were in many respects, and it must derive from an editor or scribe aiming at a polished 'literary' text, either for a patron with refined tastes[3] or because F was to be a memorial 'to

---

the 1606 Act against profanity seems to have had only a limited effect on dramatic performance and publication, but about the time the Folio was in preparation there are signs of a literary (rather than legal) liking for expurgation (W. W. Greg, *The Sh. First Folio*, p. 152). Dr Alice Walker argues that expurgation was editorial in origin, rather than a prompt-book matter (*Textual Problems of the First Folio*, pp. 30–1).

1. *Expansions*: e.g. heele/he will; hee's/he is; tis/it is; ist/is it; too't/to it; a would a/he would haue; a has/he hath; ile nere/I will neuer; giues (= give us)/ giue me; thou wot, wot thou, thou wot, wot ta/Thou wilt not? thou wilt not?; a wil not out, a tis/he will not out, he is. *Modernizations*: e.g. band/Bond; yeere/ eare; afore/before; other/others; and/if (frequently). *Apparent solecisms altered*: e.g. Trauers who (F whom) I sent (I. i. 28); A calls me enow/He call'd me euen now (II. ii. 76); things . . . who (F which) (III. i. 83–4); I see/I saw (III. ii. 28); There is (F are) many complaints (v. i. 36); this (F these) eight yeares (v. i. 43); beards wags (F wag) (v. iii. 34). To such grammatical scrupulousness Shaaber adds the changes from singular to plural of nouns of number (cf. collations at II. iv. 162; III. ii. 205) and the modernization of out-of-date or unfamiliar prepositional usages (cf. collations at I. ii. 159; IV. iii. 48; IV. v. 132), though one can hardly know whether this is deliberate policy on F's part or merely the compositor setting the 'proper' forms automatically. The above examples are far from exhaustive. Occasionally the process is reversed, e.g. F 'I pra'ye' for Q 'I pray you' (II. i. 28), 'you'l tell' for 'you will tell' (II. ii. 36–7), 'th'art' for 'thou art' (III. ii. 174).

2. 'Perhaps the most likely person to have devilled for Heminge and Condell is the book-keeper of the King's Company. He would have all the relevant documents under his care and probably possessed a more intimate knowledge of their nature and quality than anyone else' (W. W. Greg, *The Sh. First Folio*, p. 78).

3. This, though problematical, is not inconceivable. Having considered the question of private-transcript 'copy', Greg concludes, 'It is possible . . . that, by the time the First Folio was being got together, a few private transcripts were

keepe the memory of so worthy a Friend, & Fellow aliue, as was our SHAKESPEARE'.

It has often been argued that F was printed quite independently of Q, from a manuscript made for stage use or for reading and at one remove or more from Shakespeare's foul papers. There is impressive evidence for this view, ably presented by Matthias Shaaber.[1] He concludes that 'the copy for F was neither Q nor a corrected copy of Q nor simply a prompt-book. It was rather a prompt-book which had been transcribed and, in some important and many insignificant ways, quite thoroughly overhauled to impart to the result what may be called a certain degree of literary finish.'[2] An amendment to this view will be propounded later but first the evidence for it needs presenting.

### (v) *The Folio Text independent of the Quarto?*

(a) If Q were F's source, and the numerous variants in F which are not attributable to the editor's or compositors' errors or corrections were due to the editor's annotating Q by reference to a manuscript, the amount of work must have been formidable and the result hard for the printers to follow. As Shaaber comments, 'Naturally printers prefer printed copy, but the more it is marked up the less preferable it is'.[3]

(b) Many features of F seem unlikely if the compositor had Q under his eyes. Normal prose in Q often appears in short irregular phrases in F.[4] Many of Q's S.D.s are altered or omitted, even when correct, necessary, and plain on the page. The forms of proper names differ strikingly; here, apart from evident Q errors which F would correct, one would expect virtual identity. Some changes

---

already abroad' (*The Sh. First Folio*, p. 154). F removes most of the directions intended for stage effects—for instance, that which brings in Rumour '*painted full of Tongues*' (Induc. 1), or Falstaff's page '*bearing his sword and buckler*' (I. ii. 1), or the command '*shout*' (IV. ii. 86). These are perhaps thought unnecessary for a reading.

1. In New Var., pp. 507–15, and further in 'The Folio Text of *2 Henry IV*', *Sh. Q.*, vi. 135–44.

2. New Var., p. 515.

3. 'The Folio Text of *2 Henry IV*', *Sh. Q.*, vi. 135–6. On a comparison of Q sig. C2v and the corresponding portion of F (II. i. 81–123, 'by her owne' to 'if a man') he shows that a very heavy quantity of editorial work would have been necessary to produce F's readings out of Q's. The degree of change between Q and F is much greater than it is when passages of F unquestionably *are* printed from Q copy. My own reckoning, on extensive comparisons of prose and verse, is that *2 Henry IV* F differs from Q nearly twice as much in readings, spellings, and punctuation, as *1 Henry IV* F differs from Q5, which was demonstrably its source.

4. Cf. collations at II. i. 179–80; II. ii. 150–1, 154–5, 158–9; III. ii. 141, 146, 151; IV. iii. 3–4; V. i. 6, 16–17, 24, 28, 34, 49–52, 55–6; V. iii. 104, 106.

are venial normalizations or variants—Lombard for Lumbert, Whitsun for Wheeson, Henrie for Harrie, Germane for Iarman, Cotsall for Cotsole, Double for Dooble, Bezonian for Besonian, and Fang for Phang.[1] Doubtless authentic corrections, however derived, occur in Basingstoke for Billingsgate (II. i. 166), Stamford for Samforth (III. ii. 38), Sure-card for Soccard (III. ii. 86), and Hinckley for Hunkly (v. i. 22). Gowre (Q Gower) and Pointz (Q Poynes) seem F's preferred spellings. But one would not expect Dombledon for Dommelton (I. ii. 29) and Dombe for Dumbe (II. iv. 86), and far less Bare for Barnes (III. ii. 19), Amurah (twice) for Amurath (v. ii. 48) and particularly Couitha for Couetua (v. iii. 99)—these seem to be from another source than Q: Couitha has all the signs of misread script (*e :i* and *tu :th* errors, both graphically easy). These variants would seem to be set up from manuscript rather than print.

(*c*) Comparing two texts one should, as Shaaber remarks, soon feel sure that one was or was not set up from the other. To compare, say, Qa and Qb of *2 Henry IV* in the portions they have in common, or Q5 of *1 Henry IV* with the F text, is to see unmistakably that the later derives from the earlier. This conviction is markedly lacking in the greater part of Q and F *2 Henry IV*. Here and there one finds passages, even fairly long ones, where divergences are few— but these are usually passages in verse, of normal spelling and punctuation, where printing-house practice would produce virtual identity anyway. Despite some similarities, to read Q and F in detail against each other quite fails to produce the expected conviction that F is set from Q, and compels the conclusion that similarities are quite outweighed by divergences unlikely if Q were F's direct copy.

(*d*) Finally, some of F's variants seem due directly to MS copy. Compositors have their vagaries, and deductions from apparent evidence can be misleading, but certain readings look significant. The most striking is F's 'ioyne' for Q's 'win' (IV. v. 179), a nonsense-variant quite unlikely to arise from a misreading of Q, or from anything collated into Q, but entirely explicable as a misreading of a MS 'winne'. There are other apparent MS readings which would scarcely be inserted into a Q (supposing an editor were collating Q with a MS) because, compared with the Q readings, they look wrong, unnecessary, or odd.[2] There are others, apparently authen-

---

1. Yet everywhere else in F the spelling is 'phang(e)'—*Tw.N.*, I. v. 196; *Mer.V.*, III. iii. 7; *AYL.*, II. i. 6; *John*, II. i. 353; *Tim.*, IV. iii. 23; *Lr*, III. vii. 58. So 'Fang' in II. i and 'Fanglesse' at IV. i. 218 (for Q's 'phanglesse') are abnormal to F.

2. As well as the variants of proper names (cf. (*b*), above) there are such read

tic or equally possible readings in F, which only a very scrupulous collator would insert in a Q copy.[1] And finally there are variants which for technical reasons would be unlikely to arise from Q copy.[2]

So far, then, F would seem to have been set up from MS copy, and that not only in the parts missing from Q. Since to some extent F shows cognizance of stage practice, the MS would seem in some degree, though not consistently, to derive from a prompt-book; and since F is so far refined, the MS would seem to have aimed at literary polish.

## (vi) *The Folio Text not independent of the Quarto?*

But for the opposed view, that F was set up from a Q thoroughly edited by collation with the kind of MS just defined, there is also impressive evidence. Q would, on the face of it, be the easiest copy to use for F, provided the passages missing from it were added from some MS source. Besides these general considerations, Dr Alice Walker has added others based on common errors, typographical similarities, and other apparently shared features.[3]

The argument from common errors carries weight, though it is not conclusive. The mere fact of common errors does not necessarily prove that the later text borrows from the earlier; Shakespeare's mercurial mind, ranging rapidly over its ideas, would certainly now and then unconsciously substitute one word for another, and unless the change were evidently wrong it might pass unsuspected by different readers, scribes, editors, or compositors.[4] Shake-

---

ings as the following (the bracketed, correct, versions are Q's): 'them' (for 'men', Induc. 8); 'head' (for 'hard', I. i. 36); 'Speake' (for 'Spoke' or ? 'Spake', I. i. 59); 'aduenture' (for 'a venter', I. i. 59), 'tucke' (for 'tickle', II. i. 59); 'heart-deere-*Harry*' (for 'hearts deere Harry', II. iii. 12); 'wee' (for 'one', II. iv. 28); 'huisht with bussing Night, flyes' (for 'husht with buzzing night-flies', III. i. 11); 'tooke their course' (for 'take their courses', IV. ii. 103). F's 'pernitious' (for 'vertuous', II. ii. 71) could have originated in a MS 'vertuous' preceded by some confusing pen-strokes.

1. E.g. 'ill' (for 'bad', I. i. 41); 'continuantly' (for 'continually', II. i. 25); 'pra'ye' (for 'pray you', II. i. 28); 'viz.' (for 'with', II. ii. 15); 'one other' ( or 'another', II. ii. 17); 'sayth hee' (for 'saide he', II. iv. 88); 'beginnings' (for 'beginning', III. i. 85); 'tine' (for 'tinie', v. i. 26); and 'tyne' (for 'tiny', v. iii. 55).

2. F's 'euill' (for 'ill', I. ii. 163) is incorrect; and it would hardly arise from Q unless by a fluke, since Q's 'ill angell' is a single two-word line at the foot of the page, and hard to misread. F's 'I marry' (for 'Yea ioy', II. iv. 47) looks as though an expurgating editor had something (e.g. 'Yea Iesu') other than Q's harmless phrase before him, something Q misread from foul papers but which needed purgation in the editor's copy.

3. *Textual Problems of the First Folio*, 1953, pp. 94–120.

4. Such plausible substitution might account for QF's 'hole' (for 'hold',

speare's handwriting might be unclear, and different readers might misread it alike; this could have happened with QF's 'inuincible' (for 'invisible', III. ii. 307) and 'appeare' (for 'appear'd', IV. i. 36). Or punctuation which is haphazard, or acceptable by Elizabethan standards (though not by modern), might result in other apparent common errors; so might irregular features in Shakespeare's MS—confusion of speakers, for instance, or the setting of prose as verse. In other words, errors common to two texts may get there not by contamination of one by the other but by independent derivation from a common source.

Yet others are harder to account for without invoking such contamination—the absence from corrected Q and also from F of IV. i. 93 and 95, the common 'imagine' at IV. ii. 19, the spelling of 'dowlny' (Q), 'dowlney' (F), and 'dowlne' (QF) at IV. v. 31–2, the common attribution to Shallow of III. ii. 148 (which would seem to be Falstaff's) and to Pistol of V. v. 17, 19 (which would seem to be Shallow's). Separately, each of these and other similarities might well be accounted a fluke: collectively, they suggest F's dependence on Q.

The evidence for and against such dependence is exasperatingly ambiguous. Of the play's twenty-one scenes (counting Induction and Epilogue), about one-third offer no real evidence—except (and it is an important exception) that, as aforesaid, if one text does depend upon another, one should soon feel sure of this, and uncertainty itself tells against dependence. In the remaining two-thirds the balance looks about two to one against dependence—though double weight against does not necessarily negative single weight for. The ambiguity of the evidence may be indicated from II. i, a scene in which Dr Walker finds striking common typographical features.[1] Yet against this there are F details that look unlike even a carefully edited Q.[2] Act II, scene ii is odder. Here, in ll. 101–30, is the passage on which Miss Walker bases her most extended argument for dependence,[3] and indeed, though the evidential features

Induc. 35), 'bor[r]owed' (for 'borrower's', II. ii. 109), 'rage' (for 'rags', IV. i. 34), 'At' (for 'And', IV. i. 180) and 'thy friends' (for 'my friends', IV. v. 204). Actually, it is by no means certain that 'hole' and 'rage' are errors at all.

1. Common spellings of 'impudent sawcines' (II. i. 110–11), 'boldnes' and 'impudent sawcinesse' (II. i. 122–3), and 'maner' (II. i. 108)—F's almost invariable usage elsewhere is 'manner'.

2. The substitution of 'continuantly' for 'continually' (II. i. 25) is doubtless correct, but is unlikely as a deliberate correction; 'Henrie' for 'Harrie' (II. i. 133), 'Gowre' (thrice) for 'Gower', and 'tucke' for 'tickle' (II. i. 59) do not suggest direct setting-up from Q. 'Basingstoke' for 'Billingsgate' (II. i. 166) must be authentic correction.

3. A. Walker, *Textual Problems*, pp. 113–16. She points out the common capital

can be explained otherwise, such a cluster of them needs something like special pleading to dispose of. Yet in the same scene, indeed in the same passage, the differences are very numerous, of alternative readings, of words added or omitted, and of eccentric lineation in F of Q's prose (cf. collation, II. ii. 150–1, 154–5, 158–9). Act IV, scene i, though depending on MS to supply the missing ll. 55–79 and 103–39, otherwise shows the most apparent signs of any scene of dependence on Q, both in some noticeable common punctuation[1] and in a cluster of controversial common readings.[2] In such passages one is certainly inclined to look on Q as F's basis. Yet further in IV. ii there are variations such as cast the matter into doubt again, and the same is true of IV. iii and IV. iv. A crowning instance of the exasperating situation may be cited from IV. v; here at ll. 31–2 occur the striking spellings of 'dowlny/dowlney' and 'dowlne' (which look strong for dependence)—yet at l. 179 the 'win/ioyne' variant looks conclusive against it. And so one goes on.

## (vii) *The Answer?*

'The answer must logically be that for some reason an annotated quarto was transcribed to form a manuscript which was used as printer's copy for the Folio.'[3] Professor Bowers's conclusion is nearly my own also. This kind of solution seems the only way to reconcile the cumulatively impressive signs of Q's influence on F with the high degree of variation F shows from Q, and the unmistakable signs that F's compositors were reading (sometimes misreading) script.

The ingredients of F's copy must, it would seem, have been a

---

of 'Wen' (l. 101) but not of 'dogge' (l. 102), the common brackets ('(saies he)', l. 108), the common error ('bor[r]owed cap', l. 109), the vagary of 'breuitie' in one line but 'breuity' in the next (ll. 117–18), the separate setting of 'Peace' (l. 116), the common absence of speech-prefix for *Prince* (l. 119), and the error by which Q's *Poynes* (l. 128) is not in F, which apparently takes Poins to be already speaking (as indeed, from the absence in QF of the Prince's speech-prefix at l. 119, he appears to be doing).

1. The most striking is 'Feare you not, that if' (l. 185); cf. also '(in these great affaires)' (l. 6); 'haue in him, touch ground' (l. 17); 'Doue, and very blessed spirite' (l. 46); '(present now,)' (l. 83, Q; '(present now)', F); 'euery slight, and false . . .' (l. 190); 'that may repeate, and history . . .' (l. 203); 'He doth unfasten so, and shake . . .' (l. 209); 'greete his grace (my lord) we come' (l. 228). These are all admissible Elizabethan punctuations, but the identity of the two texts is interesting.

2. 'guarded with rage' (l. 34); 'so appeare' (l. 36); the omission of ll. 93, 95; 'At either end' (l. 180). Early in the next scene occurs the most striking of the common errors, 'th'imagine voice' (IV. ii. 19).

3. Fredson Bowers, 'A Definitive Text of Shakespeare', in *Studies in Sh.*, 1953, p. 26.

quarto and a virtually full MS showing some cognizance of stage practice.[1] These ingredients appear to have been combined in a transcript made either from an elaborately annotated Q or (which seems more likely) from a Q and a MS concurrently, the scribe keeping his eye on both in varying degrees. The transcript, if made with 'literary' pretensions, would be responsible for F's gentility.

This conclusion, complicated though it is, seems dictated by the nature of F's text. To object to it is easy.[2] Yet Q needed much amplification in the serious scenes and also (the evidence of F suggests) was thought to need much refinement in the comedy, together with heavy expurgation, extensive punctuation, much alteration of directions, and revision of numerous speech-prefixes and other irregularities left over in Q from the foul papers. To make a transcript from the ingredients described might well be seen as the best way of providing usable copy.[3]

Since, however, important arguments for F's dependence on Q are based on common typographical details, could these details be mediated from Q to F through a transcript? I think they could. It is important to recognize that a vast deal of typographical detail is *not* so mediated—F, as has been shown, differs from Q much more than it should were Q its direct copy. But still it seems possible that some oddities will survive transcription, partly through coincidence, partly through a degree of automatism on the part of transcriber and compositor alike, and partly, no doubt, from uncertainty as to what else to do with a word like 'dowlny'. Were Q itself F's copy, the common peculiarities would not need explaining thus —but they would be much more numerous. Were F's copy quite independent of Q, they would be very remarkable indeed. But a scribe with a printed text before him as his main source (the MS being mainly used as a check) might well preserve some features of

1. 'Virtually full' because, though restoring Q's cuts, it omits some short passages.

2. Cf. M. Shaaber's objections, in 'The Folio Text of *2 Henry IV*', *Sh. Q.*, 6, p. 143.

3. The Q involved was apparently a copy of Qa, with which F coincides in several readings as against different readings in Qb. The scene (III. i), which Qa omits, F would derive from the MS, and a most interesting variant occurs between its version and Qb's. Lines 53–6 ('O, if this were seen' to 'and die') occur in Qb but not in F. Yet this does not look like a cut in F, which seems rather to preserve the original text. F's lines are perfect verse rhythm, whereas Q's version makes 'Tis not ten yeeres gone' (l. 57; in F a perfect complement to 'With diuers Liquors' of l. 53) into a docked hemistich. If Shakespeare meant it as a separate line he would surely have written, e.g., 'It is not ten . . .' or ' 'Tis yet not ten . . .'. It looks, therefore, as if Qb preserves an addition to the original draft (perhaps inserted marginally) while the MS behind F at this point simply followed the original lines, overlooking the addition.

spelling, capitalization, lineation, and punctuation, even though losing many others. And the compositor would again preserve a proportion of these, even though losing others.

It is hard to see what kind of MS was put together with Q in the transcript. If the prompt-book, that would explain F's signs of stage practice, and also why the MS itself could not be F's copy—it would be wanted in the play-house. Yet problems arise. In the first place, it would have to include not only the passages apparently censored from Q (these it might well have, since they are dramatically necessary) but also those Q drops apparently for stage abridgement; to preserve these in a prompt-book would be odd. Secondly, F often diverges markedly from what a prompt-book would need, and seems to suggest tinkering, independent of authentic stage directions.[1] Possibly the King's Men's book-keeper, if he were the scribe, would introduce some changes from his general knowledge of productions but would not bother with methodical prompt-book collation.

The present text, therefore, takes Q decidedly as the main authority. When F's variants are of only equal merit, Q's logically prevail. Nevertheless, F's variants need weighing with care, and in fact about eighty of F's readings are here preferred to Q's. As against this, about 280 of Q's readings are preferred to F's (not counting Q's profanities, colloquialisms, and solecisms, refined away from F but retained here); of these a hundred or more are readings of equal merit, where Q's superior authority carries the day. If eighty should seem a large number of readings to be adopted from F, it should be borne in mind that even setting from printed copy, not MS, the compositor of Qb varied materially in reproducing the 165 lines in which Qb overlaps Qa—he made

---

1. Unlike Q, F provides the Lord Chief Justice with no attendants at II. i. 59. Having omitted *exit hostess and sergeant* (placed by Q prematurely after II. i. 160), F fails to insert it after l. 162. Q's entry-direction for II. ii, *Enter the Prince, Poynes, sir Iohn Russel, with other*, is changed to *Enter Prince Henry, Pointz, Bardolfe, and Page*, but in fact Bardolph and the page enter only at l. 65. F shifts the direction *Enter Bardolfe and boy* (II. ii. 65; in Q it lets Hal comment on the page's behaviour as he follows Bardolph down-stage) to l. 68, omitting *and boy* (an editor's, not a prompter's idea, surely?). F omits Peto's knocking at II. iv. 348 (an essential stage-effect; Q reads *Peyto knockes at doore*). At III. ii. 294 neither Q nor F has the necessary *Exeunt* for Bardolph and the recruits, and at the end of the scene, where Q has no *Exit*, F misleadingly adds *Exeunt*. Finally, there is the very odd entry-direction for IV. i. Here, while dropping from the entrants Q's (mute) *Bardolfe*, F adds to them *Westmerland, Coleuile*, though Westmoreland, an enemy, does not enter until ll. 24–5 (where in fact Q and F bring him on), and Colevile not until IV. iii. Possibly an editor, observing that Colevile is required three hundred and fifty lines later on, but that Q omits any entry for him there (or anywhere else), thought he should be present with the rebel forces throughout.

seven variant readings (as well as numerous variant literals and accidentals). At this rate, such a compositor would have varied about 140 times in setting Q's 3,300 lines from print, and considerably more in setting from MS. So eighty is not an unduly large number of corrections to have survived the hazards of F's chain of transmission and still be judged good enough to oust Q's readings.

## (viii) *The Dering Manuscript*

A very interesting early seventeenth-century manuscript survives, and is now in the Folger Library, Washington, of a single play combining both parts of *Henry IV*, with much abridgement and some added linking passages. The abridgement, made perhaps for Court performance, was further revised by the hand of Sir Edward Dering (1598–1644) of Surrenden in Kent, possibly for private theatricals. The text is based on Q5 (1613) of Part 1 and Qb of Part 2. In a few readings it coincides with F, but it shows no real signs of F influence. Sir Edward's revisions appear to date from 1623 or 1624; they include the marking of acts and scenes, not identical with those of F. About three-quarters of the text (up to Act IV, scene 8) is from Part 1. The remainder is a drastically abridged and garbled version of Part 2. Dering's IV. 9 is from Induction and I. i; IV. 10 from II. i; V. 1 from II. iii; V. 2 from III. i; V. 3 from III. i and IV. iv; V. 4, 5, 6, 7, 8 from IV. iv–v; V. 9 from V. ii; V. 10 from V. ii and V. As will be evident from the borrowings from the third, fourth, and fifth acts of Part 2, the main theme is the decline of the King and the accession of the Prince. Little is seen of the rebels and nothing of the Archbishop, little of Falstaff and the Hostess, virtually nothing of Eastcheap life or of the Lord Chief Justice, and nothing at all of Gloucestershire. The text has no authority. It was edited in 1845 by J. O. Halliwell(-Phillips) for the Shakespeare Society. Insofar as it coincides with *2 Henry IV* it is described and fully collated by Shaaber, New Var., pp. 645–50.

### 11. EDITORIAL METHODS

(i) Q is taken as the most authoritative text, Qb supplying Act III, scene i, missing from Qa. F, however, has sufficient authority to supply not only the passages missing from both issues of Q but a number of other readings.

(ii) The British Museum copy of Q, C.12.g.20, formerly belonging to George Steevens and George III, has been used as the Q text, variant readings in other copies of Q having been checked by inquiry from the owners. The F text used was that of the Kökeritz–Prouty facsimile; no variant readings (as distinct from other typographical features) turned up in the Folio copies Dr Charlton Hinman collated for his *Printing and Proof Reading of the First Folio* (1963), but one has come to light during the preparation of this edition—'bo' occurs for 'no' (v. v. 13) in the Elizabethan Club copy at Yale, and perhaps in other copies too.

For other editions I consulted in the first place the original Cambridge, original Arden, New Variorum, and London Shakespeare collations, but checked readings by the relevant editions.

(iii) The collation notes record (*a*) all significant departures from Q in the text of this edition, including punctuation changes which affect the sense; (*b*) all significant differences between Qa and Qb, and between Q and F; (*c*) interesting editorial emendations and conjectures, whether acceptable or not. The collation mostly ignores (*a*) accidentals, minor literals, spelling- or italicization-details, and minor variants of proper names; (*b*) variant forms of stage-directions later than F, and of locations; (*c*) alternative Elizabethan spellings provided they are unambiguous—these are silently modernized (e.g. to/too, lose/loose, then/than). The lemmas are given in modernized form, even though the citations following are in the original. A modernized text can hardly avoid this discrepancy, but whenever the modernization is misleading the original is given also in brackets. The first edition to give an accepted reading is given first, any conjecture or later edition following. A collation such as that at Induction, l. 40, '*Exit*.] Q (*exit Rumours.*), F.', means that Q originates the reading, in the form in parentheses, whereas F has it as in the present text. 'Subst.' (=substantially) means that the reading is as cited except for variations immaterial to the point under consideration. F's splitting of Q's lines is noted only if not clearly due to F's column-width.

(iv) A few words, where Shakespeare perhaps chose between alternative forms, are left unmodernized provided that the reader will not be jolted with unfamiliarity: 'vildly' (for 'vilely'), though retained in some New Arden volumes, is not adopted, nor are, e.g., 'accompt' (I. i. 167), 'berod' (I. ii. 169), 'dowlny' and 'dowlne' (IV. v. 31, 32), 'swound' (IV. v. 233); but milder archaisms are retained, like 'strond' (I. i. 62) and 'lanthorn' (I. ii. 48). 'And' (= if) is not changed to 'an'.

(v) In the verse of this edition, -ed indicates the syllabic past verb-ending, 'd the non-syllabic. An exception, however, is made in the case of words like 'denied', where the apostrophe would look awkward; here the -ed is or is not an extra syllable as the metre requires. In the prose, the -ed is silent or syllabic according to modern usage. Contracted Q forms which affect pronunciation (e.g. II. iv. 70, 'foule-mouthdst') are rendered in the nearest modern equivalent (e.g. 'foul-mouth'dst').

(vi) The punctuation of Q is very light and loose indeed; that of F is thorough and indeed excessive. The present text has been punctuated lightly but, it is hoped, sufficiently to avoid confusion or hesitation about meaning and syntax.

(vii) Additions to the directions of QF are indicated by square brackets, as also with act- and scene-numbers.

## 12. REFERENCES AND ABBREVIATIONS

The abbreviated titles of Shakespeare's works are those of C. T. Onions, *A Shakespeare Glossary*. Line-numbers and texts of passages cited or quoted are from W. G. Clark and W. A. Wright's Globe edition of the *Works of Shakespeare*, 1864. Quotations from the Bible, unless otherwise attributed, are from the Bishops' Bible, 1568. Q means the Quarto of 1600; Qa the Quarto issue without Act III, scene i, Qb the Quarto issue with it. F means the First Folio of 1623. F1 is used only where the First has to be distinguished from the later Folios, F2, F3, and F4. References to later editions and editors are given as in the New Variorum edition by M. A. Shaaber. In the collation, numerals are added after editors' names only when a particular edition is indicated. Unnumbered references are to the first editions. The place of publication, except where given otherwise, is London.

| | |
|---|---|
| Abbott | E. A. Abbott, *A Shakespearian Grammar*, 3rd edn, 1870. |
| Alexander | *The Complete Works of William Shakespeare*, ed. Peter Alexander, London and Glasgow, 1951. |
| Anders | H. R. D. Anders, *Shakespeare's Books*, Berlin, 1904. |
| Arber | See *SR*. |
| Ax | Hermann Ax, *The Relation of Shakespeare's Henry IV to Holinshed*, Freiburg-im-Breisgau, 1912. |
| Betterton | Thomas Betterton, *The Sequel of Henry the Fourth*, 1721. |
| Bond | See Lyly. |
| Brome (Shepherd) | Richard Brome, *Dramatic Works* [ed. R. H. Shepherd], 3 vols., 1873. |
| Bullen | After a writer's name (e.g. Middleton, Bullen) this signifies the edition by A. H. Bullen. |
| Bullen 1904 | *The Works of William Shakespeare*, ed. A. H. Bullen, vol. v, Stratford-upon-Avon, 1904. |
| Bulloch | John Bulloch, *Studies on the Text of Shakespeare*, 1878. |

| Cambr. 1, 2 | *The Works of William Shakespeare*, ed. W. G. Clark, J. Glover, and W. A. Wright, 1st edn, vol. iv, Cambridge, 1864; 2nd edn, vol. iv, Cambridge, 1891. |
| Capell | *Mr William Shakespeare His Comedies, Histories, and Tragedies*, ed. Edward Capell, vol. v, 1768. |
| Capell (Notes) | Edward Capell, *Notes and Various Readings to Shakespeare*, 2 vols., 1779–80. |
| Capell's Errata | Errata page following Notes on *2 Henry IV* in *Notes and Various Readings to Shakespeare*, 1779, i. 184. |
| Chambers (*El. St.*) | E. K. Chambers, *The Elizabethan Stage*, 4 vols., Oxford, 1923. |
| Chambers (*W. Sh.*) | E. K. Chambers, *William Shakespeare*, 2 vols., Oxford, 1930. |
| Chapman (Shepherd) | *The Comedies and Tragedies of George Chapman now first collected* [ed. R. H. Shepherd], 3 vols., 1873. |
| Chester, ed. 1957 | *The Second Part of King Henry the Fourth*, ed. Allan Chester (The Pelican Shakespeare), Baltimore, 1957. |
| Clarke, ed. 1865 | *The Plays of Shakespeare*, ed. Charles and Mary Cowden Clarke, vol. ii, 1865. |
| Coleridge | *Coleridge's Shakespearean Criticism*, ed. Thomas Middleton Raysor, 2 vols., Cambridge, Mass., 1930. |
| Collier 1, 2, 3 | *The Works of Shakespeare*, ed. J. P. Collier, 1st edn, vol. iv, 1842; 2nd edn, vol. iii, 1858; 3rd edn, vol. iv, 1876. |
| Cotgrave | Randle Cotgrave, *A Dictionarie of the French and English Tongues*, 1611. |
| Cowl | *The Second Part of King Henry the Fourth*, ed. R. P. Cowl (The Arden Shakespeare), 1923. |
| Craig | *The Complete Works of William Shakespeare*, ed. W. J. Craig (The Oxford Shakespeare), 1892. |
| Daniel (*C.W.*) | Samuel Daniel, *Ciuile Wars*, 1595. |
| Daniel, George | *Henry IV, Part 2*, ed. George Daniel, n.d. |
| Daniel, P. A. | 'Some Remarks on the Introductory Scene of the Second Part of Shakespeare's *Henry IV*' [by Karl Hagena]. With a Commentary by P. A. Daniel. *New Shakespeare Society's Transactions*, 1877–9. |
| Dekker (Bowers) | Thomas Dekker, *Dramatic Works*, ed. Fredson Bowers, 4 vols., Cambridge, 1953–61. |
| Dekker (Grosart) | Thomas Dekker, *Non-Dramatic Works*, ed. A. B. Grosart, 5 vols., 1884–6. |
| Deighton | *Henry IV, Second Part*, ed. K. Deighton, 1893. |
| Delius 3 | *Shakespeares Werke*, ed. Nicolaus Delius, 3rd edn, vol. i, Elberfeld, 1872. |
| Dering | See Intro., p. lxxxiv. |
| Dyce 1, 2 | *The Works of William Shakespeare*, ed. A. Dyce, 1st edn, vol. iii, 1857; 2nd edn, vol. iv, 1864. |
| Dyson | *A Booke Containing all such Proclamations as were published during the Raigne of the late Queene Elizabeth. Collected . . . by . . . Humfrey Dyson . . .*, 2 vols., 1618. |
| EETS | The Early English Text Society. |

Fabyan Robert Fabyan, *The New Chronicles of England and France*, ed. Sir Henry Ellis, 1811.

Farmer Richard Farmer, contributor to *Var. '73*.

F.V. *The Famous Victories of Henry the Fifth*, ed. P. A. Daniel, Shakspere-Quarto Facsimiles 39, 1887.

Globe *The Works of Shakespeare*, ed. W. G. Clark and W. A. Wright (The Globe Edition), 1864.

Gould George Gould, *Corrigenda and Explanations of the Text of Shakespeare*, 1884.

Greene (Collins) Robert Greene, *Plays and Poems*, ed. J. C. Collins, 2 vols., Oxford, 1905.

Greene (Grosart) Robert Greene, *Life and Complete Works*, ed. A. B. Grosart, 15 vols., 1881–6.

Hall Edward Hall, *The Vnion of the Two Noble and Illustre Famelies of Lancaster and Yorke*, 1809 edn.

Halliwell *The Works of William Shakespeare*, ed. J. O. Halliwell, vol. x, 1861.

Hanmer 1, 2 *The Works of Shakespear*, ed. Sir Thomas Hanmer, 1st edn, vol. iii, Oxford, 1743; 2nd edn, vol. iii, Oxford, 1770.

Hardyng *The Chronicle of Iohn Hardynge . . . together with the Continuation by Richard Grafton*, ed. Sir Henry Ellis, 1812 edn.

Harvey Gabriel Harvey, *Complete Works*, ed. A. B. Grosart, 3 vols., 1884–5.

Hart Alfred Hart, *Shakespeare and the Homilies*, Melbourne, 1934.

Hazlitt's *Dodsley* *A Select Collection of Old English Plays, originally published by Robert Dodsley*, revised by W. Carew Hazlitt, 15 vols., 1874–6.

Hemingway *The Second Part of King Henry IV*, ed. S. B. Hemingway (The Yale Shakespeare), New Haven, 1921.

Herr J. G. Herr, *Scattered Notes on the Text of Shakespeare*, Philadelphia, 1879.

Heywood, Thomas (Shepherd) Thomas Heywood, *Dramatic Works* [ed. R. H. Shepherd], 6 vols., 1874.

Holinshed (or Hol.) Raphael Holinshed, *Chronicles of England, Scotland, and Ireland*, 6 vols., 1807–8 edn.

Hudson *The Harvard Shakespeare*, ed. H. N. Hudson, vol. xi, Boston, 1880.

Hunt. L. Q. *The Huntington Library Quarterly*, San Marino, California.

Irving *The Works of Shakespeare*, ed. Henry Irving and Frank Marshall, vol. iii, 1888.

*JEGP* *Journal of English and Germanic Philology*, Urbana, Illinois.

Johnson *The Plays of William Shakespeare*, ed. Samuel Johnson, vol. iv, 1765.

Jonson (H. & S.) Ben Jonson, ed. C. H. Herford and Percy and Evelyn Simpson, 11 vols., Oxford, 1925–52.

Jorgensen Paul A. Jorgensen, *Shakespeare's Military World*, Berkeley, 1956.

Keightley *The Plays of Shakespeare*, ed. Thomas Keightley, vol. iii 1864.

Kinnear     Benjamin Gott Kinnear, *Cruces Shakespearianae*, 1883.

Kittredge     *The Complete Works of Shakespeare*, ed. G. L. Kittredge, Boston, 1936.

Knight 1, 2     *Works of William Shakespeare*, Pictorial Edition, ed. Charles Knight, 1st edn, vol. i, 1839; 2nd edn, vol. i, 1867.

Kyd (Boas)     *The Works of Thomas Kyd*, ed. F. S. Boas, Oxford, 1901.

Lettsom     W. N. Lettsom, 'New Readings in Shakespeare', in *Blackwood's Magazine*, lxxiv, 1853, pp. 181–202, 303–24, 451–74.

Linthicum     M. Channing Linthicum, *Costume in the Drama of Shakespeare and his Contemporaries*, Oxford, 1936.

Lobban     *2 Henry IV*, ed. J. H. Lobban (Granta Shakespeare), Cambridge, 1915.

Lyly (Bond)     John Lyly, *Complete Works*, ed. R. W. Bond, Oxford, 1902.

Mackail     J. W. Mackail, 'A Crux in 2 Henry IV', in *TLS*, 30 Sept. 1926, p. 654.

Madden     D. H. Madden, *The Diary of Master William Silence*, 2nd edn, 1907.

Malone     *The Plays and Poems of William Shakespeare*, ed. Edmond Malone, vol. v, 1790.

Malone (Suppl. 1780)     Edmond Malone, *Supplement to the Edition of Shakespeare's Plays Published in 1778*, 2 vols., 1780.

Mal. Soc.     The Malone Society edition.

Marlowe     Christopher Marlowe, *Works*, gen. ed. R. H. Case, 6 vols., 1930–3.

Marston     *The Plays of John Marston*, ed. H. Harvey Wood, 3 vols., Edinburgh, 1934–9.

Mason     John Monck Mason, *Comments on the Last Edition of Shakespeare's Plays* (i.e. *Var. '78*), 1785.

Maxwell     J. C. Maxwell, '2 Henry IV, II. iv. 91 ff.' (i.e. II. iv. 81–2, this edn), *MLR*, vol. 42, 1947, p. 485.

McIlwraith     A. K. McIlwraith, '"Forestald Remission"', *TLS*, 19 January 1933, p. 40.

Middleton (Bullen)     Thomas Middleton, *Works*, ed. A. H. Bullen, 8 vols., 1885–6.

Mitford     John Mitford, 'Conjectural Emendations', in *The Gentleman's Magazine*, n.s. xxii, 1844, pp. 115–36, 451–72; xxiii, 1845, pp. 115–32, 571–85.

*MLN*     *Modern Language Notes*, Baltimore.

*MLR*     *The Modern Language Review*, Cambridge.

Monro     *The London Shakespeare*, ed. John Monro, vol. iv, London and New York, 1957.

Morgann     Maurice Morgann, *An Essay on the Dramatic Character of Sir John Falstaff*, 1777.

Nashe (McKerrow)     Thomas Nashe, *Works*, ed. R. B. McKerrow, 5 vols., 1904–10.

*N.C.S.*     *The Second Part of the History of Henry IV*, ed. J. Dover Wilson (New Cambridge Shakespeare), Cambridge, 1946.

Neilson                 *The Complete Dramatic and Poetic Works of William Shake-*
                        *speare,* ed. W. A. Neilson (Cambridge Edition),
                        Boston, 1906.

Noble                   Richmond Noble, *Shakespeare's Biblical Knowledge,* 1935.

*NQ*                    *Notes and Queries.*

*OED*                   *A New English Dictionary,* Oxford, 1884–1928.

Onions                  C. T. Onions, *A Shakespeare Glossary,* 2nd edn, revised,
                        Oxford, 1919.

Peele (Bullen)          George Peele, *Works,* ed. A. H. Bullen, 2 vols., 1888.

*PMLA*                  *Publications of the Modern Language Association of America,*
                        Menasha, Wisconsin.

Pope 1, 2               *The Works of Shakespear,* ed. Alexander Pope, 1st edn,
                        vol. iii, 1723; 2nd edn, vol. iv, 1728.

*PQ*                    *The Philological Quarterly,* Iowa City.

Rann                    *Dramatic Works of William Shakespeare,* ed. Joseph Rann,
                        vol. iii, 1789.

*RES*                   *The Review of English Studies.*

Ridley                  *Henry IV, Second Part,* ed. M. R. Ridley (New Temple edn),
                        1934.

Rowe 1, 3               *The Works of Mr William Shakespear,* ed. Nicholas Rowe,
                        1st edn, vol. iii, 1709; 3rd edn, vol. iv, 1714.

*SAB*                   *The Shakspere Allusion-Book,* rev. J. Munro, re-issued with
                        a preface by Sir Edmund Chambers, 2 vols., Oxford,
                        1932.

Schmidt                 A. Schmidt, *Shakespeare-Lexicon,* rev., 2 vols., Berlin and
                        Leipzig, 1923.

*Sh. Ass. B.*           *The Shakespeare Association Bulletin,* New York.

*Sh. Q.*                *The Shakespeare Quarterly,* New York.

*Sh.'s Engl.*           *Shakespeare's England; an Account of the Life and Manners of
                        his Age,* 2 vols., Oxford, 1916–17.

Shaaber                 *The Second Part of Henry the Fourth,* ed. Matthias A.
                        Shaaber (New Variorum edn), Philadelphia, 1940.

Sisson                  *William Shakespeare: The Complete Works,* ed. C. J. Sisson,
                        [1954].

Sisson                  C. J. Sisson, *New Readings in Shakespeare,* 2 vols., Cam-
    (*New Readings*)    bridge, 1956.

Singer 1, 2             *The Dramatic Works of William Shakespeare,* ed. S. W.
                        Singer, 1st edn, vol. v, Chiswick, 1826; 2nd edn, vol. v,
                        1856.

*SP*                    *Studies in Philology,* Chapel Hill, North Carolina.

Spurgeon                Caroline Spurgeon, *Shakespeare's Imagery and What It Tells
                        Us,* Cambridge, 1935.

*SR*                    *A Transcript of the Registers of the Company of Stationers of
                        London, 1554–1640 A.D.,* ed. Edward Arber, 5 vols.,
                        1875.

Staunton                *The Plays of Shakespeare,* ed. Howard Staunton, vol. i, 1858.

Steevens                *The Plays of William Shakespeare,* with notes by Samuel
                        Johnson and George Steevens, ed. Isaac Reed, vol. ix,
                        1793.

| | |
|---|---|
| Stow | John Stow, *Chronicles of England*, 1580; *Annales of England*, 1592. |
| STS | Scottish Text Society. |
| *subst.* | substantially. |
| Sugden | Edward H. Sugden, *A Topographical Dictionary to the Works of Shakespeare*, Manchester, 1925. |
| Theobald 1, 2 | *The Works of Shakespeare*, ed. Lewis Theobald, 1st edn, vol. iii, 1733; 2nd edn, vol. iv, 1740. |
| Thirlby | Styan Thirlby, contributor to Theobald's edition, 1733. |
| Tilley | M. P. Tilley, *A Dictionary of the Proverbs in England in the Sixteenth and Seventeenth Centuries*, Ann Arbor, 1950. |
| Tillyard | E. M. W. Tillyard, *Shakespeare's History Plays*, 1944. |
| *TLS* | *The Times Literary Supplement*. |
| Tollet | George Tollet, contributor to *Var. '78*. |
| Tyrwhitt | Thomas Tyrwhitt, *Observations and Conjectures upon some Passages of Shakespeare*, Oxford, 1766. |
| *Var. '73* | *The Plays of William Shakespeare*, ed. Samuel Johnson and George Steevens, vol. v, 1773. |
| *Var. '78* | *The Plays of William Shakespeare*, ed. Samuel Johnson and George Steevens, vol. v, 1778. |
| *Var. '03* | *The Plays of William Shakespeare*, ed. Isaac Reed, vol. xii, 1803. |
| Vaughan 1, 2 | Henry H. Vaughan, *New Readings and New Renderings of Shakespeare's Tragedies*, 1st edn, 2 vols., 1878–81; 2nd edn, 3 vols., 1886. |
| Walker | Wm S. Walker, *A Critical Examination of Shakespeare's Text*, 3 vols., 1860. |
| Walker, A. | Alice Walker, *Problems of the First Folio*, Cambridge, 1953. |
| Warburton | *The Works of Shakespear*, ed. Wm Warburton, vol. iv, 1747. |
| Webster | John Webster, *Complete Works*, ed. F. L. Lucas, 4 vols. 1927. |
| White 1, 2 | *The Works of William Shakespeare*, ed. R. G. White, vol. vi, Boston, 1859; *Comedies, Histories, Tragedies, and Poems* (Riverside Shakespeare), vol. ii, Boston, 1883. |
| Wilson (*Fortunes*) | John Dover Wilson, *The Fortunes of Falstaff*, Cambridge, 1943. |
| Wilson (*MSH*) | John Dover Wilson, *The Manuscript of Shakespeare's Hamlet*, 2 vols., Cambridge, 1934. |
| Wilson (N.C.S.) | *The Second Part of the History of Henry IV*, ed. John Dover Wilson (The New Cambridge Shakespeare), Cambridge, 1946. |
| Winstanley | *Henry IV, Part 2*, ed. L. Winstanley, New York, 1918. |

# THE SECOND PART OF
# KING HENRY THE FOURTH

## THE ACTORS' NAMES[1]

RUMOUR *the Presenter*.
KING HENRY *the Fourth*.
PRINCE HENRY, *afterwards crowned King Henry the Fifth*.
PRINCE JOHN OF LANCASTER. ⎫ Sons to Henry the
HUMPHREY [DUKE] OF GLOUCESTER. ⎬ Fourth, and brethren
THOMAS [DUKE] OF CLARENCE. ⎭ to Henry the Fifth.
[HENRY PERCY, EARL OF] NORTHUMBERLAND. ⎫
THE ARCHBISHOP OF YORK.  Opposites
[LORD] MOWBRAY.  against
[LORD] HASTINGS.  King
LORD BARDOLPH.  Henry
TRAVERS.  the
MORTON.  Fourth.
[SIR JOHN] COLEVILE. ⎭
[EARL OF] WARWICK. ⎫
[EARL OF] WESTMORELAND.
[EARL OF] SURREY.
[SIR JOHN BLUNT.]
GOWER.  ⎬ Of the King's party.
HARCOURT.
[THE] LORD CHIEF JUSTICE.
[A SERVANT *of the Lord Chief Justice*.] ⎭
POINS. ⎫
[SIR JOHN] FALSTAFF.
BARDOLPH.
PISTOL.  ⎬ Irregular Humourists.
PETO.
[*Falstaff's*] PAGE. ⎭
[ROBERT] SHALLOW. ⎫ Both Country Justices.
SILENCE. ⎭
DAVY, *Servant to Shallow*.
FANG *and* SNARE, *two sergeants*.
[RALPH] MOULDY. ⎫
[SIMON] SHADOW.
[THOMAS] WART.  ⎬ Country Soldiers.
[FRANCIS] FEEBLE.
PETER] BULLCALF. ⎭

1. This list is from F, with the addition of the words in brackets.

2

[LADY NORTHUMBERLAND,] NORTHUMBERLAND'S WIFE.
[LADY PERCY,] PERCY'S WIDOW.
HOSTESS QUICKLY.
DOLL TEARSHEET.
[*Speaker of the*] EPILOGUE.
[FRANCIS *and other*] *Drawers.*
*Beadles* [*and Other Officers*], *Grooms,* [*Porter, Messenger, Soldiers, Lords, Musicians, Attendants.*]

[SCENE: *England*]

# THE SECOND PART OF
# [KING] HENRY THE FOURTH

## INDUCTION

*[Warkworth. Before Northumberland's castle.]*

*Enter* RUMOUR *painted full of tongues.*

*[Rum.]* Open your ears; for which of you will stop
    The vent of hearing when loud Rumour speaks?
    I, from the Orient to the drooping West,
    Making the wind my post-horse, still unfold
    The acts commenced on this ball of earth.       5

---

*Title.*] KING *Hanmer; not in QF.*     FOURTH] fourth, / *continuing to his death, and coro-* / nation of Henry the / fift. *Q;* Fourth, / Containing his Death: and the Coronation / of King Henry the Fift. *F.*     INDUCTION] *F (Actus Primus. Scæna Prima.* / INDVCTION.), *Johnson; not in Q.*     *Location.*] *Capell, subst.*     S.D. *painted full of tongues*] *Q; not in F.*     1. *Rum.*] *Capell; not in QF.*

Heading.] Stage-directions originating later than F are enclosed in the text in square brackets.

*Induction*] Act- and scene-divisions occur first in F. An induction is a scene or monologue introductory to the main action.

Location.] Capell inferred this from ll. 35–7. Holinshed relates (iii. 26) that Northumberland, absent from Shrewsbury, was marching thither too late but, hearing that Westmoreland was moving against him, withdrew to Warkworth Castle in Northumberland, the Percys' principal seat.

Rumour . . . tongues] Rumour, Report, or Fame (like Supposition in *1H4*, v. ii. 8), was personified as a figure adorned with tongues and eyes. Details are given in Shaaber and in T. W. Craik, *Studies in the Tudor Inter-*

*lude,* 1952. Virgil's Fama (*Aen.,* iv. 181–90) was perhaps the source; she has many eyes, tongues, and ears, and sings alike of truth and falsehood. In Stephen Hawes's *Pastime of Pleasure,* Fame is 'A goodly lady, envyroned about / With tongues of fire' (EETS, vol. 173, ll. 156–7). In 1553 the Revels Office made payment 'for payntinge of a cote and a Capp w*i*th Ies tonges and eares for fame' (A. Feuillerat, *Documents Relating to the Revels,* 1914, p. 142); and Holinshed writes of a pageant under Henry VIII in 1519, 'Then entered a person called Report, apparelled in crimsin sattin full of toongs' (iii. 634): cf. also Butler, *Hudibras,* II. i. 45–54.

4. *still*] ever, continually.

4–5. *unfold . . . acts*] 'In the theatrical sense: Rumour is the Presenter' (Wilson, N.C.S.).

Upon my tongues continual slanders ride,
The which in every language I pronounce,
Stuffing the ears of men with false reports.
I speak of peace, while covert enmity
Under the smile of safety wounds the world;               10
And who but Rumour, who but only I,
Make fearful musters, and prepar'd defence,
Whiles the big year, swoln with some other grief,
Is thought with child by the stern tyrant War,
And no such matter? Rumour is a pipe                      15
Blown by surmises, jealousies, conjectures,
And of so easy and so plain a stop
That the blunt monster with uncounted heads,
The still-discordant wav'ring multitude,
Can play upon it. But what need I thus                    20
My well-known body to anatomize
Among my household? Why is Rumour here?
I run before King Harry's victory,
Who in a bloody field by Shrewsbury
Hath beaten down young Hotspur and his troops,           25
Quenching the flame of bold rebellion
Even with the rebels' blood. But what mean I
To speak so true at first? My office is
To noise abroad that Harry Monmouth fell

6. tongues] *Q;* Tongue, *F.*    8. men] *Q;* them *F.*    13. Whiles] *Q;* Whil'st *F.*
grief] *Q;* griefes *F.*    14–15. War, . . . matter?] *F;* Warre? . . . matter. *Q.*
16. jealousies, conjectures] *Q* (Iealousies coniectures), *F.*    19. wav'ring] *Q;*
wauering *F.*    27. rebels'] *QF* (rebels), *Theobald 2;* rebel's *Globe.*

9–20. *I . . . it*] This vividly suggests
the 'unquiet time' in which, enthroned
by 'covert enmity' and 'the still-discordant wav'ring multitude', Henry
must maintain his rule.

12. *fearful . . . defence*] G. B. Harrison's *Second Elizabethan Journal* (1931)
describes preparations repeatedly
made against expected Spanish in-
vasions in 1595–7, and vividly conveys
what Shakespeare has in mind.

16. *jealousies*] 'suspicious apprehensions of evil, mistrust. Now *dial.*' (*OED,*
Jealousy, 5).

17.] So easily and straightforwardly

to be played upon (the stops of a pipe
are the vent-holes producing the
notes).

18. *monster . . . heads*] A frequent
image in classical and Elizabethan
literature (cf. Anders, p. 276); e.g.
*Cor.,* II. iii. 18—'the many-headed
multitude', and IV. i. 1–2—'the beast /
With many heads'; also Dekker, *Guls
Hornebook* (Grosart, ii. 243). For proverbial instances see Tilley, M1029,
M1308.

29. *Harry Monmouth*] Prince Hal
was born at and named after Monmouth.

Under the wrath of noble Hotspur's sword,    30
And that the King before the Douglas' rage
Stoop'd his anointed head as low as death.
This have I rumour'd through the peasant towns
Between that royal field of Shrewsbury
And this worm-eaten hold of ragged stone,    35
Where Hotspur's father, old Northumberland,
Lies crafty-sick. The posts come tiring on,
And not a man of them brings other news
Than they have learnt of me. From Rumour's tongues
They bring smooth comforts false, worse than true
    wrongs.                    *Exit.*    40

34. that] *Q;* the *F.*    35. hold] *Theobald;* hole *QF.*    36. Where] *F;* When *Q.*
40. *Exit.*] *Q (exit Rumours.), F.*

33. *peasant*] rustic (and credulous).

35. *hold*] QF's 'hole' may result from the common *d : e* misreading, or may be what Shakespeare wrote, his mind running on 'worm-eaten'. A subconscious 'hole / hold' pun is not unlikely.

*ragged stone*] 'Castles and city walls were falling to pieces in Shakespeare's day' (Wilson, N.C.S., citing *John,* II. i. 259, and *R2,* III. iii. 52, v. v. 21).

37. *crafty-sick*] Holinshed (iii. 23) and Daniel (*C.W.,* iii. 97) mention 'the sickness of Northumberland' (*1H4,* IV. iv. 14) as the reason why he was not at Shrewsbury, but do not attribute it to craft. Yet from *Richard II* on, Northumberland had been a Machiavellian, and his unforeseen abandonment of Hotspur had a somewhat specious air.

*tiring on*] riding to exhaustion (with perhaps a sense also of 'tearing on', 'galloping hard').

# ACT I

## SCENE I.—[*The same.*]

### *Enter* LORD BARDOLPH.

*L. Bard.*  Who keeps the gate here, ho?

### *Enter the* PORTER.

Where is the Earl?

*Porter.*  What shall I say you are?
*L. Bard.*                         Tell thou the Earl
That the Lord Bardolph doth attend him here.
*Porter.*  His lordship is walk'd forth into the orchard.
Please it your honour knock but at the gate,                    5
And he himself will answer.

### *Enter* NORTHUMBERLAND.

*L. Bard.*                         Here comes the Earl.
                                                   [*Exit Porter.*]

### ACT I

#### *Scene* 1

Act I] *Actus Primus. F* [*before Induction*], *Theobald; not in Q.*      Scene I] *Pope;*
*Scena Secunda. F; not in Q.*      Location.] *Pope, subst.*      S.D.] *Q (Enter the Lord*
*Bardolfe at one doore.), Dyce; Enter Lord Bardolfe, and the Porter. F.*      Bardolph] *Rowe*
[*passim*]*; Bardolfe QF* [*passim, except for Bardolf at F 1. iii. 69*].      1. S.D. *Enter the*
*Porter*] *F, subst.* [*before l. 1*], *Dyce; not in Q.*      6. S.D. *Enter*] *Q (Enter the Earle), F.*
6. S.D. *Exit Porter.*] *Dyce; not in QF.*

S.D.] 'This is an interesting example of the entrance, in rapid succession, of three different characters by three different approaches to the outer stage.... Bardolph ... must have used a side door [cf. Q, *Enter the lord Bardolfe at one doore.*]. It seems most likely that the gate kept by the porter ... would have been represented by the entrance to the inner stage; the orchard gate, presumably smaller, would have been represented more appropriately by [the other] side door' (Shaaber). Some editors bring the porter in on the balcony, above, since instead of seeking Northumberland himself he asks Lord Bardolph to do so. But the point about the three different entrances remains unaffected.

7

*North.*  What news, Lord Bardolph? Every minute now
    Should be the father of some stratagem.
    The times are wild; contention, like a horse
    Full of high feeding, madly hath broke loose,        10
    And bears down all before him.
*L. Bard.*                       Noble Earl,
    I bring you certain news from Shrewsbury.
*North.*  Good, and God will!
*L. Bard.*                As good as heart can wish.
    The King is almost wounded to the death;
    And, in the fortune of my lord your son,        15
    Prince Harry slain outright; and both the Blunts
    Kill'd by the hand of Douglas; young Prince John
    And Westmoreland and Stafford fled the field;
    And Harry Monmouth's brawn, the hulk Sir John,
    Is prisoner to your son. O, such a day,        20
    So fought, so follow'd, and so fairly won,
    Came not till now to dignify the times
    Since Caesar's fortunes!
*North.*                How is this deriv'd?
    Saw you the field? Came you from Shrewsbury?

---

7. *North.*] Q (*Earle*), F (*Nor.*) [*so also at ll. 13, 23, 28, 33, 55, 60*].    Every] *Q ;*
Eu'ry *F.*    13. God] *Q ;* heauen *F.*    21. follow'd] *Q* (followed), *F.*

---

7. *Every minute now*] B. T. Spencer, '*2H4* and the Theme of Time' in *U. Toronto Q.*, July 1944, p. 397, points out how aware the serious characters are of human life as conditioned by Time, past, present, and future.

8. *stratagem*] Though this word could have its modern sense, the meaning here is rather 'deed of blood or violence' (*OED*); cf. *3H6*, II. v. 89— 'What stratagems, how fell, how butcherly'.

16–17. *both . . . Douglas*] In *1H4*, V. iii. 13, Shakespeare shows only one Blunt, Sir Walter, slain by Douglas. Holinshed gives two varying accounts of his death as though he were two persons, though in the list of the slain he counts only one (iii. 26). Daniel particularizes Sir Walter and another Blunt as having been killed at Shrewsbury (*C.W.*, iii. 111, 112).

18. *Stafford fled*] Rumour is running true to form; Stafford in fact did not flee but was killed at Shrewsbury (*1H4*, V. iii. 7; Hol., iii. 26; Daniel, *C.W.*, iii. 113).

19. *brawn*] 'boar (or swine) as fattened for the table. *dial.*' (*OED*, Brawn. *sb.* 4). Many comparisons applied to Falstaff 'recall the chief stock-in-trade of the victuallers and butchers of Eastcheap, namely, meat of all kinds' (Wilson, *Fortunes*, p. 27); cf. 'that damned brawn', *1H4*, II. iv. 123.

*hulk*] 'large ship of burden or transport, (hence) big, unwieldy person' (Onions). For the double sense combined, see II. iv. 63.

23. *fortunes*] triumphs.

*L. Bard.*  I spake with one, my lord, that came from thence,
    A gentleman well bred, and of good name,          26
    That freely render'd me these news for true.
*North.*  Here comes my servant Travers whom I sent
    On Tuesday last to listen after news.

*Enter* TRAVERS.

*L. Bard.*  My lord, I over-rode him on the way,          30
    And he is furnish'd with no certainties
    More than he haply may retail from me.
*North.*  Now, Travers, what good tidings comes with you?
*Travers.*  My lord, Sir John Umfrevile turn'd me back
    With joyful tidings, and, being better hors'd,          35
    Out-rode me. After him came spurring hard
    A gentleman almost forspent with speed,
    That stopp'd by me to breathe his bloodied horse
    He ask'd the way to Chester, and of him
    I did demand what news from Shrewsbury.          40
    He told me that rebellion had ill luck,
    And that young Harry Percy's spur was cold.
    With that he gave his able horse the head,
    And bending forward struck his armed heels
    Against the panting sides of his poor jade          45
    Up to the rowel-head; and starting so

28. whom] *F;* who *Q.*     29. S.D.] *F;* [*against ll. 25–6*] *Q.*     33. with] *Q;* fro *F.*
36. hard] *Q;* head *F.*     41. ill] *F;* bad *Q.*     44. forward] *Q;* forwards *F.*
armed] *Q;* able *F.*

27. *these news*] 'News' could be singular or plural.

30. *over-rode*] 'out-rode (not "overtake" as *OED* glosses). Bardolph-Umfrevile met Travers, turned him back (l. 34) and outrode him (l. 36)' (Wilson, N.C.S.).

33. *tidings comes*] 'Tidings', like 'news' (l. 27), could be singular or plural.

34. *Sir John Umfrevile*] Lord Bardolph's part in this scene may originally have been Umfrevile's. Q heads l. 161 *Vmfr.* (editors change this to *Travers* or *Lord Bardolph*—F omits the line entirely), and at I. iii. 81 Lord

Bardolph is found to be ignorant of news given here at ll. 134–5. Perhaps a transference of parts took place (imperfectly) to save actor-power.

41. *ill*] Q reads 'bad', but it seems more likely that this is an error by attraction from the 'had' immediately before than that F's 'ill', which fits with Northumberland's echo of the news at l. 51, is wrong.

43. *able*] active, vigorous.

45. *jade*] weary hack; used here in commiseration, as in *1H4*, II. i. 6—'poor jade is wrung in the withers out of all cess'.

He seem'd in running to devour the way,
Staying no longer question.

*North.*                    Ha? Again!
Said he young Harry Percy's spur was cold?
Of Hotspur, Coldspur? that rebellion          50
Had met ill luck?

*L. Bard.*          My lord, I'll tell you what:
If my young lord your son have not the day,
Upon mine honour, for a silken point
I'll give my barony, never talk of it.

*North.* Why should that gentleman that rode by Travers    55
Give then such instances of loss?

*L. Bard.*                    Who, he?
He was some hilding fellow that had stol'n
The horse he rode on, and, upon my life,
Spoke at a venture. Look, here comes more news.

*Enter* MORTON.

*North.* Yea, this man's brow, like to a title-leaf,    60
Foretells the nature of a tragic volume.
So looks the strond whereon the imperious flood
Hath left a witness'd usurpation.
Say, Morton, didst thou come from Shrewsbury?

*Mor.* I ran from Shrewsbury, my noble lord,    65
Where hateful death put on his ugliest mask
To fright our party.

---

48. *North.*] *Q (Earle), F [so also at ll. 67, 83, 93, 136]*.    55. should that] *Q;* should the *F*.    59. Spoke] *Q;* Speake *F*.    a venture] *Q* (a venter); aduenture *F*.    62. whereon] *Q;* when *F*.

47. *devour the way*] Parallels are found in Catullus, *Odes*, xxxv. 7—'viam vorabit'; *Job*, xxxix. 27 (Genevan)—'He [the war-horse] swalloweth the grounde for fierceness and rage'; and Jonson, *Sejanus*, v. x. 763–4 (H. & S., iv. 465–6).

53. *point*] cord or lace for tying garments.

57. *hilding*] worthless.

60–1. *title-leaf . . . volume*] The title-page of *Richard III* (1597) may serve as an example: *The Tragedy of King Richard the third. Containing, His treacher-* ous *Plots against his brother Clarence: the pittiefull murther of his innocent nephewes: his tyrannicall vsurpation: with the whole course of his detested life, and most deserued death.* Middleton & Dekker perhaps imitated this simile in *The Roaring Girl*, 1611—'As many faces there (fill'd with blith lookes) / Shew like the promising titles of new bookes, / (Writ merily)' (I. ii. 21–3; Bowers, iii. 17).

62. *strond*] A variant of 'strand'.

63. *witness'd usurpation*] signs of forcible encroachment.

*North.*                     How doth my son, and brother?
    Thou tremblest, and the whiteness in thy cheek
    Is apter than thy tongue to tell thy errand.
    Even such a man, so faint, so spiritless,                    70
    So dull, so dead in look, so woe-begone,
    Drew Priam's curtain in the dead of night,
    And would have told him half his Troy was burnt:
    But Priam found the fire ere he his tongue,
    And I my Percy's death ere thou report'st it.               75
    This thou wouldst say, 'Your son did thus and thus;
    Your brother thus; so fought the noble Douglas'—
    Stopping my greedy ear with their bold deeds:
    But in the end, to stop my ear indeed,
    Thou hast a sigh to blow away this praise,                  80
    Ending with 'Brother, son, and all are dead'.
*Mor.*  Douglas is living, and your brother, yet;
    But, for my lord your son—
*North.*                     Why, he is dead.
    See what a ready tongue suspicion hath!
    He that but fears the thing he would not know              85
    Hath by instinct knowledge from others' eyes
    That what he fear'd is chanced. Yet speak, Morton;
    Tell thou an earl his divination lies,
    And I will take it as a sweet disgrace,
    And make thee rich for doing me such wrong.                 90

---

79. my] *Q;* mine *F.*     83. son—] *Q* (sonne:), *Rowe 3;* Sonne. *F.*     dead.] *F;*
dead? *Q.*     86. others'] *QF* (others), *Capell;* other's *Warburton.*     87. chanced]
*Q;* chanc'd *F.*     88. an] *Q;* thy *F.*

67–103.] 'Act I, scene i, is . . . a harsh
reminder of what is involved in the
hard game of power politics—the
desperate resolve . . . and the penalties
for failure; and for some thirty lines,
throughout Northumberland's elaborate rhetoric of protestation against ill
news, the word "dead" (or "death")
tolls with monotonous insistence'
(L. C. Knights, *Some Shn Themes*, pp.
52–3).

70–3. *Even . . . burnt*] This may echo
'Drawe mee like old *Priam* of *Troy,* /
Crying, the house is a fire, the house is
a fire / As the torch ouer my head'

(Kyd, *Span. Trag.*, 1602, Mal. Soc.,
ll. 2230–2, III. xii *bis*). A play called
*Jeronimo*, entered as new (Henslowe's
*Diary*, ed. Greg, Pt 1, li (Errata) and
p. 50), was acted 7 January 1597; it
was probably *The Spanish Tragedy* re-
novated with additions, of which this is
one. The *Iliad* offers no parallel. In the
*Aeneid*, ii. 268–97, Hector appears in a
night vision to Aeneas, weeping and
warning him of danger, and Aeneas
awakes to find Troy on fire.

88.] Though I am an earl, do
not shrink from calling my forecast
lies.

*Mor.* You are too great to be by me gainsaid,
    Your spirit is too true, your fears too certain.
*North.* Yet, for all this, say not that Percy's dead.
    I see a strange confession in thine eye:
    Thou shak'st thy head, and hold'st it fear or sin          95
    To speak a truth. If he be slain, say so:
    The tongue offends not that reports his death;
    And he doth sin that doth belie the dead,
    Not he which says the dead is not alive.
    Yet the first bringer of unwelcome news          100
    Hath but a losing office, and his tongue
    Sounds ever after as a sullen bell,
    Remember'd tolling a departing friend.
*L. Bard.* I cannot think, my lord, your son is dead.
*Mor.* I am sorry I should force you to believe          105
    That which I would to God I had not seen;
    But these mine eyes saw him in bloody state,
    Rend'ring faint quittance, wearied, and out-breath'd,
    To Harry Monmouth, whose swift wrath beat down
    The never-daunted Percy to the earth,          110
    From whence with life he never more sprung up.
    In few, his death, whose spirit lent a fire

---

96. say so:] *F; not in Q.*    103. tolling] *Q;* knolling *F.*    106. God] *Q;* heauen
*F.*    109. Harry] *Q; Henrie F.*

---

92. *spirit*] intuition.

94. *strange*] reluctant, 'unwilling to
accede to a request' (*OED*, strange *a.*
†11).

98. *he . . . dead*] A familiar idea; e.g.
Thomas Heywood (Shepherd, ii. 303),
*1 Fair Maid of the West*, III. i. 24—
'Tis more then sinne thus to bely the
dead'; cf. Middleton, *Michaelmas
Term*, IV. iv. 37–8 (Bullen, i. 307).

102. *sullen bell*] Cf. Sonnet lxxi—
'Than you shall hear the surly sullen
bell / Give warning to the world that I
am fled'. 'Nearly all [Sh.'s] references
are to the passing or to the funeral bell.
It is clear that its slow sound and
sorrowful association has profoundly
impressed him, and all the force of the
peculiar emotional effect of its heavy,

saddening reiteration is summoned up
in the adjective "sullen"' (Spurgeon,
p. 383): cf. *OED*, sullen, *a.* 3b.

107–11.] The unhistorical idea that
Hal killed Hotspur arises from the
chronicles' ambiguity. Holinshed
writes that Hotspur was slain by 'the
other on his [the King's] part', and
this may be misread as meaning the
Prince. Daniel makes Hotspur and
Hal meet in combat (*C.W.*, iii. 97). In
*1 Henry IV* only Falstaff is present besides the combatants, and he is to be
allowed the credit of the killing (*1H4*,
v. iv. 161–2). But by ignoring that fact
and letting Morton give an eyewitness
account, Shakespeare achieves a most
vivid rendering.

108. *quittance*] exchange of blows.

Even to the dullest peasant in his camp,
Being bruited once, took fire and heat away
From the best-temper'd courage in his troops:          115
For from his metal was his party steel'd,
Which once in him abated, all the rest
Turn'd on themselves, like dull and heavy lead:
And as the thing that's heavy in itself
Upon enforcement flies with greatest speed,            120
So did our men, heavy in Hotspur's loss,
Lend to this weight such lightness with their fear
That arrows fled not swifter toward their aim
Than did our soldiers, aiming at their safety,
Fly from the field. Then was that noble Worcester      125
Too soon ta'en prisoner, and that furious Scot,
The bloody Douglas, whose well-labouring sword
Had three times slain th'appearance of the King,

---

116. metal] *Q* (mettal), *F* (Mettle).     steel'd] *F;* steeled *Q.*     126. Too] *F;*
So *Q.*

114. *Being bruited once*] Immediately it was reported.

114-25. *fire . . . field*] This whole passage is notable for the alliance of concrete and abstract senses, in *fire, heat, best-temper'd, metal, steel'd, abated, turn'd, dull,* and *heavy.* W. H. Clemen comments: 'Shakespeare has ceased to think of the images as something separable, they are continually at his disposal, are more easily associated with everything, and follow each other more rapidly and smoothly. . . . *Metal,* often used by Shakespeare to designate masculine courage and strength of character, is here felt in its original significance and may thus point to *steel'd,* upon which in turn the *lead* in the third line is dependent. But before *lead* stands *heavy,* and out of this *heavy lead* develops a further image which in its turn now produces the image of the flying arrows through the notion of flying' (*Devel. of Sh.'s Imagery,* 1951, pp. 76-7).

115. *best-temper'd*] of the finest temper, having the hardness and elasticity steel should have.

*courage*] Both abstract, and concrete (= man of courage [*OED,* courage, *sb.* 1c]); cf. 'fears' as both 'dangers' and 'dangerous men' at IV. v. 195, and as both 'cowardice' and 'cowards' at *1H4,* I. iii. 87.

116. *metal*] Q's 'mettal' and F's 'mettle' are 'differentiated spellings of the same word' (Onions). Both senses now distinct are here combined.

117-18.] Hotspur's metal/mettle had given an edge, as of steel, to the spirit of his troops. This edge being lost through his death ('reduced to a lower temper'—Johnson), their spirits like soft-metalled blades 'turn'd on themselves' and bent (probably with the secondary sense of 'turned back', 'fled'): *abate* = 'To turn the edge; to blunt . . . *Obs.*' (*OED,* abate, *v*[1]. 8).

120. *enforcement*] compulsion, propulsion.

123. *fled*] As an occasional past form of 'fly' (*OED,* Flee, *v.* 6), *fled* can suggest both the flying of arrows and the fleeing of soldiers.

128.] Holinshed writes that Douglas killed three decoys 'apparelled in the

Gan vail his stomach, and did grace the shame
Of those that turn'd their backs, and in his flight,          130
Stumbling in fear, was took. The sum of all
Is that the King hath won, and hath sent out
A speedy power to encounter you, my lord,
Under the conduct of young Lancaster
And Westmoreland. This is the news at full.          135
*North.* For this I shall have time enough to mourn.
In poison there is physic; and these news,
Having been well, that would have made me sick,
Being sick, have in some measure made me well.
And as the wretch whose fever-weaken'd joints,          140
Like strengthless hinges, buckle under life,
Impatient of his fit, breaks like a fire
Out of his keeper's arms, even so my limbs,
Weaken'd with grief, being now enrag'd with grief,
Are thrice themselves. Hence, therefore, thou nice
     crutch!          145
A scaly gauntlet now with joints of steel
Must glove this hand: and hence, thou sickly coif!
Thou art a guard too wanton for the head
Which princes, flesh'd with conquest, aim to hit.

---

137. these] *Q;* this *F.*     143. keeper's] *QF* (keepers), *Rowe;* keepers' *conj. Delius.*
144. Weaken'd] *F* (Weak'ned), *Pope;* Weakened *Q.*

kings sute' (iii. 26), a feat reflected in *1H4,* v. iii. 7–8, 19–27, and v. iv. 25–8.

129. *vail his stomach*] abate his courage.

131. *Stumbling . . . took*] A loose version (and, through brevity, misleading) of 'The earle of Dowglas, for hast, falling from the crag of an hie mounteine, . . . was taken' (Hol., iii. 26), and 'falling from a hill, he was so bruis'd / That the pursuers took him' (*1H4,* v. v. 21–2).

137. *In . . . physic*] Wilson (N.C.S.) quotes *Lucr.,* 530–2—'The poisonous simple sometimes is compacted / In a pure compound; being so applied, / His venom in effect is purified'.

141. *under life*] under the weight of the living man.

143. *keeper's*] 'Nurse; one who has charge of the sick' (*OED,* Keeper, *sb.* 1e).

144. *grief . . . grief*] suffering . . . sorrow, grievance. 'A word of wide meaning, including pain, worry, grievance, and sorrow' (Wilson, N.C.S.).

145. *nice*] unmanly; perhaps also, trivial.

146. *scaly*] of scale-armour, made of overlapping metal pieces.

147. *coif*] nightcap.

148. *guard too wanton*] too effeminate a trimming, 'with play on the meaning "defence" ' (Onions).

149. *flesh'd with conquest*] by their taste of blood and victory made eager for more (cf. *OED,* Flesh, *v.* 1, 2a, 2c).

Now bind my brows with iron, and approach          150
The ragged'st hour that time and spite dare bring
To frown upon th'enrag'd Northumberland!
Let heaven kiss earth! Now let not Nature's hand
Keep the wild flood confin'd! Let order die!
And let this world no longer be a stage          155
To feed contention in a ling'ring act;
But let one spirit of the first-born Cain
Reign in all bosoms, that, each heart being set
On bloody courses, the rude scene may end,
And darkness be the burier of the dead!          160
*L. Bard.* This strained passion doth you wrong, my lord.
*Mor.* Sweet earl, divorce not wisdom from your honour;
          The lives of all your loving complices
          Lean on your health; the which, if you give o'er
          To stormy passion, must perforce decay.          165
          You cast th'event of war, my noble lord,
          And summ'd the account of chance, before you said
          'Let us make head'. It was your presurmise
          That in the dole of blows your son might drop.

155. this] *Q;* the *F.*      161. *L. Bard.*] *Pope, subst.; Vmfr. Q; Tra. Capell; not in F.*
This . . . lord.] *Q; not in F.*      162. *Mor.*] *Wilson (N.C.S.), conj. Daniel; Bard. QF,*
*subst.*      honour;] *Q* (honor,)*; Honor. F.*      163. The] *Wilson (N.C.S.), conj.*
*Daniel; Mour.* The *QF, subst.*      164. Lean on your] *F;* Leaue on you *Q.*
which,] *Theobald;* which *QF.*      164–5. o'er / To . . . passion, must] *F;* ore, /
To . . . passion must *Q.*      166–79.] *F; not in Q.*

150–60.] Shakespeare's command
over rant has already appeared in
Hotspur's outbursts (*1H4*, I. iii. 93–
107, 194–207).
      151. *ragged'st*] roughest.
      153–60.] Outcries for the subversion
of order express the moral upheaval
suffered, in the tragedies, by the victims of tragic despair (Macbeth, Lear,
Timon) and, in the histories, by the
foes of national harmony. This invoca-
tion of universal fratricide is an early
pointer to the rebels' moral bank-
ruptcy, only partly relieved later by
the Archbishop's noble intentions; its
violence goes some way towards excusing the Gaultree manœuvre. See also
note on ll. 200–1.
      161.] Q gives this line to *Vmfr[evile]*.

If Bardolph took Umfrevile's part
(see l. 34, note) he should have this
line. Line 162 ends in Q with a comma
and seems to belong with what follows,
to be spoken by Morton. Perhaps
Shakespeare or a reviser meant to
substitute *Bard.* but failed to delete
*Vmfr.*, so that Q's compositor set *Vmfr.*
for l. 161, *Bard.* for l. 162, and *Mour.*
for ll. 163 ff. F's editor doubtless realized that *Vmfr.*'s appearance is anoma-
lous, and excised the line.
      166. *cast th'event*] reckoned up the
outcome.
      168. *make head*] raise an army;
resist by arms; cf. *1H4*, I. iii. 284—
'To save our heads by raising of a
head'.
      169. *dole*] dealing out.

You knew he walk'd o'er perils, on an edge,        170
More likely to fall in than to get o'er.
You were advis'd his flesh was capable
Of wounds and scars, and that his forward spirit
Would lift him where most trade of danger rang'd.
Yet did you say 'Go forth'; and none of this,        175
Though strongly apprehended, could restrain
The stiff-borne action. What hath then befall'n,
Or what hath this bold enterprise brought forth,
More than that being which was like to be?

*L. Bard.*  We all that are engaged to this loss        180
Knew that we ventur'd on such dangerous seas
That if we wrought out life 'twas ten to one;
And yet we ventur'd for the gain propos'd,
Chok'd the respect of likely peril fear'd,
And since we are o'erset, venture again.        185
Come, we will all put forth, body and goods.

*Mor.*  'Tis more than time. And, my most noble lord,

---

170–1. edge, / More] *Steevens, Capell's Errata;* edge / More *F; not in Q.*        178.
brought] *F2;* bring *F1; not in Q.*        181. ventur'd] *F;* ventured *Q.*        182. 'twas]
*Q;* was *F.*        183. ventur'd . . . propos'd,] *QF;* ventur'd, . . . propos'd *Capell.*
186. forth, body] *F* (forth; Body,)*;* forth body *Q.*

170–1. *he walk'd . . . o'er*] Shakespeare is recalling Worcester's first mooting of insurrection to Hotspur—'to o'erwalk a current roaring loud, / On the unsteadfast footing of a spear' (*1H4*, i. iii. 192–3). The reminiscence of *1H4* and the notions of falling in or getting over once again suggest Worcester's metaphor of the perilous sword-bridge of mediaeval romances. In *Mabinogion* (Everyman Lib., 'Kilhwch and Olwen', p. 103), 'Osla Gyllellvawr . . . bore a short broad dagger' which, laid over a torrent, 'would form a bridge sufficient for the armies of . . . Britain'. Lancelot crosses a dangerous bridge in Chrétien de Troyes' *Lancelot* (Everyman Lib., pp. 308–9)—'The bridge across the cold stream consisted of a polished gleaming sword; but the sword was stout and stiff, and was as long as two lances. At each end there was a tree-trunk in which the sword was firmly fixed. . . [He] preferred to maim himself rather than fall from the bridge and be plunged in the water . . . [so] he passes over with great pain and agony, being wounded in the hands, knees and feet'. See also H. R. Patch, *The Other World*, 1950, for sword-bridge references and the illustration facing p. 306. For *edge* as 'sword', see *Cor.*, v. vi. 113—'Stain all your edges on me'.

172. *advis'd*] aware.

174. *trade of danger*] trafficking in, or interchange of, danger.

182. *wrought out*] won through with.

184. *respect*] consideration.

185. *o'erset*] overturned; perhaps also, overstaked—i.e. our foes have outbid our stake (*OED*, Set, *v.* 35—'To stake . . . welfare or existence').

186. *put forth*] '(a) i.e. to sea; (b) invest' (Wilson, N.C.S.).

I hear for certain, and dare speak the truth,
The gentle Archbishop of York is up
With well-appointed pow'rs. He is a man                    190
Who with a double surety binds his followers.
My lord your son had only but the corpse,
But shadows and the shows of men, to fight;
For that same word 'rebellion' did divide
The action of their bodies from their souls,                195
And they did fight with queasiness, constrain'd,
As men drink potions, that their weapons only
Seem'd on our side; but, for their spirits and souls,
This word 'rebellion'—it had froze them up,
As fish are in a pond. But now the Bishop                  200
Turns insurrection to religion;
Suppos'd sincere and holy in his thoughts,
He's follow'd both with body and with mind,
And doth enlarge his rising with the blood
Of fair King Richard, scrap'd from Pomfret stones;         205
Derives from heaven his quarrel and his cause;
Tells them he doth bestride a bleeding land,
Gasping for life under great Bolingbroke;
And more and less do flock to follow him.
*North.*  I knew of this before, but, to speak truth,       210
This present grief had wip'd it from my mind.
Go in with me, and counsel every man
The aptest way for safety and revenge:

---

188. dare] *Q; do F.*     189–209.] *F; not in Q.*     192. corpse] *F* (Corpes), *Halliwell; not in Q.*     201–2. religion; ... thoughts,] *Rowe;* Religion, ... Thoughts: *F; not in Q.*     208. Bolingbroke] *F (Bullingbrooke), Pope; not in Q.*

189–91. *The gentle ... followers*] The successive phases in Holinshed (iii. 36) by which Northumberland, the Archbishop, and others conspire, then the Archbishop and Mowbray prevail upon their friends, and then the Archbishop's followers flock to York (all this in 1405) are dramatically compressed here into a concurrent action following closely on Shrewsbury.

*gentle*] well-born (but implying noble character also).

191. *double surety*] i.e. by bodily and spiritual allegiance.

192. *corpse*] i.e. soulless bodies. 'Corpes' and 'corps' were plural as well as singular.

200–1. *But now ... religion*] In the eyes of Elizabeth and her ministers this was the most sacrilegious form of insurrection, as well as the most dangerous.

202. *Suppos'd*] Being considered (Morton is not implying scepticism).

204. *enlarge*] enhance.

205. *Pomfret*] The castle where Richard was murdered.

Get posts and letters, and make friends with speed:
Never so few, and never yet more need.      *Exeunt.* 215

SCENE II.—[*London. A street.*]

*Enter* SIR JOHN FALSTAFF, *with his* PAGE *bearing his
sword and buckler.*

*Fal.* Sirrah, you giant, what says the doctor to my water?
*Page.* He said, sir, the water itself was a good healthy
      water; but, for the party that owed it, he might have
      moe diseases than he knew for.
*Fal.* Men of all sorts take a pride to gird at me. The brain      5

215. and] *Q; nor F.*

*Scene* II

SCENE II] *Var. '73; Scena Tertia. F; not in Q.      Location.*] *Pope, subst.*      S.D.] *Q*
(*Enter sir Iohn alone, with his page bearing his sword and buckler.*), *Pope; Enter Falstaffe,
and Page. F.*      I. *Fal.*] *Q* (*Iohn*) [*so also at ll. 5, 66, 79, 86, 186, 200, 206, 224, 229,
235, 237*], *F* [*throughout scene*].      4. moe] *Q; more F.*

214. *posts*] couriers.

*Scene* II

S.D.] *Q*'s *alone* perhaps means 'in
advance of his attendant', as also in
the S.D. to Qb III. i—*Enter the King in
his night-gowne alone* (where again a
page attends him). Wilson (N.C.S.)
brings Falstaff in hobbling, with a
stick, because of his painful toe (l. 246)
and suggests that his entry is an absurd
parody of Northumberland's with the
'nice crutch' (I. i. 145). Falstaff's
sword and buckler are doubtless an
oblique allusion to the renown accru-
ing from his supposed slaying of Hotspur (*1H4*, v. iv. 156-7). In Henry
Medwall's *Nature* (printed c. 1516-20)
there is an entrance which curiously
parallels the comic pomposity of Falstaff's, when Pryde comes in boasting
of his apparel and accoutrements,
with his 'sworde or trayne . . . so heuy
that I am fayne / to puruey suche a
lad / . . . a praty boy / . . . He maketh
me laugh with many a toy / . . . He

occupyeth no great place'; he orders
his page, 'Come behynd and folow
me' (C. ii⟨r⟩–iii⟨r⟩; cited in B. Spivak,
'Falstaff and the Psychomachia', *Sh.
Q.*, viii, Autumn 1957, p. 457). The
similarity suggests some interlude- or
morality-situation.

1. *giant*] The Page's diminutive
stature is mentioned affectionately by
Shallow at v. iii. 30, 55. The word, and
Viola's phrase about Maria in *Tw.N.*,
I. v. 218—'some mollification for your
giant'—suggests some diminutive boy
actor in the company.

3. *party that owed*] person who
owned: *party*, now facetious in this
sense, was not so then.

4. *moe*] 'more in number (as distinguished from *more*, greater in
amount)' (*OED*, Mo, C. *adj.* 2).

5–30.] 'Falstaff has a trick of voice
that recalls the great prose writers of
the seventeenth century, the doctors
and divines. He shows . . . the same
curious combination of abandon and
economy, the fine frenzy blended with

of this foolish-compounded clay, man, is not able to
invent anything that intends to laughter more than I
invent, or is invented on me; I am not only witty
in myself, but the cause that wit is in other men. I
do here walk before thee like a sow that hath over-            10
whelmed all her litter but one. If the Prince put thee
into my service for any other reason than to set me
off, why then I have no judgment. Thou whoreson
mandrake, thou art fitter to be worn in my cap than
to wait at my heels. I was never manned with an            15
agate till now, but I will inset you, neither in gold
nor silver, but in vile apparel, and send you back
again to your master for a jewel,—the juvenal the
Prince your master, whose chin is not yet fledge. I
will sooner have a beard grow in the palm of my            20
hand than he shall get one off his cheek; and yet he

6. foolish-compounded] *Pope;* foolish compounded *QF, subst.*      clay, man]
*Pope;* clay-man *QF, subst.*      7. intends] *Q;* tends *F.*      10–11. overwhelmed] *Q*
(ouerwhelmd), *Rowe 3;* o'rewhelm'd *F.*      16. inset] *Q* (in-set); sette *F.*      18.
jewel,—the] *Dyce;* iewell, the *Q;* Iewell. The *F.*      19. fledge. I] *Q* (fledge, I),
*Cowl, conj. Vaughan;* fledg'd, I *F.*      21. off] *Q;* on *F;* of *Sisson, conj. Collier.*
and] *Q; not in F.*

and wrought into an inevitable rhyth-
mic movement. . . . His words have the
air of being spoken extempore, and
yet being under the strictest control;
and so, by some sort of equal and opposite tension, acquire a new momen-
tum' (R. W. David, *The Janus of Poets*,
1935, p. 40). Ludwig Borinsky points
out how Falstaff becomes the 'actor of
his own role', and his style a means of
self-realization ('Sh.'s Comic Prose',
in *Sh. Survey*, 8, 1955).

6. *foolish-compounded clay, man*] man,
compounded of folly, created from
clay.

7. *intends*] 'to tend or incline. *Obs.*'
(*OED*, Intend, *v.* 24). F's 'tends' may
be error or sophistication.

13–14. *Thou whoreson mandrake*] You
confounded midget; *whoreson* 'sometimes express[es] jocular familiarity'
(*OED*). On the mandrake, see III. ii.
309, note.

14. *worn . . . cap*] i.e. as jewel or

brooch. Men of fashion wore elaborate
jewellery as hat-ornaments (Linthicum, p. 221); c . *Timon*, III. vi. 122–3
—'He gave me a jewel th'other day,
and now he has beat it out of my
hat'.

15–16. *manned with an agate*] 'attend-
ed by a cameo' (Wilson, N.C.S.)
Agates, worn as jewels, were carved
with tiny figures; 'an agate very vilely
cut' is how Beatrice describes a short
man (*Ado*, III. i. 65).

17. *vile*] mean.

18. *jewel*] i.e. '(*a*) brooch, (*b*) darling' (Wilson, N.C.S., citing *Wiv.*, III.
iii. 45—'my heavenly jewel', and
*Oth.*, I. iii. 195—'for your sake, jewel').
Falstaff seems to mean, 'Hal is ridicul-
ing me; I'll get even with him by sending you back, ill-dressed, like a *bad*
ornament'. *Jewel* and *juvenal* (slurred
as *ju'nal*) make a barely passable
jingle.

19. *fledge*] covered with down.

will not stick to say his face is a face-royal. God may
finish it when He will, 'tis not a hair amiss yet. He
may keep it still at a face-royal, for a barber shall
never earn sixpence out of it. And yet he'll be crow-   25
ing as if he had writ man ever since his father was a
bachelor. He may keep his own grace, but he's almost out of mine, I can assure him. What said Master
Dommelton about the satin for my short cloak and
my slops?                                              30

*Page.* He said, sir, you should procure him better assur-
ance than Bardolph: he would not take his bond and
yours, he liked not the security.

---

22. God] *Q;* Heauen *F.*     23. 'tis] *Q;* it is *F.*     25. he'll] *Q;* he will *F.*     27.
he's] *Q;* he is *F.*     29. Dommelton] *Q; Dombledon F; Dumbleton Malone.*
30. my] *Q; not in F.*     31. *Page.] Q (Boy), F, subst. [so henceforth throughout scene].*
32. Bardolph] *QF1* (Bardolfe), *F4.*     bond] *Q* (band), *F.*

---

22. *face-royal*] royal face, 'first-rate
face' (Wilson, N.C.S.), leading to puns
on *face* as the 'head' of a coin (cf. *LLL.,*
v. ii. 617—'the face of an old Roman
coin'), and on *royal* as both a coin,
worth 10s., and the monarch's face
stamped on it. Johnson comments,
'that is, a face exempt from the touch
of vulgar hands. So a *stag-royal* is not to
be hunted, a *mine-royal* is not to be
dug'.
   23. *a hair*] A quibble; = 'an iota'
(*OED, sb.* 5).
   24. *keep . . . face-royal*] i.e. it will
remain a *royal* face (worth its full 10s.)
since not a sixpence will need to be
spent at the barber's.
   26. *writ*] designated himself.
   27. *grace*] A quibble; (*a*) title ('Your
Grace'); (*b*) favour.
   29. *Dommelton*] 'Dom(m)el' ('dum-
mel(l)', 'dumble', with many variants,
and derivations like 'dummel-head')
is widely distributed for a blockhead
(Wright, *Engl. Dial. Dict.,* 'Dummel').
Some such term may have been
intended.
   29–30. *short cloak . . . slops*] The
*short cloak* sounds like the fashionable
full - sleeved waist - length garment

called the 'Dutch cloak' (Linthicum,
p. 195); *slops* are baggy breeches (*ibid.,*
p. 209). Falstaff is showing the attributes of Pride, particularly the vanity
of extravagant apparel, on which
moralists were voluble, and Stow's
comment may be relevant—'This time
[Henry IV's reign] was used exceeding
pride in garments, gowns with deepe
and broade sleeues' (*Annales,* p. 519).
In Medwall's *Nature* (printed 1516–
20) Pride boasts, 'Than haue I suche a
short gown / Wyth wyde sleues that
hang a down / They wold make some
lad in thys town / a doublet and a cote /
Som me[n] wold thynk y$^t$ this were
pryde / But yt ys not so' (C. ii$^v$). (For
another parallel with *Nature* see S.D.
to this scene, note.) Falstaff's apparel
marks him out as overweening; Elizabeth's Privy Council periodically in-
veighed against 'unordinate excesse in
apparell, contrary both to the good
lawes of the Realme, and to her
Maiesties former admonitions, and to
the confusion of degrees of all estates,
. . . and finally to the impoverishing of
the Realme' (e.g. Humphry Dyson,
*Proclamations,* 1618, for 13 Feb. 1587
and 6 July 1597).

*Fal.* Let him be damned like the glutton! Pray God his
tongue be hotter! A whoreson Achitophel! A ras-    35
cally yea-forsooth knave, to bear a gentleman in
hand, and then stand upon security! The whoreson
smooth-pates do now wear nothing but high shoes
and bunches of keys at their girdles; and if a man is
through with them in honest taking up, then they    40
must stand upon security. I had as lief they would
put ratsbane in my mouth as offer to stop it with

---

34. *Fal.*] Q (*sir Iohn*) [*so also at ll. 52, 57, 102*], F.      Pray God] Q; may F.
35-6. rascally yea-forsooth] F, *subst.;* rascall yea forsooth Q.      36. gentleman]
Q (gentle man), F.      38. smooth-] F; smoothy- Q.

---

34. *glutton*] The Dives-and-Lazarus
parable of the glutton who went to
hell (*Luke*, xvi. 19) seems, like that of
the Prodigal Son (cf. II. i. 142-3), to
have impressed Falstaff; he refers to it
also at *1H4*, III. iii. 35-6, and IV. ii.
26-7. As Professor J. C. Maxwell
points out to me, it also combines in an
associative complex with the idea of
Bardolph's fiery nose. In *1 Henry IV* the
sight of Bardolph prompts Falstaff to
think of hell and Dives (*1H4*, III. iii.
35-6). Here the complex works in
reverse—thoughts of Dives and hell-
fire (l. 34) prompt those of Bardolph
(l. 49).

34-5. *Pray . . . hotter*] As in Part 1,
Falstaff shows himself well-read in the
Bible; this reference is to the rich man
in hell—'Then he cryed, and said . . .
send to Lazarus that he may dippe y^e
tip of his finger in water, and coole my
tongue; for I am tormented in this
flame' (*Luke*, xvi. 24).

35. *Achitophel*] The treacherous
counsellor who deserted David for
Absalom ('the treason was great';
*2 Sam.*, xv. 12).

35-6. *rascally yea-forsooth knave*] Falstaff alludes to tradesmen's (Puritans')
servile complaisance and mild oaths.
Hotspur had already scoffed at the
latter (*1H4*, III. i. 251-9); cf. Jonson,
*Poetaster*, IV. ii. 33-4 (H. & S., iv. 263)
—'your citie mannerly word (for-

sooth) vse it not too often'; also T.
Heywood, *1 Edward 4* (Shepherd, i.
49).

36-7. *bear . . . hand*] encourage with
hopes.

37. *stand upon*] insist on.

38. *smooth-pates*] i.e. city (Puritan)
tradesmen who, despising the long
locks of fashion, cropped their hair
short; known later as Roundheads.

*high shoes*] '"To stand upon one's
pantofles" [high cork-soled shoes] indicated pride' (Linthicum, p. 252).
Joseph Hall's *Virgidemiae*, 1598, satir-
izes teetering dandies who 'tread on
corked stilts a prisoners-pace' (Bk IV,
sat. vi, l. 11). 'They haue corked
shooes', Stubbes writes, 'and fine
pantofles, which beare them vp a
finger or two from the ground; wherof
some be of white leather, some of
black, and some of red, some of black
veluet, some of white, some of red,
some of green, raced, carued, cut, and
stitched all ouer with silk, and laid on
with golde, siluer, and such like: . . . to
go abroad in them . . . is rather a let or
hinderance to a man than otherwise'
(*Anat. of Abuses*, ed. Furnivall, 1877,
Pt I, pp. 57-8).

39. *bunches of keys*] Tokens of important affairs.

39-40. *is through . . . taking up*] has
agreed with them on an honest bar-
gain.

security. I looked a should have sent me two and
twenty yards of satin, as I am a true knight, and he
sends me 'security'! Well, he may sleep in security,        45
for he hath the horn of abundance, and the lightness
of his wife shines through it; and yet cannot he
see, though he have his own lanthorn to light him.
Where's Bardolph?

*Page.* He's gone into Smithfield to buy your worship a        50
horse.

*Fal.* I bought him in Paul's, and he'll buy me a horse in
Smithfield. And I could get me but a wife in the
stews, I were manned, horsed, and wived.

43. a] *Q;* hee *F.*        44. a] *Q; not in F.*        45. Well, he] *F;* well he *Q.*        47. it;]
*F;* it: wheres Bardolf, *Q.*        49. Where's Bardolph?] *F;* [*after* it; *in l. 47*] *Q.*
50. into] *F;* in *Q.*        53. And] *Q;* If *F.*        but] *Q; not in F.*

45. *sleep in security*] Apparently part
of Falstaff's recurrent Biblical idiom.
H. E. Cain suggests that 'the expression was of religious and ecclesiastical
origin and . . . referred to a kind of
spiritual blindness' ('A Note on *2H4*,
I. ii. 35–47'; *Sh. Ass. B.*, xiv, 1939, pp.
51 ff.). 'The sleep of error, or sin, and
of security' (heedlessness) and spiritual lethargy is harped upon in Archbishop Sandys's 11th sermon (*Sermons
of Edwin Sandys*, ed. J. Ayre, Parker
Soc., 1841, pp. 208, 210–12).

46. *horn of abundance*] Like other
horns, this one, the cornucopia or horn
of plenty (the horn of the nymph
Amalthea, set among the stars for fruit-
fulness: Ovid, *Metam.*, ix. 87–8), was
associated with cuckoldry; cf. Ford &
Dekker, *Sun's Darling*, IV. i (Ford's
*Works*, ed. Dyce, 1869, iii. 154)—
'*Ray*[*bright*]: . . . Plenty, Summer's
daughter, empties daily / Her cornucopia fill'd with choicest viands.
*Fol*[*ly*]: Plenty's horn is always full in
the city' (the reference being to pros-
perity and cuckoldry); also Middleton, *Family of Love*, v. i. 123–5 (Bullen,
iii. 98). It was a recurrent jest that
citizens' wives, starved of romance,
were unfaithful, and fertile in illegiti-
mate offspring.

*lightness*] infidelity.

47–8. *and yet . . . light him*] i.e. he
cannot see (*a*) his own cuckold's horn,
(*b*) his wife's 'lightness', though it
shines through his own (lant)horn.
*Lanthorn* as a variant of lantern arose
probably from popular etymology,
lanterns having been made generally
of horn (*OED*, Lantern, *sb.*).

50. *Smithfield*] Really 'Smoothfield',
a level space north of Newgate and
west of Aldgate, where animals were
sold from early times until 1855. 'The
allusions . . . to the horses sold in
Smithfield that occur in the drama are
not generally flattering' (Cowl); cf.
ll. 52–4, note.

52–4. *I bought . . . wived*] The nave of
old St Paul's was a popular place of
business, where 'masterless men set up
their bills for service' and were engaged (*Sh.'s Engl.*, ii. 166). Falstaff
alludes to the proverb (Tilley, W276),
'A man must not make choice of 3.
things in 3. places. Of a wife in Westminster. Of a seruant in Paules. Of a
horse in Smithfield. Least he chuse a
queane, a knaue or a iade' (S[imon]
R[obson], *Choise of Change*, 1585, sig.
L.iii^v). Fynes Moryson gives it also
as a common saying (*Itinerary*, 1907,
iii. 463).

*Enter* LORD CHIEF JUSTICE *and* SERVANT.

*Page.* Sir, here comes the nobleman that committed the     55
    Prince for striking him about Bardolph.

*Fal.* Wait close, I will not see him.

*Ch. Just.* What's he that goes there?

*Servant.* Falstaff, and't please your lordship.

*Ch. Just.* He that was in question for the robbery?     60

*Servant.* He, my lord: but he hath since done good service
    at Shrewsbury, and, as I hear, is now going with
    some charge to the Lord John of Lancaster.

*Ch. Just.* What, to York? Call him back again.

*Servant.* Sir John Falstaff!     65

*Fal.* Boy, tell him I am deaf.

*Page.* You must speak louder, my master is deaf.

*Ch. Just.* I am sure he is, to the hearing of anything good.
    Go pluck him by the elbow, I must speak with him.

*Servant.* Sir John!     70

*Fal.* What! A young knave, and begging! Is there not
    wars? Is there not employment? Doth not the King
    lack subjects? Do not the rebels need soldiers?
    Though it be a shame to be on any side but one, it is
    worse shame to beg than to be on the worst side, were     75

---

54. S.D. *Lord*] *Q; not in* F.     *and Servant*] F; *not in* Q.     55. nobleman] *Q* (noble
man), F.     58. *Ch. Just.*] *Q* (*Iustice*), F.     60. *Ch. Just.*] *QF* (*Iust.*), subst. [*so
throughout scene except at ll. 177, 199, 202, 222, 226*].     71. begging] *Q;* beg *F.*
73. need] *Q;* want *F.*

---

54. S.D.] Nowhere in *1 Henry IV* was
Falstaff so evidently confronted by a
champion of the opposing side. This
confrontation, and the fact that the
Lord Chief Justice is not worsted, are
pointers to the play's course. 'The law,
now bodied forth in the half-legendary
figure of the Lord Chief Justice, becomes a formidable person in the
drama. The opening encounter between these two, in which Falstaff
makes believe not to see or hear his
reprover, is symbolic of Falstaff's
whole attitude to law—he ignores its
existence as long as he can. But the
voice which he at first refuses to hear is
the voice which will pronounce his

final sentence' (Harold Jenkins, *Structural Problem in 'Henry IV'*, 1956,
p. 23).

56. *striking . . . Bardolph*] In Elyot's
*Gouernour* Hal threatens but does not
strike the Chief Justice; the striking
was a later accretion. *The Famous Victories* S.D. reads *He giueth him a boxe on
the eare.*

60. *in question*] under judicial exam-
ination.

64. *to York*] In *1H4*, v. v. 36–7, the
King despatches Prince John and
Westmoreland 'Towards York . . . /
To meet Northumberland and the
prelate Scroop': see ll. 203–5, be-
low.

it worse than the name of rebellion can tell how to
make it.

*Servant.* You mistake me, sir.

*Fal.* Why, sir, did I say you were an honest man? Setting
my knighthood and my soldiership aside, I had lied     80
in my throat if I had said so.

*Servant.* I pray you, sir, then set your knighthood and
your soldiership aside, and give me leave to tell you
you lie in your throat, if you say I am any other than
an honest man.     85

*Fal.* I give thee leave to tell me so? I lay aside that which
grows to me? If thou get'st any leave of me, hang me.
If thou tak'st leave, thou wert better be hanged. You
hunt counter. Hence! Avaunt!

*Servant.* Sir, my lord would speak with you.     90

*Ch. Just.* Sir John Falstaff, a word with you.

*Fal.* My good lord! God give your lordship good time of
day. I am glad to see your lordship abroad, I heard
say your lordship was sick. I hope your lordship goes
abroad by advice; your lordship, though not clean     95
past your youth, have yet some smack of age in you,
some relish of the saltness of time; and I most

79. sir, did] *Q;* sir? Did *F.*     man? Setting] *F;* man, setting *Q.*     86. me so?]
*F;* me, so *Q.*     87. me? If] *F;* me, if *Q.*     89. hunt counter] *Q;* Hunt-counter
*F.*     92. God] *Q; not in F.*     of] *Q;* of the *F.*     96. have] *Q;* hath *F.*     age]
*F;* an ague *Q.*     97. time] *F;* time in you *Q.*

79–80. *Setting . . . aside*] i.e. Divesting
myself of knighthood and soldiership,
and assuming therefore that I could be
capable of lying.

80–1. *lied in my throat*] lied foully. A
familiar tag; Tilley, T268, gives many
examples. '*The lie in the throat* was a lie
uttered deliberately; *the lie in the teeth*
was one for which some excuse was
allowed on the ground of its having
proceeded from haste or some palliat-
ing cause' (J. Hunter, ed. 1871).

87. *grows to*] incorporates with.

88–9. *You hunt counter*] = (*a*) You're
a catchpole, and (*b*) you've got the
wrong man. In *Err.,* Antipholus of
Ephesus is jailed by 'A hound that
runs counter' (IV. ii. 39), i.e. a ser-

geant or catchpole; and there and
here the phrase presumably quibbles
on the Counter, or debtors' prison.
'To hunt counter' as a hunting term
means to follow the scent 'back-
wardes the same way that the chase is
come' (Turbervile, *Booke of Hunting,*
1575, p. 243).

96. *smack of age*] Falstaff enjoys
deflecting his own failings on to others,
as when he calls the Gad's Hill
travellers 'caterpillars', 'gorbellied
knaves', and 'fat chuffs' (*1H4,* II. ii.
88–94).

97. *saltness*] For *saltness* as maturity
Cowl quotes Middleton, *Spanish Gipsy,*
III. i. 41–4 (Bullen, vi. 158)—'*Rod-*
[*erigo*]: The freshness of the morning

humbly beseech your lordship to have a reverend
care of your health.

*Ch. Just.*  Sir John, I sent for you before your expedition    100
to Shrewsbury.

*Fal.*  And't please your lordship, I hear his Majesty is
returned with some discomfort from Wales.

*Ch. Just.*  I talk not of his Majesty. You would not come
when I sent for you.                                            105

*Fal.*  And I hear, moreover, his Highness is fallen into
this same whoreson apoplexy.

*Ch. Just.*  Well, God mend him! I pray you let me speak
with you.

*Fal.*  This apoplexy, as I take it, is a kind of lethargy,    110
and't please your lordship, a kind of sleeping in the
blood, a whoreson tingling.

*Ch. Just.*  What tell you me of it? Be it as it is.

*Fal.*  It hath it original from much grief, from study, and
perturbation of the brain; I have read the cause of           115
his effects in Galen, it is a kind of deafness.

100. for] *Q; not in F.*     100–1. expedition to] *Q;* Expedition, to *F.*     102. And't]
*Q;* If it *F.*     105. you.] *Q;* you? *F.*     108. God] *Q;* heauen *F.*     you] *Q;*
*not in F.*     110. as I take it, is] *Q* (as I take it? is); is (as I take it) *F.*     111. and't
...of] *Q;* a *F.*     in] *Q;* of *F.*

be upon you both! *San[cho]*: The saltness of the evening be upon you
single!' But this is mere antithetical
quipping. The metaphors being of
taste (*smack, relish*), *saltness* perhaps
refers to the tang of meat preserved
in brine beyond its natural span.
Elsewhere saltness can mean youthful vitality; cf. *Wiv.*, II. iii. 50,
'We have some salt of our youth in
us'.

100. *I sent for you*] 'It appears that
the Lord Chief Justice had taken
up the case of the Gad's Hill robbery
and summoned Falstaff to the
Court of King's Bench' (Wilson,
N.C.S.).

103. *returned ... Wales*] In *1H4*, v. v.
39–40, the King announced that 'Myself and you, son Harry, will towards
Wales, / To fight with Glendower and
the Earl of March'.

107. *apoplexy*] paralysis; cf. ll. 110–
12. Writers hostile to Henry describe
the disease as leprosy, inflicted as
God's punishment for Richard II's
murder. Hall and Holinshed denounce
this as monkish foolishness. Holinshed
makes no mention of the King's sickness until 1412 (iii. 57).

114. *it original*] its origin. 'Its' as
possessive pronoun appears in books
just before 1600 but not in the Bible or
any of Shakespeare's works in his lifetime (*OED*, Its).

*grief ... study*] For *grief*, see I. i. 144,
note; *study* = mental concentration.
Henry's illness is indeed related to the
stress of his troubled reign.

116. *Galen*] The writings of Claudius
Galenus (A.D. 129–99), the famous
Greek physician. Falstaff is a well-
read man; for the range of his knowledge see his numerous Biblical refer-

*Ch. Just.* I think you are fallen into the disease, for you
    hear not what I say to you.

*Fal.* Very well, my lord, very well. Rather, and't please
    you, it is the disease of not listening, the malady of    120
    not marking, that I am troubled withal.

*Ch. Just.* To punish you by the heels would amend the
    attention of your ears, and I care not if I do become
    your physician.

*Fal.* I am as poor as Job, my lord, but not so patient.    125
    Your lordship may minister the potion of imprison-
    ment to me in respect of poverty; but how I should
    be your patient to follow your prescriptions, the
    wise may make some dram of a scruple, or indeed a
    scruple itself.    130

*Ch. Just.* I sent for you when there were matters against
    you for your life, to come speak with me.

*Fal.* As I was then advised by my learned counsel in the
    laws of this land-service, I did not come.

*Ch. Just.* Well, the truth is, Sir John, you live in great    135
    infamy.

*Fal.* He that buckles himself in my belt cannot live in
    less.

*Ch. Just.* Your means are very slender, and your waste is
    great.    140

---

119. *Fal.*] *F; Old. Q.*    123. do become] *Q;* be *F.*    137. himself] *Q;* him *F.*
139. are] *Q;* is *F.*    is] *Q; not in F.*

---

ences and the notes, e.g. on III. ii. 253–
5, 260–4, 264–6; IV. iii. 94–100, 107–8,
114–15; and in *1 Henry IV* the allusions
to Diana's foresters (*1H4*, I. ii. 29),
King Cambyses (II. iv. 425), and so
on.

  122. *punish . . . heels*] Strictly, put in
irons, or the stocks; more generally,
put in prison.

  125.] 'Slandered by Satan, . . .
reduced to absolute poverty, . . . urged
to curse God and die, . . . in all his suf-
ferings [Job] did not sin with his lips
[and] his patience became a proverb'
(Noble, p. 271): cf. *Job*, i–ii.

  126–7. *minister . . . poverty*] give me a
dose of imprisonment since I suffer

from poverty (and so am too poor to
pay a fine).

  129. *make . . . scruple*] feel a particle of
doubt. *Dram* and *scruple* carry on the
medical metaphor started by *minister
the potion.* A dram in apothecaries'
weight was 60 grains ($\frac{1}{8}$ oz.) and a
scruple a third of a dram.

  134. *laws . . . land-service*] rules of
military service. Between Gad's Hill
and Shrewsbury, Falstaff was on military duty and so immune from a
civilian summons.

  136–8. *infamy . . . less*] 'Perhaps some
lost jest here; he speaks of infamy as if
it were a material in which he clothes
himself' (Wilson, N.C.S.).

*Fal.* I would it were otherwise, I would my means were
    greater and my waist slenderer.

*Ch. Just.* You have misled the youthful Prince.

*Fal.* The young Prince hath misled me. I am the fellow
    with the great belly, and he my dog.    145

*Ch. Just.* Well, I am loath to gall a new-healed wound.
    Your day's service at Shrewsbury hath a little gild-
    ed over your night's exploit on Gad's Hill. You may
    thank th'unquiet time for your quiet o'er-posting
    that action.    150

*Fal.* My lord!—

*Ch. Just.* But since all is well, keep it so: wake not a
    sleeping wolf.

*Fal.* To wake a wolf is as bad as smell a fox.

*Ch. Just.* What! You are as a candle, the better part    155
    burnt out.

*Fal.* A wassail candle, my lord, all tallow—if I did say of
    wax, my growth would approve the truth.

*Ch. Just.* There is not a white hair in your face but
    should have his effect of gravity.    160

*Fal.* His effect of gravy, gravy, gravy.

---

142. waist] *QF* (waste), *Hanmer 2.*    slenderer] *F;* slender *Q.*    149. th'] *Q;*
the *F.*    151. lord!—] *Theobald, subst.;* lord. *Q;* Lord? *F.*    154. smell] *Q;*
to smell *F.*    159. in] *Q;* on *F.*

---

144–5. *the fellow . . . dog*] Not satis-
factorily elucidated; apparently another lost jest here.

149. *your quiet o'er-posting*] i.e. your
offence's being quietly passed over; cf.
*2H6,* III. i. 255–6—'His guilt should be
but idly posted over, / Because his purpose is not executed'.

152–3. *wake . . . wolf*] Echoing the
proverb, 'It is evil waking of a sleeping
dog' (Tilley, W7).

154. *smell a fox*] A proverbial tag;
Tilley, F628, illustrates the phrase,
'As rank as a fox'. Cowl suggests that
Falstaff has in mind the Lord Chief
Justice's scheming at l. 206, but the
audience knows nothing about this
and the allusion is probably to his
legal shrewdness in general.

157. *wassail candle*] large fat candle

lighted at festivities and meant to last
the night through.

*tallow*] Tallow, used for candles, is
made of animal fat.

158. *my growth would approve*] i.e. my
'waxing' would prove.

160, 161. *gravity, gravy*] Both said
with a broad a. Lyly's *Endimion,* v. ii.
107–8, has a similar pun—'digge an
old wife out of the graue that shall be
answerable to his grauitie' (Bond, iii.
71). Kökeritz cites 'gravity-grave' as a
jingle of nearly identical sounds (*Sh.'s
Pronunciation,* 1955, p. 76).

161. *gravy*] fat from hot meat; 'every
hair has its own drop of sweat' (Wilson,
N.C.S.). *OED* (Gravy 2b) gives '*to
stew in one's own gravy,* to be bathed in
sweat'. Falstaff may have a 'hair/hare'
pun in mind.

*Ch. Just.*  You follow the young Prince up and down, like
    his ill angel.

*Fal.*  Not so, my lord, your ill angel is light, but I hope he
    that looks upon me will take me without weighing.     165
    And yet in some respects, I grant, I cannot go. I
    cannot tell—virtue is of so little regard in these
    costermongers' times that true valour is turned
    bearherd; pregnancy is made a tapster, and his
    quick wit wasted in giving reckonings; all the     170
    other gifts appertinent to man, as the malice of this
    age shapes them, are not worth a gooseberry. You
    that are old consider not the capacities of us that are
    young; you do measure the heat of our livers with

---

163. ill] *Q;* euill *F.*     167. tell—] *Q* (tell,), *Rowe;* tell. *F.*     168. costermongers']
*Q* (costar-mongers), *F* (Costor-mongers), *Theobald 2;* costermonger's *White;*
coster-monger *Capell.*     times] *Q; not in F.*     169. bearherd] *Q* (Berod), *F*
(Beare-heard).     and] *Q;* and hath *F.*     171. this] *F;* his *Q.*     172. them,
are] *F;* the one *Q.*     174. do] *Q; not in F.*

---

163. *ill angel*] attendant spirit of evil
(like the Good and Bad Angels in
Marlowe's *Faustus*).

164. *your . . . light*] A quibble on (*a*)
Satan as 'transformed into an angel of
light' (*2 Cor.*, xi. 14); and (*b*) light,
clipped, bad money. The *angel* was a
gold coin, of varying worth from
6s. 8d. to 10s., so called because it por-
trayed St Michael slaying the dragon.
Puns on it, and on its being good, bad,
or light, are, as Shaaber remarks, 'hard
to escape in Elizabethan comedy'.

165. *take . . . weighing*] accept me at
full value without putting me on the
scales.

166. *go*] A quibble: (*a*) pass current;
cf. Dekker, *1 Honest Whore*, III. i. 52–3
(Bowers, ii. 59)—'*Fust*[*igo*]: Ile so
batter your crowne, that it shall scarce
go for fiue shillings'; (*b*) travel afoot.

167. *cannot tell*] don't know what
to think. Johnson suggested a play on
*tell* in the sense 'count as good money'
(like *go*, immediately above).

169. *bearherd*] The bear-leader's
occupation was accounted low. Q's
'berod' conveys the pronunciation.
'Berrord' occurs in *Ado*, II. i. 43, and

'Berard' and 'Bearard' in *2H6*, v. i. In
F the word is spelt 'Beare-heard' here
and at *Shr.*, Induction ii. 21, but it may
originally have been 'bearward'.

*pregnancy*] quickness of intellect.

169–70. *tapster . . . reckonings*] An
example is Francis the tapster, whose
eloquence is merely 'the parcel of a
[tavern-] reckoning' (*1H4*, II. iv.
113).

172. *not . . . gooseberry*] This phrase
seems not to be recorded elsewhere,
but it is paralleled by similar tags and
has a proverbial ring; e.g. *Troil.*, v. iv.
13—'not proved worth a blackberry'.

174–5. *measure . . . galls*] This echoes
Lyly, *Euphues, Anatomy of Wit* (Bond,
i. 192–3) and, Dr T. W. Craik suggests to me, in its echo of Euphues'
dissolute youth may reflect Falstaff's
vision of himself as the prodigal-
gallant: 'Doe you measure the hotte
assaultes of youth, by the colde skir-
mishes of age? whose yeares are subiect to more infirmities then our youth,
we merry, you melancholy, . . . wee
bolde, you fearefull, we in all pointes
contrary vnto you, and ye in all pointes
vnlike vnto us'. Lyly's *Loues Metamor-*

the bitterness of your galls; and we that are in the    175
vaward of our youth, I must confess, are wags too.

*Ch. Just.* Do you set down your name in the scroll of
youth, that are written down old with all the characters of age? Have you not a moist eye, a dry hand,
a yellow cheek, a white beard, a decreasing leg, an    180
increasing belly? Is not your voice broken, your
wind short, your chin double, your wit single, and
every part about you blasted with antiquity? And
will you yet call yourself young? Fie, fie, fie, Sir
John!    185

*Fal.* My lord, I was born about three of the clock in the
afternoon, with a white head, and something a
round belly. For my voice, I have lost it with hal-
looing, and singing of anthems. To approve my
youth further, I will not: the truth is, I am only old    190
in judgment and understanding; and he that will
caper with me for a thousand marks, let him lend
me the money, and have at him! For the box of the
ear that the Prince gave you, he gave it like a rude

177. *Ch. Just.*] *Q (Lo.), F (Iust.), Rowe.*    182. your chin double,] *Q; not in F.*
184. yet] *Q; not in F.*    186–7. about . . . afternoon,] *Q; not in F.*    188–9.
hallooing] *QF (hallowing), Dyce 2.*    190. further] *Q; farther F.*    193. him!
For] *F, subst.;* him for *Q.*    193–4. the ear] *Q (the yeere);* th'eare *F.*

*phosis,* IV. ii. 72–3 (Bond, iii. 323), is
similar—'That old man measureth the
hot assault of loue with the cold skir-
mishes of age'. The liver was taken to
be the seat of passion and love; cf.
below, IV. iii. 103–4 and v. v. 31, and
*Wiv.,* II. i. 120–1—'*Ford:* Love my
wife! *Pistol:* With liver burning hot'.

176. *vaward*] vanguard, forefront.

*wags too*] high-spirited, as well as
youthful.

178–9. *characters*] (*a*) letters; and (*b*)
characteristics.

179. *moist*] rheumy (as a sign of old
age).

*dry hand*] i.e. the contrary of the
moist hand supposedly typical of
youth and 'the precedent of pith and
livelihood' (*Ven.,* 25–6); cf. *Oth.,* III.
iv. 36–7—'*Oth.* Give me your hand:

this hand is moist, my lady. *Des.* It yet
has felt no age nor known no sorrow'.

186–7. *about . . . afternoon*] Falstaff
seems to mean 'when the day was well
on, fully mature, growing towards
sundown'; 'in the afternoon of her best
days' (*R3,* III. vii. 186) = 'as she is
getting on in life'.

192. *marks*] The mark was the value
of 13s. 4d., not a coin.

193–4. *box of the ear*] Cf. l. 56, note.
'Falstaff introduces the topic to "approve" his "judgment and understanding"' (Wilson, N.C.S.). Q's 'box
of the yeere' may reproduce Shakespeare's spelling; *ear* was often pronounced, and spelt, with a 'y', as in the
phrase 'as long as donkeys' years'.
This form was not a vulgarism; it
occurs in the MS of Ralegh's poems.

prince, and you took it like a sensible lord. I have    195
checked him for it, and the young lion repents
—[*Aside*] marry, not in ashes and sackcloth, but in
new silk and old sack.

*Ch. Just.* Well, God send the Prince a better companion!

*Fal.* God send the companion a better prince! I cannot    200
rid my hands of him.

*Ch. Just.* Well, the King hath severed you and Prince
Harry: I hear you are going with Lord John of
Lancaster, against the Archbishop and the Earl of
Northumberland.    205

*Fal.* Yea, I thank your pretty sweet wit for it. But look
you pray, all you that kiss my lady Peace at home,
that our armies join not in a hot day; for, by the
Lord, I take but two shirts out with me, and I mean
not to sweat extraordinarily. If it be a hot day, and    210
I brandish anything but a bottle, I would I might
never spit white again. There is not a dangerous
action can peep out his head but I am thrust upon
it. Well, I cannot last ever; but it was alway yet the

---

197. S.D.] *Wilson (N.C.S.)*; *not in QF.*    199. *Ch. Just.*] Q (*Lord*), F (*Iust.*), *Rowe*
[*so ll. 202, 222, 226*].    199, 200. God] *Q;* heauen *F.*    202–3. and Prince
Harry] *F; not in Q.*    206. Yea] *Q;* Yes *F.*    208–9. by the Lord] *Q;* if *F.*
210. and] *Q;* if *F.*    211. a] *Q;* my *F.*    bottle,] *F;* bottle. *Q.*    I would] *Q;*
would *F.*    214–21. but . . . motion] *Q; not in F.*

---

195. *sensible*] A quibble: (*a*) reasonable; (*b*) capable of physical feeling.

197. *ashes and sackcloth*] An echo of
*Matt.*, xi. 21—'they had repented long
agone in sackecloth and ashes'; similarly *Luke*, x. 13.

198. *silk . . . sack*] 'To mourn in sack
and claret' (Tilley, S13) was an ironical proverbial tag.

*old sack*] Sack was a white Spanish
wine, and old sack was preferred; cf.
Henry Porter, *Two Angry Women of
Abington* (Mal. Soc., ll. 852–3)—
'*Phil*[*ip*]: . . . Neighbour tis an olde
prouerbe and a true, / Goose giblets
are good meate, old sacke better then
new'.

212. *spit white*] Probably *white* here
=clear, colourless (as still in phrases

like 'white wine'). Editors have produced a varied (though not very en-
lightening) gallery of white-spitting
Elizabethans (cf. Cowl, Shaaber). One
spat white, it seems, through too little
drink, or too much drink, or being
healthy, or being unhealthy. Probably
Falstaff uses 'white' either to fortify
'spit', meaning only, as Shaaber suggests, 'Would I might never spit
again', or to invoke the notion of his
good healthy life, as in, e.g. *Batman
vppon Bartholome*—'The whitte spettle
not knottie, signifieth health' (ed.
1582, lib. vii, addition to cap. 30, fol.
97). He would then mean, 'Would I
might never again give signs of the
vigour and health I pride myself
upon'.

trick of our English nation, if they have a good  215
thing, to make it too common. If ye will needs say I
am an old man, you should give me rest. I would
to God my name were not so terrible to the enemy
as it is—I were better to be eaten to death with a
rust than to be scoured to nothing with perpetual  220
motion.

*Ch. Just.* Well, be honest, be honest, and God bless your
expedition!

*Fal.* Will your lordship lend me a thousand pound to
furnish me forth?  225

*Ch. Just.* Not a penny, not a penny; you are too impatient to bear crosses. Fare you well: commend me to
my cousin Westmoreland.

[*Exeunt Lord Chief Justice and Servant.*]

*Fal.* If I do, fillip me with a three-man beetle. A man can
no more separate age and covetousness than a can  230
part young limbs and lechery: but the gout galls the
one, and the pox pinches the other; and so both the
degrees prevent my curses. Boy!

*Page.* Sir?

*Fal.* What money is in my purse?  235

*Page.* Seven groats and two pence.

---

222. God] *Q*; heauen *F*.   228. S.D.] *Capell, subst.; Exit. F2; not in QF.*   230.
a] *Q*; he *F*.   233. curses. Boy!] *F* (curses. Boy?), *Hanmer;* curses, boy. *Q*.

---

220–1. *perpetual motion*] Edmund
Jentill wrote to Lord Burghley in
October 1594, claiming to have invented a 'perpetuall motion', able to
'dryve a myll'. In Jonson's *Silent
Woman*, v. iii. 63 (H. & S., v. 258),
Morose complains of a tumult, crying
out, 'The perpetuall motion is here,
and not at *Eltham*'—this refers to a
*perpetuum mobile* set up at Eltham by a
German inventor, Cornelius Drebbel
(Jonson, H. & S., x. 43, fn. 63). Cowl
cites further Elizabethan examples.

227. *crosses*] A quibble: (*a*) money
(Elizabethan silver coins bore a cross
on the obverse); (*b*) afflictions (echoing *Luke*, xiv. 27—'whosoeuer doth not
bear his crosse'). See also II. i. 119–20,
note.

229. *fillip . . . beetle*] flip me with a
sledgehammer. A beetle is an out-
sized hammer or ram for driving
stakes or flattening paving-stones; a
three-man beetle had three handles
and needed three men to wield it.

230–1. *age . . . lechery*] Tilley, M568,
illustrates the proverb, 'Old men are
covetous by nature'. Dekker, *2 Honest
Whore*, II. i. 79–80 (Bowers, ii. 155),
has a similar idea—'Letchery loues
to dwell in the fairest lodging, and
Couetousnesse in the oldest build-
ings'.

232–3. *both . . . curses*] 'Both stages of
life have their own curses which anti-
cipate mine' (Wilson, N.C.S.).

236. *groats*] Coins worth four-
pence.

*Fal.* I can get no remedy against this consumption of the
purse; borrowing only lingers and lingers it out, but
the disease is incurable. Go bear this letter to my
Lord of Lancaster; this to the Prince; this to the     240
Earl of Westmoreland;—and this to old mistress
Ursula, whom I have weekly sworn to marry since
I perceived the first white hair of my chin. About it;
you know where to find me. [*Exit Page.*] A pox of
this gout! or a gout of this pox! for the one or the     245
other plays the rogue with my great toe. 'Tis no
matter if I do halt; I have the wars for my colour,
and my pension shall seem the more reasonable.
A good wit will make use of anything; I will turn
diseases to commodity.                    *Exit.*     250

SCENE III.—[*York. The Archbishop's palace.*]

*Enter the* ARCHBISHOP, THOMAS MOWBRAY [*the*] *Earl Marshal,
the* LORDS HASTINGS *and* BARDOLPH.

*Arch.* Thus have you heard our cause, and known our means,
And, my most noble friends, I pray you all
Speak plainly your opinions of our hopes:

243. of] *Q;* on *F.*     244. S.D.] *Capell; not in QF.*     245–6. the other] *Q;*
th'other *F.*     246. 'Tis] *Q;* It is *F.*     250. S.D.] *F (Exeunt), Capell; not in Q.*

*Scene* III

SCENE III] *Var. '73; Scena Quarta. F; not in Q.     Location.*] *Theobald, subst.*
S.D.] *Capell, subst.; Enter th'Archbishop, Thomas Mowbray (Earle Marshall) the Lord
Hastings, Fauconbridge, and Bardolfe. Q; Enter Archbishop, Hastings, Mowbray, and
Lord Bardolfe. F.     1. Arch.*] *Q (Bishop), F (Ar.).     cause*] *Q; causes F.*
known] *Q;* kno *F.*

237–8. *I . . . purse*] Tilley, P263,
illustrates the proverb, 'He is purse-
sick and lacks a physician'.

239–41. *Go . . . Westmoreland*] Falstaff is carrying things on at a high
level—a mark of post-Shrewsbury
prestige, presumably. The letter to the
Prince is the impudent missive
delivered at II. ii. 94–127.

241–2. *mistress Ursula*] It is not clear
whether or not this is Mistress

Quickly, to whom Falstaff has sworn
marriage on 'Wednesday in Wheeson
week' (II. i. 86–7), called 'Nell' in *H5*,
II. i. 20.

244–50. *A pox . . . commodity*] In
morality-play and other treatments,
Gluttony was traditionally 'Full
of diseases' (Spenser, *F.Q.*, I. iv.
23).

247. *colour*] pretext.

250. *commodity*] advantage.

And first, Lord Marshal, what say you to it?

*Mowb.*  I well allow the occasion of our arms,                      5
But gladly would be better satisfied
How in our means we should advance ourselves
To look with forehead bold and big enough
Upon the power and puissance of the King.

*Hast.*  Our present musters grow upon the file                    10
To five and twenty thousand men of choice;
And our supplies live largely in the hope
Of great Northumberland, whose bosom burns
With an incensed fire of injuries.

*L. Bard.*  The question then, Lord Hastings, standeth thus—
Whether our present five and twenty thousand             16
May hold up head without Northumberland.

*Hast.*  With him we may.

*L. Bard.*                            Yea, marry, there's the point:
But if without him we be thought too feeble
My judgment is, we should not step too far                   20
Till we had his assistance by the hand;
For in a theme so bloody-fac'd as this
Conjecture, expectation, and surmise
Of aids incertain should not be admitted.

*Arch.*  'Tis very true, Lord Bardolph, for indeed            25
It was young Hotspur's case at Shrewsbury.

*L. Bard.*  It was, my lord; who lin'd himself with hope,
Eating the air and promise of supply,

---

5. *Mowb.*] Q (*Marsh.*), F (*Mow.*).      18. Yea] Q; I F.      21–4.] F; *not in* Q.
25. *Arch.*] Q (*Bish.*) [*also at l. 76*], F [*Ar. at l. 76*].      26. case] F; cause Q.
27. lin'd] F; lined Q.      28. and] Q; on F.

5. *allow*] grant, admit.

8. *forehead . . . big*] This expressive metaphor recalls the 'moody frontier' (forehead) of defiance put up by the Percys in *1H4*, I. iii. 19.

12. *supplies*] reinforcements.

*largely*] amply, abundantly.

14. *incensed*] The original meaning (= kindled) and the current figurative (= enraged) are equally present.

26. *case*] Q's 'cause' may be right; cf. *OED*, Cause, *sb.* 10—'the case as it concerns anyone', citing *Lucr.*,

1295, 'The cause craves haste'.

27. *lin'd*] strengthened, as lining strengthens a garment.

28. *air and promise*] Q's 'particularly forceful hendiadys' (Dodds, *MLR*, xlii. 381) is less usual than F's reading but more Shakespearean. Hotspur fed himself on insubstantial undertakings of help. The idea is repeated in *Ham.*, III. ii. 99—'I eat the air, promise-crammed'. Tilley, M226, cites the proverb, 'A man cannot live upon air (like a chameleon)'.

Flatt'ring himself in project of a power
Much smaller than the smallest of his thoughts,          30
And so, with great imagination
Proper to madmen, led his powers to death,
And winking leap'd into destruction.

*Hast.* But, by your leave, it never yet did hurt
To lay down likelihoods and forms of hope.          35

*L. Bard.* Yes, if this present quality of war—
Indeed the instant action, a cause on foot—
Lives so in hope, as in an early spring
We see th'appearing buds; which to prove fruit
Hope gives not so much warrant, as despair          40
That frosts will bite them. When we mean to build,

29. in] *Q;* with *F.*          36–55.] *F; not in Q.*          36–7.] *As Rowe, subst.* (Yes, if . . .
War, / Indeed the . . . Action, a . . . foot,) *;* Yes, if . . . warre, / Indeed . . . action:
a . . . foot, *F;* Yes, in . . . war;— / Indeed the . . . action, (a . . . foot) *Malone;* Yes,
in . . . war, / Indeed, the . . . action. A . . . foot *Kittredge;* Yes, if . . . war / Impede
the . . . act; a . . . foot *Pope;* Yes, if the . . . war / Impede the present action. A . . .
foot *Capell;* Yes, in . . . war, / Indeed of . . . action; a . . . foot *Var.* '73, *conj. Johnson;*
Yes, in . . . war: / Indeed the . . . act and . . . foot *Collier 2;* Yes, in . . . war, /
Indeed the . . . act, and . . . foot, *Collier 3;* Yes, if . . . war, / This instant action and
. . . foot *Dyce 2;* Yes, if . . . war / Needed the . . . action. A . . . foot *Neilson;* Yes, if
. . . war / Impel the . . . action. A . . . foot *conj. Steevens in Var.* '78; [Yes, in . . .
war,] Indeed the instanc'd action [: a . . . foot] *conj. Tollet in Var.* '78; Yes, if this
prescient . . . war / Induc'd . . . action [: a . . . foot] *conj. Mason;* Yes, of this
present . . . war, / Indeed the . . . action: [a . . . foot] *conj. Bulloch;* Yes, if . . .
war / Denied . . . action: [a . . . foot] *Herr;* Yes, if . . . war / End in . . . action:
a . . . foot *conj. Camb. 2;* Yes, if . . . war / Indeed . . . action. A . . . foot *Wilson*
(*N.C.S.*), *conj. Mackail;* Yes, if . . . war's / Indeed . . . action. A . . . foot *conj. Wilson*
(*N.C.S.*)*; not in Q.*          38. hope,] *Rowe;* hope: *F; not in Q.*

29. *project*] anticipation.

30. *Much smaller*] i.e. Which proved in fact to be much smaller.

33. *winking*] shutting his eyes to the truth.

36–9. *Yes . . . buds*] The chief crux of the play. None of the emendations is really convincing. Dropped lines have been suspected. *Indeed* has been claimed as a verb (= 'bring to realization') but this makes very forced sense. With punctuation somewhat modernized, the text as it stands in F allows two reasonable explanations: (*a*) 'Yes, it *does* hurt, if this state of war, this imminent action in fact, the campaign already on foot, lives on hopes like those we form in spring at the sight of the buds—when indeed our hopes of good fruit are less likely to be realized than our fears of a frosty blight'; or (*b*) 'I agree, provided that this state of war we are in, &c., lives on hopes only insofar as in spring we view the buds hopefully, fully aware that they are likely to be blighted by frost'. Bardolph is a cautious realist, and therefore explanation (*a*) is perhaps the likelier.

39. *which . . . fruit*] i.e. and that these will bear fruit.

41–62.] 'An application of the Parable of the Builder. . . *Luke,* xiv. 28–30' (Noble, p. 176): 'For which of

We first survey the plot, then draw the model,
And when we see the figure of the house,
Then must we rate the cost of the erection,
Which if we find outweighs ability,                           45
What do we then but draw anew the model
In fewer offices, or at least desist
To build at all? Much more, in this great work—
Which is almost to pluck a kingdom down
And set another up—should we survey                           50
The plot of situation and the model,
Consent upon a sure foundation,
Question surveyors, know our own estate,
How able such a work to undergo,
To weigh against his opposite; or else                        55
We fortify in paper and in figures,
Using the names of men instead of men,
Like one that draws the model of an house
Beyond his power to build it, who, half-through,
Gives o'er, and leaves his part-created cost                  60
A naked subject to the weeping clouds,
And waste for churlish winter's tyranny.

*Hast.*  Grant that our hopes, yet likely of fair birth,
    Should be still-born, and that we now possess'd
    The utmost man of expectation,                            65
    I think we are a body strong enough,
    Even as we are, to equal with the King.

*L. Bard.*  What, is the King but five and twenty thousand?
*Hast.*  To us no more; nay, not so much, Lord Bardolph;

---

47. least] *F;* last *Capell; not in Q.*     55. opposite;] *Theobald;* Opposite? *F; not in Q.*     56. We] *F;* Bard. We *Q.*     58. one] *F;* on *Q.*     an] *Q;* a *F.*     59. through] *Q* (thorough), *F.*     66. we are a] *F;* we are so, *Q;* we're so a *conj. Collier;* we are so a *Kittredge.*

you minding to buylde a towre, sitteth not down before, and counteth the cost, whether he haue sufficient to performe it. Lest that after he hathe laid the fundation, and is not able to performe it, all that beholde it, beginne to mocke him, Saying, this man began to buylde, and was not able to make an end' (Genevan).

43. *figure*] design.

47. *offices*] rooms, apartments; cf. *Timon,* II. ii. 159–60.

*at least*] i.e. 'carrying our reductions to the limit'.

55. *his opposite*] adverse factors.

60. *part-created cost*] partly-built object of his expense.

61. *naked subject*] '(*a*) exposed object; (*b*) helpless victim' (Wilson, N.C.S.).

For his divisions, as the times do brawl, 70
Are in three heads: one power against the French;
And one against Glendower; perforce a third
Must take up us. So is the unfirm King
In three divided, and his coffers sound
With hollow poverty and emptiness. 75

*Arch.* That he should draw his several strengths together
And come against us in full puissance
Need not be dreaded.

*Hast.* If he should do so,
He leaves his back unarm'd, the French and Welsh
Baying him at the heels: never fear that. 80

*L. Bard.* Who is it like should lead his forces hither?

*Hast.* The Duke of Lancaster, and Westmoreland;
Against the Welsh, himself and Harry Monmouth;
But who is substituted 'gainst the French
I have no certain notice.

*Arch.* Let us on, 85
And publish the occasion of our arms.
The commonwealth is sick of their own choice;
Their over-greedy love hath surfeited.
An habitation giddy and unsure
Hath he that buildeth on the vulgar heart. 90
O thou fond many, with what loud applause

---

71. Are] *F*; And *Q*; Stand *conj. Vaughan.* 78. be] *F*; to be *Q.* 78–80. If . . .
that] *As F [verse]; prose, Q.* 79–80. He . . . Baying] *F*; French and Welch he
leaues his back vnarmde, they baying *Q*; To *French,* and *Welsh,* he leaves his back
unarm'd, / They baying *Capell*; To the French and Welsh he leaves his back
unarm'd, / They baying *Ridley.* 84. substituted 'gainst] *F*; substituted
against *Q*; substitute against *Ridley.* 85–108. Arch. Let . . . worst.] *F; not in Q.*

71. *Are*] Q's 'And' looks like an *r/n*
and *e/d* misreading.

81.] Lord Bardolph is here ignorant
of what he was told at i. i. 134–5; cf.
i. i. 34, note.

82. *Duke of Lancaster*] This title belonged to Hal, who succeeded his
father in it (Hol., iii. 1). But John was
born at Lancaster and Holinshed calls
him 'the lord Iohn of Lancaster' (iii.
37) and 'duke' (of Bedford, however:
Hol., iii. 58). Stow says, of Henry IV's
coronation, that 'his second sonne was

there made duke of Lancast[er]'
(*Annales*, p. 513), and Shakespeare
seems to think of John as being next to
Hal, though the second son was, in
fact, Thomas.

84. *substituted*] delegated.

89–90.] Cf. *Luke,* vi. 49—'But he
that heareth, & doeth it not, is like a
man that without foundation built an
house vpon the earth: against which
the flood did beate vehemently, and it
fell immediately'.

91–3.] Apparently an echo of

Didst thou beat heaven with blessing Bolingbroke,
Before he was what thou wouldst have him be!
And being now trimm'd in thine own desires,
Thou, beastly feeder, art so full of him              95
That thou provok'st thyself to cast him up.
So, so, thou common dog, didst thou disgorge
Thy glutton bosom of the royal Richard;
And now thou wouldst eat thy dead vomit up,
And howl'st to find it. What trust is in these times?   100
They that, when Richard liv'd, would have him die
Are now become enamour'd on his grave.
Thou that threw'st dust upon his goodly head,
When through proud London he came sighing on
After th'admired heels of Bolingbroke,                105
Cry'st now, 'O earth, yield us that King again,
And take thou this!' O thoughts of men accurs'd!
Past and to come seems best; things present, worst.
*Mowb.*  Shall we go draw our numbers and set on?
*Hast.*  We are time's subjects, and time bids be gone.    *Exeunt.*

92, 105. Bolingbroke] F (*Bullingbrooke*), *Pope*; *not in Q.*     109. *Mowb.*] F (*Mow.*);
*Bish. Q.*     110. S.D.] Q (*ex.*); *not in F.*

Daniel's lines on the fickleness of the
populace in fluctuating from Richard
II to Bolingbroke; cf. *C.W.*, i. 71,
Appendix I, p. 204.

91. *fond*] foolish.

94. *trimm'd*] decked out.

95–100.] This forceful passage combines those images of surfeit and dis-
gusting canine gluttony which, Spurgeon suggests (pp. 120, 195), reflect
Shakespeare's fastidiousness.

99.] This derives, like similar echoes
(Tilley, D455), from *Prov.*, xxvi. 11—
'As a dogge turneth againe to his owne
vomite, so a foole turneth to his foolish-
nes'; similarly *2 Peter*, ii. 22.

103–5.] A reminiscence of *R2*, v. ii.

1–35, when 'rude misgovern'd hands
from window tops / Threw dust and
rubbish on King Richard's head' as he
followed the triumphant Bolingbroke.
Both passages may echo *2 Sam.*, xvi. 13
—'And as Dauid and his men went by
the way, Semei went along on the
hilles side ouer against him, and curst
as he went, and threw stones at him,
and cast dust'.

109.] Having cut all the Archbishop's preceding speech, Q transfers to him this colourless line to get
him off the stage.

110. *time's subjects*] For the stress
on time, see Intro., p. lii, and I. i. 7,
note.

# ACT II

SCENE I.—[*Eastcheap. Near the Boar's Head Tavern.*]

*Enter* HOSTESS, *with two Officers,* FANG [*with her*] *and*
SNARE [*following*].

*Host.* Master Fang, have you entered the action?

*Fang.* It is entered.

*Host.* Where's your yeoman? Is't a lusty yeoman? Will a
    stand to't?

*Fang.* Sirrah—Where's Snare?                            5

*Host.* O Lord, ay! Good Master Snare.

*Snare.* Here, here.

*Fang.* Snare, we must arrest Sir John Falstaff.

### ACT II

#### *Scene* 1

ACT II SCENE I] *F* (*Actus Secundus. Scœna Prima*); *not in Q.*    Location.] *Wilson*
(*N.C.S.*); *London. Pope; A Street in London. Theobald.*    S.D.] *F, subst.; Enter
Hostesse of the Tauerne, and an Officer or two. Q.*    *with her*] *Capell; not in QF.
following*] *Capell; not in QF.*    1. Fang] *Q* (Phang), *F* [*so also throughout scene,
except l. 54*].    3. Is't] *Q;* Is it *F.*    Will a] *Q;* Will he *F.*    4. to't] *Q;* to it *F.*
6. O Lord, ay] *Q* (O Lord I), *Theobald;* I, I *F.*

S.D.] Fang (= seize) and Snare are
respectively the sergeant and his yeoman, characters who often bear descriptive names, like '*Sergeant* Ambush
*and yeoman* Clutch' in Dekker & Webster's *Westward-Ho*, III. ii. S.D. (Bowers,
ii. 350).

1, 6. *Master*] As a blunder (or high
strategy?) the Hostess confers a title
not warranted by the constable's
rank, on which see l. 45, note. She
likewise bestows an archbishopric on
the Lord Chief Justice at II. i. 68
and a captaincy on Pistol at II. iv.
135.

5. *Sirrah*] This might be addressed to
(*a*) some other 'officer'—but there are

no signs of any; (*b*) Fang's 'Boy'
(Capell's suggestion)—but there are
no signs that Fang has one; (*c*) Snare,
thought by Fang to be present though
in fact lagging (Shaaber's suggestion);
(*d*) the Hostess, since 'sirrah' was used
for either sex (*OED*, Sirrah. 2). Since it
is the Hostess who answers, (*d*) is the
likeliest.

7. Snare] 'The delay in Snare's
entry was perhaps designed to draw
attention to an extraordinary figure
and get-up' (Wilson, N.C.S.). If he
also played the first beadle (v. iv) he
would be cadaverously thin, as that
scene makes clear; cf. v. iv head-note.
But there is no telling.

*Host.* Yea, good Master Snare, I have entered him and
    all.                                                          10

*Snare.* It may chance cost some of us our lives, for he will
    stab.

*Host.* Alas the day, take heed of him—he stabbed me in
    mine own house, most beastly in good faith. A cares
    not what mischief he does, if his weapon be out; he      15
    will foin like any devil, he will spare neither man,
    woman, nor child.

*Fang.* If I can close with him, I care not for his thrust.

*Host.* No, nor I neither; I'll be at your elbow.

*Fang.* And I but fist him once, and a come but within my      20
    vice,—

*Host.* I am undone by his going, I warrant you, he's an
    infinitive thing upon my score. Good Master Fang,
    hold him sure; good Master Snare, let him not
    'scape. A comes continuantly to Pie Corner—saving      25

9. Yea] *Q; I F.*     11. for] *Q; not in F.*     14. most beastly in good faith]
*Q; and that most beastly F.*     A] *Q; he F.*     15. does] *Q; doth F.*     20.
And] *Q; If F.*     and a] *Q; if he F.*     21. vice] *F;* view *Q.*     22. by]
*Q; with F.*     going, I warrant you,] *Q;* going: I warrant *F.*     he's] *Q;*
he is *F.*     23. score. Good] *F;* score, good *Q.*     25. A] *Q* (a); he *F.*     con-
tinuantly] *F;* continually *Q.*

13–18. *stabbed . . . weapon . . . foin . . .
thrust*] Equivoques. For a similar play
on *stab,* cf. *Caes.,* I. ii. 277–8—'If
Caesar had stabbed their mothers,
they would have done no less'. *Foin* =
to thrust with a weapon (a fencing
term); cf. II. iv. 228.

21. *vice*] Q perhaps misread 'vice'
as 'vue' (Wilson, N.C.S.).

22. *going*] i.e. to the wars (without
paying his bill).

23. *infinitive*] '[Mistress Quickly's]
vocabulary is large and far from illiter-
ate. She aspires to be an artist in words,
and fails not in ideal but in execution'
(E. D. Hanscom, Tudor Sh., 1912,
quoted in Shaaber). *OED*'s other examples of *infinitive* for 'infinite' or
'infinity' are from Hardyng's *Chronicle*
(c. 1470) and Gervase Markham's
*Honorable Tragedie of Sir Richard
Grinuile,* 1595 (sigs. A3ʳ and E4ᵛ). Fal-

staff's 'two or three and fifty' buckram
men are probably an echo of Markham's work (New Arden, *1H4,* II. iv.
184, note), and this may be another.

25. *continuantly*] F's fine word is
surely Shakespeare's. It = 'incon-
tinently', 'any moment now'. 'He is, to
the knowledge of Mistress Quickly, on
his way to Pie Corner, and may therefore be expected to come upon the
scene immediately' (Cowl).

*Pie Corner*] 'The corner of Giltspur
Street and Cock Lane in W. Smithfield. It was so called from the cooks'
shops which stood there, at which pigs
were dressed during Bartholomew
Fair' (Sugden).

25–6. *saving . . . manhoods*] Apolo-
getic formula for mentioning a questionable subject. References to Pie
Corner often mention its squealing
pigs and reeking cookery; e.g. Mas-

your manhoods—to buy a saddle, and he is indited
to dinner to the Lubber's Head in Lumbert Street to
Master Smooth's the silkman. I pray you, since my
exion is entered, and my case so openly known to the
world, let him be brought in to his answer. A hun-      30
dred mark is a long one for a poor lone woman to
bear, and I have borne, and borne, and borne, and
have been fubbed off, and fubbed off, and fubbed off,
from this day to that day, that it is a shame to be
thought on. There is no honesty in such dealing, un-    35
less a woman should be made an ass, and a beast, to
bear every knave's wrong.

*Enter* FALSTAFF, BARDOLPH, *and* PAGE.

Yonder he comes, and that arrant malmsey-nose
knave Bardolph with him. Do your offices, do your
offices, Master Fang and Master Snare, do me, do     40
me, do me your offices.

27. Lubber's . . . Lumbert] *Q;* Lubbars . . . Lombard *F.*      28. pray you] *Q;*
pra'ye *F.*      31. one] *QF;* Lone *Theobald* [= Loan] *;* score *Collier* 2; ow'n' *White.*
33–4. and fubbed off, from] *Q;* from *F.*      37. S.D.] *Q* [*after l. 41*] (*Enter sir Iohn,
and Bardolfe, and the boy.*), *Capell, subst.; Enter Falstaffe and Bardolfe. F.*      39. knave]
*Q; not in F.*

singer, *City Madam*, I. i. 152 (*Works*,
Mermaid edn, i. 408)—'Fie on them
[hired cooks]! they smell of Fleet-Lane
and Pie-Corner'.
    26. *buy a saddle*] Smithfield with its
animal market being close by, 'there
were many saddlers' shops in the neighbourhood of Pie-Corner' (Sugden).
    *indited*] A not-infrequent catachresis
in comedy for 'invite'; Benvolio teases
the Nurse with 'She will indite him to
some supper' (*Rom.*, II. iv. 135).
    27. *Lubber's*] A Quicklyism (= big,
clumsy fellow) for 'Libbard's', 'Leopard's'. The sign of the Leopard fitted
the silkman's shop since embroidered
garments often figured the lion's or
leopard's head. Cotgrave gives 'Mas-
quine. *The representation of a Lyon's
head, &c, upon the elbow, or knee of some
old-fashioned garments*'. Sherwood's *Dic-
tionarie English and French*, 1632, repeats
this, though reading 'a Libbard's

head'. Cf. also *LLL.*, v. ii. 550–1—
'*Costard.* I Pompey am—. *Boyet.* With
libbard's head on knee'.
    *Lumbert Street*] Lombard Street was
'so called of the *Longobards* . . . assemb-
ling there twise euery day . . . vntill . . .
1568 [when they] began to make their
meetings at . . . the Royall Exchange'
(Stow, *Survey*, ed. Kingsford, i. 201). It
runs from the Mansion House to
Gracechurch Street.
    29. *case*] For a convincing suggestion
that 'my case so openly known' is a
sexual equivoque see the argument by
Mr Anthony Baker in *NQ*, New Ser.,
Vol. 13, No. 4, April 1966.
    31. *mark*] See I. ii. 192, note.
    *one*] mark, score, reckoning.
    38. *malmsey-nose*] Malmsey was a
strong, sweet, red wine. Onions cites
'"Malmesey", a jolly red nose', from
*The Dictionary of the Canting Crew*
(c. 1700).

*Fal.* How now, whose mare's dead? What's the matter?

*Fang.* Sir John, I arrest you at the suit of Mistress Quickly.

*Fal.* Away, varlets! Draw, Bardolph! Cut me off the villain's head! Throw the quean in the channel!　45

*Host.* Throw me in the channel? I'll throw thee in the channel. Wilt thou, wilt thou, thou bastardly rogue? Murder! Murder! Ah, thou honeysuckle villain, wilt thou kill God's officers and the King's? Ah, thou　50 honeyseed rogue! thou art a honeyseed, a man queller, and a woman queller.

*Fal.* Keep them off, Bardolph!

*Fang.* A rescue! A rescue!

*Host.* Good people, bring a rescue or two. Thou wot, wot　55

43. Sir John] *F; not in Q.*　43–4. Mistress Quickly] *Q, corr.* (mistris *Quickly*); mistris, quickly *Q, uncorr.*; Mist. *Quickly F.*　47–8. in the channel] *Q;* there *F.* 49. Ah] *Q* (a)*;* O *F.*　50. Ah] *Q* (a)*;* O *F.*　54. *Fang*] *F;* Offic. *Q.*　55. or two] *Q; not in F.*　55–6. Thou . . . ta?] *Q* (thou wot, wot thou, thou wot, wot ta,)*;* Thou wilt not? thou wilt not? *F.*

42. *whose . . . dead?*] what's the fuss? Proverbial: Tilley, M657.

43–4. *Quickly*] The name occurs once in *1H4*, at III. iii. 106; this is its first occurrence in Part 2. Kökeritz thinks that as it could be pronounced 'quick-lie' that is what it means (*Sh.'s Pronunciation*, p. 124). But surely the point is a tavern hostess's bustle.

45. *varlets*] Falstaff's abuse is appropriate—*varlet* = 'sergeant', as well as 'knave'; e.g. 'one o' the varlets o' the citie, a serieant' (Jonson, *E.M.I.*, IV. ix. 70–1; H. & S., iii. 386).

*Draw, Bardolph*] 'There is perhaps a hint [of the stage-handling] in the fact that almost every word Falstaff says is by way of putting Bardolph up to active measures of defence' (Shaaber).

46. *quean*] slut, '*spec.* a harlot, strumpet (espec. in 16th–17th c.)' (*OED*, Quean. 1).

*channel*] gutter.

48. *bastardly*] Expressive overlap of 'bastard' and 'dastardly'.

49, 51. *honeysuckle, honeyseed*] Shots at 'homicidal', 'homicide'.

50. *God's . . . King's*] Officers main-

taining 'the King's peace', which is also God's; Sir Thomas Smith, *De Republica Anglorum*, 1583 (Bk 3, ch. 3, p. 92), says, 'The Prince . . . must see iustice executed against all malefactors & offenders against the peace, which is called Gods and his'.

51–2. *man queller*] Equivalent to 'man-killer'. 'Quail, crush, conclude, and quell' is Bottom's curtain-line in *MND.*, v. i. 292.

54. *A rescue*] Fang is either shouting for help to foil an escape, or denouncing Bardolph's intervention. 'Rescue' or 'A rescue' was a cry for help in averting arrest, as in Dekker, *1 Honest Whore*, IV. iii. 141 (Bowers, ii. 84)—'*Geo[rge]:* A rescue Prentises, my maister's catch-pold'. 'Bring a rescue' was also a recognized phrase, as in l. 55 and Barry's *Ram Alley*, III. i (Hazlitt's *Dodsley*, x. 326)—'do you bring / A rescue, goodman knight?'.

55–6. *wot . . . ta*] Dialectal for 'wilt . . . thou'. F's lamentable version is uncomprehending refinement by someone apparently taking 'wot' for 'wilt not'.

thou, thou wot, wot ta? Do, do, thou rogue! Do,
thou hempseed!

*Page.* Away, you scullion! you rampallian! you fustilarian! I'll tickle your catastrophe!

*Enter* LORD CHIEF JUSTICE *and his men.*

*Ch. Just.* What is the matter? Keep the peace here, ho!        60
*Host.* Good my lord, be good to me, I beseech you stand
to me.
*Ch. Just.* How now, Sir John? What are you brawling here?
Doth this become your place, your time, and business?
You should have been well on your way to York.        65
Stand from him, fellow, wherefore hang'st thou upon
him?
*Host.* O my most worshipful lord, and't please your
Grace, I am a poor widow of Eastcheap, and he is
arrested at my suit.
*Ch. Just.* For what sum?        70

58. Page] *Q (Boy), F; Fal. F3.*        58–9. fustilarian] *Q;* Fustillirian *F.*        59.
tickle] *Q;* tucke *F.*        59. S.D.] *Q; Enter. Ch. Iustice. F.*        60. Ch. Just.]
*Q (Lord), F (Iust.), Rowe [so also subst. at ll. 107, 117, 128].*        What is] *Q;*
What's *F.*        63. Ch. Just.] *Q (Lord), F [so also subst. at ll. 70, 78, 132, 163, 165,
168, 173, 176, 181, 184, 189].*        What] *QF; what, Pope; what! Keightley.*        66.
thou upon] *Q;* vpon *F;* thou on *Pope.*

57. *hempseed*] Another shot at 'homicide', with the component sense of
'gallows-bird'; 'the fruit of hempseed' = the hangman's rope, in Field-
ing, *Jon. Wild,* IV. xiv.
58. *rampallian*] ruffian (used generally of men, sometimes of women).
58–9. *fustilarian*] '? comic formation
on the word 'fustilugs' = a fat frowsy
woman' (Onions).
59. *tickle .. catastrophe*] make your
backside tingle. A current phrase;
Cowl gives examples, with variants.
61–2. *stand to*] stand by, stand up
for.
63. *What*] For what, Why.
68. *Grace*] 'A title usually reserved
for royalties, dukes, and archbishops'
(Shaaber). The Hostess blunders
again over rank; cf. notes to ll. 1, 6 of
this scene, and II. iv. 135.

*Eastcheap*] 'A street running E. from
the junction of Cannon St. and
Gracechurch St. to Gt. Tower St.'
(Sugden). Its meaty associations make
it an appropriate setting for Falstaff.
'This East cheape is now a flesh market
of Butchers there dwelling . . . it had
sometime also Cookes mixed amongst
the Butchers, and such other as sold
victuails readie dressed of all sorts. . .
In the yeare 1410, vpon the euen of *St
Iohn Baptist,* the kinges sonnes,
*Thomas,* and *Iohn,* being in Eastcheape
at supper, (or rather at breakfast, for it
was betwixt 2. and 3. of the clocke
after midnight) a greate debate happened between their men and other of
the court, which lasted one houre,
even till the Mayor and Sheriffes with
other cittizens appeased the same'
(Stow, *Survay,* 1598, p. 170).

*Host.* It is more than for some, my lord, it is for all I have.
    He hath eaten me out of house and home, he hath
    put all my substance into that fat belly of his: but I
    will have some of it out again, or I will ride thee
    a-nights like the mare.                                          75
*Fal.* I think I am as like to ride the mare if I have any
    vantage of ground to get up.
*Ch. Just.* How comes this, Sir John? Fie! what man of
    good temper would endure this tempest of exclama-
    tion? Are you not ashamed to enforce a poor widow     80
    to so rough a course to come by her own?
*Fal.* What is the gross sum that I owe thee?
*Host.* Marry, if thou wert an honest man, thyself and the
    money too. Thou didst swear to me upon a parcel-
    gilt goblet, sitting in my Dolphin chamber, at the     85
    round table, by a sea-coal fire, upon Wednesday in
    Wheeson week, when the Prince broke thy head for
    liking his father to a singing-man of Windsor—thou
    didst swear to me then, as I was washing thy wound,
    to marry me, and make me my lady thy wife. Canst     90
    thou deny it? Did not goodwife Keech the butcher's
    wife come in then and call me gossip Quickly?—
    coming in to borrow a mess of vinegar, telling us she

---

71. all] *Q;* all: all *F.*     75. a-nights] *Q* (a nights)*;* o'Nights *F.*     78. Fie] *F;*
*not in Q.*     what] *Q;* what a *F.*     86. upon] *Q;* on *F.*     87. Wheeson] *Q;*
Whitson *F.*     88. liking his father] *Q;* lik'ning him *F.*

---

72. *eaten . . . home*] Proverbial;
Tilley, H784.

74–5. *ride . . . mare*] press you hard in
your sleep like the nightmare.

76. *ride the mare*] 'The allusion is . . . a
wanton one' (Malone, ed. 1790).

79. *temper*] disposition.

84–5. *parcel-gilt goblet*] *parcel-gilt* =
partly gilded, '*esp.* of silver ware, as
bowls, cups, etc., having the inner
surface gilt' (*OED*). Falstaff swore his
oath on a vessel he adored.

85. *Dolphin chamber*] Inn-rooms had,
and often still have, fancy names, like
the 'Half-moon' and 'Pomgarnet' of
*1H4*, II. iv. 30, 42.

86. *sea-coal*] mineral coal, as op-

posed to charcoal; borne by sea to
London, generally from Newcastle.

87. *Wheeson*] '"W(h)issun" is a
north-country and midland form'
(Onions); cf. 'Peesel' for 'Pistol' at
II. iv. 158.

88. *liking*] likening.

*singing-man of Windsor*] See Appendix III.

91. *Keech*] Animal fat the butcher
rolls up for tallow. In *H8*, I. i. 55–7, the
butcher's son, Wolsey, is a 'keech' big
enough to obscure the sun's rays.

92. *gossip*] 'neighbour', more or less;
a familiar term of address.

93. *mess*] small quantity, enough for
a dish.

had a good dish of prawns, whereby thou didst
desire to eat some, whereby I told thee they were ill        95
for a green wound? And didst thou not, when she
was gone downstairs, desire me to be no more so
familiarity with such poor people, saying that ere
long they should call me madam? And didst thou
not kiss me, and bid me fetch thee thirty shillings? I        100
put thee now to thy book oath, deny it if thou canst.

*Fal.* My lord, this is a poor mad soul, and she says up and
down the town that her eldest son is like you. She
hath been in good case, and the truth is, poverty
hath distracted her. But for these foolish officers, I        105
beseech you I may have redress against them.

*Ch. Just.* Sir John, Sir John, I am well acquainted with
your manner of wrenching the true cause the false
way. It is not a confident brow, nor the throng of
words that come with such more than impudent        110
sauciness from you, can thrust me from a level consideration. You have, as it appears to me, practised
upon the easy-yielding spirit of this woman, and
made her serve your uses both in purse and in
person.        115

*Host.* Yea, in truth, my lord.

*Ch. Just.* Pray thee, peace. Pay her the debt you owe her,
and unpay the villainy you have done with her; the
one you may do with sterling money, and the other
with current repentance.        120

---

96. thou not] *Q;* not thou *F.*        97-8. so familiarity] *Q;* familiar *F.*        102. mad]
*F;* made *Q.*        112. You . . . me,] *Q;* I know you ha' *F.*        113-15. and . . .
person] *Q; not in F.*        116. Yea, in truth] *Q;* Yes in troth *F.*        117. Pray thee]
*Q;* Prethee *F.*        118. with] *Q; not in F.*

---

96. *green*] unhealed.

98. *familiarity*] This, Shaaber points
out, may be something of a stock
malapropism; 'his familiaritie seruant'
occurs in Munday's *John a Kent*, 1594
(Mal. Soc., l. 348).

99. *madam*] i.e. as being married
to a knight; cf. 'my lady' (l. 90).
William Harrison's *Description of England*, 1577, says, 'How soeuer one
be dubbed or made Knight, his
wife is by and by called *Madame*,

or Ladye' (Bk II, ch. 2; Hol., i. 267).

101. *book oath*] Bible oath.

112. *you . . . me*] F's compositor
seems bent on saving space hereabouts; this may explain the tinkering.

113-15. *and . . . person*] Cut from F,
perhaps to save space, or as improper.

118. *the villainy . . . done*] As Wilson
(N.C.S.) observes, Falstaff's slander of
immorality (ll. 102-3) is here returned
back on himself.

119-20. *sterling . . . current*] Both

*Fal.* My lord, I will not undergo this sneap without reply. You call honourable boldness impudent sauciness; if a man will make curtsy and say nothing, he is virtuous. No, my lord, my humble duty remembered, I will not be your suitor. I say to you  125
I do desire deliverance from these officers, being upon hasty employment in the King's affairs.

*Ch. Just.* You speak as having power to do wrong; but answer in th'effect of your reputation, and satisfy the poor woman.                                                    130

*Fal.* Come hither, hostess.                    [*Takes her aside.*]

### Enter GOWER.

*Ch. Just.* Now, Master Gower, what news?

*Gower.* The King, my lord, and Harry Prince of Wales
Are near at hand: the rest the paper tells. [*Gives a letter.*]

*Fal.* As I am a gentleman!                                          135

*Host.* Faith, you said so before.

*Fal.* As I am a gentleman! Come, no more words of it.

*Host.* By this heavenly ground I tread on, I must be fain to pawn both my plate and the tapestry of my dining-chambers.                                                    140

*Fal.* Glasses, glasses, is the only drinking; and for thy

123. make] *Q; not in F.*     124. my humble] *Q;* your humble *F.*     126. do] *Q; not in F.*     129. th'effect] *Q;* the effect *F.*     131. S.D. *Takes her aside*] *Capell, subst.; not in QF.*     Enter *Gower*] *F (Enter M. Gower), Malone;* enter a messenger *Q [at end of l. 132].*     133. Harry] *Q;* Henrie *F.*     134. S.D.] *Dyce; not in QF.*     136. Faith] *Q;* Nay *F.*

imply authenticity, validity. 'The chief justice seems addicted to numismatic punning' (Sidney Lee, ed. 1908); cf. 'bear crosses' at I. ii. 227.

121. *sneap*] snub, rebuke.

123. *curtsy*] obeisance, bow (by either sex); cf. Epil., l. 1.

128. *having power*] being empowered, entitled.

129. *in . . . . reputation*] as befits the reputation you claim.

135. *As I am a gentleman*] An oath of dubious value, both in this particular instance and in general. Middleton's discrediting of it is decisive, in *The Family of Love,* I. iii. 30 ff. (Bullen, iii.

23); discussing swearers of meaningless oaths, Club says, 'after their honesty was gone, then came they to their gentility, and swore *as they were gentlemen*; and their gentility they swore away so fast, that they had almost sworn away all the ancient gentry out of the land'.

138. *By . . . tread on*] Another expressive overlap (cf. l. 48), of 'By this ground I tread on' and 'By this heavenly light' (as in *Oth.,* IV. iii. 65).

*fain*] content (as the lesser of two evils).

141. *Glasses*] Glass drinking-ware was replacing that of metal; William

walls, a pretty slight drollery, or the story of the
Prodigal, or the German hunting, in waterwork, is
worth a thousand of these bed-hangers and these fly-
bitten tapestries. Let it be ten pound if thou canst.     145
Come, and 'twere not for thy humours, there's not a
better wench in England. Go, wash thy face, and
draw the action. Come, thou must not be in this
humour with me, dost not know me? Come, come,
I know thou wast set on to this.                          150

---

144. hangers] *Q;* hangings *F.*     145. tapestries] *F;* tapestrie *Q.*     146. and
'twere] *Q;* if it were *F.*     there's] *Q;* there is *F.*     148. the] *Q;* thy *F.*     149.
dost . . . me? Come,] *Q; not in F.*

---

Harrison's *Description of England,* 1577
(Bk II, ch. 6; Hol., i. 280–1), records
that 'our gentilitie as lothing those
mettals [gold and silver] . . . do now
generallie choose rather the Venice
glasses both for our wine and beere.
. . . And as this is seene in the gentilitie,
so in the wealthie communaltie the
like desire of glasse is not neglected.
. . . The poorest also will haue glasse if
they may'. A letter from the Earl of
Shrewsbury, 1580, shows his lordship
much in Mistress Quickly's predi-
cament—'I wold haue you bye me
glasses to drink in: Send me word
what olde plat yeldes the ounce, for I
wyll nott leve me a cuppe of sylvare
to drink in butt I wyll see the next
terms my creditors payde' (cited
by Steevens, 1793, from Edmund
Lodge's *Illus. of Brit. History,* 1791, II.
252).

*only*] only proper, best.

142. *drollery*] comic painting (specifically, one in the Dutch manner);
*OED*'s earliest example of the
word. Evelyn notes (*Diary,* 13 August
1641), 'We arrived late at Roterdam,
where was their annual marte or
faire, so furnished with pictures
(especially Landskips and Drolleries,
as they call those clounish repre-
sentations)'.

142–3. *the story . . . Prodigal*] *Luke,* xv.
11–32; a frequent subject for wall
decorations, and 'the most frequently

mentioned Parable of the Gospels in
the plays' (Noble, p. 277).

143. *the German hunting*] i.e. hunting
scene, of Dutch/German provenance.
No particular illustration has been
identified, though the reference looks
specific. Such scenes were imported
from the **Continent**; Hall (pp. 586–7)
records complaints under Henry VIII
that 'the Dutchemen bryng ouer . . .
lether and Weynskot ready wrought,
with . . . painted clothes so that if it
were wrought here, Englishmen
mighte haue some worke & lyuynge by
it'. Similarly it was said in the House
of Commons in 1601 that 'Painting of
Cloth is decayed, and not *One Hundred*
Yards of new Painted Cloth made here
in a Yeare, by reason of so much
painted *Flanders* pieces brought from
thence' (Anno 1601, 12 December,
*Historical Collections,* by Heywood
Townshend, 1680).

*waterwork*] 'imitation tapestry,
painted in size or distemper on the
walls. . . . *Obs.*' (*OED,* Waterwork. 4).

144. *hangers*] Q's word ('a piece of
tapestry hanging' [*OED,* Hanger. 2a])
is as acceptable as F's.

145. *ten pound*] 'A large advance on
the thirty shillings of l. 100' (Wilson,
N.C.S.).

146. *humours*] moods.

147. *wash thy face*] 'The poor dame
has been crying' (Rolfe, ed. 1880).

148. *draw*] withdraw.

*Host.* Pray thee, Sir John, let it be but twenty nobles;
　　i'faith, I am loath to pawn my plate, so God save
　　me, la!

*Fal.* Let it alone, I'll make other shift: you'll be a fool
　　still.　　　　　　　　　　　　　　　　　　　　　155

*Host.* Well, you shall have it, though I pawn my gown.
　　I hope you'll come to supper. You'll pay me all
　　together?

*Fal.* Will I live? [*To Bardolph*] Go, with her, with her!
　　Hook on, hook on!　　　　　　　　　　　　160

*Host.* Will you have Doll Tearsheet meet you at supper?

*Fal.* No more words, let's have her.

　　　　　　*Exeunt Hostess, Fang*[, *Snare, Bardolph, and Page*].

*Ch. Just.* I have heard better news.

*Fal.* What's the news, my lord?

*Ch. Just.* Where lay the King tonight?　　　　165

*Gower.* At Basingstoke, my lord.

---

151. Pray thee] *Q;* Prethee *F.*　　152. i'faith, I am loath] *Q;* I loath *F.*　　152–
3. so . . . me] *Q;* in good earnest *F.*　　156. though] *Q;* although *F.*　　157–
8. all together?] *Q* (al together.), *F* (altogether?), *Rowe.*　　159. S.D.] *Capell*
[*after* with her, with her!], *White; not in QF.*　　162. S.D.] *Capell, subst.; exit
hostesse and sergeant. Q* [*after l. 160*]*; not in F.*　　163. better] *Q;* bitter *F.*　　164.
lord] *Q;* good Lord *F.*　　165. tonight] *Q;* last night *F.*　　166. *Gower*] *Q*
(*Mess.*), *F* (*Mes.*), *Rowe.*　　Basingstoke] *F;* Billingsgate *Q.*

---

151. *twenty nobles*] That is, £6 13s. 4d.,
the noble being a gold coin worth
6s. 8d. The Hostess wants a 10 per
cent instalment of the 100 marks
owing.

156–8.] Comic though this scene is,
one is touched by Mistress Quickly's
exploited kindness.

159. *Will I live?*] Sure as I live!

161. *Doll*] 'A regular name for a
prostitute at this time; cf. Doll Common in *The Alchemist*' (Wilson,
N.C.S.); also Dorothea (Doll) Target
in Dekker's *2 Honest Whore*, and Doll
in Dekker & Webster's *Northward
Ho.*

*Tearsheet*] Not all critics are content
with this name; Coleridge suggested
'Tearstreet', in view of II. ii. 159. But in
Dekker & Middleton's *Roaring Girl*, v.
i. 118 (Bowers, iii. 85), a character

says, 'I am cal'd by those that haue
seen my valour, *Tear-cat*', and Doll's
name seems meant to show equivalent
prowess (and temper) in another
sphere. *A mery geste of Robyn Hoode*
(printed W. Copland, c. 1560) provides a parallel ('she is a trul of trust, to
serue a frier at his lust / a prycker a
prauncer a terer of shefes'; Mal. Soc.,
*Collections*, I. 2, p. 132); the (undated)
reprint by Edward White (1577–1624)
reads 'shetes' for 'shefes' and is doubtless correct. In Beaumont & Fletcher's
*Valentinian*, III. i (Glover & Waller, iv.
44), a whore is 'a kind of Kicker out of
sheets'.

165. *tonight*] F's change to 'last
night' is not needed; *OED* gives 'Tonight. *adv.* 3. last night'; cf. *Rom.*, I. iv.
50—'I dreamt a dream tonight'.

166. *Basingstoke*] A town in Hamp-

*Fal.* I hope, my lord, all's well. What is the news, my lord?

*Ch. Just.* Come all his forces back?

*Gower.* No, fifteen hundred foot, five hundred horse
    Are march'd up to my Lord of Lancaster,        170
    Against Northumberland and the Archbishop.

*Fal.* Comes the King back from Wales, my noble lord?

*Ch. Just.* You shall have letters of me presently.
    Come, go along with me, good Master Gower.

*Fal.* My lord!                              175

*Ch. Just.* What's the matter?

*Fal.* Master Gower, shall I entreat you with me to
    dinner?

*Gower.* I must wait upon my good lord here, I thank you,
    good Sir John.                        180

*Ch. Just.* Sir John, you loiter here too long, being you
    are to take soldiers up in counties as you go.

*Fal.* Will you sup with me, Master Gower?

*Ch. Just.* What foolish master taught you these manners,
    Sir John?                             185

*Fal.* Master Gower, if they become me not, he was a fool
    that taught them me. This is the right fencing
    grace, my lord; tap for tap, and so part fair.

*Ch. Just.* Now the Lord lighten thee, thou art a great
    fool.                        *Exeunt.*   190

169. *Gower*] Q (*Mess.*), F (*Mes.*), *Rowe.*     174. Gower] Q; *Gowre* F [*so also at*
*ll. 177, 183*].     179–80.] *As* Q; I . . . heere. / I . . . *Iohn.* F.     181–2.] *As* F,
*prose;* **Sir** . . . long, / Being . . . vp / In . . . go. Q [*irregular lines*].     182. counties]
Q; Countries *F.*     190. S.D.] *F; not in* Q.

**shire,** 46 miles S.W. of London, on the
Great West Road. The chronicles do
not mention any stay by Henry here.

Q's 'Billingsgate' is a curious aberra-
tion or misreading.

    173. *presently*] immediately.

SCENE II.—[*London. A room in the Prince's house.*]

*Enter* PRINCE HENRY *and* POINS.

*Prince.* Before God, I am exceeding weary.

*Poins.* Is't come to that? I had thought weariness durst
    not have attached one of so high blood.

*Prince.* Faith, it does me, though it discolours the com-
    plexion of my greatness to acknowledge it. Doth it      5
    not show vilely in me to desire small beer?

*Poins.* Why, a prince should not be so loosely studied as to
    remember so weak a composition.

*Prince.* Belike then my appetite was not princely got, for,
    by my troth, I do now remember the poor creature      10
    small beer. But indeed, these humble considerations
    make me out of love with my greatness. What a dis-
    grace is it to me to remember thy name! or to know

---

*Scene* II

SCENE II] *F* (*Scena Secunda*); *not in Q.*      Location.] Wilson (*N.C.S.*); *London.*
*Pope*; *London. Another Street. Malone.*      S.D.] *Rowe*; *Enter the Prince, Poynes,*
*sir Iohn Russel, with other. Q*; *Enter Prince Henry, Pointz, Bardolfe, and Page. F.*
1. Before God] *Q*; Trust me *F.*      2. Is't] *Q*; Is it *F.*      4. Faith, it does] *Q*;
It doth *F.*      10. by my] *Q*; in *F.*

---

1.] Hal's despondency is a significant stage in his and the play's evolution. In *F.V.*, on the contrary, he longs
for his father's death (sc. i. 95; vi. 14–
16, 41–3, 50–1).

3. *attached*] Sometimes = 'attacked',
but here in the legal sense of 'taken
into custody'; cf. IV. ii. 109. Hal's rank
should exempt him from common
fates.

4–5. *discolours . . . complexion*] Hal's
mind passes to the pallor weariness
brings, with the sense also of 'casts a
shadow over my splendour as prince'.

6. *small beer*] thin beer. It was sometimes recommended as a morning
draught after a bad night, as in
Middleton, *Old Law*, II. i. 229–33
(Bullen, ii. 154)—'*Sim[onides]:* I shall
ne'er drink at home, I shall be so
drunk abroad. *But[ler]:* But a cup of
small beer will do well next morning.
*Sim:* I grant you.'

7. *loosely studied*] lax in what he
attends to.

10. *creature*] 'Applied, after *1 Tim.*,
iv. 4 ("every creature of God is
good"), to food and other things
which minister to the material comfort of man' (*OED*, Creature. 1c).

12–13. *What . . . name*] Dramatists
make much of forgetfulness of friends'
names by those aspiring to better
themselves. In Middleton's *Your Five
Gallants*, II. iii. 83–7 (*Works*, Bullen,
iii. 165), Bungler describes how to cut
acquaintance—'If I be disposed, I'll
forget any man in a seven-night, and
yet look him in the face; nay, let him
ride but ten mile from me, and come
home again, it shall be at my choice
whether I'll remember him or no'; cf.
Jonson, *Devil is an Ass*, II. viii. 6–
10 (H. & S., vi. 206), and Field,
*Amends for Ladies*, I. i. 200–6 (Peery,
p. 167).

thy face tomorrow! or to take note how many pair of
silk stockings thou hast—viz. these, and those that     15
were thy peach-coloured ones! or to bear the inven-
tory of thy shirts—as, one for superfluity, and another for use! But that the tennis-court keeper knows
better than I, for it is a low ebb of linen with thee
when thou keepest not racket there; as thou hast not     20
done a great while, because the rest of thy low countries have made a shift to eat up thy holland. And

15. viz.] *F;* with *Q.*     16. ones] *F;* once *Q.*     17–18. another] *Q;* one other *F.*
20. keepest] *Q;* kept'st *F.*     21. thy] *F;* the *Q.*     22. made . . . to] *F; not in Q.*
22–7. And . . . strengthened.] *Q; not in F.*

15. *silk stockings*] 'Long silk stockings
were affected by men of fashion in an
age when as much store was set by a
good leg as by a good face' (Cowl).

16. *peach-coloured*] 'A deep fresh
pink. . . . Allusions to it in the drama
are in connexion with gallants and
would-be courtiers' (Linthicum, p.
40).

*bear*] sc. in mind.

17. *shirts*] Like stockings, shirts were
expensive items. Stubbes, as usual, is
censorious: '[Englishmen's] Shirtes,
which all in a manner doe werre . . .
are eyther of Camericke, Holland,
Lawne, or els of the finest cloth that
maye bee got. And of these kindes of
Shirts euerie one now doth weare
alike. . . . I haue heard of [silk-
embroidered] Shertes that haue cost
some ten shillynges, some twentie,
some fortie . . and (which is horrible
to heare) some ten pounde a peece'
(*Anat. of Abuses*, ed. Furnivall, 1877,
Pt I, p. 53).

18. *tennis-court*] Tennis was popular,
though sober citizens frowned on it,
and there were many courts in London; cf. *The Puritan Widow*, II. i. 71–6—
'*Widow:* How now, Simon? where's
my sonne Edmund? *Simon:* Verily,
Madame, hee is at vaine Exercise,
dripping in the Tennis-court. *Widow:*
At Tennis-court? . . . Oh, wicked
Edmund' (*Sh. Apocrypha*, ed. Tucker
Brooke, p. 229): and *Lingua*, III. iv—

'*Ana[mnestes]*. . . . I . . . sought you in
every alehouse, inn, tavern, dicing-
house, tennis-court, stews, and in suchlike places' (Hazlitt's *Dodsley*, ix. 391).

19–20. *it is . . . racket*] only when your
supply of shirts runs out do you give up
your games (with a pun on *racket* as
'uproar').

20–1. *as . . . while*] Players changed
frequently while playing, and Poins's
one spare shirt was not enough; cf.
Fletcher, *Honest Man's Fortune*, III. i
(Glover & Waller, x. 241)—'How long
doth that [a lord's affection] last?
perhaps the changing of some three
shirts in the Tennis-Court'; and Jonson, *Cynthia's Revels*, II. i. 66–8 (H. &
S., iv. 65).

21–2. *the rest . . . holland*] Dizzy punning on (*a*) *rest* as 'repose' and 'remainder'; (*b*) *low countries* as 'Nether-
lands', 'lower regions' (of the body),
and 'low haunts' (the stews, where
Poins begets bastards; l. 23); (*c*) *shift*
as 'contrivance', 'shirt', and 'change
of clothing'; (*d*) *eat up* as 'consume' and
'overrun' (the allusion being to 'the
relation between Holland and the rest
of the Low Countries—one of the out-
standing questions of the age'; Wilson,
N.C.S.); (*e*) *holland* as 'linen' and
'Holland' (source of fine linen). Per-
mutations among these could be endless, but the comprehensive sense is
'Your other low habits have put you to
pawning your shirts' (Shaaber).

God knows whether those that bawl out the ruins of
thy linen shall inherit his kingdom: but the mid-
wives say the children are not in the fault; where-          25
upon the world increases, and kindreds are mightily
strengthened.

*Poins.* How ill it follows, after you have laboured so hard,
you should talk so idly! Tell me, how many good
young princes would do so, their fathers being so sick          30
as yours at this time is.

*Prince.* Shall I tell thee one thing, Poins?

*Poins.* Yes, faith, and let it be an excellent good thing.

*Prince.* It shall serve, among wits of no higher breeding
than thine.          35

*Poins.* Go to, I stand the push of your one thing that you
will tell.

*Prince.* Marry, I tell thee it is not meet that I should be
sad now my father is sick; albeit I could tell to thee,
as to one it pleases me for fault of a better to call my          40
friend, I could be sad, and sad indeed too.

*Poins.* Very hardly, upon such a subject.

*Prince.* By this hand, thou thinkest me as **far in** the devil's
book as thou and Falstaff, for obduracy and persis-
tency. Let the end try the man. But I tell thee, my          45
heart bleeds inwardly that my father is so sick; and

---

23. bawl] *Q* (bal), *Pope; not in F.*          out] *Q; out of Pope;* out from *Capell; not in F.*
25-6. fault; whereupon] *Theobald;* fault whereupon *Q; not in F.*          30. being] *Q;*
lying *F.*          31. at this time] *Q; not in F.*          ·33. faith] *Q; not in F.*          36-7. you
will] *Q;* you'l *F.*          38. Marry] *Q* (Mary); Why *F.*          43. By this hand] *Q;
not in F.*

---

22-7. *And . . . strengthened*] Not in F;
perhaps cut as profane.

23-4. *whether . . . kingdom*] whether
your offspring, howling from baby-
clothes made from the scraps of your
shirts, shall go to heaven; an echo
of *Matt.*, xxv. 34—'Come, ye blessed
of my father, inherit the kingdom,
which hath ben prepared for you
from the foundation of the world'
(Noble, p. 177).

23. *out*] out of.

25. *not . . . fault*] not to be blamed for
being bastards (presumably, there-

fore, not to be denied God's blessing).

25-7. *whereupon . . . strengthened*]
which is the way the world multiplies,
and a fine reinforcement of one's
family it is!

28. *so hard*] i.e. with such exertion of
your wits.

33. *an excellent . . . thing*] Presumably,
'something better than your recent
quips'.

36. *stand the push of*] can stand up to.

45. *Let . . . man*] Proverbial as
'The end crowns (tries) all'; Tilley,
E116.

keeping such vile company as thou art hath in reason
taken from me all ostentation of sorrow.

*Poins.* The reason?

*Prince.* What wouldst thou think of me if I should weep?          50

*Poins.* I would think thee a most princely hypocrite.

*Prince.* It would be every man's thought; and thou art a
blessed fellow, to think as every man thinks. Never a
man's thought in the world keeps the roadway better
than thine: every man would think me an hypocrite          55
indeed. And what accites your most worshipful
thought to think so?

*Poins.* Why, because you have been so lewd, and so much
engraffed to Falstaff.

*Prince.* And to thee.          60

*Poins.* By this light, I am well spoke on; I can hear it with
mine own ears. The worst that they can say of me is
that I am a second brother, and that I am a proper
fellow of my hands, and those two things I confess I
cannot help. By the mass, here comes Bardolph.          65

*Enter* BARDOLPH *and* PAGE.

*Prince.* And the boy that I gave Falstaff—a had him from
me Christian, and look if the fat villain have not
transformed him ape.

*Bard.* God save your Grace!

61. By this light] *Q*; Nay *F.*          spoke on] *Q*; spoken of *F.*          65. By the mass] *Q*;
Looke, looke *F.*          65. S.D.] *Q* (*Enter Bardolfe and boy*), Rowe [*after l. 68*], Capell;
*Enter Bardolfe. F* [*after l. 68*].          66. a] *Q*; he *F.*          67. look] *Q*; see *F.*          69. God]
*Q*; not in *F.*

48. *ostentation*] show; not meant in
the opprobrious sense, which occurs
only in *LLL.*, v. ii. 409—'blown me full
of maggot ostentation'.

56. *accites*] induces, excites, but also
with a quibble, *accite* being a legal
term for 'cite', 'summon'; cf. v. ii. 141.
'Poins's "thought" is represented as a
magistrate ("most worshipful"), sitting in judgment on Hal's conduct'
(Wilson, N.C.S.).

58. *lewd*] loose-living (referring in a
general way to his low tastes and associations), not meant as licentious.

59. *engraffed*] closely attached to.

60. *And to thee*] 'The quiet bitterness
of this escapes Poins. It is Hal's last
word to him in private' (Wilson,
N.C.S.).

63. *second brother*] younger son, without inheritance (and therefore dependent on his wits).

63–4. *proper . . . hands*] fine fighting
fellow. Tilley, M163, illustrates as proverbial, 'He is a tall man of his hands'
(i.e. a good fighter).

68. *ape*] The Page is either guying
Bardolph or is fantastically dressed.

*Prince.* And yours, most noble Bardolph!                              70

*Poins.* [*To Bardolph*] Come, you virtuous ass, you bashful
    fool, must you be blushing? Wherefore blush you
    now? What a maidenly man-at-arms are you be-
    come! Is't such a matter to get a pottle-pot's maiden-
    head?                                                     75

*Page.* A calls me e'en now, my lord, through a red lattice,
    and I could discern no part of his face from the win-
    dow. At last I spied his eyes, and methought he had
    made two holes in the ale-wife's new petticoat, and
    so peeped through.                                        80

---

71. *Poins*] *QF*; *Bard.* Theobald.     71. S.D.] *This edn; to the Boy* Johnson.     virtu-
ous] *Q*; pernitious *F*.     74. Is't] *Q*; Is it *F*.     76. *Page*] *Q* (*Boy*), *F* [*so throughout
scene*].     A calls] *Q*; He call'd *F*.     e'en now] *Q* (enow), *Cambridge*; euen
now *F*.     79. wife's] *QF* (wiues), *Capell*.     new] *F*; red *conj.* Monro; *not in Q.*
80. so] *Q*; *not in F.*

---

71. Poins] Following Theobald,
many editors wrongly give this to
Bardolph, thinking that the 'maidenly
man-at-arms' quip is addressed by
him to the Page. But the Page is no
man-at-arms, and the quip is directed
at Bardolph for his crimson face. The
Page readily seconds the jest.

71–2. *you virtuous . . . blushing*]
Tilley, B480, illustrates as proverbial,
'Blushing (bashfulness) is virtue's
colour (is a sign of grace)'.

*virtuous*] F's 'pernitious' must be
misreading of MS, or inadvertence, or
uninformed tinkering.

74–5. *get . . . maidenhead*] knock off a
pot of ale—an accepted jest; cf. *Muce-
dorus* (Hazlitt's *Dodsley*, vii. 234)—
'*Mouse* [*the Clown*]: . . . I call'd for
three pots of ale . . . Now, sirrah, I had
taken the maidenhead of two of them
—now, as I was lifting the third to my
mouth . . .'. *Pottle-pot* = two-quart
tankard.

76. *red lattice*] i.e. window of an ale-
house. Ale-houses had red lattice-
work windows (later, patterns imitat-
ing these on the wall, the origin of the
frequent name 'Chequers'). William
Harrison's *Description of England*, 1577,
II. xii (Hol., i. 315–16), remarks that

formerly country houses 'did vse much
lattise [but now] lattises are . . .
growne into less vse, bicause glasse is
come to be . . . within a verie little so
good cheape if not better then the
other'. References abound; e.g. Wilkins, *Miseries of Enforced Marriage*
(Hazlitt's *Dodsley*, ix. 510)—'*Ilford*:
Be mild in a tavern? 'tis treason to the
red lattice'; Marston, *Antonio &
Mellida*, v (Wood, i. 58)—'*Bal[urdo]*:
I am not as wel knowne by my wit as
an alehouse by a red lattice'.

79. *ale-wife's new petticoat*] The Page
is rather forcing his jest; Bardolph's
eyes peered from his red face, which
merged with the red lattice, as though
through holes in the barmaid's (red)
petticoats; Monro cogently suggests
that *new* is a misreading of MS 'red'.
The petticoat's redness is implied, for
clearly the ale-wife is disreputable; red
gowns or petticoats were associated
with prostitutes—cf. New Arden *1H4*,
I. ii. 10 and note, and *The Penniles Parliament of Thred-Bare Poets* (C. Hindley,
*Old Book Collector's Miscellany*, 1872, ii.
4)—'men must have care lest, conversing too much with red petticoats,
they banish their hair from their heads
. . . (i.e. by reason of Lues Venerea)'

*Prince.* Has not the boy profited?

*Bard.* Away, you whoreson upright rabbit, away!

*Page.* Away, you rascally Althaea's dream, away!

*Prince.* Instruct us, boy; what dream, boy?

*Page.* Marry, my lord, Althaea dreamt she was delivered      85
of a firebrand; and therefore I call him her dream.

*Prince.* A crown's-worth of good interpretation! There
'tis, boy.

*Poins.* O, that this blossom could be kept from cankers!
Well, there is sixpence to preserve thee.                     90

*Bard.* And you do not make him be hanged among you,
the gallows shall have wrong.

*Prince.* And how doth thy master, Bardolph?

*Bard.* Well, my lord. He heard of your Grace's coming to
town—there's a letter for you.                                95

*Poins.* Delivered with good respect. And how doth the
martlemas your master?

*Bard.* In bodily health, sir.

*Poins.* Marry, the immortal part needs a physician, but
that moves not him; though that be sick, it dies not. 100

---

81. Has] *Q;* Hath *F.*      82. rabbit] *F;* rabble *Q.*      88. 'tis] *Q;* it is *F.*      89.
this] *Q;* this good *F.*      91. And] *Q;* If *F.*      be] *F; not in Q.*      92. have wrong]
*Q;* be wrong'd *F.*      94. my] *Q;* my good *F.*

---

83. *Althaea's dream*] Althaea, wife of
Œneus, king of Calydon, is here confused with Hecuba, who before the
birth of Paris dreamed that she was
delivered of a firebrand (Ovid, *Hero-
ides*, xvi). Althaea was told that her
new-born son Meleager would live as
long as a brand placed by the Fates on
the fire was unburnt. She saved the
brand until, on Meleager's killing her
brothers, she cast it on the fire (Ovid,
*Metam.*, viii).

89. *cankers*] canker-worms.

90. *to preserve thee*] This alludes to the
cross which figured on Elizabethan
silver coins; cf. I. ii. 227, and Brome,
*Damoiselle*, IV. i (Shepherd, i. 444).

94–5. *He . . . you*] This is one of the
three letters to important recipients
which the highly-placed Falstaff sends
off at I. ii. 239–41.

96. *good respect*] proper ceremony
(ironical).

97. *martlemas*] The Feast of St Martin, 11 November. The reference is,
perhaps, like 'latter spring' and 'All-
hallown summer' (*1H4*, I. ii. 178),
directed to Falstaff's autumnal mel-
lowness ('i.e. hale old man'—Ridley;
'St Martin's Summer, a season of fine
mild weather occurring about Martinmas' [*OED*, Martin³, 3c]), but doubtless also to 'the prodigious plenty of
Martlemas' (*Sh.'s Engl.*, i. 356), the
vast meaty associations of Martinmas,
when animals were slaughtered to be
preserved for the winter. Falstaff is
Hal's 'sweet beef' at *1H4*, III. iii. 199.

99–100.] An allusion to *Matt.*, ix. 12
—'They that be whole neede not a
Physician, but they that are sicke'
(Noble, p. 177).

*Prince.* I do allow this wen to be as familiar with me as
my dog, and he holds his place, for look you how
he writes—[*Reads*] 'John Falstaff, Knight.'

*Poins.* Every man must know that, as oft as he has occasion to name himself: even like those that are kin to      105
the King, for they never prick their finger but they
say, 'There's some of the King's blood spilt'. 'How
comes that?' says he that takes upon him not to
conceive. The answer is as ready as a borrower's cap
—'I am the King's poor cousin, sir'.      110

*Prince.* Nay, they will be kin to us, or they will fetch it
from Japhet. But the letter:—'Sir John Falstaff,
Knight, to the son of the King nearest his father,
Harry Prince of Wales, greeting.'

102. how] *Q; not in F.*      103. writes—[*Reads*] 'John] *Sisson;* writes. | *Poynes
Iohn Q;* writes. | *Poin. Letter. Iohn F.*      John] *QF;* Sir John *conj. Capell.*      103–
4. Falstaff . . . Every] *Sisson;* Falstaffe Knight, euery *QF subst.*      104. has] *Q;*
hath *F.*      107. There's] *Q;* there is *F.*      108–9. that?' . . . The] *F4* (that? (says
he . . . conceiue) the), *Rowe* (that? says he . . . conceiue: the); that (saies he)
. . . conceiue the *Q;* that (sayes he) . . . conceiue? the *Ff1–3.*      109. borrower's]
*Theobald, conj. Warburton;* borowed *QF subst.*      111. or] *Q;* but *F.*      112. the]
*Q;* to the *F.*

101. *wen*] lump, 'swoln excrescence
of a man' (Johnson).

102. *holds his place*] stands upon his
rank.

103. *John . . . Knight*] Though QF
give this to Poins, Sisson's suggestion
that it belongs to the Prince is attrac-
tive. There may have been an Old-
castle/Falstaff alteration in MS which
caused a dislocation and also the accidental loss of the 'Sir' which one would
expect (and Capell conjectured) before *John*, and which occurs when Hal
repeats the title in l. 112.

109. *borrower's*] Theobald's emendation is clearly right; cf. *Timon,* II. i. 16–
19—'Importune him for my moneys;
be not ceas'd / With slight denial, nor
then silenc'd when / "Commend me to
your master", and the cap / Plays in
the right hand, thus'.

112. *Japhet*] i.e. If they cannot claim
direct royal kinship they will do so as
descending from Japhet, father of all
Europeans; cf. *Gen.,* x. 5—'Of these

[offspring of Japhet, Noah's third son]
were the isles of the Gentiles deuided
in their landes' (i.e. the peoples of
Europe).

112–27.] Falstaff 'holds his place'
indeed. His letter is a mixture of pomposity and impudence. Dover Wilson
points out that the addressee's name,
expressed with due etiquette, should
come first, the writer's name following
humbly at the end, and that the
Caesar parody is presumptuous, the
libel on Poins bare-faced, the spiritual
advice flippant, and the subscription
highflown (*Fortunes,* pp. 105–6). The
address is, as Poins says, a 'certificate',
a licence issued by a sovereign to a
subject, and Falstaff is clearly getting
above himself. But this need not be
taken too seriously; the main point is
that his sense of style rarely deserts
him, and here in short space he parodies epistolary formality, oracular
gravity, pious ejaculation (ll. 122–3),
mealy-mouthed Puritanism (l. 124),

*Poins.* Why, this is a certificate!                                    115

*Prince.* Peace! 'I will imitate the honourable Romans in
      brevity.'

*Poins.* He sure means brevity in breath, short-winded.

[*Prince.*] 'I commend me to thee, I commend thee, and
      I leave thee. Be not too familiar with Poins, for he      120
      misuses thy favours so much that he swears thou art
      to marry his sister Nell. Repent at idle times as thou
      mayst, and so, farewell.

            Thine by yea and no—which is as much as to
            say, as thou usest him—Jack Falstaff with my      125
            familiars, John with my brothers and sisters,
            and Sir John with all Europe.'

*Poins.* My lord, I'll steep this letter in sack and make
      him eat it.

*Prince.* That's to make him eat twenty of his words. But      130

---

116. Romans in] *QF;* Roman in *Warburton;* Roman's *or* Roman in's *Anon, conj.
apud Cambridge.*      118. He sure] *Q;* Sure he *F.*      119. *Prince*] *Theobald; not
in QF.*      126. familiars] *F;* family *Q.*      sisters] *Q; Sister F.*      128. *Poins*]
*Q; not in F.*      I'll] *Q; I will F.*

---

and *miles-gloriosus* effrontery (ll. 125–
7).

116–17. *Romans in brevity*] Brutus,
says Plutarch, affected the 'brief com-
pendious manner of speech of the
Lacedaemonians', and perhaps the
trait was thought general. Warburton's emendation 'Roman' may be
what Shakespeare intended; the reference then would be to Caesar's terse
despatch after Zela—'veni, vidi, vici'
—parodied in ll. 119–20 and quoted at
IV. iii. 41–2.

119. *Prince*] QF have no speech-
heading, so Poins seems to continue.
But surely the Prince should read his
own letter. Perhaps Shakespeare wrote
ll. 116–27 as continuous text, with l.
118 merely as a parenthetical inter-
jection, and so did not repeat the
Prince's speech-prefix.

119–20. *I commend me . . . leave
thee*] 'I send you my regards, I think
well of you, I am going away' (Wilson,
*Fortunes*, p. 105).

122–3. *Repent . . . mayest*] 'Pious
wishes were common in letters of the

age' (Wilson, N.C.S.); the piety here
is parody. Its nonchalance is echoed
by Parolles—'When thou hast leisure, say thy prayers' (*All's W.*, I. i.
227).

124. *by yea and no*] Part of Falstaff's frequent Puritan idiom, a
parody of citizens' (Puritans') oaths;
cf. I. ii. 35–6, note. In J. Cooke's *How a
Man May Choose*, III. iii (Hazlitt's *Dodsley*, ix. 61) a Puritan lady swears,
'Brother, by yea and nay'; Thomas
Heywood, *I If You Know Not Me*
(Shepherd, i. 271, 273) has, '*Vnder the
yea and nay, men often buy | Much cozen-
age*'. The fussy Shallow, though hardly a Puritan, uses the phrase at III.
ii. 8.

128–9.] The dramatists sometimes
make a rogue eat his words or other
document. The Summoner in *Sir John
Oldcastle* has to swallow the process he
comes to serve on Sir John (Mal. Soc.,
ll. 565–85), and Mannering the seals
of his commission for victual-raising in
Greene's *Pinner of Wakefield* (Grosart,
xiv. 128).

do you use me thus, Ned? Must I marry your sister?

*Poins.* God send the wench no worse fortune! But I never
said so.

*Prince.* Well, thus we play the fools with the time, and
the spirits of the wise sit in the clouds and mock us.    135
Is your master here in London?

*Bard.* Yea, my lord.

*Prince.* Where sups he? Doth the old boar feed in the old
frank?

*Bard.* At the old place, my lord, in Eastcheap.    140

*Prince.* What company?

*Page.* Ephesians, my lord, of the old church.

*Prince.* Sup any women with him?

*Page.* None, my lord, but old Mistress Quickly, and
Mistress Doll Tearsheet.    145

*Prince.* What pagan may that be?

*Page.* A proper gentlewoman, sir, and a kinswoman of
my master's.

*Prince.* Even such kin as the parish heifers are to the
town bull. Shall we steal upon them, Ned, at sup-    150
per?

---

132. God . . . wench] *Q; May the Wench haue F.*    137. Yea] *Q; Yes F.*
150–1.] *As Q [continuous prose]; Towne-Bull? / Shall . . . Supper? F [irregular lines].*

---

138–9.] Tilley, B483, illustrates as
proverbial, 'He feeds like a boar in a
frank'; *frank* = sty, pen for hogs. At I.
i. 19 Falstaff is a 'brawn', at II. iv. 227
a boar-pig, and so on. This allusion
is the nearest Shakespeare comes to
naming the Boar's Head Tavern—'the
olde Tauerne in Eastcheap' of *F.V.*
(sc. i. 89; ii. 66). 'This famous hostelry
. . . was on the N. side of Gt Eastcheap.
. . . The tavern abutted at the back on
St Michael's in Crooked Lane, and
was just where the statue of William IV
now stands' (Sugden). There is no
evidence that it existed in Henry IV's
time; the first reference to it as a
tavern dates from a lease of 1537 (*Sh.'s
Engl.*, ii. 172).

140. *Eastcheap*] Cf. II. i. 68, note.

142. *Ephesians*] boon companions,
like Trojans or Corinthians; cf. *1H4*,
II. i. 77 and II. iv. 13, and *Wiv.*, IV.
v. 19—'It is thine host, thine
Ephesian, calls'; see following note.

*of the old church*] The allusion is perhaps to the unregenerate Ephesians,
with the sensual faults St Paul warns
them against (particularly indulgence
in wine: *Ephes.*, v. 18) before they 'put
off the old man' and put on the new
(*Ephes.*, iv. 22–4). The Page hardly
seems to allude (unless ironically, and
the irony would be lost on the stage) to
'the prime church of the Ephesians',
whose conditions St Paul laid down,
and which was the Puritan court of
appeal for purity of life; Mistress
Purge in Middleton's *Family of Love*,
I. iii. 111–13 (Bullen, iii. 27) says, 'I
cannot find that either plays or players
were allowed in the prime church of
Ephesus by the elders'.

146. *pagan*] harlot; *OED*'s first
example in this sense.

147. *proper*] respectable.

150. *town bull*] parish bull. Tilley,

*Poins.* I am your shadow, my lord, I'll follow you.

*Prince.* Sirrah, you boy, and Bardolph, no word to your
 master that I am yet come to town—there's for your
 silence.           155

*Bard.* I have no tongue, sir.

*Page.* And for mine, sir, I will govern it.

*Prince.* Fare you well; go.  [*Exeunt Bardolph and Page.*]
 This Doll Tearsheet should be some road.

*Poins.* I warrant you, as common as the way between 160
 Saint Albans and London.

*Prince.* How might we see Falstaff bestow himself tonight in his true colours, and not ourselves be seen?

*Poins.* Put on two leathern jerkins and aprons, and wait
 upon him at his table as drawers.    165

*Prince.* From a god to a bull? A heavy descension! It was
 Jove's case. From a prince to a prentice? A low
 transformation, that shall be mine, for in everything the purpose must weigh with the folly. Follow
 me, Ned.         *Exeunt.* 170

---

154–5.] *As* Q; Master ... Towne. / There's ... silence. F [*irregular lines*]. 154.
come to] Q; *in* F. 158–9.] *As* Q [*except for S.D.*]; Fare ... go. / This ... Rode. F
[*irregular lines*]. 158. you] Q; ye F. 158. S.D.] *Capell, subst.; not in* QF.
164. leathern] Q; Leather F. 165. as] Q; like F. 166. descension] Q;
declension F.

B716, cites the ironical proverb, 'The
town bull is as much a bachelor as he',
and, 'To be a great whore-master, to
be the town bull'. Doll in Dekker &
Webster's *Northward Ho*, IV. i. 164
(Bowers, ii. 452), likewise is 'a towne
cowe'.

159. *road*] i.e. whore. Tilley illustrates as proverbial the phrases 'as
common as the highway' (H457) and
'as common as the cartway' (C109);
Skeat (*NQ*, 10th Ser., ix, 1908, p. 264)
provides a *Piers Plowman* parallel (A
Text, Pt I, Passus iii. 127)—'Heo [she]
is ... / As Comuyn as the Cart-wei to
knaues and to alle'. The basic idea is,
probably, 'object indiscriminately
tramped or ridden over'; cf. Wilkins,
*Miseries of Enforced Marriage*, III (Hazlitt's *Dodsley*, ix. 522)—'*Sis*[*ter*]: Shall
I be left then like a common road, /

That every beast that can but pay his
toll / May travel over?'—and W. B.
Yeats, *Crazy Jane on God*—'Though like
a road / That men pass over, / My
body makes no moan.'

160–1. *as common ... London*] See
l. 159, note. St Albans being on
Watling Street, then as now the main
route to the Midlands, the way to
London was particularly busy.

162. *bestow*] 'behave' (Onions).

164–5.] 'This was a plot very unlikely to succeed where the prince and
the drawers were all known, but it produces merriment, which our author
found more useful than probability'
(Johnson).

166. *From ... bull*] For love of
Europa, Jupiter transformed himself
into a bull; Ovid, *Metam.*, ii. 846–76.
*heavy descension*] grievous descent.

SCENE III.—[*Warkworth. Northumberland's castle.*]

*Enter* NORTHUMBERLAND, LADY NORTHUMBERLAND,
*and* LADY PERCY.

*North.* I pray thee, loving wife and gentle daughter,
 Give even way unto my rough affairs;
 Put not you on the visage of the times
 And be like them to Percy troublesome.
*Lady N.* I have given over, I will speak no more.     5
 Do what you will, your wisdom be your guide.
*North.* Alas, sweet wife, my honour is at pawn,
 And, but my going, nothing can redeem it.
*Lady P.* O yet, for God's sake, go not to these wars!
 The time was, father, that you broke your word    10
 When you were more endear'd to it than now;
 When your own Percy, when my heart's dear Harry,
 Threw many a northward look to see his father
 Bring up his powers; but he did long in vain.
 Who then persuaded you to stay at home?     15
 There were two honours lost, yours and your son's.
 For yours, the God of heaven brighten it!
 For his, it stuck upon him as the sun
 In the grey vault of heaven, and by his light
 Did all the chivalry of England move      20

*Scene* III

SCENE III] *F* (*Scena Tertia.*); *not in Q.*   Location. Warkworth.] Capell.   *North-umberland's Castle.*] Theobald.   S.D.] *Q* (*Enter Northumberland his wife, and the wife to Harry Percie.*), *F* (*Enter Northumberland, his Ladie, and Harrie Percies Ladie.*), Rowe.
1. pray thee] *Q*; prethee *F.*   2. even] *Q*; an euen *F.*   5. *Lady N.*] *QF* (*Wife*), Rowe, subst. [*so also at l. 50*].   9. *Lady P.*] *Q* (*Kate*), *F* (*La.*), Rowe, subst. [*so subst. also at l. 53*].   God's] *Q*; heauens *F.*   10. that] *Q*; when *F.*   11. endear'd] *F*; endeere *Q.*   12. heart's dear Harry] *Q*; heart-deere-*Harry F.*   14. powers] *Q*; Powres *F*; pow'rs *Pope.*   17. the ... heaven] *Q*; may heauenly glory *F.*

2.] Make my hard position as easy as you can.

11. *endear'd*] bound by honourable attachment.

18. *stuck*] Used for 'the fixity and lustre of a heavenly body in its sphere' (Shaaber, quoting *Ham.*, v. ii. 268–9— 'Your skill shall, like a star i'th' darkest night, / Stick fiery off indeed'); and

*Ant.*, v. ii. 79–80—'His face was as the heav'ns, and therein stuck / A sun and moon').

19. *grey*] Often used for 'blue', as in *Tit.*, II. ii. 1—'The hunt is up, the morn is bright and grey', and Peele, *Old Wives' Tale* (Bullen, i. 318)—'The day is clear, the welkin bright and grey'.

To do brave acts. He was indeed the glass
Wherein the noble youth did dress themselves.
He had no legs that practis'd not his gait;
And speaking thick, which nature made his blemish,
Became the accents of the valiant;                    25
For those that could speak low and tardily
Would turn their own perfection to abuse,
To seem like him. So that in speech, in gait,
In diet, in affections of delight,
In military rules, humours of blood,                  30
He was the mark and glass, copy and book,
That fashion'd others. And him—O wondrous him!
O miracle of men!—him did you leave,
Second to none, unseconded by you,
To look upon the hideous god of war                   35
In disadvantage, to abide a field
Where nothing but the sound of Hotspur's name
Did seem defensible: so you left him.
Never, O never, do his ghost the wrong
To hold your honour more precise and nice             40
With others than with him! Let them alone.
The Marshal and the Archbishop are strong:

23-45. He . . . grave.] F; not in Q.        32. wondrous him!] Rowe; wondrous!
him, F; not in Q.

21. glass] Like 'mirror' (e.g. Myrroure for Magistrates), frequently used
for 'example', 'model'; cf. Sir Thomas
More (Mal. Soc.), ll. 752–3)—'Ile be
thy glasse, dresse thy behauiour according to my cariage'; and Ham., III.
i. 161—'the glass of fashion'.

24. speaking thick] i.e. speaking im-
petuously. Cf. Cymb., III. ii. 58–60—
'Say and speak thick— / Love's counsellor should fill the bores of hearing /
To the smothering of the sense'. 'The
phrase has been interpreted . . . as
meaning either "having a defect of
speech" . . . or "having a guttural
accent". . . . [It] in fact means simply
"rapid, or hurried, speech", a frequent Elizabethan sense. . . . Over-
haste in speaking, of course, might
lead to want of clarity in enunciation

["which nature made his blemish"].
. . . The origin of the stage tradition of
stuttering this part was Schlegel's
translation of the word thick by stottern,
after which German actors stuttered
the part and set a fashion' (Sisson, New
Readings). Shakespeare is recalling the
impulsive, crowded utterance he had
given Hotspur, appropriate to his
name (or perhaps the Northumbrian
burr?). No such characteristic appears
in the chronicles.

29. affections of delight] inclinations to
pleasure.

30. humours of blood] caprices of temperament.

31. mark] guiding sign.

36. abide a field] face a battle.

38. defensible] 'furnishing the means
of defence' (Malone).

Had my sweet Harry had but half their numbers,
Today might I, hanging on Hotspur's neck,
Have talk'd of Monmouth's grave.

*North.*                               Beshrew your heart,
Fair daughter, you do draw my spirits from me          46
With new lamenting ancient oversights.
But I must go and meet with danger there,
Or it will seek me in another place,
And find me worse provided.

*Lady N.*                              O, fly to Scotland,     50
Till that the nobles and the armed commons
Have of their puissance made a little taste.

*Lady P.*  If they get ground and vantage of the King,
Then join you with them like a rib of steel,
To make strength stronger: but, for all our loves,     55
First let them try themselves. So did your son;
He was so suffer'd; so came I a widow,
And never shall have length of life enough
To rain upon remembrance with mine eyes,
That it may grow and sprout as high as heaven          60
For recordation to my noble husband.

*North.*  Come, come, go in with me. 'Tis with my mind
As with the tide swell'd up unto his height,
That makes a still-stand, running neither way.
Fain would I go to meet the Archbishop,                65
But many thousand reasons hold me back.
I will resolve for Scotland. There am I,
Till time and vantage crave my company.          *Exeunt.*

45. *grave*] Lady Percy, as well as Morton (cf. I. i. 109), knows that Hal, not Falstaff, killed Hotspur. The play's 'dramatic ambiguity' can have it one way for comic make-believe, the other for serious truth.

52. *taste*] trial.

57. *so suffer'd*] allowed to do so.

59.] To water with tears the plant of memory.

67–8.] As at Shrewsbury, Northumberland's defection seals the rebellion's fate. In Holinshed he flees to Berwick only after 'too much hast of the Archbishop' has fatally precipitated matters (Hol., iii. 38).

SCENE IV.—[*London. The Boar's Head Tavern in Eastcheap.*]

*Enter two* DRAWERS[, FRANCIS *and another*].

*Francis.* What the devil hast thou brought there—apple-johns? Thou knowest Sir John cannot endure an apple-john.

*Scene* IV

SCENE IV] F (*Scæna Quarta.*); *not in* Q.     *Location. London.*] *Capell.     The . . . Eastcheap.*] *Theobald.*     S.D. *Enter two Drawers*] F; *Enter a Drawer or two.* Q. *Francis and another*] *Hemingway; not in* QF.     1. *Francis*] Q; 1. *Drawer.* F [*so also at l. 10*].     the devil] Q; *not in* F.

'The finest tavern scene ever written' (Masefield, *Sh.*, 1911, p. 117). More Hogarthian than anything in *1 Henry IV*, it is proof that Falstaff will not do as a king's companion, yet its Hogarthian quality includes irresistible appreciation of human beings, however coarse or absurd. 'The whole scene of broad comedy through which there flickers, as a glance of firelight, a touch of natural unforced sentiment . . . is a creation of sheer genius, and lifts Shakespeare as high above his fellows as does any of his great tragic scenes, for they tried in play after play to make such scenes come to life, and yet did nothing like this, seemingly thrown out carelessly' (J. B. Priestley, *English Comic Characters*, 1925, p. 77). As Herford notes (ed. 1928), this is the last time the company assembles at Eastcheap.

Location.] Cf. II. ii. 138–9, note.

Speech-headings.] The distribution of speeches in ll. 1–21 raises some problems. They alternate in Q between Francis and a Drawer, in F between 1 and 2 Drawer (ll. 13–14 being omitted, however). Q also has *Enter Will* before l. 19, but gives him nothing to say. The speeches here at ll. 1, 4, and 10 are distributed as in Q; at ll. 13, 15, 19, and 21 they are distributed as seems most probably Shakespeare's intention. The evidence is that (*a*) ll. 13–14 sound like a new warning about an imminent development; (*b*) 'Sirrah' (l. 15) seems an address to a

new hearer, not to the companion whom Francis has addressed twice already; (*c*) l. 21 should presumably be spoken by the Second Drawer, since he has been ordered to find Sneak's noise. Q's *Enter Will* should perhaps have been put in before the Drawer's speech not at l. 19 but at l. 13, so that it is he who brings the warning: F perhaps, saving an acting part, cut his entry and his ll. 13–14. It would be to him in Q that Francis would address his 'Sirrah' (l. 15), and he would naturally reply (l. 19). Q's '*Francis*' before l. 21 seems wrong, since he is not the one to 'find out Sneak', and F's '2. *Draw.*' seems right.

1–2. *apple-johns*] 'Apple-John (so called because it is ripe about S. John's Day [24 June]). A kind of apple said to keep two years, and to be in perfection when shrivelled and withered' (*OED*). Since no apple can be gathered so early, Mr I. I. Jeffries, once a professional fruit-grower, suggests, privately, that 'if the name has anything to do with St John's Day, it would perhaps be more likely that the apple *kept* to around that date. It was famed for its long-keeping qualities'

2–3. *Sir . . . apple-john*] Falstaff's dislike may be sufficiently explained by ll. 4–8, but Jonson uses *apple-john* in a way which seems equivalent to 'apple-squire', i.e. pimp; viz., *Bart. Fair*, 1. iii. 55 (H. & S., vi. 24, and x. 180, note) —'She may call you an Apple-*Iohn*, if you vse this' (i.e. if you throw your

*2 Draw.* Mass, thou sayst true. The Prince once set a dish
of apple-johns before him, and told him there were     5
five more Sir Johns; and, putting off his hat, said, 'I
will now take my leave of these six dry, round, old,
withered knights'. It angered him to the heart; but
he hath forgot that.

*Francis.* Why then, cover, and set them down, and see if     10
thou canst find out Sneak's noise. Mistress Tearsheet
would fain hear some music.

*Enter* THIRD DRAWER.

*3 Draw.* Dispatch! The room where they supped is too
hot, they'll come in straight.

*Francis.* Sirrah, here will be the Prince and Master Poins     15
anon, and they will put on two of our jerkins and
aprons, and Sir John must not know of it; Bardolph
hath brought word.

*3 Draw.* By the mass, here will be old utis; it will be an
excellent stratagem.     20

*2 Draw.* I'll see if I can find out Sneak.     *Exit [with third*
*Drawer].*

---

4. 2 *Draw.*] *Q* (*Draw.*), *F.*     Mass] *Q; not in F.*     7–8. old, withered] *Q*; old-
wither'd *F.*     12. hear] *Q;* haue *F.*     S.D.] *Alexander, conj. Ridley; Enter Will. Q*
[*after l. 18*]; *not in F.*     12–13. music. / [S.D.] / *3 Draw.* Dispatch] *Alexander, conj.
Ridley;* musique. / *Dra.* Dispatch *Q;* music. Dispatch *Pope;* Musique. *F.*     13–
14.] *Q; not in F.*     15. *Francis*] *Q;* 2. *Draw. F.*     18–19. word. / *3 Draw.*]
*Alexander;* word. / *Enter Will.* / *Dra. Q;* word. / 1. *Draw. F.*     19. By the mass] *Q;*
Then *F.*     old] *Q corr., F;* oll *Q uncorr.*     21. 2 *Draw.*] *F; Francis Q.*     21. S.D.
with third *Drawer*] *Alexander, subst.; not in QF.*

---

wife and a rival together). Wilson
(N.C.S.) suggests also that the
shrivelled apple, like the 'withered
elder', might signify impotence (cf.
l. 256).

11. *Sneak's noise*] Sneak's band (of
musicians). In *F.V.* the Prince sends
three times for 'a noyse of Musitians'
(sc. ii. 99; iv. 91; vi. 107). About 1613,
Thomas Heywood's *1 Iron Age*, III. i
(Shepherd, iii. 312), has, 'Where's this
great sword and buckler man of
Greece? / Wee shall haue him one of
Sneakes noise, / And come peaking
into the Tents of the *Greeks*, / With will

you haue any musicke Gentlemen?' If,
as this continuing repute suggests, the
band really existed, or its name was a
popular tag, one need not explain
Sneak's name on such grounds as that,
e.g., 'references to the fiddlers are
generally contemptuous' (Cowl).

19. *old utis*] a high old time; 'utis' is
either, or both, (*a*) the dialectal 'Utis
(*Wor[cester]*) Noise, confusion, din'
(Wright, *Engl. Dial. Dict.*; similarly
*OED*, Utas[2]); (*b*) jollification, period
of festivity (*OED*, Utas[1]. I.c), i.e.
strictly the 'octave', eighth day, or
eight days, of a festival.

*Enter* HOSTESS *and* DOLL TEARSHEET.

*Host.* I'faith, sweetheart, methinks now you are in an
excellent good temperality. Your pulsidge beats as
extraordinarily as heart would desire, and your
colour I warrant you is as red as any rose, in good          25
truth, la! But i'faith you have drunk too much canaries, and that's a marvellous searching wine, and it
perfumes the blood ere one can say, 'What's this?'
How do you now?

*Doll.* Better than I was—hem!          30

*Host.* Why, that's well said—a good heart's worth gold.
Lo, here comes Sir John.

*Enter* FALSTAFF[, *singing*].

*Fal.* 'When Arthur first in court'—Empty the jordan.

21. S.D. *Enter . . . Tearsheet.*] *Q* (*Enter mistris Quickly, and Doll Tere-sheet.*), F
(*Enter Hostesse, and Dol.*), *Capell.*          22. *Host.*] *Q* (*Quickly*) [*so also subst. at l. 31*], F.
I'faith] *Q; not in F.*          25–6. in . . . la] *Q* (in . . . law); *not in F.*          26. i'faith] *Q;
not in F.*          28. one] *Q; wee F.*          this?] *Capell;* this, *Q;* this. *F.*          30. *Doll*] *Q*
(*Tere.*) [*so also at ll. 39, 42*], F (*Dol.*) [*so throughout scene*].          31. that's] *Q;* that
was *F.*          32. Lo] *Q;* Looke *F.*          32. S.D. *Enter Falstaff*] *Q* (*enter sir Iohn*), F.
*singing*] *Capell; not in QF.*          33. *Fal.*] *Q* (*sir Iohn*), F (*Falst.*).

23–4. *temperality . . . pulsidge . . .
extraordinarily*] Editors translate these
as 'temper', 'pulse', 'ordinarily', but
Mistress Quickly's speech has surely a
richer flavour. *Temperality* seems to
combine 'temper' and 'quality', *pulsidge* conveys 'an impression of fulness
that is extremely apt' (Clarke, *Sh. Key,*
1879, p. 63), and *extraordinarily* suggests 'much better than usual'.

26–7. *canaries*] 'Canary' is a sweet
wine; Mistress Quickly's plural may
arise from confusion with 'canaries', a
lively dance.

28. *perfumes*] Editors translate this as
'inflames', 'perfuses', 'pervades'. All
these, together with the sense of
spirituous fragrance 'searching' the
blood, get somewhere near the Hostess's remarkable use of language.

30. *hem*] Probably a hiccough; or
perhaps some professional sound of
invitation, as in Dekker, *1 Honest*

*Whore,* IV. iii. 31–3 (Bowers, ii. 80)—
'*Wife.* . . . What said he *George,* when
he passde by thee? *Geo*[*rge*]. Troth
Mistris nothing: not so much as a Bee,
he did not hum: not so much as a
Bawd he did not hem'. 'Hem' was also
a drinking cry; at III. ii. 212–13, Shallow's drinking watchword is, 'Hem,
boys'; in *1H4,* II. iv. 17, 'Hem' is a call
to swallow a draught; and in Eliot's
*Ortho-epia Gallica,* 1593, Pt ii. 41,
drinkers cry, 'Hem, ha-hem!' while
quaffing. An actress will make any
noise she considers suitable.

31. *a good . . . gold*] A characteristic
overlap of 'A good heart conquers ill
fortunes' (Tilley, H305) and 'A good
name is better than riches (gold)'
(Tilley, N22).

33–4. *When . . . king*] Falstaff is
garbling the ballad *Sir Lancelot du Lake*
—'When Arthur first in court began /
And was approved king' (Child, *Engl.*

[*Exit Francis.*]—'And was a worthy king'—How
　　now, Mistress Doll?　　　　　　　　　　　　　　35

*Host.* Sick of a calm, yea, good faith.

*Fal.* So is all her sect; and they be once in a calm they are
　　sick.

*Doll.* A pox damn you, you muddy rascal, is that all the
　　comfort you give me?　　　　　　　　　　　　　40

*Fal.* You make fat rascals, Mistress Doll.

*Doll.* I make them? Gluttony and diseases make them, I
　　make them not.

*Fal.* If the cook help to make the gluttony, you help to

---

34. S.D.] *Capell* (*Exit* Drawer.), *Alexander.*　　36. good faith] *Q;* good-sooth *F.*
37. and] *Q;* if *F.*　　39. A . . . you, you] *Q;* You *F.*　　42. them, I] *F;* I *Q.*
44. cook help to] *Q;* Cooke *F.*

---

*and Scot. Ballads*, 1861, i. 55). The first
extant version occurs c. 1586 in
Deloney's *Garland of Good Will*
(Thomas Deloney, *Works*, ed. Mann,
1912, p. 323).

33. *Empty . . . jordan*] Victor Hugo,
claiming to be one who enjoys Shakespeare unsqueamishly, observes, 'Falstaff m'est proposé, je l'accepte, et
j'admire le *empty the jordan*' (*Wm Sh.*,
1864, p. 372); *jordan* = chamber-pot.
Tavern rooms, says Earle, are 'not
furnisht with beds apt to be defil'd, but
more necessary implements, Stooles,
Table, and a Chamber-pot' ('A
Tavern', in *Microcosmographie*). G. B.
Harrison (*Penguin Sh.*) points out that
sanitary arrangements and habits
were so crude that Lord Mountjoy's
delicate behaviour evoked his secre-
tary's admiring comment—'He . . .
was so modest in the necessities of
nature, as my selfe . . . and (I thinke)
his most familiar friends, never heard
or saw him use any liberty therein, out
of the priveledge of his private chamber, except perhaps in Irish journeys,
where he had no with-drawing roome'
(Fynes Moryson, *Itinerary*, 1907, ii.
263).

36. *calm*] 'Calm' and 'qualm' being
pronounced alike, Mistress Quickly
does not so much blunder as produce a

potential Irish bull, of which Falstaff
takes advantage. Owen Price, *English
Orthographie*, 1668, gives '*qualm*, sudden fit, *calm*, still quiet' as words of like
sound and different sense (A. J. Ellis,
*Early Engl. Pronunciation*, 1871, iii.
969).

37. *sect*] = both 'sex' (*OED*, Sect.
sb.[1] 1d.) and 'profession' (that of a
courtesan). As well as the joke, 'even in
calm waters they are seasick', Falstaff seems to mean 'women who are
quiet must be ailing' and 'courtesans
not plying their trade are out-of-
sorts'.

39. *muddy*] Combined with *rascal*
(see next note) it meant a deer sluggish
and out of season; cf. 'A dull and
muddy-mettl'd rascal' in *Ham.*, II. ii.
594.

41. *You . . . rascals*] You tempt us to
loose-living and so we grow bloated.
*Fat rascals* is an oxymoron, a 'rascal'
being a young deer 'leane & out of
season' (Puttenham, *Arte of English
Poesie*, Bk III, ch. xvii).

42. *Gluttony and diseases*] Gluttony
was naturally associated with a swollen
figure; and 'to grow fat and bloated,
is one of the consequences of the
venereal disease' (Monck Mason,
*Comments on the Last Edition* [Var. 1778]
*of Sh.'s Plays*, 1785, p. 189).

make the diseases, Doll; we catch of you, Doll, we     45
catch of you; grant that, my poor virtue, grant that.

*Doll.* Yea, joy, our chains and our jewels.

*Fal.* 'Your brooches, pearls, and ouches'—for to serve
bravely is to come halting off, you know; to come
off the breach, with his pike bent bravely; and to     50
surgery bravely; to venture upon the charged
chambers bravely;—

*Doll.* Hang yourself, you muddy conger, hang yourself!

*Host.* By my troth, this is the old fashion; you two never
meet but you fall to some discord. You are both i'     55

47. Yea, joy] *Q*; I marry *F*.     52. bravely;—] *Rowe* (bravely—), *Capell*; braue-
ly. *QF*.     53.] *Q*; *not in F*.     54. By my troth] *Q*; Why *F*.     55-6. i'good
truth] *Q*; in good troth *F*.

47. *joy*] 'pet' (Wilson, N.C.S.). But
the word is odd, and F's change arose
presumably from some actual profanity in the copy F's editor had before
him which he would feel bound to
purge—possibly 'Iesu'. An *e/o* error
and misreading of long 's' and 'u' as
'y' would turn 'Iesu' into 'joy' (Ridley,
ed. 1934).

*our chains . . . jewels*] i.e. You get
from us the valuables we have been
given.

48. *Your . . . ouches*] Capell was the
first to mark this as a quotation. It has
the air of being one, but whence it
comes is uncertain. In Percy's *Reliques*
the ballad of *The Boy and the Mantle*, 'as
revised and altered by a modern hand',
contains the line 'With brooches, rings
and owches', but this seems to borrow
from the play rather than vice versa;
the authentic version is merely 'With
brauches and ringes'. There may,
however, be a loose recollection of the
ballad, as there is of *Sir Lancelot du
Lake* in ll. 33-4, perhaps crossed with
one of Spenser, *F.Q.*, III. iv. 23—'Gold,
amber, yuorie, perles, owches, rings'.
*Ouch* = (*a*) gem, brooch; (*b*) car-
buncle, sore. For the latter sense cf.
Chapman, *Widow's Tears*, I (*Works*,
Shepherd, iii. 14), where a 'diseased
lord' has 'as many aches [pron.

aitches] in's bones, as there are ouches
in's skinne'. *OED* does not record
similar double senses for *pearls*, but
this context suggests they existed.
Hilda Hulme, *Explorations in Sh.'s
Language*, 1962, p. 197, cites from
Nicholas Udall's trans. of the *Apoph-
thegms of Erasmus*, 'little pimples . . .
[which] budden out in the noses and
faces . . . & are called the Saphires and
Rubies of the Tauerne'.

48–52. *to serve . . . bravely*] Military
ideas, e.g. of serving, occupying, using
weapons, and firing bullets, lent themselves to equivoques; cf. II. i. 13–18,
II. iv. 110–15, 145. Dekker, *2 Honest
Whore*, v. ii. 226–33 (Bowers, ii. 211),
has a similar extravaganza of improprieties; and cf. Donne, *Elegie XX*,
'Loves Warre'—'neare thrusts, pikes,
stabs, yea bullets hurt not here'. Partridge, *Sh.'s Bawdy*, is fully informa-
tive.

53.] F omits, perhaps in error for
the much more improper preceding
speech.

*conger*] An abusive term, as in Dekker, *Shoemaker's Holiday*, I. iv. 111
(Bowers, i. 36)—'goe you sowst
cunger'. The conger haunts muddy
waters. It may, like a good many
fishy metaphors, have had a sexual
implication.

good truth as rheumatic as two dry toasts, you cannot one bear with another's confirmities. What the
goodyear! one must bear, [*To Doll*] and that must be
you—you are the weaker vessel, as they say, the
emptier vessel.                                                       60

*Doll.* Can a weak empty vessel bear such a huge full hogs-
head? There's a whole merchant's venture of Bordeaux stuff in him; you have not seen a hulk better
stuffed in the hold. Come, I'll be friends with thee,
Jack, thou art going to the wars, and whether I shall      65
ever see thee again or no there is nobody cares.

*Enter* DRAWER.

*Draw.* Sir, Ancient Pistol's below, and would speak with
you.

58. S.D.] *Rowe* [*after l. 60*], *Hudson; not in QF.*     61. *Doll*] Q (*Dorothy*) [*but Doll.
as catchword after l. 60*] F.     67. Pistol's] Q; *Pistoll is* F.

56. *rheumatic*] 'She means "choleric"
(hot and dry, like "toast"); the rheumatic "humour" or "complexion" is
cold and wet' (Wilson, N.C.S.). Mistress Quickly is uncertain of her
humours; she calls Falstaff 'rheumatic' again at *H5*, II. iii. 40 (where
she seems to have the Church of Rome
in mind), and Dr Caius 'phlegmatic'
(for ?choleric) in *Wiv.*, I. iv. 79.

*dry toasts*] 'Which cannot meet but
they grate one another' (Johnson).

57. *confirmities*] 'Mistress Quickly
turns the Genevan of *Rom.*, xv. 1 ("We
which are strong, ought to beare the
infirmities [Bishops' Bible, 'frail-
nesse'] of the weake") topsyturvy'
(Noble, p. 65).

57–8. *What the goodyear*] What the
devil; 'a meaningless expletive . . .
possibly deriving from early modern
Dutch *wat goedtjaar* [which] probably
arose from . . . *good year* as an exclamation = "as I hope for a good year"'
(*OED*). *Goodyear* occurs also 'as de-
noting some undefined malefic power
or agency' (ibid.); e.g. *Lr*, v. iii. 24—
'The goodyears shall devour them,
flesh and fell'.

58–9. *one . . . vessel*] 'A woman is the
weaker vessel' is proverbial; Tilley,
W655. It derives from the Genevan of
*1 Pet.*, iii. 7—'giuing honour vnto the
woman [Bishops' Bible, 'the wife'],
as vnto the weaker vessel' (Noble, p.
178). 'Women are made to bear' (*Shr.*,
II. i. 201) is a common tag, with the
objects implied of (*a*) troubles (as
here); (*b*) children; (*c*) men—see
ll. 61–2.

60. *emptier vessel*] Mistress Quickly
may be echoing the proverb, 'Empty
vessels sound most' (Tilley, V36), or
there may be the same equivoque as in
l. 61.

61. *empty vessel*] Besides the mer-
cantile idea there is a sexual one, of a
body 'unoccupied' (see ll. 145–6). In
*Oth.*, IV. ii. 83 ('to preserve this vessel
for my lord'), 'this vessel' = this body
of mine.

62–3. *merchant's . . . stuff*] merchant-
man's cargo of Bordeaux wine.

63. *hulk*] Cf. I. i. 19, note.

67. *Ancient Pistol*] Ensign (standard-
bearer) Pistol. He is well named, the
early pistol being erratic, stupend-
ously noisy, and less dangerous than it

*Doll.* Hang him, swaggering rascal, let him not come
    hither: it is the foul-mouth'dst rogue in England.    70
*Host.* If he swagger, let him not come here. No, by my
    faith! I must live among my neighbours, I'll no
    swaggerers. I am in good name and fame with the
    very best. Shut the door, there comes no swaggerers
    here. I have not lived all this while to have swagger-    75
    ing now. Shut the door I pray you.
*Fal.* Dost thou hear, hostess?
*Host.* Pray ye pacify yourself, Sir John, there comes no
    swaggerers here.
*Fal.* Dost thou hear? It is mine ancient.    80
*Host.* Tilly-fally, Sir John, ne'er tell me: and your ancient
    swagger, a comes not in my doors. I was before
    Master Tisick the debuty t'other day, and, as he said

71–2. No . . . faith] *Q; not in F.*    72. among] *Q;* amongst *F.*    78. Pray ye] *Q;*
'Pray you *F.*    81. ne'er] *Q;* neuer *F.*    and] *Q* (&)*; not in F.*    82. swagger, a]
*This edn, conj. Maxwell;* swaggrer *Q;* Swaggerer *F.*    83. debuty] *Q;* Deputie *F.*
t'other] *Q;* the other *F.*

sounded (Jorgensen, 'My Name is
Pistol Call'd', *Sh. Q.*, i, 1950, pp. 73–
5). For equivocal senses of the name
see ll. 109–15, note. 'Bardolph as corporal and Pistol as "ancient" . . . are
singularly imperfect representatives of
their ranks. Their titles, if not intended
as gross misapplications of esteemed
offices (for which Captain Falstaff is
to blame), seem to be self-conferred
honorifics' (Jorgensen, *Sh.'s Military
World*, 1956, p. 65).

69. *swaggering rascal*] *Swaggering* is
hectoring; the word, though hardly
the performance, was a fashionable
novelty—'Swaggering is a new worde
amongst them, and rounde headed
custome giues it priuiledge with much
imitation' (Chapman, *Achilles Shield*,
1598; quoted *OED*, Swagger, *v.*).
Pistol is the 'Roaring Boy', 'swearing three-pil'd oathes in a Tauerne'
(Dekker, *Devil's Last Will and Testament*, Grosart, iii. 354), and he be-
haves like the 'roaring devil i' th' old
play' to which he is compared in *H5*,
IV. iv. 75 (D. C. Boughner, 'Pistol and
the Roaring Boys', *Sh. Ass. B.*, xi.

226–37). Nashe admonishes the type
—'You that beare the name of souldiers, and liue baselie swaggering in
euerie ale-house, hauing no other
exhibition [maintenance] but from
harlots and strumpets; seeke some
newe trade, and leaue whoring and
quarrelling, least besides the nightly
guilt of youre owne banqurout con-
sciences, Bridewell or Newgate prooue
the ende of your caueleering' (*Terrors
of the Night*, McKerrow, i. 384).

78. *pacify*] satisfy; or perhaps, keep
quiet.

81. *Tilly-fally*] Fiddlesticks.

81–2. *and . . . comes*] Q and F make
sense, but Q's is rather lame sense, and
F's solution looks perfunctory. The
emendation, proposed by J. C. Maxwell (*MLR*, 1947, p. 485), follows the
train of thought of l. 71—'If he
swagger, let him not come here': Mistress Quickly does not know Pistol but
is estimating him from Doll's account.
If Shakespeare wrote 'swagger a', this
might well look like 'swaggrer' (cf.
Wilson, *MSH*, p. 110).

83. *Tisick*] A phthisic is a consump-

to me—'twas no longer ago than Wednesday last, i'
good faith—'Neighbour Quickly,' says he—Master     85
Dumb our minister was by then—'Neighbour
Quickly,' says he, 'receive those that are civil, for',
said he, 'you are in an ill name'—now a said so, I can
tell whereupon. 'For', says he, 'you are an honest
woman, and well thought on, therefore take heed     90
what guests you receive; receive', says he, 'no swaggering companions': there comes none here. You
would bless you to hear what he said. No, I'll no
swaggerers.

*Fal.* He's no swaggerer, hostess, a tame cheater, i'faith,     95
you may stroke him as gently as a puppy greyhound.
He'll not swagger with a Barbary hen, if her feathers
turn back in any show of resistance. Call him up,
drawer.                                        [*Exit Drawer.*]

*Host.* Cheater, call you him? I will bar no honest man     100
my house, nor no cheater, but I do not love swaggering, by my troth, I am the worse when one says
'swagger'. Feel, masters, how I shake, look you, I
warrant you.

---

84. 'twas] *Q;* it was F.     Wednesday] *F;* wedsday *Q.*     84–5. i'good
faith—'Neighbour] *Kittredge;* I good faith neighbor *Q;* 'I'good faith, neighbour *Cambridge;* Neighbour F.     86. Dumb] *Q* (Dumbe); *Dombe* F.     88.
said he] *Q;* sayth hee *F.*     a] *Q;* hee *F.*     95. i'faith,] *Q;* hee: *F.*     97.
He'll] *Q;* hee will F.     99. S.D.] *Capell; not in QF.*     102. by my troth]
*Q; not in* F.

---

tive cough. The worthy official must
be somewhat decrepit.

*debuty*] The deputy of the ward was
its most responsible citizen, charged
with its good government.

86. *Dumb*] The phrase 'dumb dogs'
(from *Isaiah,* lvi. 10—'His watchmen
are ignorant, they are dumb dogs,
they cannot bark') was applied,
especially by Puritans, to unzealous
preachers. John Rainold, for instance,
urges ministers to be diligent, and
deplores 'the *ignorance* of many, that
are *dumbe dogges,* & cannot barke' (*Pro-
phecie of Obadiah,* 1613, p. 29).

87. *civil*] well-behaved.

88–9. *I . . . whereupon*] 'I know now

why he said so, it was for admitting
such riotous fellows as your ancient'
(Deighton, ed. 1893).

92. *companions*] fellows (contemptuous).

95. *tame cheater*] petty gamester or
sharper; cf. Beaumont & Fletcher,
*Fair Maid of the Inn,* IV. ii (Glover &
Waller, ix. 199)—'you . . . will be
drawn into the net by this decoy duck,
this tame cheater'.

97. *swagger*] i.e. be obstreperous.

*Barbary hen*] guinea fowl. The dramatists often use 'guinea-hen' dis-
paragingly for a woman, sometimes in
the sense of prostitute. Falstaff presumably has this in mind.

*Doll.* So you do, hostess.                                    105
*Host.* Do I? Yea, in very truth do I, and 'twere an aspen
    leaf. I cannot abide swaggerers.

*Enter Ancient* PISTOL, BARDOLPH, *and* PAGE.

*Pist.* God save you, Sir John!
*Fal.* Welcome, Ancient Pistol! Here, Pistol, I charge
    you with a cup of sack; do you discharge upon mine    110
    hostess.
*Pist.* I will discharge upon her, Sir John, with two
    bullets.
*Fal.* She is pistol-proof, sir; you shall not hardly offend
    her.                                                       115
*Host.* Come, I'll drink no proofs, nor no bullets; I'll
    drink no more than will do me good, for no man's
    pleasure, I.
*Pist.* Then to you, Mistress Dorothy! I will charge you.
*Doll.* Charge me? I scorn you, scurvy companion.          120
    What, you poor, base, rascally, cheating, lack-linen
    mate! Away, you mouldy rogue, away! I am meat
    for your master.

105. *Doll.*] *Q* (*Teresh.*), *F* (*Dol.*).    106. and 'twere] *Q; if it were F.*    107. S.D.
*Ancient*] *Q; not in F.    Bardolph, and Page.*] *Rowe; and Bardolfes boy. Q; and Bardolph
and his Boy. F.*    108. God save] *Q; 'Saue F.*    114. -proof, sir;] *Capell; proofe: sir,
Q; -proofe (Sir) F.    not*] *Q; not in F.*    116. bullets; I'll] *Q; Bullets: I will F.*
120. *Doll.*] *Q* (*Doro.*) [*so also at ll. 125, 136*], *F* (*Dol.*).

106–7. *an aspen leaf*] A proverbial
simile; Tilley, L140.
    109–15.] As at ll. 48–52, the military
terms allow quibbles. *Pistol* prompts
the same equivoques as occur (*a*) at
l. 158, and (*b*) in Webster, *Duchess of
Malfi*, II. ii. 39–40 (Lucas, ii. 58), on
'a Switzer . . . / With a Pistoll in his
great cod-piece'. *Charge* means (*a*) load
for action (a military-and-sexual
quibble), and (*b*) toast—cf. Fletcher,
*Valentinian*, v. viii (Glover & Waller,
iv. 89), 'And thus I give the first
charge [pledge] to ye all'. *Discharge*
means (*a*) go off like a firearm, and (*b*)
toast in your turn. *Bullets* carries on the
quibbling.
    114. *pistol-proof*] 'Implies, I sup-
pose, that she is past bearing' (Wilson,

N.C.S.)—certainly past bearing Pistol.
    114–15. *you . . . offend her*] whatever
you do you will not do her any harm.
Equivocal.
    *shall not hardly*] A colloquialism
('shan't hardly') still heard.
    116–18.] The Hostess is excusably
muddled by the preceding exchanges.
Whether she thinks *proofs* and *bullets*
relate to drinking is not clear. *OED*
gives no instance of 'proof' as applied
to spirits before 1705 (Proo , *sb.* 11).
*For no man's pleasure* suggests that the
conversation is still vaguely in the area
of sexual innuendo.
    120. *Charge*] Doll takes this as frank
sexual provocation.
    122–3. *meat . . . master*] A proverbial

*Pist.* I know you, Mistress Dorothy.

*Doll.* Away, you cutpurse rascal, you filthy bung, away!          125
By this wine, I'll thrust my knife in your mouldy
chaps and you play the saucy cuttle with me. Away,
you bottle-ale rascal, you basket-hilt stale juggler,
you! Since when, I pray you, sir? God's light, with
two points on your shoulder? Much!          130

*Pist.* God let me not live, but I will murder your ruff for
this.

*Fal.* No more, Pistol! I would not have you go off here.
Discharge yourself of our company, Pistol.

*Host.* No, good Captain Pistol, not here, sweet captain.          135

*Doll.* Captain! Thou abominable damned cheater, art
thou not ashamed to be called captain? And captains were of my mind, they would truncheon you

127. and] *Q;* if *F.*      129. God's light] *Q;* what *F.*      131. God . . . but] *Q;*
not in *F.*      133. *Fal.*] *Q (sir Iohn), Pope; not in F.*      133–4.] *Q; not in F.*      137.
And] *Q;* If *F.*

phrase (Tilley, M837), with, often, a
sexual meaning.

124. *I know you*] i.e. There's plenty I
could tell about you.

125. *bung*] pickpocket (lit., purse).

127. *play . . . cuttle*] Meaning uncertain; in a general sense, 'if you play
any of your tricks'. In thieves' cant a
'cuttle' or 'cuttle-bung' was the knife
for purse-slitting; perhaps also a cutpurse or cut-throat.

128. *bottle-ale*] Meaning uncertain;
perhaps 'cheap', or 'small-beer', or
'frothy'. Marston, *Scourge of Villainie*,
Sat. vi, 1–2, has, 'Why, thou bottle-
ale, / Thou barmy froth!'

*basket-hilt stale juggler*] The gist is,
'swashbuckling, out-of-date, impos-
tor'. *Basket-hilt* (a vaguely derisive
term) = having a hilt of basket-like
curved steel strips to defend the hand;
in Dekker, *Satiromastix*, iv. ii. 16
(Bowers, i. 354), Crispinus and
Fannius are 'that paire of Basket-
hiltes'.

129. *Since when*] sc. have you set up
as a soldier?

129–30. *with . . . shoulder*] all tagged
out. *Points* were tags or laces for fasten-

ing garments, here for attaching the
armour for the chest and arms.

130. *Much*] 'Exclamation indicating
incredulity' (Wilson, N.C.S.).

131. *murder*] tear, tear off; cf. l. 141.

*your ruff*] In Dekker & Middleton's
*Roaring Girl*, v. i. 314 (Bowers, iii. 90),
Moll says, 'How many are whores, in
small ruffes and still lookes?' (implying the answer, 'None'). From this it
would seem that whores wore big
ruffs. Drunken bullies in the dramatists often tear the clothes of such as
Doll; e.g. Jonson, *Bart. F.*, iv. v. 82–3
(H. & S., vi. 106)—'KNO[CKHUM] . . .
ha! doe you know who I am? shall I
teare ruffe, slit wastcoat, make ragges
of petticoat?' A 'young rank whore', in
Field's *A Woman's a Weather-cocke*, i. ii.
60 (Peery, p. 79), will 'Put on my
fighting wastcoate, and the Ruffe /
That feares no tearing'.

133–4.] F omits, probably as indecent; cf. ll. 109–15, notes.

135. *Captain Pistol*] 'Quickly hopes
to pacify him by giving him a commission' (Wilson, N.C.S.).

138–9. *truncheon you out*] cudgel you
out of the ranks with their truncheons

out, for taking their names upon you before you
have earned them. You a captain? You slave! For    140
what? For tearing a poor whore's ruff in a bawdy-
house? He a captain? Hang him, rogue, he lives
upon mouldy stewed prunes and dried cakes. A
captain? God's light, these villains will make the
word as odious as the word 'occupy', which was an    145
excellent good word before it was ill sorted: therefore captains had need look to't.

*Bard.*  Pray thee go down, good ancient.

*Fal.*  Hark thee hither, Mistress Doll.

*Pist.*  Not I! I tell thee what, Corporal Bardolph, I could    150
tear her! I'll be revenged of her.

*Page.*  Pray thee go down.

*Pist.*  I'll see her damned first! To Pluto's damnèd lake,

---

144. God's light] *Q; not in F.*    145–6. word as . . . sorted] *Q;* word Captaine
odious *F.*    147. to't] *Q;* to it *F.*    151. of] *Q;* on *F.*    152. *Page] Q (Boy), F*
[*so also at l. 222*].    153. damnèd] *Rowe;* damnd *Q;* damn'd *F.*

---

(which captains bore as signs of
authority). As Wilson (N.C.S.) notes,
Captain Fluellen uses his on Pistol in
*H5*, v. i.

139–40. *for taking . . . them*] Pistol is
not in fact guilty of this, but Doll aims
at the many bogus Elizabethan captains, often satirized in the drama.
'The uniform of a captain was easily
imitated, for it consisted of nothing
more distinctive than a rapier, scarf,
and plumes' (Cowl).

143. *stewed . . . cakes*] i.e. scraps of
brothel-fare and pastry-cooks' throw-
outs. Stewed prunes and brothels were
often associated; cf. Dekker, *Seven
Deadly Sinnes* (Grosart, ii. 44)—'a
house where they set stewed Prunes
before you' (= a brothel); *Captain
Underwit*, IV. ii (Bullen, *Old Engl. Plays*,
ii. 377)—'they [bawds] keepe themselves so in health and so soluble with
stewd prunes'; and *Meas.*, II. i. 88–90.
The term was used of bawds themselves, and Falstaff compares Mistress
Quickly to 'a stewed prune' (*1H4*, III.
iii. 128). 'Prunes, raisins of the sun, and
currants', boiled in broth, were part of
the cure for venereal disease (W.

Clowes, *The Cure of . . . Lues Venerea*,
1596, p. 161), and seem to have been
thought a preventative against it; but
dramatists also exploited the pun in
'stews'.

145–6. *as the . . . sorted*] F purges,
probably as indecent; see l. 61, note.

145. *occupy*] For the 'odious' sense,
see Thomas Heywood, *2 If You Know
Not Me* (Shepherd, i. 311)—'*Hob[son]*.
Bones-a-me, knave, a prentise must
not occupy for himself but for his
master. . . . *John.* And he cannot
occupy for his master, without the consent of his mistris. . . . I hope the sub-
urbs tolerates any man or woman to
occupy for themselves'. Jonson complains that 'Many, out of their owne
obscene Apprehensions, refuse proper
and fit words; as *occupie, nature*, and the
like: So the curious industry in some of
having all alike good, hath come
neerer a vice, then a vertue' (*Discoveries*, ll. 1545–8; H. & S., viii.
610).

153–7.] So far, Pistol seems merely
the Roaring Boy, innocent of theatrical tastes. At this precise moment he
develops an addiction to dramatic

by this hand, to th'infernal deep, with Erebus and
tortures vile also! Hold hook and line, say I! Down,     155
down, dogs! Down, faitors! Have we not Hiren
here?                                          [*Draws his sword.*]
*Host.* Good Captain Peesel, be quiet, 'tis very late i'

154. by this hand] *Q; not in F.*     th'] *Q; the F.*     with] *Q; where F.*     156.
faitors] *Q* (faters), *Capell; Fates F.*     157. S.D.] *Wilson (N.C.S.), subst.; clapping
his Hand to his Sword. Capell; not in QF.*     158. 'tis] *Q; it is F.*     158–9. i'faith] *Q;
not in F.*

gobbets, which affects almost every
subsequent speech (S. Musgrove, 'The
Birth of Pistol', *RES*, New ser., x. 56).
Shakespeare seems to be seized by a
novel idea, and Pistol grows another
quality (as Mistress Quickly rapidly
changes from the 'most sweet wench'
of *1H4*, i. ii. 46). Shakespeare draws
some of Pistol's idiom from Eliot's
*Ortho-epia Gallica*, 1593. Perhaps he
was sampling Eliot at this moment,
and was prompted to develop Pistol's
new line by coming upon the passage
given in Appendix I, p. 231 (with, particularly, the reference to Trojans,
Caesar, and, above all, Cannibals;
cf. ll. 163–4).

153–5. *Pluto's . . . also*] Typical
dramatic rant of the early 1590s.
Malone suggested a burlesque of
Peele's *Battle of Alcazar*, iv. ii. (Mal.
Soc., ll. 1230–54)—'You dastards of
the night and Erybus, / Fiends, Fairies,
hags that fight in beds of steele, /
Range through this armie with your
yron whips, / . . . Descend and take to
thy tormenting hell, / The mangled
bodie of that traitor king / . . . / Then
let the earth discouer to his ghost, /
Such tortures as vsurpers feele below /
. . . / Damnd let him be, damnd and
condemnd to beare / All torments,
tortures, plagues, and paines of hell'.
'Plutoes loathsome lake' occurs in
Greene's *Alphonsus*, iii. ii. 87 (Mal.
Soc., l. 946), 'Ile downe to hell, and
. . . / Knock at the dismall gates of
*Plutos* court' in Kyd, *Span. Trag.*, iii.
xiii. 109–10 (Boas, p. 72), and 'Ile
dragge thy cursed ghoast / Through all
the riuers of foule *Erebus*' in *Locrine*,

iii. vi. 65–6 (Mal. Soc., ll. 1345–
6). And so on, and so on, ad infini-
tum.

155. *Hold . . . line*] A proverbial tag
(Tilley, H589) from angling; meaning, more or less, 'May things go
right!' Pistol may be ranting at ran-
dom, but a similar association in *Lr*,
ii. vi. 8 ('Nero is an angler in the lake
of darkness') suggests that this follows
on 'Pluto's damnèd lake'.

156. *faitors*] rogues: originally =
'doer', 'agent', but generally pejora-
tive in 16th c.

156–7. *Have . . . here*] Pistol apparently brandishes his sword (*Hiren*
sounds like 'iron', said in Elizabethan
English with a strong 'r'). He is also
vociferating a tag (almost certainly)
from a lost play by Peele, *The Turkish
Mahamet and Hyrin [Irene] the Fair
Greek* (c. 1594). The words, or variants
of them, occur in other plays, e.g. Jonson, Chapman, and Marston, *East-
ward-Hoe*, ii. i. 107–8 (H. & S., iv. 539)
—'*Qu[ickesilver]: . . . hast thou not Hyren
here?*'; Dekker, *Satiromastix*, iv. iii. 243–
4 (Bowers, i. 366); and John Day, *Law
Tricks* (Mal. Soc., ll. 1330–1). At the
same time he is insulting Doll, since
*Hiren* implies 'harlot', as in *Merrie Conceited Iests of George Peele*, c. 1607 ('How
George read a Play-booke to a Gentleman')—'the famous play of the Turkish *Mahomet*, and *Hyrin* the faire
Greeke, in Italian called a Curtesan,
. . . in England, . . . a Whore, . . . a
Puncke'.

158. *Peesel*] 'A current colloquial
pronunciation of Pistol', admitting the
'pizzle' equivoque (Kökeritz, 'Pun-

faith; I beseek you now, aggravate your choler.

*Pist.* These be good humours indeed! Shall pack-horses,    160
And hollow pamper'd jades of Asia,
Which cannot go but thirty mile a day,
Compare with Caesars and with Cannibals,
And Troyant Greeks? Nay, rather damn them with
King Cerberus, and let the welkin roar!        165
Shall we fall foul for toys?

*Host.* By my troth, captain, these are very bitter words.

*Bard.* Be gone, good ancient, this will grow to a brawl
anon.

*Pist.* Die men like dogs! Give crowns like pins! Have we    170
not Hiren here?

*Host.* O' my word, captain, there's none such here.
What the goodyear, do you think I would deny
her? For God's sake be quiet.

*Pist.* Then feed and be fat, my fair Calipolis!        175
Come, give's some sack.

---

160–6.] *Divided as Pope; prose, QF.*    162. mile] *Q;* miles *F.*    163. Caesars] *Q;*
*Cæsar F.*    164. Troyant] *Q* (troiant)*; Troian F.*    167. captain] *Q corr., F*
(Captaine)*; captane Q uncorr.*    170. Die . . . crowns] *F;* Men like dogges giue
crownes *Q.*    172. O'] *Q* (A), *Theobald;* On *F.*    174. For God's sake] *Q;* I pray *F.*
175–7.] *As Capell; prose, QF.*    176. give's] *Q* (giues), *Capell;* giue me *F.*

ning Names', *MLN*, 1950, pp. 240–3).

159. *beseek*] Perhaps meant as a
blunder, perhaps as a provincialism;
it was a northern and North-Midland
form (*OED*).

160. *good humours*] fine goings-on;
*humour* was a catchword for freaks of
temperament or conduct.

160–2. *Shall . . . day*] Pistol mal-
treats Marlowe's famous lines wherein
Tamburlaine urges on the captive
kings who drag his chariot —'Holla, ye
pamper'd jades of Asia! / What, can ye
draw but twenty miles a day?' (*2
Tamb.*, IV. iii. 1–2).

163–4. *Caesars . . . Troyant Greeks*] An
echo of Eliot's *Ortho-epia Gallica*, 1593
(cf. Appendix I, pp. 231–2).

165. *King Cerberus*] Pistol confers
royal rank on the three-headed dog
which guarded the underworld.

*let . . . roar*] A frequent tag.

166.] Shall we quarrel over trifles?

170. *Die . . . dogs*] A proverbial ranting tag; Tilley, D509.

*Give . . . pins*] Pistol outvies heroes
like Tamburlaine, who distributed
kingdoms to their followers.

173. *What the goodyear*] Cf. ll. 57–8,
note.

175. *feed . . . Calipolis*] Parody of
Peele's *Battle of Alcazar* (Mal. Soc.),
ll. 584–618), in which Muly Mahamet
enters '*with lyons flesh vpon his sworde*'
and offers it to his starving mother,—
'Hold thee, Calypolis, feede and faint
no more / This flesh I forced from a
lyonesse / . . . / Feede then and faint not
faire Calypolis / . . . / Feede and be
fat that we may meete the foe'.
Other dramatists made play with it
also: cf. Dekker, *Satiromastix*, IV. i. 150
(Bowers, i. 352), Marston, *What You
Will*, v. i. 1 (Wood, ii. 285), and
Thomas Heywood, *The Royall King*
(Shepherd, vi. 30).

*Si fortune me tormente sperato me contento.*
Fear we broadsides? No, let the fiend give fire!
Give me some sack; and sweetheart, lie thou there!
                                        [*Lays down his sword.*]
Come we to full points here? And are etceteras nothings?

*Fal.* Pistol, I would be quiet.                                    181

*Pist.* Sweet knight, I kiss thy neaf. What! we have seen
      the seven stars.

*Doll.* For God's sake, thrust him downstairs, I cannot
      endure such a fustian rascal.                                185

*Pist.* Thrust him downstairs? Know we not Galloway
      nags?

---

177. *contento*] *Q; contente F.*     178–80.] *As Pope; prose, QF.*     179. sweet-
heart, lie] *Q corr.* (sweet hart, lie), *F, subst.;* sweet hartlie *Q uncorr.*     179. S.D.]
*Johnson; not in QF.*     180. nothings] *Q* (no things); nothing *F.*     184. For
God's sake] *Q; not in F.*

---

177. Si . . . contento] If fortune torments me, hope contents me. This is
also Pistol's curtain-line at v. v. 96.
He garbles a motto current in Spanish,
Italian, and French; which language
he thinks he is speaking is uncertain.

178. *give fire*] shoot.

179. *sweetheart . . . there*] For the
sentiment, cf. Jonson, *E.M.O.*, III. i.
80–1 (H. & S., iii. 510), when Shift
addresses his rapier—'Sell my rapier?
no, my deare, I will not bee diuorc't
from thee'. For the gesture, cf. *Rom.*,
III. i. 5–8—'Thou art like one of these
fellows that when he enters the confines of a tavern claps me his sword
upon the table and says, "God send
me no need of thee!"' Cowl gives
further parallels.

180.] Pistol's meaning is as near no-
meaning as may be; approximately,
'Is this where we come to a stop, with
nothing to follow?' *Etceteras* and
*nothings* are doubtless sexual quibbles,
the former deputizing for a coarse
word (cf. *Rom.*, II. i. 38—'An open
etcetera'; *OED*, Etcetera, 2b), the
latter (equivalent to the circle O)
meaning the same thing (cf. *Ham.*, III.
ii. 128).

182. *Sweet . . . neaf*] Courtliness col-

lapses into the plebeian, *neaf* being
dialectal for 'fist'.

183. *the seven stars*] Pistol's remark
means that they have enjoyed themselves by night; cf. Falstaff's 'We have
heard the chimes at midnight' (III. ii.
209) and 'we that go by the moon and
the seven stars' (*1H4*, I. ii. 16). *The
seven stars* are usually said to be 'the
seauen Starres, called the *Pleiades*'
(Dekker, *King's Entertainment*; Bowers,
ii. 301). But since Ursa Major (Sep-
tentriones, the Great Bear, the Big
Dipper, Charles's Wain) more evidently contains seven stars, and is a
familiar point of reference in the night
sky (since it points to the Pole Star),
one would rather think that is what is
intended. The Fool's 'The reason why
the seven stars are no moe than seven'
(*Lr.*, I. v. 38) suggests they are clearly
discernible as seven, which is more
evident of the stars in Ursa Major than
in the Pleiades.

186–7. *Know . . . nags*] i.e. We know
a harlot when we see one. 'Doll is like
a Galloway nag, because anyone may
ride her' (Sugden). '*Galway* Nagges
[are] a certaine race of little Horses in
*Scotland* [which] indure the chase with
good courage' (Gervase Markham,

*Fal.* Quoit him down, Bardolph, like a shove-groat shil-
ling. Nay, and a do nothing but speak nothing, a
shall be nothing here.                                    190
*Bard.* Come, get you downstairs.
*Pist.* What! shall we have incision? shall we imbrue?
                              [*Snatches up his sword.*]
Then death rock me asleep, abridge my doleful days!
Why then let grievous, ghastly, gaping wounds
Untwind the Sisters Three! Come, Atropos, I say!     195
*Host.* Here's goodly stuff toward!
*Fal.* Give me my rapier, boy.
*Doll.* I pray thee, Jack, I pray thee do not draw.
*Fal.* [*Drawing*] Get you downstairs.
*Host.* Here's a goodly tumult! I'll forswear keeping     200

189. and a . . . a] *Q;* if hee . . . hee *F.*     192–5.] *As Capell; prose, QF.*     192.
S.D.] *Capell, subst.; Rowe, subst.* [*after l. 195*]; *not in QF.*     195. Untwind] *Q*
(vntwinde), *F1* (vntwin'd); untwine *F3.*     196. goodly] *Q;* good *F.*     198.
pray thee . . . pray thee] *Q;* prethee . . . prethee *F.*     199. S.D.] *Rowe* [*after*
downstairs.] *not in QF.*

*Cavelarice,* 1607, Bk III, ch. i, p. 7). The
term could be mildly abusive; a
drunken Scot is called 'my *Galloway*
Nag' in Jonson, *Bart. Fair,* IV. iv. 4 (H.
& S., vi. 96). But *nag* also = prostitute,
as in 'Yon ribaudred nag of Egypt'
(*Ant.,* III. x. 10); and Wilson (N.C.S.)
cites *Willobie his Avisa,* 1594, sig. \*4ᵛ,
'they may for an Angell and a great
deale less haue hired nagges to ride at
their pleasure, such as make a sinneful
gaine of a filthy carkasse'.

    188. *Quoit*] Pitch, like a quoit.

    188–9. *shove-groat shilling*] coin
slithering along a shuffle-board. *Shove-
groat* resembled shuffle-board, a coin
being propelled along a smooth
marked board. Edward IV shillings
were often used (*Sh.'s Engl.,* ii. 467).

    192. *incision . . . imbrue*] blood-letting
(a surgical term) . . . shed blood.

    193. *death . . . asleep*] A fragment from
a poem attributed by Hawkins, *History of Music,* 1776 (iii. 30), to Anne
Boleyn, but by F. M. Padelford, *Early
16th c. Lyrics* (pp. 102, 148), to Anne's
brother George, as they both awaited
execution in 1536. It begins, 'O Death!

rocke me on slepe, / Bringe me on
quiet reste'. It occurs likewise in
Arnold Cosbie's *Vltimum Vale to the
Vaine World,* written as he lay in the
Marshalsea awaiting execution in
1591 (ed. J. P. Collier, 1863, p. 19).

    *abridge . . . days*] This is the tenor of
the song quoted but does not occur in
it; it mocks the vein of many laments,
e.g. *1 Tamburlaine,* v. ii. 223—'abridge
thy baneful days'.

    193–5. *abridge . . . Atropos*] Perhaps a
double echo of Sabren's speeches in
the last scene of *Locrine*—'I my selfe . . ./
Meane to abridge my former destenies'
(Mal. Soc., ll. 2244–5), and 'Sweet
*Atropos,* cut off my fatall thred' (ibid.,
l. 2228). Pistol is as well-versed in
classical legend and alliterative
style as are Pyramus and Thisbe in
*MND.*

    195. *Untwind*] Undo the spinning of
(obsolete for 'untwine').

    *the Sisters Three*] The Fates, Clotho,
Lachesis, Atropos. The first held the
spindle on which life's thread was
spun, the second drew the thread, the
third cut it.

house afore I'll be in these tirrits and frights! [*Falstaff thrusts at Pistol.*] So! Murder, I warrant now!
Alas, alas, put up your naked weapons, put up your
naked weapons.          [*Exit Bardolph, driving Pistol out.*]

*Doll.* I pray thee, Jack, be quiet, the rascal's gone. Ah,     205
you whoreson little valiant villain, you!

*Host.* Are you not hurt i' th' groin? Methought a made
a shrewd thrust at your belly.

[*Enter* BARDOLPH.]

*Fal.* Have you turned him out a-doors?

*Bard.* Yea, sir, the rascal's drunk. You have hurt him,     210
sir, i' th' shoulder.

*Fal.* A rascal, to brave me!

*Doll.* Ah, you sweet little rogue, you! Alas, poor ape,
how thou sweat'st! Come, let me wipe thy face.
Come on, you whoreson chops! Ah, rogue, i'faith, I     215

201. afore] *Q;* before *F.*     201–2. S.D.] *Wilson (N.C.S.); not in QF.*     204.
S.D.] *Collier 3; Exeunt* Pistol *and* Bardolph. *Capell; not in QF.*     205. pray thee]
*Q;* prethee *F.*     rascal's] *Q;* Rascall is *F.*     207. a] *Q;* hee *F.*     208. S.D.]
*Capell; not in QF.*     209. a-] *Q* (a); of *F;* o' *Cambridge.*     210. Yea] *Q;* Yes *F.*
211. i' th'] *Q* (i'th); in the *F.*     212. rascal, to . . . me!] *Theobald;* rascall to . . .
me? *Q;* Rascall to . . . me. *F.*     213. Ah, you] *Q* (A you), *F.*     215. Ah]
*Q* (a), *F.*     i'faith] *Q; not in F.*

201. *tirrits*] Perhaps a Quicklyism
telescoping 'terrors' and 'fits'; but
various dialect words are similar (e.g.
'ter', anger; 'tirr', to snarl, or be worked up; 'tirrivee', rage, commotion;
'tirry', agitated; 'terry', to provoke,
torment: Wright, *Engl. Dial. Dict.*).

206. *whoreson . . . villain*] Terms
(here) of appreciation, like 'rogue',
'ape', in l. 213.

209. *a-doors*] 'Phonetic reduction
apparently of both *of doors, o' doors,* . . .
and *at doors*' (*OED,* † A-doors).

210. *the rascal's drunk*] This is as good
a place as any for bringing to bear on
this episode *Proverbs*, xxiii. 29–33
(Genevan)—'To whome is wo? to
whome is sorowe? to whome is strife?
to whome is murmuring? to whome
are woundes without cause? & to
whome is the rednes of the eyes? Euen
to them that tarie long at wine. . . .

Loke not thou upon the wine when it
is red & when it sheweth his colour in
the cuppe, or goeth downe pleasantly.
. . . Thine eyes shall lock upon strange
women and thine heart shal speake
lewde things. Yea, thou shalt be as he
that lieth down in the midst of the sea,
or as he that sleepeth upon the top of a
mast'. (For the echo of this last sentence cf. III. i. 18–20, and note.) This is
closely resumed in the *Homily against
Gluttony and Drunkenness* (*Certain Sermons appoynted by the Queenes Maiestie,*
1574, 2nd tome, pp. 207 ff.). Direct
from the Bible, or via pulpit repetition
of the homilies, it might well influence
the audience's views of Boar's-Head
life.

213. *ape*] = fool; a playful expostu-
lation, like 'mad-headed ape', *1H4,*
II. iii. 80.

215. *chops*] fat cheeks. 'Fafelu . .

love thee. Thou art as valorous as Hector of Troy,
worth five of Agamemnon, and ten times better
than the Nine Worthies. Ah, villain!

*Fal.* A rascally slave! I will toss the rogue in a blanket.

*Doll.* Do, and thou dar'st for thy heart. And thou dost,     220
I'll canvass thee between a pair of sheets.

*Enter* MUSICIANS.

*Page.* The music is come, sir.

*Fal.* Let them play. Play, sirs! [*Music.*] Sit on my knee,
Doll. A rascal bragging slave! The rogue fled from
me like quicksilver.          225

*Doll.* I'faith, and thou followedst him like a church.
Thou whoreson little tidy Bartholomew boar-pig,
when wilt thou leave fighting a-days, and foining
a-nights, and begin to patch up thine old body for
heaven?          230

218. Ah] *Q* (a), *F*.     219. A] *F; Ah Q.*     220. and . . . And] *Q; if . . . if F.*
221. S.D.] *Q* (*enter musicke.*) [*after l. 221*], *F* (*Enter Musique*), *Dyce.*     223. S.D.]
*Singer 2; not in QF.*     226. I'faith] *Q; not in F.*     228–9. a- . . . a-] *Q* (a . . . a);
on . . . on *F.*

*Puffed vp; fat cheeked; a chops'* (Cotgrave).

215, 218. *Ah, rogue . . . Ah, villain*] Q reads 'a rogue', 'a villain', but Doll is still addressing Falstaff, appreciatively.

216. *Hector*] The most valiant and honourable of the Trojans.

217. *Agamemnon*] The Greek general was popularly esteemed; cf. J. Cooke, *Greene's Tu Quoque* (Hazlitt's *Dodsley*, xi. 213)—'This is the captain of brave citizens; / The Agamemnon of all merry Greeks'. He is mentioned as a popular stage figure in *Captain Underwit*, II. i (Bullen, *Old Engl. Plays*, ii. 339)—'like Cavaliers with tilting feathers, / Gaudy as *Agamemnons* in the play'.

217–18. *ten . . . Worthies*] High praise indeed; the Nine Worthies were generally reckoned to be three Pagans —Hector, Alexander, Julius Caesar; three Jews—Joshua, David, Judas Maccabeus; and three Christians— Arthur, Charlemagne, Godfrey of Bouillon.

220. *for thy heart*] at the risk of thy life.

221. *I'll . . . sheets*] i.e. I'll toss you about too, between the sheets (with a play on 'canvas' as sheet-material).

226. *thou . . . church*] An odd comparison, perhaps drawn from Nashe, *Summer's Last Will*, l. 1031 (McKerrow, iii. 266), where Bacchus has a 'paunch . . . built like a round church'. Doll is either ironical ('You didn't budge an inch') or simply joking ('you looked like a great building lurching about').

227. *tidy*] 'bonny; fat, plump . . . Now *dial*.' (*OED*, Tidy. a.2).

*Bartholomew boar-pig*] Bartholomew Fair, on St Bartholomew's Day (24 August), was a great occasion for the dressing and cooking of pig-flesh. *Boar-pig* = young boar.

228. *foining*] thrusting; cf. II. i. 13–18, note.

*Enter*[*, behind,*] *the* PRINCE *and* POINS *disguised*
[*as drawers*].

*Fal.* Peace, good Doll, do not speak like a death's-head,
do not bid me remember mine end.

*Doll.* Sirrah, what humour's the Prince of?

*Fal.* A good shallow young fellow; a would have made a
good pantler, a would ha' chipped bread well.          235

*Doll.* They say Poins has a good wit.

*Fal.* He a good wit? Hang him, baboon! His wit's as
thick as Tewkesbury mustard; there's no more conceit in him than is in a mallet.

*Doll.* Why does the Prince love him so, then?          240

*Fal.* Because their legs are both of a bigness, and a plays
at quoits well, and eats conger and fennel, and

230. S.D. *behind*] *Var.* '78; *not in QF.*    *the*] *F; not in Q.*    *disguised*] *F; not in Q.*
*as drawers*] *Capell, subst.; not in QF.*    233. humour's] *Q;* humor is *F.*    234–5.
a would . . . a] *Q;* hee would . . . hee *F.*    235. ha'] *Q* (a), *Cambridge;* haue *F.*
236. has] *Q;* hath *F.*    237. wit's] *Q;* Wit is *F.*    238. there's] *Q;* there is *F.*
240. does] *Q;* doth *F.*    241. a plays] *Q;* hee playes *F.*

231. *death's-head*] skull, used as a *memento mori.*

233. *humour*] disposition.

235. *pantler*] pantryman.

*chipped bread*] Pantlers chipped the hard crust off loaves; cf. Fletcher, *Bloody Brother*, III. ii (Waller, iv. 286)— 'poor Paul the Pantler, / That thus am clipt, because I chipt / The cursed Crust of Treason / With Loyal Knife'. Andrew Boorde advises that 'Burnt breade, and harde crustes, & pasty crustes, doth ingendre color [choler], aduste and melancholy humours; wherfore chyp the vpper crust of your breade' (*Dyetary of Helth*, 1542, EETS, Extra ser., x, 1870, p. 261).

238. *Tewkesbury mustard*] 'Excellent mustard' was associated with Tewkesbury (Fynes Moryson, *Itinerary*, 1907, III. i. 54), and it was apparently invoked proverbially; Brome, *City Wit*, III. i (*Works*, Shepherd, i. 310) has, 'Ile lay all my skill to a messe of *Tewksbury* Mustard she sneezes thrice within these three houres'. Still, Falstaff's analogy is odd; 'He's as sharp, as if he

liv'd upon Tewksbury-Mustard' (Tilley, M1333) shows that, as one would expect, sharpness rather than thickness was the usual ground of comparison between mustard and wit.

*conceit*] invention, imagination, wit.

239. *a mallet*] a wooden (therefore heavy and solid) hammer. *OED* gives as proverbial, '*As sad* (i.e. dull) *as any mallet*', and quotes Milton, *Colasterion* (*Works*, 1851, iv. 357)—'I amaze me, though the fancy of this doubt be as obtuse and sad as any mallet'. For a similar image cf Tilley, B220—'As dull as a Beetle' (heavy hammer); Lyly, *Midas*, I. ii. 66 (Bond, iii. 121)— 'Thou hast a beetle head'; and *Shr.*, IV. i. 160–'beetle-headed . . . knave'.

241. *legs*] 'Legs were important to men of fashion until the trousers eclipsed them' (Wilson, N.C.S.); cf. II. ii. 15, note.

242. *eats . . . fennel*] has a good digestion and a dull wit. Conger-eel, unless well cooked or pickled, was considered a heavy, indigestible food, liable to blunt the wits. Beaumont &

drinks off candles' ends for flap-dragons, and rides
the wild mare with the boys, and jumps upon joint-
stools, and swears with a good grace, and wears his          245
boots very smooth like unto the sign of the Leg, and
breeds no bate with telling of discreet stories, and

246. boots] *Q;* Boot *F.*

Fletcher, *Philaster,* ii. i (Glover &
Waller, i. 93), list 'freshe Porke,
Conger, and clarified Whay' as 'dul-
lers of the vital spirits'. *Fennel,* a fra-
grant yellow herb, was 'used as a sauce
with fish hard of digestion' (Beisley,
*Sh.'s Garden,* 1864, p. 158).

243. *drinks . . . flap-dragons*] i.e. per-
forms acts of bravado; cf. Beaumont
& Fletcher, *Monsieur Thomas,* ii. ii
(Glover & Waller, iv. 110)—'carowse
her health in Cans and candles ends'.
A flap-dragon was a small object float-
ing on liquor. Either the object was
aflame and had itself either to be
dodged while the liquor was drunk or
else extinguished in the mouth (perhaps also swallowed—as presumably
here); or the liquor was aflame and the
object had to be gulped out of it (as
raisins are in the game of snap-
dragon). It is not surprising that 'our
Flemish corporal was lately choked
at Delft with a flap-dragon' (W. R.,
*Match at Midnight,* ii. i [Hazlitt's
*Dodsley,* xiii. 44]).

243–4. *rides . . . mare*] Tilley, M655,
gives many examples of 'To ride (shoe)
the wild mare'. These were two different games, sometimes confused.
*Riding the wild mare* could be either
playing see-saw (which, though most
editors propose it, seems an unlikely
pastime for Poins) or (much likelier),
'A play among boys, wherein the person who acts the mare, slides over the
shoulders of several others, who are
linked together; and is strapped with
leathern aprons, and the like, while he
is getting over' (Wright, *Engl. Dial.
Dict.,* Mare, *sb.* 2(1)). Dr Harold
Brooks calls my attention to an account
by his father, the Rev. Jospeh Barlow

Brooks, in *Lancashire Bred* [1949], p. 54,
which runs, 'This game was a great
favourite in our school yard and I
think it was common in our county
and in Yorkshire. . . . Four or five boys
arrange in turn to jump onto the
backs of four or five other boys and
remain [in] the saddle until the under
boys sink under their weight. [These
latter boys] fix themselves tightly one
behind the other, with heads in back-
sides, the first being supported by the
school-yard wall. The jumpers take a
considerable run, especially the first as
he must try to land on the first back
and thus give plenty of room for the
others who follow'.

244–5. *jumps . . . stools*] A sign of
boisterous spirits; cf. Jonson, *Silent
Woman,* iv. i. 101–2 (H. & S., v. 221)—
'If [she love] actiuitie, be seene . . .
leaping ouer stooles, for the credit of
your back', and Middleton, *Chaste
Maid,* iii. iii. 119–21 (Bullen, v. 70–1)
—'when you come to your inn, / If you
leapt over a joint-stool or two, / 'Twere
not amiss' (spoken to a foolish gallant).
*Joint-stool* = one made of parts joined
and fitted together.

245–6. *wears . . . smooth*] Having a
good leg, Poins wore well-fitting
boots. Those whose legs were indif-
ferent would wear ruffled boots; cf.
Marston, *Antonio & Mellida,* v. i
(Wood, i. 56–7)—'when I see one . . .
wears a ruffled boot, I feare the
fashion of his legge'.

246. *like . . . Leg*] as smooth as the
well-booted leg shown as a sign over a
bootmaker's shop.

247. *breeds . . . stories*] Since the tenor
of Falstaff's comments is that Poins is a
brainless boon companion, the sense

such other gambol faculties a has that show a weak
mind and an able body, for the which the Prince
admits him: for the Prince himself is such another,   250
the weight of a hair will turn the scales between
their avoirdupois.

*Prince.* Would not this nave of a wheel have his ears cut
off?

*Poins.* Let's beat him before his whore.   255

*Prince.* Look whe'er the withered elder hath not his poll
clawed like a parrot.

*Poins.* Is it not strange that desire should so many years
outlive performance?

*Fal.* Kiss me, Doll.   260

*Prince.* Saturn and Venus this year in conjunction!
What says th'almanac to that?

*Poins.* And look whether the fiery Trigon his man be not

---

248. a has] *Q; hee hath F.*   251. a] *Q; an F.*   the scales] *F; scales Q.*
255. Let's] *Q; Let vs F.*   256. whe'er] *Q (where), Neilson; if F.*   262. th']
*Q; the F.*

---

253. *nave of a wheel*] Falstaff is circular (*nave* = hub, boss), and, quibblingly, a 'knave' as well.

253–4. *have ... off*] 'A Star-Chamber penalty for defaming royalty' (Winstanley, ed. 1918).

255. *beat him*] 'The punishment for incontinence' (Wilson, N.C.S.), usually applied to prostitutes but here proposed for the equally erring client.

256. *withered elder*] A seeming quibble; (*a*) decrepit old man; (*b*) sapless elder-tree (cf. 'dead elm', l. 328).

256–7. *his poll ... parrot*] 'Doll is rumpling his hair' (A. Chester, ed. 1957).

may be (as appears on the face of it), 'being harmless in his stories he causes no offence (*no bate* = no strife). But the other, sarcastic, sense—'he breeds no annoyance in his hearers by being tamely discreet', i.e. he delights them with improper stories—seems more appropriate to Falstaff's scandal-mongering.

261. *Saturn ... conjunction*] *Conjunction* = 'apparent proximity of two planets or other heavenly bodies' (*OED*, Conjunction 3). As 'the patriarch of the gods' (Wilson, N.C.S.), Saturn governed old age with its morose wits and appetites, and no planet could be more opposed to Venus. Their conjunction, Johnson observes, 'was indeed a prodigy. The astrologers, says *Ficinus*, remark, that *Saturn* and *Venus* are never conjoined'. Apparently the astrologers are wrong, but excusably so, since the conjunction is rarely observable, being low on or below the horizon.

262. *What ... that*] Almanacs with astrological and other predictions were (as they still are) sold cheaply to the credulous.

263. *fiery Trigon*] The zodiac's twelve signs were divided into four trigons (= triangles) or triplicities. One (which Bardolph's face recalls) consisted of the three fiery signs—Aries, Leo, Sagittarius; the others, respectively, were of three airy,

lisping to his master's old tables, his note-book, his
counsel-keeper.                                                    265
*Fal.* Thou dost give me flattering busses.
*Doll.* By my troth, I kiss thee with a most constant heart.
*Fal.* I am old, I am old.
*Doll.* I love thee better than I love e'er a scurvy young
boy of them all.                                                  270
*Fal.* What stuff wilt have a kirtle of? I shall receive
money a-Thursday, shalt have a cap tomorrow. A
merry song! Come, it grows late, we'll to bed.
Thou't forget me when I am gone.
*Doll.* By my troth, thou't set me a-weeping and thou     275
sayst so. Prove that ever I dress myself handsome
till thy return, —Well, hearken a' th'end.
*Fal.* Some sack, Francis.
*Prince.* ⎫
*Poins.*  ⎭ [*Coming forward*] Anon, anon, sir.
*Fal.* Ha! A bastard son of the King's? And art not thou     280
Poins his brother?

264. master's] *F*; master, *Q*.     267. By my troth] *Q*; Nay truely *F*.     271. wilt]
*Q*; wilt thou *F*.     272. a-] *Q*; on *F*; o' *Capell*.     shalt] *Q*; thou shalt *F*.     273.
we'll] *Q*; wee will *F*.     274. Thou't] *Q*; Thou wilt *F*.     275. By my troth] *Q*;
*not in F*.     thou't] *Q*; Thou wilt *F*.     and] *Q*; if *F*.     277. a' th'] *Q* (a'th);
the *F*.     279. S.D.] *Capell*; *not in QF*.     281. Poins his] *Q*; *Poines,* his *F*.

three watery, and three earthy signs.
　264. *lisping ... tables*] i.e. whispering
love to his master's old confidante. For
'tables', 'table-book', as a notebook for
assignations, cf. Dekker, *2 Honest
Whore*, i. i. 84–5 (Bowers, ii. 139)—
'*Lod.* A pox on her, I was sure her
name was in my Table-booke once'.
Hilda Hulme (*Explorations in Sh.'s
Language*, 1962, p. 137) shows that
there was an Elizabethan equivoque
by which the woman is the 'tables'
(tablet) on whom the man uses his
'pen'. To lisp, or 'speak in the soft
voice of a lover' (Monck Mason,
p. 190), a mode of address hardly
expected from Bardolph, was that in
which the deceiver reputedly coaxed
his victims, as Chaucer's Friar 'lipsed
for his wantownesse, / To make his
Englissh sweete upon his tonge'; cf.

Beaumont & Fletcher, *Mad Lover*, i. i
(Glover & Waller, iii. 11)—'He . . . /
Lisps when he lists to catch a Cham-
bermaid'.
　268. *I am old*] The theme of Time.
　271. *kirtle*] gown consisting of bodice
and skirt.
　277. *hearken a' th'end*] Proverbial;
Tilley, E125. One of many variants of
the Latin 'respice finem'. Doll means,
'Wait for the outcome, and then judge
my faithfulness'.
　279. *Anon, anon, sir*] Coming, sir.
The drawer's habitual cry, as in *1H4*,
ii. iv. 36 ff.
　281. *Poins his*] Poins's. Some editors
follow F, reading 'Poins, his'; but Falstaff seems to mean, 'You two, though
only drawers, look just like Hal and
Poins: one of you—Hal's double—
must be an unacknowledged bastard

*Prince.* Why, thou globe of sinful continents, what a life
    dost thou lead!

*Fal.* A better than thou—I am a gentleman, thou art a
    drawer.         285

*Prince.* Very true, sir, and I come to draw you out by the
    ears.

*Host.* O the Lord preserve thy good Grace! By my troth,
    welcome to London! Now the Lord bless that sweet
    face of thine! O Jesu, are you come from Wales?    290

*Fal.* Thou whoreson mad compound of majesty, by this
    light flesh and corrupt blood [*Leaning his hand upon
    Doll*], thou art welcome.

*Doll.* How! You fat fool, I scorn you.

*Poins.* My lord, he will drive you out of your revenge and    295
    turn all to a merriment, if you take not the heat.

*Prince.* You whoreson candle-mine you, how vilely did
    you speak of me even now, before this honest, virtu-
    ous, civil gentlewoman!

*Host.* God's blessing of your good heart! and so she is, by    300
    my troth.

*Fal.* Didst thou hear me?

*Prince.* Yea, and you knew me, as you did when you ran
    away by Gad's Hill; you knew I was at your back,
    and spoke it on purpose to try my patience.    305

288. good] *F; not in Q.*   By my troth] *Q; not in F.*   289. the Lord] *Q;* Heauen
*F.*   290. O Jesu] *Q;* what *F.*   292. light flesh] *F;* light, flesh *Q.*   292–3.
S.D.] *Rowe; not in QF.*   298. even] *F; not in Q.*   299. gentlewoman] *Q* [*first
state*] (gentle- / woman), *F;* gentle- / oman *Q* [*second state*].   300. God's blessing
of] *Q;* 'Blessing on *F.*   303. Yea] *Q;* Yes *F.*

of the King's, and the other a brother
of Poins'.

   282. *sinful continents*] (*a*) sinful parts
of the world; (*b*) receptacles of sin
(*continent* = that which contains); (*c*)
sinful contents (*continent* = that which
is contained).

   290. *from Wales*] A reminder, in the
tavern frivolity, that Hal is a responsible leader; cf. i. iii. 83.

   291. *compound*] mass, lump.

   291–2. *by . . . blood*] Trying to divert attention from himself to Doll
(cf. ll. 295–6), Falstaff 'jokingly extends the common oath *by this light*

by adding *flesh and blood*' (Delius, ed.
1857).

   296. *if . . . heat*] Probably, 'if you do
not show yourself angry', though perhaps, 'if you do not strike while the
iron is hot'.

   297. *candle-mine*] 'inexhaustible magazine of tallow' (Johnson).

   298. *honest*] chaste.

   300. *God's . . . heart*] Proverbial;
Tilley, G266.

   303–4. *you knew . . . Hill*] Hal sarcas-
tically recalls Falstaff's claim, 'By the
Lord, I knew ye as well as he that made
ye' (*1H4*, ii. iv. 295).

*Fal.* No, no, no, not so; I did not think thou wast within
    hearing.

*Prince.* I shall drive you then to confess the wilful abuse,
    and then I know how to handle you.

*Fal.* No abuse, Hal, o'mine honour, no abuse.          310

*Prince.* Not?—to dispraise me, and call me pantler, and
    bread-chipper, and I know not what?

*Fal.* No abuse, Hal.

*Poins.* No abuse?

*Fal.* No abuse, Ned, i'th'world, honest Ned, none. I dis-          315
    praised him before the wicked [*Turns to the Prince*]
    that the wicked might not fall in love with thee:
    in which doing, I have done the part of a careful
    friend and a true subject, and thy father is to give
    me thanks for it. No abuse, Hal; none, Ned, none;          320
    no, faith, boys, none.

*Prince.* See now whether pure fear and entire cowardice
    doth not make thee wrong this virtuous gentle-
    woman to close with us. Is she of the wicked? Is
    thine hostess here of the wicked? Or is thy boy of the          325
    wicked? Or honest Bardolph, whose zeal burns in
    his nose, of the wicked?

*Poins.* Answer, thou dead elm, answer.

*Fal.* The fiend hath pricked down Bardolph irrecover-

---

310. o'] *Q* (a), *Cambridge; on F.*    312. chipper] *Q*; chopper *F.*    315. i'th'] *Q*
(i'th); in the *F.*    316. S.D.] *Sisson; not in QF.*    317. thee] *Q*; him *F.*
321. faith] *Q*; *not in F.*    325. thy] *Q*; the *F.*

316. *the wicked*] Mockery of Puritan
idiom for non-Puritans; cf. Overbury,
*Characters; A Button-Maker of Amster-
dame*—'most of the wicked (as he calls
them) be there . . .'; and Butler, *Hudibras*, II. ii. 251–2.

317. *thee*] F reads, more expectedly,
'him'; but Falstaff changes his address
during the speech from Poins to Hal
('thy father', l. 319), and may as well
do so here as later. For a precisely
similar change of address see II. i.
72–4.

326. *zeal*] Another Puritan key-
word; cf. Dekker, *If This Be Not a
Good Play*, v. iv. 262 (Bowers, iii. 210)

—'*Pur[itan].* Tis a burning zeale must
consume the wicked'; and Jonson,
*Alchemist*, III. i. 4–5 (H. & S., v. 340–1)
—'*Ana[nias].* In pure zeale, / I doe
not like the man: He is a *heathen*'.

328. *dead elm*] rotten support (for
your friends). The elm is a big tree,
dangerous when rotten, and it traditionally supported the vine (Virgil,
*Georgics*, i. 2–3)—'. . . ulmisque
adiungere vites'. Shakespeare twice
uses it for the man on whom the
woman is dependent—*Err.*, II. ii. 176,
*MND.*, IV. i. 49.

329. *pricked down*] marked on his
list.

able, and his face is Lucifer's privy-kitchen, where   330
he doth nothing but roast malt-worms. For the
boy, there is a good angel about him, but the devil
attends him too.

*Prince.* For the women?

*Fal.* For one of them, she's in hell already, and burns   335
poor souls. For th'other, I owe her money, and
whether she be damned for that I know not.

*Host.* No, I warrant you.

*Fal.* No, I think thou art not, I think thou art quit for
that. Marry, there is another indictment upon   340
thee, for suffering flesh to be eaten in thy house,

---

332–3. devil attends] *This edn;* diuel blinds *Q;* Deuill outbids *F;* devil's behind
conj. Wilson (*N.C.S.*); devil bloats conj. A. Walker.     335. she's] *Q;* shee is *F.*
336. th'other] *Q;* the other *F.*

---

330. *Lucifer's privy-kitchen*] Like any
nobleman, Lucifer would have a kit-
chen for his own service; cf. Nabbes,
*Spring's Glory* (Bullen, *Old Engl. Plays*,
New ser., ii. 230)—'Shrovetide. At any
Noblemans house, I can licke my
fingers in a privy kitchin'.

331. *malt-worms*] topers.

332. *good angel*] An allusion to the
belief, expressed in *Matt.*, xviii. 10,
that every individual has a guardian
angel—'See that ye despise not one of
these little ones; for I say vnto you,
that in heauen their Angels alwayes
beholde the face of my Father which is
in heauen' (Genevan).

333. *attends him too*] Q's 'blinds' and
F's 'outbids' are both unconvincing,
and editors are hesitant. The discrepancy is odd. Wilson (N.C.S.) suggests that Shakespeare perhaps wrote
'diuels behind', which was misread as
'diuels blynd' and then altered to
'diuel blinds'. In both Q and F the
'too' is unsuitable. Sisson reads 'to't'
and eases the sense. But the trouble
must lie in the verb; F's compositor
took it as 'outbids' and perhaps in his
copy it began with some minim-
strokes, before the longer strokes taken
as 'bl' (Q) or 'tb' (F). This possibility
tells against Dr Alice Walker's proposed 'bloats' (i.e. 'smokes', 'kippers'),

but would be satisfied by 'attends',
which also would make sense of 'too',
calling up the familiar picture of the
soul accompanied by both good and
bad angels. Cf. *Wiv.*, I. iii. 50–1 (Q
text)—'She hath legions of angels. / As
many diuels attend her'.

335. *burns*] infects (with venereal
disease).

337. *damned*] Falstaff may be thinking of theological condemnations of
money-lending.

339–40. *quit for that*] (*a*) forgiven,
through your charity; (*b*) repaid, insofar as you ever will be!—i.e. you've
said goodbye to it.

341–4. *flesh . . . eaten . . . vict'lers . . .
mutton*] A double sense lurks in all
these; e.g. 'was the duke a flesh-
monger' (= dealer in flesh), *Meas.*, v.
i. 337; men 'Are all but stomachs,
and we all but food: / They eat us
hungrily', *Oth.*, III. iv. 104–5; 'This
informer came into *Turnball-street* to a
Victualling-house, and there falls in
league with a Wench . . . this . . . fellow
informs against the Bawd that kept the
house', Webster, Rowley, and Heywood, *Cure for a Cuckold*, IV. i. 120–30
(Lucas, iii. 70); 'a laced mutton' (= a
woman), *TGV*, I. i. 103, and 'the duke
. . . would eat mutton on Fridays',
*Meas.*, III. ii. 191–2.

contrary to the law, for the which I think thou wilt
howl.

*Host.* All vict'lers do so. What's a joint of mutton or two
in a whole Lent?                                          345

*Prince.* You, gentlewoman,—

*Doll.* What says your Grace?

*Fal.* His Grace says that which his flesh rebels against.

> *Peto knocks at door.*

*Host.* Who knocks so loud at door? Look to th'door
there, Francis.                                          350

> *Enter* PETO.

*Prince.* Peto, how now, what news?

*Peto.* The King your father is at Westminster,
    And there are twenty weak and wearied posts
    Come from the north; and as I came along
    I met and overtook a dozen captains,                 355
    Bareheaded, sweating, knocking at the taverns,
    And asking every one for Sir John Falstaff.

---

344. vict'lers] *Q* (vitlars), *F* (Victuallers), *Kittredge.*     What's] *Q*; What is *F.*
348. S.D.] *Q*; *not in F.*     349. to th'] *Q* (too'th); to the *F.*     350. S.D.] *F*; *not in*
*Q.*     352. Westminster] *Qa,F*; Weminster *Qb.*

342. *contrary to the law*] The sale of
meat in Lent was forbidden by law,
though ineffectively. With despairing
consistency the Privy Council proclamations for nearly every year from
1588 command, 'First her Maiesties
pleasure is, vpon her vnderstanding of
the great disorders heretofore and
especially the last Lent committed in
killing and eating flesh in the time of
Lent', that innkeepers shall be under
£100 bond not to prepare meat dishes
save for customers specially licensed to
eat them (Humfrey Dyson, *A Booke
Containing all such Proclamations as were
published during the Raigne of the late
Queene Elizabeth,* 1618).

348. *His Grace . . . against*] 'i.e. His
"grace" (politeness) calls her a lady
[gentlewoman] but his manhood
knows her to be something very different' (Wilson, N.C.S.). There may
also lurk contrasts between (*a*)

spiritual grace and fleshly lusts, based
on *Galatians,* v. 17—'For the flesh
lusteth against the Spirit, and the
Spirit against the flesh'; and (*b*) 'His
Grace' (his princely condition) and
his common human desires.

352-7.] The sudden urgency strikingly offsets the timeless leisure of the
scene hitherto. Wilson (N.C.S.) stresses the extreme haste indicated by *bare-
headed* (l. 356) and cites Percy Mac-
quoid in *Sh.'s Engl.,* ii. 109—'The hat
was a great asset in a well-dressed
man's attire; . . . he sat at church and
at meals with it on, and only removed
it with most profuse ceremony on
meeting a lady, instantly replacing it;
he remained uncovered only at court
and in the presence of royalty.
Ophelia remarks on Hamlet's hatless
appearance—"with his doublet all
unbrac'd; / No hat upon his head"
(*Ham.,* ii. i. 78–9)'.

*Prince.*  By heaven, Poins, I feel me much to blame,
    So idly to profane the precious time,
    When tempest of commotion, like the south    360
    Borne with black vapour, doth begin to melt
    And drop upon our bare unarmed heads.
    Give me my sword and cloak. Falstaff, good night.
                          *Exeunt Prince and Poins.*

*Fal.*  Now comes in the sweetest morsel of the night, and
    we must hence and leave it unpicked. [*Knocking*   365
    *within. Exit Bardolph.*] More knocking at the door?

              [*Enter* BARDOLPH.]

    How now, what's the matter?
*Bard.*  You must away to court, sir, presently.
    A dozen captains stay at door for you.
*Fal.*  [*To the Page*] Pay the musicians, sirrah. Farewell,   370
    hostess; farewell, Doll. You see, my good wenches,
    how men of merit are sought after; the undeserver
    may sleep, when the man of action is called on.
    Farewell, good wenches: if I be not sent away post,
    I will see you again ere I go.                375
*Doll.*  I cannot speak; if my heart be not ready to burst—

358. to blame] Q (too blame), F.    363.] *As Q;* Giue ... Cloake: / *Falstaffe* ... night. / F.    363. S.D.] *Q; Exit. F; Exeunt* Prince, Poi. Pet. *and* Bar. *Capell.* 365–6. S.D. *Knocking within.*] *Capell, subst., Dyce; not in QF.    Exit Bardolph.*] *This edn; not in QF.*    366. S.D. *Enter Bardolph*] *Capell; not in QF.*    370. S.D.] *Capell* [*after* sirrah.]; *not in QF.*

358. *to blame*] Q's 'too blame' could mean 'too blameworthy' (cf. 'too wilful-blame', *1H4*, III. i. 177; 'The Contents [of Edgar's supposed letter] ... / Are too blame', *Lr*, I. ii. 44 [F text]). But Hal is not comparing degrees of blameworthiness but feeling himself much in fault; so Q's 'too' = to.

360. *south*] The south wind supposedly brought storms; cf. *1H4*, v. i. 3–6—'The southern wind / ... Foretells a tempest and a blustering day'.

363. S.D.] F sends only Hal off here, Q Hal and Poins. Capell added Bardolph and Peto, and most editors follow. But Hal and Poins belong to-

gether and should depart so, whilst Falstaff's entourage bustles around, taking farewell of Mistress Quickly and Doll. This is the last we see of Poins.

368. *presently*] at once.

370. *Pay ... sirrah*] A page carried his master's purse (cf. I. ii. 235) and paid incidental expenses.

372–3. *the undeserver ... on*] Chapman apparently echoes this, in an inverse sense, in *May Day*, I. i. 370–1 (*Comedies*, ed. Parrott, p. 174)—'that employment should go with the undeserver, while men of service sleep at home'.

374. *post*] posthaste.

　　　Well, sweet Jack, have a care of thyself.
*Fal.* Farewell, farewell.

　　　　　　　*Exit [with Bardolph, Peto, Page, and Musicians].*

*Host.* Well, fare thee well. I have known thee these
　　　twenty-nine years, come peascod-time, but an　　　380
　　　honester and truer-hearted man—Well, fare thee
　　　well.

*Bard.* [*At the door*] Mistress Tearsheet!

*Host.* What's the matter?

*Bard.* Bid Mistress Tearsheet come to my master.　　385

*Host.* O, run Doll, run; run good Doll; come. She comes
　　　blubbered. [*To Doll*] Yea, will you come, Doll?　*Exeunt.*

---

378. S.D. *Exit*] *Qb,F; not in Qa.　　with . . . Musicians*] *This edn; not in QF; Exeunt
Fal. and Bar. Capell.*　　383. S.D.] *Wilson (N.C.S.), Capell, subst.; not in QF.*
386–7. come . . . Doll?*] *Q; not in F.*　　387. S.D. *To Doll*] *Sisson; not in QF.*

---

378. S.D.] Qb,F mark *exit* for Falstaff only, but this seems the right
moment for his fellows also to leave.
This is the last we see of Peto.

380. *peascod-time*] time when peas are
podding. The precision with which
Mistress Quickly dates a 29-year-old
meeting is entirely touching.

380–1. *an honester . . . man*] 'Falstaff is
neither honest nor true-hearted, as she
has known to her cost, but he has her
admiration and affection, and so she
uses the words of praise that come most
easily to her tongue' (Priestley, *Engl.
Comic Characters*, 1925, p. 80). 'These
valedictory words (printed also in the

folio to indicate a broken speech, as if
unfinished from incapacity to express
all she feels of admiration) uttered by
hostess Quickly after nearly thirty
years' experience of Sir John's honesty
and truth, serve better than pages of
commentary upon his powers of fascination. The hostess's blind idolatry,
Bardolph's toughly worshipping attachment (as seen in *Henry V*) form the
handsomest excuse for the bewitch-
ment with which the Prince seeks his
society' (Clarke, ed. 1865).

387. *blubbered*] with tear-stained
face.

# ACT III

## SCENE I.—[*Westminster. The Palace.*]

*Enter the* KING *in his nightgown, with a* PAGE.

*King.* Go call the Earls of Surrey and of Warwick;
But ere they come, bid them o'er-read these letters
And well consider of them. Make good speed.

*Exit [Page].*

How many thousand of my poorest subjects
Are at this hour asleep! O sleep, O gentle sleep,            5
Nature's soft nurse, how have I frighted thee,
That thou no more wilt weigh my eyelids down,
And steep my senses in forgetfulness?
Why rather, sleep, liest thou in smoky cribs,
Upon uneasy pallets stretching thee,                        10
And husht with buzzing night-flies to thy slumber,
Than in the perfum'd chambers of the great,
Under the canopies of costly state,
And lull'd with sound of sweetest melody?

### ACT III

#### *Scene* I

ACT III SCENE I] F (*Actus Tertius. Scena Prima.*]; *not in* Q.        *Location. Westminster.*] *Dyce.        The Palace.*] *Theobald.        S.D. Enter . . . nightgown*] *Qb; Enter
the King F; not in Qa.        with a Page*] F; *alone Qb; not in Qa.        1–108.*] *Qb,F; not
in Qa.        1.* Warwick] *Qb (War.), F.        3.* S.D.] F (*Exit.*), *Rowe; not in Qb.*
*10.* pallets] *Qb; Pallads F.        11.* husht with buzzing night-flies] *Qb; huisht with
bussing Night, flies F.        14.* sound] *Qb; sounds F.*

On the omission of this scene from
Qa see Intro., p. lxxiii.
S.D. *nightgown*] dressing-gown.
5. *O . . . sleep*] An apparent echo of
Sidney's sonnet beginning 'Come
Sleepe, ô Sleepe, the certaine knot of
peace, / The baiting place of wits, the
balme of woe' (*Astrophel*, 39)—an

apparent anticipation also of *H5*, IV. i.
283–301, and *Mac.*, II. ii. 36–40. Wilson (N.C.S.) points to Daniel, *C.W.*,
iii. 115, for the idea also; cf. Appendix
I, p. 209.
9. *cribs*] hovels.
10. *pallets*] beds (often of humble
kind).

O thou dull god, why li'st thou with the vile                    15
In loathsome beds, and leav'st the kingly couch
A watch-case, or a common 'larum-bell?
Wilt thou upon the high and giddy mast
Seal up the ship-boy's eyes, and rock his brains
In cradle of the rude imperious surge,                           20
And in the visitation of the winds,
Who take the ruffian billows by the top,
Curling their monstrous heads, and hanging them
With deafing clamour in the slippery clouds,
That with the hurly death itself awakes?                         25
Canst thou, O partial sleep, give thy repose
To the wet sea-boy in an hour so rude,
And in the calmest and most stillest night,
With all appliances and means to boot,

15. li'st] *Qb*; lyest *F*.    16. leav'st] *F*; leauest *Qb*.    18. mast] *F*; masse *Qb*.
19. Seal] *Qb,F*; Seel *Craig, conj. Gould*.    22. billows] *F*; pillowes *Qb*.    24.
deafing] *Qb* (deaffing); deaff'ning *F*.    clamour] *Qb*; Clamors *F*.    slippery]
*Qb*; slipp'ry *F*.    26. thy] *F*; them *Qb*.    27. sea-boy] *F*; season *Qb*; sea's son
*Ridley*; sea-son *Chester*.

15. *vile*] low, mean in station.

17. *watch-case*] Often, from Hanmer on, interpreted as sentry-box, but no real corroboration of this sense has been offered: *OED* surmises '?A place in which one must keep watch', but cites this line only. The idea is rather that the wakeful king is enclosed in the rich bed like a restless mechanism in a watch-case ('usually of gold or silver and elaborately ornamented', Wilson, N.C.S.). Watches could sound an alarm (cf. Middleton, *A Mad World*, v. ii. 240 [Bullen, iii. 355]—'the watch rings alarm in his pocket'), and Shakespeare's mind moves thence to the wider disturbance of the 'common 'larum-bell'.

18–20.] The image of the masthead sleeper in a storm seems to reflect *Prov.*, xxiii. 34, perhaps reinforced by the *Homily Against Drunkenness* (A. Davenport, '*2H4* and the *Homily Against Drunkenness*', *NQ*, vol. 195, pp. 160–2). *Proverbs* reads (Bishops' Bible)—'Yea, thou [the drunkard] shalt be as though thou layest in the

middest of the sea, or sleepest vpon the top of the mast of a shyp'; the *Homily* reads, 'He doubtlesse is in great daunger, that sleepeth in the middest of the sea, for soone he is ouerwhelmed with waues. He is lyke to fal sodenly that sleepeth in the toppe of the maste' (*Certain Sermons appoynted by the Queenes Maiestie*, 1574, 2nd tome, p. 208). Shakespeare still more closely echoes the same sources in *R3*, III. iv. 101–3—'like a drunken sailor on a mast, / Ready with every nod to tumble down / Into the fatal bowels of the deep'. On the use of allied material, see II. iv. 210, note.

21. *visitation*] violent onset (*OED*, Visitation, 8).

24. *deafing*] Qb is more archaic, and preferable. *OED* gives 'Deaf *v.* (*arch.* or *dial.*) . . . 3. to drown (a sound) *with* a louder sound. Hence Deafing'. Cf. *John*, II. i. 147—'What cracker is this same that deafs our ears?'

*slippery*] Either 'sliding quickly by' or 'giving the clouds no hold'; or both.

25. *hurly*] tumult.

Deny it to a King? Then happy low, lie down!                30
Uneasy lies the head that wears a crown.

*Enter* WARWICK *and* SURREY.

*War.* Many good morrows to your Majesty!
*King.* Is it good morrow, lords?
*War.* 'Tis one o'clock, and past.
*King.* Why then, good morrow to you all, my lords.         35
  Have you read o'er the letters that I sent you?
*War.* We have, my liege.
*King.* Then you perceive the body of our kingdom
  How foul it is, what rank diseases grow,
  And with what danger, near the heart of it.          40
*War.* It is but as a body yet distemper'd,
  Which to his former strength may be restor'd
  With good advice and little medicine.
  My Lord Northumberland will soon be cool'd.
*King.* O God, that one might read the book of fate,        45
  And see the revolution of the times

31. S.D.] *F; Enter Warwike, Surry, and sir Iohn Blunt. Qb.*  34. o'] *Qb,F* (a),
*Theobald.*  36. letters] *F;* letter *Qb.*  41. distemper'd] *F;* distempered *Qb.*
42. restor'd] *F;* restored *Qb.*  45. O God] *Qb;* Oh Heauen *F.*

31. *Uneasy . . . crown*] A proverbial
sentiment: cf. Tilley C863—'Crowns
have cares'.

S.D.] F's S.D. omits Qb's '*sir Iohn
Blunt*'; having nothing to say, Blunt
need not enter. In l. 1 the King calls
only for Surrey and Warwick, and
though by addressing 'you all, my
lords' in l. 35 he seems to include
Blunt, this is not decisive, since 'all'
might refer to two only (e.g. *2H6*, II. ii.
26—'as all you know' [addressed to
Salisbury and Warwick]; *F.Q.*, II. i. 61
—'a locke of all their heare' [i.e. of
Mordant's and Amavia's]). 'You all'
in the southern states of the U.S.A. is a
similar usage. Perhaps up to l. 35
Shakespeare thought of using Blunt,
and afterwards forgot him. A producer will presumably leave him out.

38-40.] 'All through the distur-
bances . . . which abound in the historical plays, the picture of . . . the dis-

tempered body of the kingdom, full o
"rank diseases", is constant' (Spurgeon, p. 160).

43. *little*] a little.

45-56.] G. H. W. Rylands marks
here the 'first hint' of Shakespeare's
fully mature style, with 'the accent of
Hamlet' in its imaginative brooding
(*Words & Poetry*, 1928, pp. 150-1).

46-51. *And see . . . hips*] Similarly
Sonnet lxiv. 5-8—'When I have seen
the hungry ocean gain / Advantage on
the kingdom of the shore, / And the
firm soil win of the wat'ry main, /
Increasing store with loss, and loss
with store'. Ovid, *Metam.*, xv. 262 ff.,
may lie behind both passages, direct
or via Golding's translation (1567,
f.190ʳ)—'Euen so haue places often
tymes exchaunged theyr estate. / For I
haue seene it sea which was sub-
stanciall ground alate, / Ageine where
sea was, I haue seene the same become

Make mountains level, and the continent,
Weary of solid firmness, melt itself
Into the sea, and other times to see
The beachy girdle of the ocean                              50
Too wide for Neptune's hips; how chance's mocks
And changes fill the cup of alteration
With divers liquors! O, if this were seen,
The happiest youth, viewing his progress through,
What perils past, what crosses to ensue,                    55
Would shut the book and sit him down and die.
'Tis not ten years gone,
Since Richard and Northumberland, great friends,
Did feast together, and in two years after
Were they at wars. It is but eight years since,             60
This Percy was the man nearest my soul;
Who like a brother toil'd in my affairs,
And laid his love and life under my foot;
Yea, for my sake, even to the eyes of Richard
Gave him defiance. But which of you was by—                 65
[*To Warwick*] You, cousin Nevil, as I may remember—
When Richard, with his eye brimful of tears,
Then check'd and rated by Northumberland,

51. chance's mocks] *Wilson* (*N.C.S.*)*;* chances mockes, *Qb;* Chances mocks *F;*
chances mock, *Rowe.*     53–7.] *Qb;* With diuers Liquors. 'Tis not tenne yeeres
gone, *F.*     59. years] *F;* yeare *Qb.*     66. S.D.] *Rowe* [*after* remember—]*; not in
Qb, F.*     67. eye brimful] *F* (Eye, brim-full)*;* eye-brimme full *Qb.*

dry lond, / And shelles and scales of
Seafish farre haue lyen from any
strond, / And in the toppes of moun-
taynes hygh old Anchors haue beene
found'.

47. *continent*] dry land.

53–6. *O . . . die*] On the omission of
this from F, see Intro., p. lxxxii, fn. 3.

57–60. *ten years . . . two years . . . eight
years*] At the time of the Archbishop's
revolt (1405) only six years had passed
since Henry overthrew Richard II,
and only two since Shrewsbury.
Shakespeare, as often, uses time freely.

65. *Gave him defiance*] Northumberland never precisely did this, but,
when he and Hotspur announce that
Richard is in Flint Castle, Boling-

broke commands them to 'send the
breath of parley / Into his ruined ears'
and to deliver terms of submission
(*R2*, iii. iii. 32–44).

66. *Warwick . . . Nevil*] No Warwick
appears in *R2*, and if one had done so
he should have been a Beauchamp.
As Wilson (N.C.S.) points out, 'The
only Neville to be Earl of Warwick
was "the king-maker" (1428–71), who
figures in *H6*, whence no doubt
Shakespeare took the name'. Or
Shakespeare may confuse Warwick
with Westmoreland: 'Rafe Neuill,
earle of Westmerland' is Prince John's
fellow-general against the Archbishop (Hol. iii. 37).

68–77. *Then . . . corruption*] Richard

Did speak these words, now prov'd a prophecy?
'Northumberland, thou ladder by the which                    70
My cousin Bolingbroke ascends my throne'
(Though then, God knows, I had no such intent
But that necessity so bow'd the state
That I and greatness were compell'd to kiss)
'The time shall come'—thus did he follow it—                 75
'The time will come, that foul sin, gathering head,
Shall break into corruption'—so went on,
Foretelling this same time's condition,
And the division of our amity.

*War.*  There is a history in all men's lives                80
Figuring the nature of the times deceas'd;
The which observ'd, a man may prophesy,
With a near aim, of the main chance of things
As yet not come to life, who in their seeds
And weak beginnings lie intreasured.                         85
Such things become the hatch and brood of time;
And by the necessary form of this
King Richard might create a perfect guess

72. God] *Qb;* Heauen *F.*      73. bow'd] *F;* bowed *Qb.*      81. nature] *F;* natures
*Qb.*      84. who] *Qb;* which *F.*      85. beginnings] *F;* beginning *Qb.*

is 'check'd and rated by Northumberland' in the abdication scene (*R2,* IV.
i), when Northumberland acts in
effect as counsel for the prosecution.
The lines loosely quoted are addressed
later to Northumberland by Richard
on his way to the Tower (*R2,* v. i. 55–
9). This speech is a notable part of the
chain of prophecies and reminiscences
which unify the historical sequence.

72–4.] These lines, important in the
judgment of Bolingbroke's action,
should be taken as fact, not as hypo-
critical extenuation. *Necessity* (England's plight under Richard's misrule), together with Richard's despairing haste to yield power, virtually
thrust the crown into Bolingbroke's
hands.

75–7. *The time . . . corruption*] From
*R2,* v. i. 57–9—'The time shall not be
many hours of age / More than it is,

ere foul sin gathering head / Shall
break into corruption'.

81. *Figuring . . . deceas'd*] Reproducing the form of what has already
passed.

84. *who*] Qb's reading, less conven-
tional than F's, is probably right.
Under 'Who. 11c', *OED* notes 'Used
instead of *which* in reference to an in-
animate thing or things, chiefly with
personification', and it cites, among
other instances, *Tit.,* III. i. 37—'the
stones, / Who . . . cannot answer'.

84–5. *seeds . . . intreasured*] Perhaps
echoed in *Mac.,* I. iii. 58–9—'If you
can look into the seeds of time / And
say which grain will grow and which
will not'.

85. *intreasured*] stored as in a trea-
sury.

87. *necessary . . . this*] inevitable pattern of these causes and effects.

That great Northumberland, then false to him,
Would of that seed grow to a greater falseness, 90
Which should not find a ground to root upon
Unless on you.

*King.*                   Are these things then necessities?
Then let us meet them like necessities;
And that same word even now cries out on us.
They say the Bishop and Northumberland 95
Are fifty thousand strong.

*War.*                   It cannot be, my lord.
Rumour doth double, like the voice and echo,
The numbers of the feared. Please it your Grace
To go to bed: upon my soul, my lord,
The powers that you already have sent forth 100
Shall bring this prize in very easily.
To comfort you the more, I have receiv'd
A certain instance that Glendower is dead.
Your Majesty hath been this fortnight ill,
And these unseason'd hours perforce must add 105
Unto your sickness.

*King.*                   I will take your counsel.
And were these inward wars once out of hand,
We would, dear lords, unto the Holy Land.        *Exeunt.*

---

97. and] *Qb,F;* an *Ridley, conj. Vaughan.*    98. feared] *Qb,F;* fear'd *Pope.*
99. soul] *Qb;* Life *F.*    100. powers] *Qb;* Pow'rs *F.*    102. receiv'd] *F;*
receiued *Qb.*    105. unseason'd hours] *F* (vnseason'd howres); vnseasoned
howers *Qb.*

89–90.] A quasi-proverbial idea;
'He that once deceives is ever suspected' (Tilley, D180).

92–3.] Henry IV's practical nature
is evident in this recovery from the
melancholy of ll. 45–79.

103. *instance . . . dead*] instance =
proof. Holinshed (iii. 48) reports

Glendower's death in 1409 (the actual
date was c. 1415–16), but in 1405 he
relates that many Welshmen were
killed at Usk and Owen's son was
taken (iii. 33–4). This may be the
germ of this news.

105. *unseason'd*] late, untimely.

SCENE II.—[*Gloucestershire. Before Justice Shallow's house.*]

*Enter Justice* SHALLOW *and Justice* SILENCE, *with* MOULDY, SHADOW, WART, FEEBLE, BULLCALF[, *and Servants, behind*].

*Shal.* Come on, come on, come on: give me your hand, sir, give me your hand, sir; an early stirrer, by the rood! And how doth my good cousin Silence?

*Sil.* Good morrow, good cousin Shallow.

*Shal.* And how doth my cousin your bedfellow? and your     5
    fairest daughter and mine, my god-daughter Ellen?

*Sil.* Alas, a black woosel, cousin Shallow!

*Shal.* By yea and no, sir: I dare say my cousin William is
    become a good scholar; he is at Oxford still, is he
    not?     10

*Scene* II

SCENE II] *F* (*Scena Secunda.*) *; not in Q.*     *Location.*] *Theobald* (*Justice* Shallow's
Seat in Gloucestershire.), *Cambridge.*     S.D. *Enter . . . Silence*] *Q ; Enter Shallow
and Silence F.*     *with . . . Bullcalf*]*F ; not in Q.*     *and . . . behind*] *Malone; not
in QF.*     1. give] *Qa,F; sir, giue Qb.*     7. woosel] *Q ; Ouzell F.*     8. no]
*Q ; nay F.*

Location.] That Shallow lives in Gloucestershire is not revealed until IV. iii. 80, 126–7. At first Shakespeare probably thought of him as living between London and York; see Appendix IV. 'From first to last Shakespeare was loyal to country life. He took it for granted as the norm, as the background before which the more formal or spectacular events were transacted. . . . Far from being a satire, the Gloucestershire scenes in *Henry IV* complete the picture of England and put the emphasis where Shakespeare meant it to be: on the life of the English countryside' (Tillyard, p. 302). 'Shakespeare . . . deliberately creates an air of homely comfort, the air of provincial old England. Shallow's sentimental harking back to the days of his youth; his grotesque deviations . . . all this is not pure silliness: it is also poetic' (Ludwig Borinski, 'Sh.'s Comic Prose', in *Sh. Survey*, 8, 1955, p. 63).

Entry-direction.] The difference between F and Q may represent a difference between production and original idea (which was, perhaps, to bring in the recruits individually; 'Let them appear as I call', Shallow replies to Falstaff's 'Let me see them, I beseech you' [ll. 95–9]). The effect is probably better if, as in F, the scarecrows are visible from the start.

7. *black woosel*] Ousel or black ousel = blackbird. 'Silence speaks with mock-modest disparagement' (Clarke, ed. 1865); 'At the court of the fair Elizabeth, blondes were fashionable and brunettes out of favour' (Winstanley, ed. 1918). The dramatists often disparage brunettes; Cowl gives many examples. Q's 'woosel' is recorded in *OED* (Woosell) as a 16th-17th c. spelling, and suggests Silence's rustic speech; cf. Bottom in *MND.*, III. i. 128–'The woosell cock, so black of hue, / With orange-tawny bill.'

8. *yea and no*] This is Shakespeare's usual form, rather than F's 'yea and nay': cf. II. ii. 124.

9–12. *Oxford . . . Court*] Oxford and Cambridge in the 16th c. often prepared young men for the London Inns

*Sil.* Indeed, sir, to my cost.

*Shal.* A must then to the Inns o'Court shortly: I was once
of Clement's Inn, where I think they will talk of mad
Shallow yet.

*Sil.* You were called 'lusty Shallow' then, cousin.            15

*Shal.* By the mass, I was called anything, and I would
have done anything indeed too, and roundly too.
There was I, and little John Doit of Staffordshire,
and black George Barnes, and Francis Pickbone,
and Will Squele, a Cotsole man—you had not four            20
such swinge-bucklers in all the Inns o'Court again;
and I may say to you, we knew where the bona-robas
were, and had the best of them all at commandment.
Then was Jack Falstaff, now Sir John, a boy, and
page to Thomas Mowbray, Duke of Norfolk.            25

*Sil.* This Sir John, cousin, that comes hither anon about
soldiers?

---

12. A . . . o'] *Q* (A . . . a); Hee . . . of *F*.      16. By the mass] *Q; not in F.*      18.
Doit] *Q* (Doyt), *F*.      19. Barnes] *Q; Bare F.*      20. Cotsole man] *Q;* Cot-sal-
man *F*.      21. o'] *Q* (a); of *F*.      22. bona-robas] *Q* (bona robes), *F*.      26.
This . . . cousin] *Qa,F;* Coosin, this sir Iohn *Qb*.

---

of Court, the select legal colleges.
'After leaving the university, the
richer student came to London to
finish his education by the study of law
at one of the Inns of Court, which were
the centre of the intellectual life of the
country. The junior members were the
pick of the universities, belonged to the
best families, . . . [and] were not too
much occupied with their studies'
(G. B. Harrison, *Sh.; Complete Works*,
1952, p. 31).

13. *Clement's Inn*] One of the Inns of
Chancery, less select than the Inns of
Court and occupied by students preparing for or unable to gain entrance
to these latter.

15.] Silence is admiringly familiar
with Shallow's life-story.

*lusty*] (*a*) lively, stalwart; (*b*)
lascivious. Both senses offer a comic-
pathetic contrast to Shallow's present
condition.

17. *roundly*] without ceremony.

20. *Cotsole*] Phonetic variant of
Cotswold. The Cotswolds were famed
for field-sports (cf. *Wiv.*, I. i. 91–2—
'How does your fallow greyhound,
sir? I heard say he was outrun on
Cotsall'), but it is not apparent that, as
commentators aver, this is implied
here.

21. *swinge-bucklers*] swash-bucklers.

22. *bona-robas*] 'smarter whores'
(Wilson, N.C.S.); 'fine showy wan-
tons' (Johnson). Florio, *A Worlde of
Wordes*, 1598, has, 'Buonarobba, as we
say, good stuffe, a good wholesome
plum-cheeked wench', and Dekker,
*2 Honest Whore*, I. i. 55–6 (Bowers, ii.
138), 'our Country Bona Robaes, ah!
are the sugrest delicious Rogues'.

24–5. *Then . . . Norfolk*] This unexpected sidelight is sometimes said to
be historically true of both Fastolfe and
Oldcastle, but the only source of the
idea seems to be the passage itself. It
is rather one of the many imaginative
retrospective touches which so extend
the living reality of the characters.

*Shal.* The same Sir John, the very same. I see him break
   Scoggin's head at the court gate, when a was a
   crack, not thus high; and the very same day did I     30
   fight with one Samson Stockfish a fruiterer, behind
   Gray's Inn. Jesu, Jesu, the mad days that I have
   spent! And to see how many of my old acquaintance
   are dead!
*Sil.* We shall all follow, cousin.     35
*Shal.* Certain, 'tis certain, very sure, very sure. Death, as
   the Psalmist saith, is certain to all, all shall die. How
   a good yoke of bullocks at Stamford fair?

28. see] *Q; saw F.*     29. Scoggin's] *Q* (Skoggins), *F* (*Scoggan's*).     a was] *Q;*
hee was *F.*     31. Samson] *Q* (Samson), *F* (*Sampson*).     32. Jesu, Jesu] *Q;* Oh *F.*
33. my] *Q; mine F.*     36–7. as . . . saith] *Q; not in F.*     38. Stamford] *F;*
Samforth *Q.*

29. *Scoggin's*] This, it has been suggested, may be Henry Scogan,
Chaucer's friend, court-poet to Henry
IV, who sent Prince Hal and his
brothers a ballad as they dined in
London (Wilson, N.C.S., citing Stow,
*Survey*, ed. Kingsford, i. 241). In the
masque *Of the Fortunate Isles*, ll. 284–7
(H. & S., vii. 717), Jonson calls him
'a fine gentleman, and a *Master* of
*Arts*, / Of *Henry* the fourth's times, that
made disguises / For the Kings sonnes,
and writ in ballad-royall / Daintily
well'. Perhaps he was mentioned in
some *Henry IV* source-play. But Shakespeare's audience would probably
associate *Scoggin* rather with John
Scoggin (Scoggan, Skoggon, &c.),
Edward IV's jester, whose name was
used generically for 'buffoon' (*OED*,
Scoggin), and prompted such 16th–
17th c. derivatives as 'scoggery', 'scog-
ginism', 'scogginist'. *The geystes of
SKOGGON*, entered *SR*, 1565–6 (Arber, i. 134), survives in 17th c. versions, which attribute it to Andrew
Boorde, c. 1490–1549.

30. *crack*] lad (in effect, young
rascal).

31. *Samson Stockfish*] Two names
comically at variance: *stockfish* is
dried cod, beaten before cooking to
soften it; cf. *Tp.*, III. ii. 78–9. 'While

the "crack" Falstaff is chastising
"Scoggin" at the palace gates . . .
"lusty" Shallow is giving battle to a
costermonger' (Wilson, N.C.S.).

31–2. *behind Gray's Inn*] i.e. in Gray's
Inn Fields, which stretched north-
wards behind Gray's Inn, an Inn of
Court north of Holborn and west of
Gray's Inn Road.

36–7. *Death . . . all*] From *Ps.*, lxxxix.
47—'What man is hee that liveth, and
shall not see death?' The idea, as
might be expected, was a common-
place; cf. Tilley, D142—'Death is
common to all'; M502, M505, etc.

37. *How*] What price (still used in
country parlance).

38. *bullocks*] This topic may owe
something to *Ecclesiasticus*, xxxviii. 22,
24–5 (Genevan), where mortality,
bullock-breeding, and rustic simplicity are conjoined—'Remember his
judgment; thine also shal be likewise,
vnto me yesterday, and vnto thee today. . . How can he get wisedome that
holdeth the plough . . . and his talke is
but of the breeding of bullockes?'
(Noble, p. 178, and A. Davenport,
'*2H4* and the *Homily Against Drunkenness*', *NQ*, vol. 195, Apr. 1950, pp. 160–
2). 'Shallow's crass simplicity, his
dense unawareness of how trite is his
moralizing and how steep the descent

*Sil.* By my troth, I was not there.

*Shal.* Death is certain. Is old Double of your town living   40
    yet?

*Sil.* Dead, sir.

*Shal.* Jesu, Jesu, dead! A drew a good bow, and dead! A
    shot a fine shoot. John a Gaunt loved him well, and
    betted much money on his head. Dead! A would   45
    have clapped i'th'clout at twelve score, and carried
    you a forehand shaft a fourteen and fourteen and a
    half, that it would have done a man's heart good to
    see. How a score of ewes now?

*Sil.* Thereafter as they be; a score of good ewes may be   50
    worth ten pounds.

*Shal.* And is old Double dead?

39. By my troth] *Q;* Truly Cousin *F.*          40, 52. Double] *Q* (Dooble), *F.*          43.
Jesu, Jesu, dead!] *Q;* Dead? See, see: *F.*          A . . . A] *Q;* hee . . . hee *F.*          44. a
Gaunt] *Q;* of Gaunt *F.*          45. A] *Q;* hee *F.*          46. i'th'] *Q* (ith); in the *F.*          47.
a fourteen] *Q;* at foureteene *F.*

from it, is the most exquisite comedy. And yet Shakespeare uses this passage to express the way he sees life and to strengthen the pattern of the present plays. Shakespeare did indeed see life as a ridiculous but fascinating blend; a blend in the present scene of men dying and bullocks sold in the busy market; while, for the pattern of the play, Shallow speaks his words just after Henry IV has been brought to the point of death: it is in this context that he speaks generally of death and then turns to Stamford Fair, reminding us that it is still flourishing' (Tillyard, p. 303).

*Stamford*] A market town in Lincolnshire, 90 miles north of London. Great horse- and stock-fairs were held there each February, Lent, and August. 'At such gatherings a price was set on livestock that remained current in the country round till the next fair' (*Sh.'s Engl.*, i. 312).

44. *John a Gaunt*] 'belonged to the golden age of the long bow, with which we won in succession Crécy, Poitiers,

and . . . Agincourt' (Wilson, N.C.S.).

46. *clapped i'th'clout*] hit the target (the clout being a square of canvas with a small white circle on it, marked in the centre with a wooden peg, the 'pin').

*twelve score*] sc. yards. Shaaber (pp. 241–3) summarizes long discussions as to whether this distance represents ordinary or extraordinary prowess, and as to whether Shallow is talking sense or nonsense. The conclusion seems to be that, while this distance was common enough, accurate shooting over it was exceptional.

47. *forehand shaft*] arrow shot with the target seen above the bow hand, as in normal target shooting.

47–8. *fourteen and a half*] sc. score yards. Shooting 280–90 yards seems not to have been exceptional, but shooting this distance with a forehand shaft, not by a high arc, would have been an extraordinary feat, almost certainly impossible.

50. *Thereafter . . . be*] The price is according to the quality.

*Sil.*  Here come two of Sir John Falstaff's men, as I think.

*Enter* BARDOLPH *and one with him.*

*Shal.*  Good morrow, honest gentlemen.

*Bard.*  I beseech you, which is Justice Shallow?  55

*Shal.*  I am Robert Shallow, sir, a poor esquire of this
county, and one of the King's justices of the peace.
What is your good pleasure with me?

*Bard.*  My captain, sir, commends him to you, my captain
Sir John Falstaff, a tall gentleman, by heaven, and a  60
most gallant leader.

*Shal.*  He greets me well, sir; I knew him a good backsword man. How doth the good knight? May I ask
how my lady his wife doth?

*Bard.*  Sir, pardon: a soldier is better accommodated than  65
with a wife.

*Shal.*  It is well said, in faith, sir, and it is well said indeed,
too. 'Better accommodated'! It is good, yea indeed
is it; good phrases are surely, and ever were, very

---

53. S.D.] *Q; Enter Bardolph and his Boy.* F [*after l. 52*].    54. *Shal.* Good] *F;* Good
*Qa corr., Qb; Bardolfe.* Good *Qa uncorr.*    58. good] *Qa,F; not in Qb.*    60. by
heaven] *Q; not in F.*    62. well, sir; I] *Q* (wel, sir, I), *Capell;* well: (Sir) I *F.*
65. accommodated] *F;* accommodate *Q.*    67. in faith] *Q; not in F.*    69. ever
were] *Q;* euery where *F.*

---

54. *Shal.*] F's reading. Uncorrected
copies of Q prefix *Bardolfe* to this
speech, as well as *Bard.* to the next.
F's *Shal.* is reasonable and its authority
sufficient to warrant the reading. As
Sisson observes (*New Readings*), 'It is
surely Shallow's place and manner to
greet the newcomers, and certainly not
for Bardolph to condescend to Shallow
and Silence'. At v. iii. 104 Shallow
greets the irrupting Pistol with
'Honest gentleman'.

56. *esquire*] gentleman, of rank just
below a knight.

59. *commends . . . you*] sends you his
regards.

60. *tall*] valiant.

62–3. *backsword man*] fencer at
single-stick, a fencing stick with a

basketwork guard for the hand, used
instead of a sword.

65. *accommodated*] Bardolph is using
a vogue-word new to the provincial
Shallow and, it would seem, part of
military jargon, as when Bobadil says,
'Hostesse, accommodate vs with another bed-staffe here, quickly: Lend
vs another bed-staffe. The woman do's
not vnderstand the wordes of *Action*'
(Jonson, *E.M.I.*, I. v. 125–8; H. & S.,
iii. 321). Jonson mentions 'Accommo-
dation' among 'the perfumed termes
of the time' (*Discoveries*, H. & S., viii.
632).

69, 71. *phrases, phrase*] Sometimes
used for a single word; cf. *Ham.*,
II. i. 111—' "beautified" is a vile
phrase'.

commendable. 'Accommodated'—it comes of 'ac-  70
commodo'; very good, a good phrase.

*Bard.* Pardon, sir, I have heard the word—phrase call
you it? By this day, I know not the phrase, but I will
maintain the word with my sword to be a soldier-like
word, and a word of exceeding good command, by  75
heaven. Accommodated: that is, when a man is, as
they say, accommodated, or when a man is being
whereby a may be thought to be accommodated;
which is an excellent thing.

*Shal.* It is very just.                                    80

*Enter* FALSTAFF.

Look, here comes good Sir John. Give me your
good hand, give me your worship's good hand. By
my troth, you like well, and bear your years very
well. Welcome, good Sir John.

*Fal.* I am glad to see you well, good Master Robert Shal-  85
low. Master Surecard, as I think?

72. Pardon] *Qa,F;* Pardon me *Qb.*      73. this] *Qa,F;* this good *Qb.*      75–6. by
heaven] *Q; not in F.*      77. is being] *Qa;* is, beeing *Qb,F, subst.*      78. whereby]
*F;* whereby, *Qa,Qb.*      a may be] *Q;* he *F.*      80. *Shal.*] *Q (Iust.), F.*
80. S.D.] *Qa,F [after l. 79], Cambridge; Enter sir Iohn Falstaffe Qb [after l. 79].*
81–2. your good] *Q;* your *F.*      82–3. By my troth] *Q;* Trust me *F.*      83. like]
*Q; looke F.*      86. Surecard] *F;* Soccard *Q.*

72–6. *phrase . . . heaven*] 'The late
eighties and nineties were years of
word-making and language-building.
. . . The dramatists, especially Shakespeare, show how nation-wide was the
interest in words. . . . That a country
Justice should pounce on the etymology of a new term . . . is not perhaps
surprising; it is less expected that the
Bardolphs of the Elizabethan world
should be verbal and grammatical
precisians' (G. Willcock and A.
Walker, *Arte of English Poesie*, 1936,
p. xciii).
74–5. *soldier-like word*] Though *OED*
offers no particularly military sense o
'accommodate', Bobadil's outburst
(see l. 65, note) shows that it was current among soldiers, who often enough
in the drama pride themselves on their

locutions; e.g. Falstaff to Mistress
Page in *Wiv.*, II. i. 13—'I will not say
pity me—'tis not a soldierlike phrase'.
75. *word . . . command*] extremely
good military term.
80.] = Quite right.
83. *like*] thrive.
85. *Master*] 'Master . . . is the title
which men giue to esquires and other
gentlemen' (Sir Thomas Smith, *De
Republica Anglorum*, 1583, i. 27).
86. *Surecard*] F's word (though not
carrying entire conviction) means
something; Q's does not. The *Oxford
Dict. Engl. Proverbs* lists several 16th–
17th c. uses of 'surecard', all meaning,
more or less, 'safe bet', 'cert.' (its
modern sense). According to Malone
(*Suppl.*, 1780), it was used by a late
17th c. translator of Suetonius to mean

*Shal.* No, Sir John, it is my cousin Silence, in commission
　　with me.

*Fal.* Good Master Silence, it well befits you should be of
　　the peace.　　　　　　　　　　　　　　　　　　　　　90

*Sil.* Your good worship is welcome.

*Fal.* Fie, this is hot weather, gentlemen. Have you pro-
　　vided me here half a dozen sufficient men?

*Shal.* Marry have we, sir. Will you sit?

*Fal.* Let me see them, I beseech you.　　　　　　　　　95

*Shal.* Where's the roll? where's the roll? where's the roll?
　　Let me see, let me see, let me see. So, so, so, so, so, so,
　　so. Yea, marry, sir: Rafe Mouldy! Let them appear
　　as I call; let them do so, let them do so. Let me see;
　　where is Mouldy?　　　　　　　　　　　　　　　　100

*Moul.* Here, and't please you.

*Shal.* What think you, Sir John? A good-limbed fellow,
　　young, strong, and of good friends.

*Fal.* Is thy name Mouldy?

---

87. Silence] *Qa* (Scilens), *Qb* (Silens), *F* [*so also subst. at ll. 89, 91; see collation also
at ll. 205–6, 282–3, and at V. iii. S.D. 4, 16*].　　93. dozen] *Q; dozen of F.*
97. Let me see, let me see, let me see] *Qa,F;* let me see, let me see *Qb.*　　97–8. so,
so, so. Yea] *Q* (so (so, so) yea)*; yea F.*　　98. Rafe] *Q; Raphe F.*　　101. and't]
*Qa;* and it *Qb;* if it *F.*

---

'boon companion', but this seems to be
uncorroborated.

87. *Silence*] On Qa's spelling
'Scilens' see Intro., p. lxviii.

*in commission*] having a commission
as Justice of the Peace.

92. *Fie . . . gentlemen*] 'A broad hint
from a thirsty soul' (Wilson, N.C.S.).

92–3. *Have . . . men*] For the recruitment scene in *F.V.* see Appendix I,
p. 230. Protests against corrupt recruiting abound in Elizabethan times.
For instance, Sir John Smythe writes
to Lord Burghley, 28 Jan. 1589/90,
about the squandering of recruits'
lives, and recommends that 'there
should be a very precise order taken in
all the musterings and trainings that
such knights and esquires as shall take
charge of bands of horsemen and foot-
men do enrol none but such as are
gentlemen, yeomen, yeomen's sons,

and artificers of some haviour' (*Hist.
MSS Comm., Salisbury Papers,* 1892, IV.
4–5). Tried before the Star Chamber
in 1596 for inciting mutiny in Essex,
Smythe again denounced the illegality
of impressment (for overseas service, at
any rate), and observed that 'there
have been 2,900 pressed out of Essex,
besides a great number of volunteers,
. . . and that not 200 have returned'.
'Pitying the destruction of his country-
men', he declares, he 'broke out into a
rage' (*State Papers, Domestic, Eliz.,
1596–97,* 19 and 28 June 1596).

93. *sufficient*] fit.

103. *of good friends*] of good kin,
family. Shallow's commendation, Wilson (N.C.S.) observes, is 'relevant
to domestic, hardly to military, service, especially under Falstaff'; yet cf.
ll. 92–3, note, for a similar contention
by Sir John Smythe.

*Moul.* Yea, and't please you.                                                    105

*Fal.* 'Tis the more time thou wert used.

*Shal.* Ha, ha, ha! most excellent, i'faith, things that are
    mouldy lack use: very singular good, in faith, well
    said, Sir John, very well said.

*Fal.* Prick him.                                                                 110

*Moul.* I was pricked well enough before, and you could
    have let me alone. My old dame will be undone
    now for one to do her husbandry and her drudgery.
    You need not to have pricked me, there are other
    men fitter to go out than I.                                                  115

*Fal.* Go to; peace, Mouldy; you shall go, Mouldy; it is
    time you were spent.

*Moul.* Spent?

*Shal.* Peace, fellow, peace—stand aside; know you
    where you are? For th'other, Sir John—let me           120
    see: Simon Shadow!

*Fal.* Yea, marry, let me have him to sit under. He's like
    to be a cold soldier.

*Shal.* Where's Shadow?

*Shad.* Here, sir.                                                                125

*Fal.* Shadow, whose son art thou?

---

105. and't] *Q; if it F.*    107. i'faith] *Q; not in F.*    108. in faith] *Q; not in F.*
110. *Fal.* Prick him.] *F; Iohn prickes him. Q [after l. 109].*    111. and] *Q; if F.*
120. th'] *Q; the F.*    121. see: Simon] *F; see Simon Q.*    122. Yea] *Q; I F.*

110. Fal. *Prick him.*] Q's compositor
took the command for a S.D. *Prick
him* = prick the name on a list, not
(*pace* an Old Vic production of the
1950's, *horribile dictu*) on the man's flesh.

111–13. *pricked . . . drudgery*] Abun-
dant word-play. *Pricked* = (*a*) vexed;
(*b*) turning sour (*OED*, Pricked. *ppl.a.*
2)—Mouldy says, in effect, 'I was
mouldy enough already'; (*c*) the sense
in Sonnet xx. 13—'She [Nature]
prickt thee out for women's pleasure';
also in Dekker, *1 Honest Whore*, v. ii.
267–8 (Bowers, ii. 101). *Undone* and
*husbandry* suggest their own equivoques; see 'do' and 'husbandry' in
Eric Partridge, *Sh.'s Bawdy.* That
*drudgery* continues the idea is evident
from Tilley, L57—'To dig another's

garden . . . to Cuckold one, to do his
work and drudgery, as they say, for
him'; cf. *All's W.,* i. iii.'49. In the circumstances, Mouldy's *old dame* is
hardly (as most editors assert) his
mother, but rather, in modern parlance, 'my old woman', i.e. wife. In
*F.V.,* sc. x, John Cobbler weeps to
leave his wife, whom Dericke refers to
as 'my dame', 'good dame'.

117. *spent*] used up.

120. *other*] others (as often).

121. *Shadow*] As well as suggesting
Shadow's physique, the name hits
at recruiting peculations; see l. 134,
note.

123. *cold*] (*a*) cool; (*b*) cowardly.

126. *son*] Rather pointless word-
play on 'sun'.

*Shad.* My mother's son, sir.

*Fal.* Thy mother's son! Like enough, and thy father's
    shadow. So the son of the female is the shadow of the
    male; it is often so indeed—but much of the father's    130
    substance!

*Shal.* Do you like him, Sir John?

*Fal.* Shadow will serve for summer. Prick him, for we
    have a number of shadows fill up the muster-book.

*Shal.* Thomas Wart!    135

*Fal.* Where's he?

*Wart.* Here, sir.

*Fal.* Is thy name Wart?

*Wart.* Yea, sir.

*Fal.* Thou art a very ragged Wart.    140

*Shal.* Shall I prick him, Sir John?

*Fal.* It were superfluous, for his apparel is built upon his
    back, and the whole frame stands upon pins: prick
    him no more.

130. much] *Q;* not *F.*    134. fill] *Q;* to fill *F.*    141. him, Sir] *Q;* him downe, /
Sir *F.*    **142.** for his] *F;* for *Q.*

128–31.] A passage of unimpress-
ive quibbles; approximately, 'Thy
mother's son—no doubt!—and called
Shadow after thy father; so the son the
mother bears is a likeness cast by the
father—but often only the dimmest
copy, with little of the paternal substance'.

133. *serve*] More word-play; (*a*) be
suitable; (*b*) be a soldier.

134. *shadows . . . muster-book*] 'The
word "shadow" was used, together
with the expression "faggot" and
"dead-head", to signify fictitious men
whose names were borne upon the
muster-rolls in order that their captain might draw their pay for his own
profit' (*Sh.'s Engl.,* i. 124). *Muster-book*
= nominal roll.

135. *Thomas Wart*] Mr E. R. Wood
informs me that in a list of *The Names
and Surnames of all the Able and Sufficient
Men in Body fit for His Majesty's Service in
the Wars within the County of Gloucester,
. . . in the Month of August, 1608,* compiled by John Smith of North Nibley,

Glos., and edited from a MS at Sher-
borne House, Glos. (London, 1902, p.
92), there appears a Thomas Warter,
carpenter, of Chipping Campden near
Stratford, aged 50–60, classed as of
'lower stature fitt to serve with a
Calyver'. A man of that name, moreover, is recorded in the Chipping
Campden parish register as buried on
18 Dec. 1624. If Shakespeare knew
him, that might account for Wart's
Christian name, the caliver-drill, and
the unexpected carpentry metaphor of
ll. 142–3. But who can tell?

140. *ragged*] tattered in dress, and,
considered as a *wart,* 'full of rough and
sharp projections' (*OED,* Ragged).

142–3. *built . . . pins*] The pricking/
pinning notion leads Falstaff into a
carpentry metaphor, Wart's rags being fastened like rough timbers;
'Don't prick (pin) him any more; his
rags are joined together on his back.
and the whole construction depends
upon pins (pegs); there's no room for
any more'. See l. 135, note.

*Shal.*  Ha, ha, ha! you can do it, sir, you can do it, I com-     145
         mend you well. Francis Feeble!

*Fee.*   Here, sir.

*Fal.*   What trade art thou, Feeble?

*Fee.*   A woman's tailor, sir.

*Shal.*  Shall I prick him, sir?                                    150

*Fal.*   You may; but if he had been a man's tailor he'd ha'
         pricked you. Wilt thou make as many holes in an
         enemy's battle as thou hast done in a woman's
         petticoat?

*Fee.*   I will do my good will, sir, you can have no more.         155

*Fal.*   Well said, good woman's tailor! Well said, courage-
         ous Feeble! Thou wilt be as valiant as the wrathful
         dove, or most magnanimous mouse. Prick the
         woman's tailor: well, Master Shallow; deep,
         Master Shallow.                                            160

*Fee.*   I would Wart might have gone, sir.

*Fal.*   I would thou wert a man's tailor, that thou mightst
         mend him and make him fit to go. I cannot put him
         to a private soldier, that is the leader of so many
         thousands. Let that suffice, most forcible Feeble.        165

*Fee.*   It shall suffice, sir.

*Fal.*   I am bound to thee, reverend Feeble. Who is next?

*Shal.*  Peter Bullcalf o'th'green!

---

146. well. Francis Feeble!] *Q*; well. / *Francis Feeble. F.*      148. *Fal.*] *Theobald;*
*Shal. QF.*     151. may; but] *Q*; may: / But *F.*     he'd ha'] *Q* (hee'd a) ; he would
haue *F.*     166. sir] *Q*; *not in F.*     167. next] *Q*; the next *F.*     168. o'th'] *Q*
(o'th) ; of the *F.*

148. *Fal.*] QF may be right in giving
this to Shallow, but Shallow's office is
to produce the recruits, Falstaff's to
question them. Shakespeare may have
put *Shal.* by mistake, or *Fal.* may have
looked like *Shal.*

149, 151. *woman's tailor . . . man's
tailor*] Women's tailoring was a trade
often treated derisively, perhaps as
seeming effeminate. In Jonson's *New
Inn*, l. 66 (H. & S., vi. 404), the silly
Nick Stuffe is '*The* Ladies *Taylor*'. In
Middleton's *Blurt, Master-Constable*,
II. ii. 21 (Bullen, i. 34), Imperia complains of her 'foolish tailor'. But the

point here lies much more in an equivoque. *Tailor* in Elizabethan English
(and later) could mean the sex organ,
male or female (Hilda Hulme, 'Three
Notes on Sh. Plays', *JEGP*, vol. 57,
1958, pp. 722–4). Here, in conjunction with *prick*, the equivoque is
apparent.

152. *pricked*] (*a*) decked you out
(*OED*, Prick, *v.* 20); (*b*) thrust you
through.

153. *battle*] army.

158. *magnanimous*] stout-hearted.

163–4. *put him to*] enlist him as.

165. *thousands*] i.e. of vermin.

*Fal.* Yea, marry, let's see Bullcalf.

*Bull.* Here, sir.                                                    170

*Fal.* Fore God, a likely fellow! Come, prick me Bullcalf
till he roar again.

*Bull.* O Lord, good my lord captain—

*Fal.* What, dost thou roar before thou art pricked?

*Bull.* O Lord, sir, I am a diseased man.                            175

*Fal.* What disease hast thou?

*Bull.* A whoreson cold, sir, a cough, sir, which I caught
with ringing in the King's affairs upon his coronation day, sir.

*Fal.* Come, thou shalt go to the wars in a gown; we will    180
have away thy cold, and I will take such order that
thy friends shall ring for thee. Is here all?

*Shal.* Here is two more called than your number; you
must have but four here, sir: and so, I pray you, go
in with me to dinner.                                                185

*Fal.* Come, I will go drink with you, but I cannot tarry
dinner. I am glad to see you, by my troth, Master
Shallow.

*Shal.* O, Sir John, do you remember since we lay all
night in the Windmill in Saint George's Field?           190

169. let's] *Q;* let vs *F.*     171. Fore God] *Q;* Trust me *F.*     me] *F; not in Q.*
173. O Lord] *Q;* Oh *F.*     174. thou art] *Q;* th'art *F.*     175. O Lord] *Q;* Oh *F.*
183. Here] *Q;* There *F.*     187. by my] *Q;* in good *F.*

171–2. *Bullcalf . . . again*] The bel-
lowing of bulls is, of course, proverbial; cf. Tilley, B715. In *1H4*, II. iv.
287, Falstaff 'roared, as ever I heard
bullcalf'.

178. *affairs*] 'To be upon the king's
affairs [business]' was an accepted
phrase—cf. Dekker, *Sir Thomas Wyat*,
I. iv. 5–6 (Bowers, i. 415); whence *the
king's affairs* came to be loosely or ig-
norantly used, as here (Cowl).

178–9. *coronation day*] i.e. coronation
anniversary, kept as a holiday.

183–4. *two . . . four*] Shallow reckons
six; only five have been seen; Falstaff is allowed four; and he takes only
three (Wart, Shadow, and Feeble).
Shakespeare often neglects such de-

tails, and the audience will hardly
notice them.

186–7. *I . . . dinner*] Evidence, as is
l. 285, that Falstaff is advancing upon
the foe with that surprising celerity he
claims in IV. iii. 34–6, and that Shakespeare had not in fact thought of him
as taking a leisurely roundabout route.
See Appendix IV.

190. *Windmill . . . Field*] St George's
Field, or Fields, lay south of the
Thames, between Southwark and
Lambeth, named after the church of
St George the Martyr: 'St George's
Road, running from the Elephant and
Castle to Westminster Bridge Road,
and St George's Church at the south
end of Blackfriars Road, preserve the

*Fal.* No more of that, good Master Shallow, no more of
    that.

*Shal.* Ha, 'twas a merry night! And is Jane Nightwork
    alive?

*Fal.* She lives, Master Shallow.             195

*Shal.* She never could away with me.

*Fal.* Never, never; she would always say she could not
    abide Master Shallow.

*Shal.* By the mass, I could anger her to th'heart. She
    was then a bona-roba. Doth she hold her own well?  200

*Fal.* Old, old, Master Shallow.

*Shal.* Nay, she must be old, she cannot choose but be old,
    certain she's old, and had Robin Nightwork by old
    Nightwork before I came to Clement's Inn.

*Sil.* That's fifty-five year ago.             205

*Shal.* Ha, cousin Silence, that thou hadst seen that that
    this knight and I have seen! Ha, Sir John, said I
    well?

*Fal.* We have heard the chimes at midnight, Master
    Shallow.             210

*Shal.* That we have, that we have, that we have; in
    faith, Sir John, we have; our watchword was 'Hem,
    boys!'—Come, let's to dinner; come, let's to dinner.
    Jesus, the days that we have seen! Come, come.

            *Exeunt [Falstaff, Shallow, and Silence].*

191–2. good ... that] *F*; master Shallow *Q*.    193. 'twas] *Q*; it was *F*.    199. By
the mass] *Q*; *not in F*.    to th'] *Q* (too'th); to the *F*.    204. Clement's Inn] *Q
corr.*, *F*; Clemham *Q uncorr.*    205–6. *Sil. . . . Silence*] *Q* (*Scilens . . . Scilens*), *F*
[*see collation also at ll. 87, 282–3*].    205. year] *Q*; yeeres *F*.    211–12. that we
have; in faith] *Q*; in faith *F*.    212–13. Hem, boys!] *Q* (Hemboies,), *F* (Hem-
Boyes.).    214. Jesus] *Q*; Oh *F*.    214. S.D.] *Q* (*exeunt.*), Capell, *subst.*; *not in F*.

name' (Sugden); a windmill appears
nearby on John Norden's map of London in 1600 (Wilson, N.C.S.). But
there seems also to have been a brothel
so named in Paris Garden Lane,
Southwark, which is doubtless what
Shallow recalls — Southwark was
known for its brothels.

193. *Nightwork*] The sense is ob-
vious; the term was common—cf.
Middleton, *A Mad World*, I. ii. 1
(Bullen, iii. 261)—'She may make

night-work on't'; Jonson, *E.M.O.*, v.
viii. 30–2 (H. & S., iii. 589)—'I
mar'le what peece of nightwork you
haue in hand . . . is this your Pandar?'

196. *away with*] put up with.

205.] See l. 15, note.

212–13. *Hem, boys!*] = Clear your
throat! Down with it!—a drinking
cry; Brome, *Jovial Crew*, 1641 (Shepherd, iii. 385), quotes 'an old Song',
ending, 'With a *heghm boy, heghm*, and
a cup of old Sack'. See II. iv. 30, note.

*Bull.* Good Master Corporate Bardolph, stand my     215
friend; and here's four Harry ten shillings in French
crowns for you. In very truth, sir, I had as lief be
hanged, sir, as go. And yet for mine own part, sir, I
do not care; but rather because I am unwilling,
and, for mine own part, have a desire to stay with     220
my friends; else, sir, I did not care, for mine own
part, so much.

*Bard.* Go to, stand aside.

*Moul.* And, good Master Corporal Captain, for my old
dame's sake stand my friend. She has nobody to do     225
anything about her when I am gone, and she is old
and cannot help herself. You shall have forty, sir.

*Bard.* Go to, stand aside.

*Fee.* By my troth I care not, a man can die but once, we
owe God a death. I'll ne'er bear a base mind—and't     230
be my destiny, so; and't be not, so. No man's too
good to serve's prince, and let it go which way it
will, he that dies this year is quit for the next.

*Bard.* Well said, th'art a good fellow.

*Fee.* Faith, I'll bear no base mind.     235

---

216. here's] *Q;* heere is *F.*     224. old] *Q corr., F; not in Q uncorr.*     225. has] *Q;*
hath *F.*     229. By my troth] *Q; not in F.*     230. God] *Q; not in F.*     I'll ne'er]
*Q;* I will neuer *F.*     230–1. and't . . . and't] *Q;* if it . . . if it *F.*     231. man's]
*Q;* man is *F.*     232. serve's] *Q;* serue his *F.*     234. th'art] *Q;* thou art *F.*
235. Faith, I'll] *Q;* Nay, I will *F.*

---

216–17. *four . . . crowns*] Harry ten
shillings (half-sovereigns coined under
Henry VII) were by the date of the
play worth only five shillings. Bullcalf
is therefore offering twenty shillings,
£1, paid in French crowns (worth
four shillings each). Mouldy's bid of
forty (l. 227) reflects his greater alarm
at going. On the assumption that four
Harry ten shillings would be worth
their original £2 and with Mouldy's
sum would make £4, some commentators have thought that when Bardolph
mentions to Falstaff a total of £3 (l.
238), he is pocketing £1 himself. But
there is no recognition of any such
trick in the text.

224. *Master . . . Captain*] Rustic difficulty with ranks; cf. l. 215.

227. *forty*] i.e. shillings.

229–33.] Feeble shows his admirable
spirit in a volley of proverbs and tags.
Tilley gives as proverbial, 'A man can
die but once' (M219), and 'I owe God
a death' (G237; with a pun on death/
debt). *I'll ne'er bear a base mind* and *No
man's too good to serve's prince*, besides
being popular tags, may echo *F.V.*,
sc. x—'doest thinke that we are so
base / Minded to die among French
men?', and 'he is not too good to
serue ye king' (see Appendix I, pp.
230–1). The conclusion echoes 'Death
pays all debts' (Tilley, D148).

*Enter* FALSTAFF *and the* JUSTICES.

*Fal.* Come, sir, which men shall I have?

*Shal.* Four of which you please.

*Bard.* Sir, a word with you. I have three pound to free
    Mouldy and Bullcalf.

*Fal.* Go to, well.                                       240

*Shal.* Come, Sir John, which four will you have?

*Fal.* Do you choose for me.

*Shal.* Marry then, Mouldy, Bullcalf, Feeble, and
    Shadow.

*Fal.* Mouldy and Bullcalf: for you, Mouldy, stay at   245
    home till you are past service; and for your part,
    Bullcalf, grow till you come unto it. I will none of
    you.

*Shal.* Sir John, Sir John, do not yourself wrong, they are
    your likeliest men, and I would have you served   250
    with the best.

*Fal.* Will you tell me, Master Shallow, how to choose a
    man? Care I for the limb, the thews, the stature,

235. S.D.] *Q; not in F.*

240.] Right! That's fine!

245–6. *stay . . . service*] 'Falstaff is
quibbling on "service": (*a*) military,
(*b*) domestic, such as Mouldy renders
his "dame", and (*c*) the kind of service
the parish bull gives' (Wilson, N.C.S.).

247. *come unto it*] Another equivoque.
*Come to it* = grow to manhood; Bullcalf is still a bull*calf.* But here *it* also
= service (on which see preceding
note).

253–5. *Care I . . . spirit*] Perhaps an
echo of *1 Sam.*, xvi. 7, when God pre-
fers David before his bigger brothers—
'The Lorde sayd vnto Samuel, Looke
not on his fashion, or on the height of
his stature . . . For man looketh on the
outwarde appearance, but the Lorde
beholdeth the hart' (Bishops'). But
more particularly, through this whole
passage Falstaff is parodying military
doctrine. His impudent rationaliza-
tion flouts one military contention by
burlesquing another. The former is

represented by, e.g., Robert Barret's
*Theorike and Practike of Moderne Warres,*
1598, which declares that the best
soldiers have 'The eyes quicke, lively,
and piercing; the head and countenance upright; the breast broad and
strong; the shoulders large; the armes
long; the fingers strong and synowie;
the belly thinne; the ribbes large; the
thigh bigge; the legge full, and the
foote leane and drie' (*op. cit.*, p. 33;
quot. G. G. Langsam, *Martial Books
and Tudor Verse,* 1951, p. 94). The doctrine Falstaff burlesques is represented
by, e.g., Thomas Proctor's *Of the
Knowledge and Conducte of Warres,* 1578
—'To sett downe a precyse order, for
the same [i.e. "the choyse of our good
souldiour"] by his shoulders, brest,
armes, thyghes, feete, or composition
of anie other parte of the bodye: I
houlde it most vayne . . . the courage
& mynde is as much to bee respected,
as the bodye' (fol. 21ᵛ; quoted by Jor-

bulk, and big assemblance of a man? Give me the
spirit, Master Shallow. Here's Wart; you see what　255
a ragged appearance it is—a shall charge you, and
discharge you, with the motion of a pewterer's
hammer, come off and on swifter than he that gibbets on the brewer's bucket. And this same half-
faced fellow Shadow; give me this man, he presents　260
no mark to the enemy—the foeman may with as
great aim level at the edge of a penknife. And for a
retreat, how swiftly will this Feeble the woman's
tailor run off! O, give me the spare men, and spare

255. Here's Wart;] Q (heres Wart,); Where's *Wart*? F.　　256. a shall] Q;
hee shall F.

gensen, *Hunt. L. Q.*, xiv. 34). Falstaff is
adept at giving his own rendering of
military doctrine; cf. New Arden
*1H4*, v. ii. 119, note. The *Myrroure for
Magistrates* (ed. L. B. Campbell, p.
470) is rather of Shallow's opinion—
'Yf you so poynted bee, to serue your
Prince in war, / . . . / Retayne such
souldiers as well made, strong, semely
are, / Brought vp to labour hard'.

254. *assemblance*] This suggests (*a*)
appearance (semblance), and (*b*)
frame, composition.

256–7. *charge . . . discharge*] load and
fire.

258. *come off and on*] This looks like
'retire and advance', but the notion of
hoisting (cf. next note) suggests a
lowering and lifting motion, i.e. 'lift
his caliver up and down' (Wilson,
N.C.S.).

258–9. *gibbets . . . bucket*] Probably
the idea is, 'swifter than a man hoisting
the brewer's yoke [for carrying pails o
liquor] onto his shoulders'. This 'allusion of doubtful meaning', as Onions
calls it, has caused much discussion.
Wilson (N.C.S.) explains *bucket* as 'the
beam of a crane or gibbet' and renders
the phrase, 'swifter than a man can
hoist with a brewer's crane'. Mr E. R.
Wood suggests, privately, that it
means a workman hanging on (as if
gibbeted) to the beam of a brewer's

hoist, so as to raise the counterpoise at
the other end (like an Egyptian
shadoof). But ingenious though these
notions are, the essential of Falstaff's
image is swiftness, and crane- or
counterpoise-hoisting seems wholly
inappropriate.

259–60. *half-faced*] pinched-faced
(thin as the 'half-face' or profile on a
coin).

260–4. *give . . . off*] Like ll. 253–5, in
effect a parody of military doctrine,
as, e.g., in Matthew Sutcliffe, *The
Practice, Proceedings, and Lawes of Armes*,
1593—'Men of meane stature are for
the most parte more vigorous and
couragious . . . and commonly excell
great bodied men in swiftnesse and
running, which is a matter in a souldier
verie requisite and commendable' (*op.
cit.*, p. 65, quoted Jorgensen, *Hunt.
L. Q.*, xiv. 34–5).

261–2. *as great aim*] as good a target.

264–6. *O . . . Bardolph*] More military parody. Sir John Smythe writes
of small-arms men (such as Falstaff's
recruits are: see next note) as 'the most
nimble to trauerse their grounds, and
to stoope to their peeces, and to take
all advauntages of groundes, and of the
smallest sorte and size of men, because
they should be the lesser markes in the
sightes of their enemies in skirmish
near at hand' (*Instructions . . . and

me the great ones. Put me a caliver into Wart's   265
hand, Bardolph.

*Bard.* Hold, Wart, traverse—thas! thas! thas!

*Fal.* Come, manage me your caliver. So, very well! Go
to, very good! Exceeding good! O, give me always
a little, lean, old, chopt, bald shot. Well said, i'   270
faith, Wart, th'art a good scab. Hold, there's a
tester for thee.

*Shal.* He is not his craft's master, he doth not do it right.
I remember at Mile-End Green, when I lay at
Clement's Inn—I was then Sir Dagonet in Arthur's   275

---

267. thas! thas! thas!] *Q;* thus, thus, thus. *F.*      270. chopt, bald] *Q* (chopt
Ballde,), *F.*      270–1. i'faith] *Q; not in F.*      271. th'art] *Q;* thou art *F.*
there's] *Q;* there is *F.*

---

*Orders Mylitarie,* 1595, p. 188; quoted
Jorgensen, *Hunt. L.Q.,* xiv. 35). As
Jorgensen remarks, 'Falstaff's knowledge of current theory is expert
enough to be perverse'.

265. *caliver*] light musket; the light-
est fire-arm after the pistol.

267. *traverse*] Probably = march to
and fro. It might = alter aim (*OED*'s
first example of this sense is 1628), but
Bardolph's barks would fit marching
better. *OED* gives, 'To traverse one's
ground, to move from side to side, in
fencing or fighting'. Cf. Daniel, *C.W.,*
iii. 77—'And vp and downe he trauers-
es his grounde' (referring to Richard
II's movements back and forth in his
cell while fending off his assailants).

*thas, thas, thas*] With a few editors
(Ridley, Kittredge, Monro), I retain
Q's spelling. As Ridley observes, 'it is
curious that so ordinary a word as *thus*
should be misspelt unless there is a
point in the misspelling (? a parody of
military drill-sergeant's accent)'.

270. *a little . . . shot*] See ll. 264–6,
note. 'The tallest and strongest men
were always preferred for the pike, and
the little nimble men for the musket
. . . Falstaff [is] echoing in part the
cant of the time' (*Sh.'s Engl.,* i. 115).

*chopt*] dried up.

*shot*] (*a*) marksman; but perhaps

also, following the derogatory epi-
thets, (*b*) 'a refuse animal left after the
best of the flock or herd have been
selected' (*OED,* Shot. *sb.³*). *OED*'s
first example is of 1796, but it records
'shoot' in this sense from 1300 on
(Shoot. *v.* 11f, g), and the word occurs
widely in dialect (H. Hulme, *Explorations in Sh.'s Language,* p. 257).

*Well said*] Well done! Often used
when nothing has been said; cf. v.
iii. 9.

271. *scab*] rascal; a term of comic
depreciation (and, of course, a pun on
Wart's name).

272. *tester*] sixpence.

274. *Mile-End Green*] A drill-ground
for citizens under training, and a place
for fairs and shows, now Stepney
Green, south of the Mile-End Road.
Most references to the military exercises there are scoffing; e.g. Barnabe
Riche, *Souldiers Wishe to Britons Welfare,* 1604 (quoted Steevens, 1793)—
'God blesse me, my countrey, and
frendes, from his direction that hath no
better experience than what hee hath
atteyned unto . . . from a traynyng at
Mile-end-greene'. Cowl gives other
examples.

*lay*] lodged, lived.

275–6. *Sir Dagonet . . . show*] Sir
Dagonet was King Arthur's fool; cf.

show—there was a little quiver fellow, and a would
manage you his piece thus, and a would about, and
about, and come you in, and come you in. 'Rah,
tah, tah', would a say; 'Bounce', would a say; and
away again would a go, and again would a come:  280
I shall ne'er see such a fellow.

*Fal.* These fellows will do well, Master Shallow. God
keep you, Master Silence: I will not use many
words with you. Fare you well, gentlemen both; I
thank you. I must a dozen mile tonight. Bardolph,  285
give the soldiers coats.

*Shal.* Sir John, the Lord bless you! God prosper your
affairs! God send us peace! At your return, visit
our house, let our old acquaintance be renewed.
Peradventure I will with ye to the court.  290

*Fal.* Fore God, I would you would, Master Shallow.

276–80. and a . . . a . . . a . . . a . . . a . . . a] *Q*; and hee . . . hee . . . hee . . . hee . . . hee
. . . he *F*.    281. ne'er] *Q*; neuer *F*.    282. will] *F*; wooll *Q*.    282–3. well . . .
Silence:] *Q* (well M. Shallow, God keep you M. Scilens,) ; well, Master *Shallow*.
Farewell Master *Silence*, *F*.    287–8. the Lord . . . God . . . God] *Q*; Heauen . . .
and . . . and *F*.    288. peace! At your] *Q* (peace at your); Peace. As you *F*.
289. our house] *Q*; my house *F*.    290. ye] *Q*; you *F*.    291. Fore God] *Q*;
*not in F*.    I] *F*; *not in Q*.    Master Shallow] *F*; *not in Q*.

Malory's *Morte Arthur*, ix. 18. The
name is used derisively in Jonson,
*E.M.O.*, IV. iv. 118–19 (H. & S., iii.
543), where Sogliardo and Shift are
'Sir Dagonet and his squire', and in
*Cynthia's Revels*, v. iv. 549 (H. & S., iv.
155). See also Beaumont & Fletcher,
*Knight of the Burning Pestle*, IV. i (Glover
& Waller, vi. 211). *Arthur's show* was
an exhibition of archery at Mile-End
Green by a society called 'The
Auncient Order, Society, & Vnitie
Laudable, of Prince Arthure, and his
knightly Armory of the Round Table'.
Richard Mulcaster, a member, de-
scribes it in his *Positions . . . for the train-
ing vp of children* (ed. 1888, ch. 26,
p. 103).

276–80. *there . . . come*] 'The handling of the fire-arms . . . was taught by
an infinity of elaborate motions, which
no doubt were parodied by Justice
Shallow when the caliver was put into

Wart's hand. . . . The description
points to the action of an alert skir-
misher, which is perfectly in accor-
dance with all that we know of the
military practice of the time. . . . If [the
musketeers] fired in close order, the
rule was that the first rank fired and
ran round the rear to reload, the
second rank fired and did likewise, and
so the remaining ranks in succession'
(*Sh.'s Engl.*, i. 114–15).

276. *quiver*] nimble.

276–80. *a would manage . . . a come*]
Representing the operations described
in the latter part of ll. 276–80, note.

279. *Bounce*] Bang; cf. Thomas Heywood, *1 Fair Maid of the West* (Shepherd, ii. 315)—'Bounce quoth the
guns'.

286. *coats*] The soldier's coat was a
linen or leather jacket which could be
strengthened with chain-mail or steel
plates.

*Shal.* Go to, I have spoke at a word. God keep you!
*Fal.* Fare you well, gentle gentlemen. *Exeunt* [*Justices*].
     On Bardolph, lead the men away. [*Exeunt Bardolph
     and recruits.*] As I return, I will fetch off these jus-     295
     tices. I do see the bottom of Justice Shallow. Lord,
     Lord, how subject we old men are to this vice of
     lying! This same starved justice hath done nothing
     but prate to me of the wildness of his youth, and the
     feats he hath done about Turnbull Street, and     300
     every third word a lie, duer paid to the hearer than
     the Turk's tribute. I do remember him at Clement's
     Inn, like a man made after supper of a cheese-
     paring. When a was naked, he was for all the world
     like a forked radish, with a head fantastically carved     305

292. God keep you] *Q* ; Fare you well *F*.
[*after l. 292*] *F*.     294. On] *F* ; *Shal*. On *Q*.
*QF*.     296–7. Lord, Lord] *Q* ; *not in F*.
304. a] *Q* ; hee *F*.

293. S.D.] *Q* (*exit*), *Cambridge; Exit*.
294–5. S.D.] *Capell, subst.; not in QF*.
300. Turnbull] *Q* ; Turnball *F*.

292. *have . . . word*] mean what I say.
293–4. Exeunt . . . *On*] Q reads
'*exit*' at the end of l. 293 and '*Shal*. On'
at the beginning of l. 294. The MS
may have read *exit Shal.*, so placed that
the compositor took *Shal.* for a speech-
prefix (Shaaber). Or if l. 294 had no
speech-prefix, being a continuation of
the preceding speech, the editor or
compositor might think Falstaff had
left and Shallow was to speak.
295. *fetch off*] fleece.
296–8. *Lord, Lord . . . lying*] Cf.
*1H4*, v. iv. 148—'Lord, Lord, how
this world is given to lying'. Falstaff
naturally deprecates any deviation
from the strictest veracity.
298–301. *This . . . lie*] A comparable
disparagement occurs in Dekker, *1
Honest Whore*, v. i. 26–7 (Bowers, ii. 90)
—'he talkes like a Iustice of peace, of a
thousand matters and to no purpose'.
300. *Turnbull Street*] Originally
Turnmill Street (the Fleet was called
Turnmill Brook hereabouts, from the
watermills it turned); 'the most disreputable street in London, a haunt of
thieves and loose women' (Sugden).

301–2. *duer . . . tribute*] rendered
more faithfully to the listener than
tribute is to the Sultan. The Turkish
rulers exacted rigorous dues from
those subject to or protected by them.
305–6. *like . . . knife*] This resembles
Gerard's *Herball*, 1597, on the mandrake (Bk II, ch. 60, p. 281)—'the idle
drones that haue little or nothing to do
but eate and drinke, haue bestowed
some of their time in caruing the
rootes of Brionie, forming them into
the shape of men & women; which
falsifying practise hath confirmed the
errour amongst the simple and vn-
learned people, who haue taken them
vpon their report to be the true Mandrake'. J. W. Lever suggests that
Shakespeare may have drawn upon
Gerard; if so, this would bear upon the
play's date. But since, by the testimony
of Gerard and others (e.g. William
Turner's *Herbal*, 1568, pp. 45ᵛ–46ʳ),
root-carving was a common diversion
or swindle, Shakespeare need not have
had a learned source for it. On this see
Intro., p. xiv, fn. 1, and on the mandrake see l. 309 and note.

upon it with a knife. A was so forlorn, that his di-
mensions to any thick sight were invisible; a was the
very genius of famine, yet lecherous as a monkey,
and the whores called him mandrake. A came ever
in the rearward of the fashion, and sung those tunes     310
to the overscutched housewives that he heard the

306. A] *Q;* Hee *F.*     307. invisible] *Rowe;* inuincible *QF.*     a] *Q;* Hee *F.*
308. genius] *Q corr., F;* gemies *Q uncorr.*     308–9. yet . . . mandrake] *Q; not
in F.*     309. A] *Q;* hee *F.*     ever] *F;* ouer *Q.*     310–13. and . . . good-nights]
*Q; not in F.*

306. *forlorn*] meagre.

307. *thick*] dull, dim.

*invisible*] QF read 'inuincible', and
many editors follow, taking the word
either as a doublet of (or error for)
'invisible' or else as meaning 'not to be
evinced, indeterminable' (Schmidt).
But all Shakespeare's other uses of 'invincible' have the normal meaning,
and 'invisible' seems preferable.
Shakespeare was erratic with his
minim-strokes (cf. Wilson, *MSH*, ii.
305–6), and a stroke or two extra in
'inuisible', 'inuisable', or perhaps
'inuiscible' (since he writes Silence as
'Scilens') could produce 'invincible'
or a 16th c. variant like 'invinsible',
'invinsable'.

308. *genius*] embodied type.

*lecherous . . . monkey*] Elizabethan
views of the morals of monkeys are
reflected in Iago's comparisons—'as
prime as goats, as hot as monkeys', and
Othello's outburst, 'Goats and monkeys' (*Oth.*, III. iii. 403, IV. i. 274).

309. *whores . . . mandrake*] In
*Genesis*, xxx. 14 (Genevan), *mandrake* is
marginally glossed, 'A kinde of herbe
whose rote hath a certeine likenes of
the figure of a man'. Gerard explains
why—'The roote is long, thick,
whitish, diuided many times into two
or three parts, resembling the legs of a
man, with other parts of his body
adioining thereto as the priuie parts, as
it hath been reported, whereas it is no
otherwise then in the rootes of carrots,
parsneps, and suchlike, forked or
deuided into two or more parts. . . For

my selfe and my seruants also haue
digged vp, planted and replanted
verie many, & yet neuer could either
perceiue shape of man or woman'
(*Herball*, 1597, p. 280). Thirty years
earlier, William Turner had also been
sceptical—'I haue in my tyme at
diuerse tymes taken vp the rootes of
the Mandrag out of the grounde, but I
neuer saw any suche thyng vpon or in
them as are in and vpon the pedlers
rootes that are comenly to be sold'
(*Herbal*, 1568, p. 46r). Sir Thomas
Browne is equally incredulous; cf.
*Pseud. Epid.*, II. 6. Illustrations in 16th
c. herbals (e.g. Wm Turner's, 1568,
Henry Lyte's, 1578, and Gerard's)
show a whiskery forked root, something like a human figure from the
waist down, with a cluster of leaves
above. From ancient times used for
love-potions, the mandrake was still
associated with sexual prowess, perhaps because of the supposed resemblance Gerard mentions.

311. *overscutched housewives*] deadbeat
whores; *housewives* = hussies. Ray's
*North-Country Words* (1674) has 'Over-
switcht housewife, i.e. a whore; a ludi-
crous word', but this is not really en-
lightening. 'Scutch' and 'switch' are
synonymous; *overscutched* should therefore mean 'well-whipped' (Doll's fate
at v. iv. 5). But it sounds as though it
meant 'worn out', and many editors
take it so. As Wilson (N.C.S.) comments, Shallow had evidently con-
sorted 'not with bona robas, but with
the lowest of the profession'.

carmen whistle, and sware they were his fancies or
his good-nights. And now is this Vice's dagger become a squire, and talks as familiarly of John a
Gaunt as if he had been sworn brother to him, and     315
I'll be sworn a ne'er saw him but once in the tilt-
yard, and then he burst his head for crowding
among the marshal's men. I saw it and told John a
Gaunt he beat his own name, for you might have
thrust him and all his apparel into an eel-skin—the     320
case of a treble hautboy was a mansion for him, a

---

314–15. a Gaunt] *Q; of Gaunt F.*     316. a ne'er] *Q; hee neuer F.*     318–19.
a Gaunt] *Q; of Gaunt F.*     320. thrust] *Q; truss'd F.*          eel-skin] *Q corr.* (eele-
skin), *F, subst.;* eele-shin *Q uncorr.*

---

312. *carmen*] Carters were noted
whistlers; their musical tastes were
reputedly free and easy. Chettle lists
*The Carman's Whistle* among 'las-
ciuious vnder songs' (*Kind-Heartes
Dreame*, ed. G. B. Harrison, 1923, p.
17); cf. Jonson, *Bart. F.*, i. iv. 70–81
(H. & S., vi. 29)—'I haue a young
Master . . . I dare not let him walke
alone, for feare of learning of vile tunes.
. . . If hee meete but a Carman i'the
streete, . . . he will whistle him and
all his tunes ouer, at night in his
sleepe'.

312–13. *fancies . . . good-nights*] im-
promptus . . . serenades; here, 'song
tunes in impromptu style' (Kittredge).
A fancy (fantasia) was a free-style
composition for viols or virginals,
'when a musician taketh a point at his
pleasure, and turneth and wresteth it
as he list' (Thos. Morley, 1597, quoted
in *Sh.'s Engl.*, ii. 38).

313. *Vice's dagger*] A reference presumably both to Shallow's lath-like
figure and to his absurd display oſ
prowess. 'The old Vice . . . / Who with
dagger of lath, / In his rage and his
wrath, / Cries "Ah, ah!" to the devil'
and offers to 'pare thy nails, dad'
(*Tw.N.*, iv. ii. 134–40) was reputedly a
favourite interlude-figure. Harsnet
remarks (*Declaration of Popish Impos-
tures*, 1603, pp. 114–15) that 'It was a
prety part in the old Church-playes,

when the nimble Vice would skip vp
like a Iacke an Apes into the deuils
necke, and ride the deuil a course, and
belabour him with his woodden dagger, til he made him roare'. In extant
plays, however, the Vices do not
assault the Devil (L. W. Cushman,
*The Devil & the Vice*, 1900, p. 69, suggests Punch-and-Judy shows as an
exception). Dr T. W. Craik has
pointed out to me that the chief comic
character (whether Vice or Fool—e.g.
Moros in William Wager's *The Longer
Thou Livest*) often bore a wooden
dagger and fought his low-comic
associates. 'This roaring devil i'the old
play, that every one may pare his nails
with a wooden dagger' (*H5*, iv. iv. 75–
7) suggests (as does the *Twelfth Night*
verse above) some actual incident,
apparently familiar to an Elizabethan
audience.

315. *sworn brother*] companion-in-
arms, pledged by a vow.

316–17. *tilt-yard*] A space in Westminster, close to Whitehall, for tourna-
ments, jousts, and sports.

320. *eel-skin*] The slim Hal is 'you
eel-skin' in *1H4*, ii. iv. 270, and Robert
Faulconbridge's skinny arms are 'eel-
skins stuff'd' in *John*, i. i. 141.

321. *case . . . hautboy*] Of the three
Elizabethan hautboys, treble, tenor,
and bass, the treble was the slenderest.
Like the modern oboe it had a long

court; and now has he land and beefs. Well, I'll be
acquainted with him if I return, and't shall go hard
but I'll make him a philosopher's two stones to me.
If the young dace be a bait for the old pike, I see no    325
reason in the law of nature but I may snap at him:
let time shape, and there an end.                    *Exit.*

322. has] *Q;* hath *F.*    I'll] *Q;* I will *F.*    be] *Q corr., F;* he *Q uncorr.*    323.
and't] *Q* (and t');* and it *F.*    324. I'll] *Q;* I will *F.*    326–7. him: let] *Q
uncorr., F;* him, till *Q corr.*    327. S.D.] *F (Exeunt.), Capell; not in Q.*

narrow case; cf. 'bow-case' as a jest at
the slim Hal in *1H4*, II. iv. 273.

324. *philosopher's two stones*] Falstaff
probably means, 'as valuable as both
the philosopher's stones put together',
i.e., a source of untold wealth. The
term 'philosopher's stone' was used for
(*a*) a method which transmuted base
metals into gold (or would have done
had it been discovered); as Face de-
fines it in Jonson, *Alch.*, II. v. 40–1 (H.
& S., v. 335), ''Tis a stone, and not a
stone; a spirit, a soul, and a body'—in
other words, a supposed principle,
method, or talisman for transmuta-
tion; (*b*) the *elixir vitae* or *aurum potabile*,
a medicine for perpetuating perfect
youth and health; cf. Beaumont &
Fletcher, *Knight of the Burning Pestle*, IV.
i (Glover & Waller, vi. 219)—'The
philosopher's stone . . . that keeps a
man ever young'. Falstaff, one would
guess, rather overestimates Shallow's
resources.

325–6. *If . . . him*] i.e. 'By the law of
nature the greater eats up the less—

the young dace makes a meal for the
old pike; and by the same law Shallow
(as slight a fellow as I am huge) is my
destined prey'; an echo of the proverb,
'The great fish eats the small' (Tilley,
F311). *Bait* = (*a*) temptation; (*b*)
food.

326–7. *him: let*] Oddly, among corrections made during the printing of
Q there occurs the change in some
copies from 'him: let' (which makes
sense) to 'him, till' (which does not).
In F's entry-direction for IV. i, but not
in Q's, '*Coleuile*' appears. If '*Coleuile*'
were included in Shakespeare's MS,
omitted in error from Q, and then
marked for insertion by the press-
corrector as Q passed through the
press (this forme of Q was much corrected; cf. Shaaber, pp. 468–9), it (or
some other correction) may have
caused an upset hereabouts in the
type, which was reset by guesswork,
*Coleuile* being again overlooked and
the correct 'him: let' corrupted to
'him, till'.

# ACT IV

## SCENE I.—[*Yorkshire.*] *Within the Forest of Gaultree.*

### *Enter the* ARCHBISHOP, MOWBRAY, HASTINGS, [*and others*].

*Arch.* What is this forest call'd?
*Hast.* 'Tis Gaultree Forest, and't shall please your Grace.
*Arch.* Here stand, my lords, and send discoverers forth
    To know the numbers of our enemies.
*Hast.* We have sent forth already.
*Arch.*                 'Tis well done.     5
    My friends and brethren in these great affairs,
    I must acquaint you that I have receiv'd
    New-dated letters from Northumberland,
    Their cold intent, tenor, and substance, thus:
    Here doth he wish his person, with such powers    10
    As might hold sortance with his quality,
    The which he could not levy; whereupon
    He is retir'd to ripe his growing fortunes

### ACT IV

#### *Scene* i

ACT IV SCENE I] *F* (*Actus Quartus. Scena Prima.*); *not in Q.*    Location. *Yorkshire.*]
*Pope.*    *Within . . . Gaultree.*] *Q* [*as end of S.D.*]; *not in F.*    S.D.] *Capell, subst.;*
*Enter the Archbishop, Mowbray, Bardolfe, Hastings, within the forrest of Gaultree.* Q;
*Enter the Arch-bishop, Mowbray, Hastings, Westmerland, Coleuile. F.*    1. Arch.] *QF*
(*Bish.*) [*so also subst. throughout scene*].    2. Gaultree] *Q;* Gualtree *F.*    12.
could] *Q corr., F;* would *Q uncorr.*

Location.] The ancient royal forest of Galtres ('Galtree' in Hol.) stretched north and north-west from York.

Entry.] Q brings on '*Bardolfe*', who has nothing to say. F omits him but adds '*Westmerland*' (who should not appear before l. 25, as in Q), and also '*Coleuile*' (who is not really wanted until he encounters Falstaff in IV. iii). It was perhaps thought in performance that Colevile should be present throughout, as a 'famous rebel' (IV. iii. 61), since at IV. iii. 64–5 he implies that he wished to urge resistance at Gaultree, not surrender.

11. *hold sortance*] accord.

        To Scotland, and concludes in hearty prayers
        That your attempts may overlive the hazard          15
        And fearful meeting of their opposite.
*Mowb.*  Thus do the hopes we have in him touch ground
        And dash themselves to pieces.

### *Enter* MESSENGER.

*Hast.*                            Now, what news?
*Mess.*  West of this forest, scarcely off a mile,
        In goodly form comes on the enemy,                  20
        And, by the ground they hide, I judge their number
        Upon or near the rate of thirty thousand.
*Mowb.*  The just proportion that we gave them out.
        Let us sway on and face them in the field.

### *Enter* WESTMORELAND.

*Arch.*  What well-appointed leader fronts us here?         25
*Mowb.*  I think it is my Lord of Westmoreland.
*West.*  Health and fair greeting from our general,
        The Prince, Lord John and Duke of Lancaster.
*Arch.*  Say on, my Lord of Westmoreland, in peace,
        What doth concern your coming.
*West.*                            Then, my lord,           30
        Unto your Grace do I in chief address
        The substance of my speech. If that rebellion
        Came like itself, in base and abject routs,
        Led on by bloody youth, guarded with rags,

18. S.D. *Enter*] *Q*; *Enter a F.*     24. S.D.] *Q* [*after l. 25*], *F.*     29–30. peace, . . . coming.] *Dyce*; peace, . . . comming? *Q*; peace: . . . comming? *F.*     30–1. *West.* Then, my lord, / Unto] *F*; *West.* Then my L. vnto *Q corr.*; *West.* Vnto *Q uncorr.*     34. rags] *Singer 2, conj. Walker*; rage *QF.*

16. *opposite*] adversary.

23. *just proportion*] exact number.

24. *sway on*] advance ('to express the uniform and forcible motion of a compact body', Johnson).

30. *What . . . coming.*] What your coming means. QF's question-mark after *coming*, a sign that the speech is an inquiry, is best rendered in a modern text by a full stop.

*Then, my lord,*] Uncorrected copies of

Q omit this; corrected ones squeeze it in as the beginning of l. 31, a clear example of correction from MS.

34. *rags*] This reading is widely accepted, for QF's 'rage'. It gives a lively image (*guarded* can mean 'trimmed'), and the rebellion is presented in terms of 'abject' disorder and beggary. But it is not clear that QF are wrong. Rebellion, allegorically personified, progressing as a monarch

And countenanc'd by boys and beggary;                    35
I say, if damn'd commotion so appear'd
In his true, native, and most proper shape,
You, reverend father, and these noble lords
Had not been here to dress the ugly form
Of base and bloody insurrection                          40
With your fair honours. You, Lord Archbishop,
Whose see is by a civil peace maintain'd,
Whose beard the silver hand of peace hath touch'd,
Whose learning and good letters peace hath tutor'd,
Whose white investments figure innocence,                45
The dove and very blessed spirit of peace,
Wherefore do you so ill translate yourself
Out of the speech of peace that bears such grace
Into the harsh and boist'rous tongue of war;
Turning your books to graves, your ink to blood,         50
Your pens to lances, and your tongue divine
To a loud trumpet and a point of war?
*Arch.*  Wherefore do I this? so the question stands.
Briefly, to this end: we are all diseas'd,
And with our surfeiting, and wanton hours,               55

36. appear'd] *Pope;* appeare *QF.*     45. figure] *Q corr., F;* figures *Q uncorr.*
55–79.] *F; not in Q.*

through a beggarly mob, preceded by bloodstained Youth and supported by boys and Beggary, might have a flanking 'guard' of Rage (just as 'rage and hot blood' are Hal's 'counsellors' at IV. iv. 63). Even if *rags* is what Shakespeare intended, the flavour of personification might have made him write 'rage'.

45. *white . . . figure*] white robes symbolize. 'Formerly all bishops wore White, and even when they travell'd' (Humphry Hody, *Hist. of Engl. Councils and Convocations*, 1701, p. 141).

46. *dove*] Reminiscent of *Matt.*, iii. 16—'the spirite of God descendyng lyke a doue'.

47. *translate*] Compressed wordplay: (a) alter from one language to another (see ll. 49–50); (b) transform (cf. *MND.*, III. i. 122—'Bottom, thou

art translated'); and (c) transfer, as bishop, from one see to another.

50–2.] 'The image of "translation", on which the whole passage is built, is itself a covert and ironical play upon the bishop's literary occupations, now so improperly set aside. "Graves" result from the "boist'rous tongue of war" and "books" from the graceful speech of peace' (Herford, ed. 1928).

52. *point*] 'short phrase sounded on an instrument as a signal' (*OED*).

54–66. *we . . . life*] Thematic statement of the ailing realm. Cf. Sonnet cxviii. 3–6, 11–12: 'As, to prevent our maladies unseen, / We sicken to shun sickness when we purge; / Even so, being full of your ne'er-cloying sweetness, / To bitter sauces did I frame my feeding; / . . . / And brought to medicine a healthful state, / Which, rank of goodness, would by ill be cur'd'.

Have brought ourselves into a burning fever,
And we must bleed for it; of which disease
Our late King Richard being infected died.
But, my most noble Lord of Westmoreland,
I take not on me here as a physician,                    60
Nor do I as an enemy to peace
Troop in the throngs of military men,
But rather show awhile like fearful war
To diet rank minds sick of happiness,
And purge th' obstructions which begin to stop          65
Our very veins of life. Hear me more plainly.
I have in equal balance justly weigh'd
What wrongs our arms may do, what wrongs we suffer,
And find our griefs heavier than our offences.
We see which way the stream of time doth run,           70
And are enforc'd from our most quiet there
By the rough torrent of occasion,
And have the summary of all our griefs,
When time shall serve, to show in articles,
Which long ere this we offer'd to the King              75

71. our most] *F; careless conj. this edn; not in Q.*        there] *F; shore Wilson (N.C.S.),
conj. Vaughan; sphere Hanmer; flow Sisson; not in Q.*

57. *bleed*] i.e. our bloodshed in battle
is a surgical 'bleeding'.

60.] This line is contradicted by ll.
64–5; Wilson (N.C.S.) thinks something may have been lost after it. But
the argument, found also in Holinshed
(cf. Appendix I, p. 193), is, 'I am not
here as a blood-letter—that is the
function of others—nor is it as an
enemy to peace that I join with men of
war. For a while I look warlike, but
this is to bring about a change of mind,
purify our nation's life, and establish
true peace' (see ll. 85–7). The Archbishop's argument may not be a good
one, but his dilemma is that facing any
spiritual leader who has to countenance war.

64. *rank . . . happiness*] minds bloated
with ease and luxury.

67. *justly*] exactly.

71. *our . . . there*] The likeliest sense
of F's reading (the passage is not in Q)

is 'our greatest quiet therein' (i.e. in
the stream of time); *most* can be adjec-
tival, as in *Meas.,* IV. i. 44—'my most
stay'. But F is clumsy, and 'shore' (Wilson, N.C.S.) fits 'stream' and 'torrent';
the graphically easy misreadings of *f* as
*t* and *o* as *e* could result in 'there' by
error. Daniel provides some support;
when  Bolingbroke  returns  from
France, he describes a river bursting
its banks and says that Bolingbroke
'Com'd [sic] to quiet shore but not to
rest' (*C.W.,* i. 88). Many editors follow
Hanmer's 'sphere', but Shakespeare
uses 'sphere' only for celestial bodies or
orbits. Yet the trouble may lie not in
F's 'there' but in 'our most', which is
rhythmically and idiomatically uneasy; 'careless' is the sort of word, not
graphically remote from 'our most',
which would give good sense with
'quiet there'.

72. *occasion*] events, occurrences.

And might by no suit gain our audience.
When we are wrong'd, and would unfold our griefs,
We are denied access unto his person,
Even by those men that most have done us wrong.
The dangers of the days but newly gone,                    80
Whose memory is written on the earth
With yet-appearing blood, and the examples
Of every minute's instance, present now,
Hath put us in these ill-beseeming arms,
Not to break peace, or any branch of it,                    85
But to establish here a peace indeed,
Concurring both in name and quality.

*West.* Whenever yet was your appeal denied?
Wherein have you been galled by the King?
What peer hath been suborn'd to grate on you,              90
That you should seal this lawless bloody book
Of forg'd rebellion with a seal divine,
⟨And consecrate commotion's bitter edge?⟩

*Arch.* My brother general, the commonwealth,
⟨To brother born an household cruelty,⟩                    95
I make my quarrel in particular.

---

80. days] *F;* daie's *Q.*          93.] *Q uncorr.; not in Q corr., F.*          94.] *F;* My brother
Generall, the common wealth *Q;* My brother general, [*shewing* Mowbray.] the
common-wealth; *Capell;* My brother-general, the common-wealth; *Var.* '73*;*
My brother, general! the commonwealth! *Knight;* My burden general is the
commonwealth; *Hudson 1;* My quarrel general, the commonwealth, *conj.*
*Johnson.*          95.] *Q uncorr.; not in Q corr., F.*

80–4. *dangers . . . Hath*] Verb-forms
in -s and -th occur with plural subjects, particularly from c. 1540 to c.
1640; being standard conversational
practice they abound in plays and
fiction—'among dramatists Ben Jonson is the only one who makes little use
of [them]' (Jespersen, *Mod. Engl.
Grammar*, II, sec. 2.242).

83. *Of . . . instance*] Which every
minute urges upon us.

90. *suborn'd . . . on*] secretly insti-
gated to harass.

91–2.] i.e. that you should authorize
with the divine seal of your approval
this forged and lawless work. There

may be a reference to the function of
bishops as licensers for the press.

93–7.] On possible cuts hereabouts,
see Intro., p. lxxii.

94–6.] Possibly corrupt — *brother
general* and *household cruelty* sound
dubious. The speech as it stands might
mean 'The grievances of my brethren
and fellow-subjects [= brother gen-
eral] and the home cruelty to my born
brother, make me take this quarrel to
myself'. If l. 95 is left out, the sense is
easier, though still a cryptic and inadequate reply to Westmoreland—'I
make the national cause my own, because these men are my brothers'.

*West.*  There is no need of any such redress,
    Or if there were, it not belongs to you.
*Mowb.*  Why not to him in part, and to us all
    That feel the bruises of the days before,          100
    And suffer the condition of these times
    To lay a heavy and unequal hand
    Upon our honours?
*West.*                  O, my good Lord Mowbray,
    Construe the times to their necessities,
    And you shall say, indeed, it is the time,         105
    And not the King, that doth you injuries.
    Yet for your part, it not appears to me
    Either from the King or in the present time
    That you should have an inch of any ground
    To build a grief on: were you not restor'd      110
    To all the Duke of Norfolk's signories,
    Your noble and right well-remember'd father's?
*Mowb.*  What thing, in honour, had my father lost,
    That need to be reviv'd and breath'd in me?
    The King that lov'd him, as the state stood then,    115
    Was force perforce compell'd to banish him,
    And then that Henry Bolingbroke and he,
    Being mounted and both roused in their seats,
    Their neighing coursers daring of the spur,
    Their armed staves in charge, their beavers down,    120
    Their eyes of fire sparkling through sights of steel,

---

102–3. To . . . hand / Upon . . . honours?] *Q;* [*one line*] *F.*    103–39. O, . . . King.]
*F; not in Q.*    116. force perforce] *Theobald;* forc'd, perforce *F; not in Q.*

97–8.] Commenting on the Archbishop's grievances, Holinshed adds 'the re orming whereof did not yet apperteine vnto him' (iii. 36). The Tudors did not countenance rebellious clerics—'it is evident that men of the Cleargie, and ecclesiastical ministers, as their successours, ought both themselues specially, and before other, to be obedient vnto their princes, and also to exhort al others vnto the same' (*Certain Sermons or Homilies*, 1574, p. 598).

102. *unequal*] unjust.

104.] Understand these times by the inevitability of circumstances.

111. *signories*] estates and honours.

115–29.] One of the best of the reminiscential passages, recalling *R2*, I. iii.

118. *roused*] raised; probably 'excited' also.

119. *daring . . . spur*] challenging the spur to prick them (or, perhaps, challenging it to give the signal for onset).

120. *armed . . . charge*] steel-tipped lances fixed for the charge.

*beavers*] visors, face-guards.

And the loud trumpet blowing them together,
Then, then, when there was nothing could have stay'd
My father from the breast of Bolingbroke,
O, when the King did throw his warder down,          125
His own life hung upon the staff he threw;
Then threw he down himself and all their lives
That by indictment and by dint of sword
Have since miscarried under Bolingbroke.

*West.*  You speak, Lord Mowbray, now you know not what.
The Earl of Hereford was reputed then          131
In England the most valiant gentleman.
Who knows on whom Fortune would then have smil'd?
But if your father had been victor there,
He ne'er had borne it out of Coventry;          135
For all the country, in a general voice,
Cried hate upon him; and all their prayers and love
Were set on Hereford, whom they doted on,
And bless'd, and grac'd, indeed more than the King.
But this is mere digression from my purpose.          140
Here come I from our princely general
To know your griefs, to tell you from his Grace
That he will give you audience; and wherein
It shall appear that your demands are just,
You shall enjoy them, everything set off          145
That might so much as think you enemies.

*Mowb.*  But he hath forc'd us to compel this offer,
And it proceeds from policy, not love.

*West.*  Mowbray, you overween to take it so.
This offer comes from mercy, not from fear;          150
For lo, within a ken our army lies,
Upon mine honour, all too confident
To give admittance to a thought of fear.
Our battle is more full of names than yours,
Our men more perfect in the use of arms,          155
Our armour all as strong, our cause the best;

---

139. indeed] *Theobald, conj. Thirlby;* and did *F; not in Q.*          140. But] *F; West.*
But *Q.*

125. *warder*] staff (held by whoever          128. *indictment*] legal accusation.
presided over a combat).          154. *battle*] army.

Then reason will our hearts should be as good.
Say you not then, our offer is compell'd.

*Mowb.* Well, by my will we shall admit no parley.

*West.* That argues but the shame of your offence:     160
A rotten case abides no handling.

*Hast.* Hath the Prince John a full commission,
In very ample virtue of his father,
To hear, and absolutely to determine,
Of what conditions we shall stand upon?     165

*West.* That is intended in the general's name:
I muse you make so slight a question.

*Arch.* Then take, my Lord of Westmoreland, this schedule,
For this contains our general grievances.
Each several article herein redress'd,     170
All members of our cause, both here and hence,
That are ensinew'd to this action
Acquitted by a true substantial form
And present execution of our wills—
To us and to our purposes confin'd     175

172. ensinew'd] *Q* (ensinewed), *F* (insinewed), *Capell* (insinew'd).     174.
wills—] *Q* (willes,), *F* (wills,), *this edn;* wills *Theobald 2.*     175. to our] *F;* our *Q.*
purposes confin'd] *This edn;* purposes confinde, *QF, subst.;* purposes, confin'd;
*Theobald 2;* properties confirm'd; *Hanmer;* properties, confin'd; *Warburton;*
purposes, confirm'd; *Capell;* purposes, consign'd; *Malone.*

161.] This abstract aphorism plays on a concrete proverb—'It is a bad sack (case) that will abide no clouting' (Tilley, S6). Of such effects in Shakespeare's mature style Clemen remarks, 'Thus a peculiar world is created, in which the concrete is continually mingled with the abstract' (*Devel. of Sh.'s Imagery*, 1951, p. 79).

162. *commission*] commis-si-on; cf. *ques-ti-on* (l. 167), *ac-ti-on* (ll. 172, 192).

163. *very ample virtue*] full authority.

164–5. *absolutely . . . upon*] unreservedly to decide on the conditions we shall insist on.

166. *intended . . . name*] signified in the title of general.

171–7.] These lines have caused much discussion, centring mainly on attempts to explain or emend QF's 'confinde' (l. 175). The argument has arisen from the practice of taking this line with what precedes rather than with what follows; that the rebels should wish the *execution of* [*their*] *wills* to be *confin'd* to them and their purposes would indeed be puzzling. But ll. 171–4, not 171–5, should be taken together, as an absolute clause, and l. 175 taken with the next two. The sense is then clear: 'If all of us involved in this action are granted a full effective pardon and the prompt satisfaction of our demands, we shall flow once more within our proper bounds, restricting ourselves to our own affairs, and support the cause of peace'. Had l. 176 preceded l. 175 no difficulty would have been felt. *Confin'd* points forward, to the image of the stream returning to its proper course after bursting forth.

We come within our aweful banks again,
And knit our powers to the arm of peace.
*West.* This will I show the general. Please you, lords,
In sight of both our battles we may meet,
And either end in peace—which God so frame!—        180
Or to the place of diff'rence call the swords
Which must decide it.
*Arch.*                        My lord, we will do so.

                                        *Exit Westmoreland.*

*Mowb.* There is a thing within my bosom tells me
That no conditions of our peace can stand.
*Hast.* Fear you not that: if we can make our peace        185
Upon such large terms, and so absolute,
As our conditions shall consist upon,
Our peace shall stand as firm as rocky mountains.
*Mowb.* Yea, but our valuation shall be such
That every slight and false-derived cause,        190
Yea, every idle, nice, and wanton reason,
Shall to the King taste of this action;
That were our royal faiths martyrs in love,
We shall be winnow'd with so rough a wind
That even our corn shall seem as light as chaff        195
And good from bad find no partition.
*Arch.* No, no, my lord, note this: the King is weary
Of dainty and such picking grievances;

180. And] *Theobald, conj. Thirlby;* At *QF.*        God] *Q;* Heauen *F.*        181. diff'-
rence] *Q;* difference *F.*        182. S.D.] *Q* [*after* decide it.], *Rowe; not in F.*        185.
not that:] *F2* (not that,), *Pope;* not, that *QF.*        189. Yea] *Q;* I *F.*        194. winnow'd] *Q;* winnowed *F.*        197–8. weary / Of dainty and] *QF, subst.;* weary of /
Such dainty and *Keightley;* weary / And dainty of *conj. Vaughan.*        198. dainty
. . . picking] *QF;* picking out such dainty *conj. Johnson.*

176.] Wilson (N.C.S.) quotes as
parallel the 'Shakespearean' pages of
*Sir Thomas More,* ll. 39–40—'whiles
they [the rebels] ar ore the banck of
their obedyenc / thus will they bere
downe all things' (A. W. Pollard and
others, *Sh.'s Hand in 'Sir Thomas More',*
1923, pp. 229 ff.).
    *aweful*] This spelling, which *OED*
records as 17th–19th c., seems worth
reviving in the 20th c. for this particular sense.

181. *diff'rence*] battle.
187. *consist*] stand firm.
189. *our valuation*] the value set on us.
193. *were . . . love*] even should
we prove our loyalty by suffering
death.
198.] This may be explained, but
awkwardly, 'Of finicky and so per-
nickety fault-finding' (the grievances
being not the rebels' complaints—
which are grave, not 'dainty'—but
the King's niggling suspicions). Per-

For he hath found, to end one doubt by death
Revives two greater in the heirs of life:                    200
And therefore will he wipe his tables clean,
And keep no tell-tale to his memory
That may repeat and history his loss
To new remembrance. For full well he knows
He cannot so precisely weed this land                        205
As his misdoubts present occasion.
His foes are so enrooted with his friends
That plucking to unfix an enemy
He doth unfasten so and shake a friend.
So that this land, like an offensive wife                    210
That hath enrag'd him on to offer strokes,
As he is striking, holds his infant up,
And hangs resolv'd correction in the arm
That was uprear'd to execution.

*Hast.*  Besides, the King hath wasted all his rods          215
On late offenders, that he now doth lack
The very instruments of chastisement;
So that his power, like to a fangless lion,
May offer, but not hold.

*Arch.*                      'Tis very true:
And therefore be assur'd, my good Lord Marshal,              220
If we do now make our atonement well,
Our peace will, like a broken limb united,

haps *such picking* mis-spells some deri-
vative of 'suspic-', 'suspec-' ('suspicious', 'suspecting', 'suspectious', 'sus-
pectful').

199. *doubt*] source of fear.

200. *heirs of life*] those who survive.

201. *tables*] tablets, records.

205–6.] i.e. he cannot cleanse the
land of every single thing which his
fears (*misdoubts*) cause him to suspect.

207–9.] Probably echoing *Matt.*,
xiii. 29 (Genevan)—'lest while ye goe
about to gather the tares, yee plucke
[Bishops' Bible, 'roote'] vp also with
them the wheate'.

210–14.] The particularity of this
illustration has attracted comment; it
looks like personal observation.

213. *hangs*] suspends in mid-action.

215. *wasted*] used up.

*rods*] Possibly echoing *Ps.*, lxxxix. 32
—'I wyl visite their offenses with the
rodde'.

218. *fangless lion*] Shakespeare may
have noticed that some of the lions in
the royal menagerie at the Tower of
London were ancient creatures; in
1598 Hentzner saw 'one lion of great
size, called Edward VI, from his having been born in that reign' (Hentzner,
*Travels in England*, trans. Horace Wal-
pole, 1797, p. 28).

219. *offer*] threaten violence.

221. *atonement*] reconciliation.

222. *like ... united*] This medical fact
was proverbial; Tilley, B515, lists 'A
broken bone (leg) is the stronger when
it is well set'.

Grow stronger for the breaking.
*Mowb.*                                        Be it so.
Here is return'd my Lord of Westmoreland.

*Enter* WESTMORELAND.

*West.*  The Prince is here at hand. Pleaseth your lordship  225
To meet his Grace just distance 'tween our armies.
*Mowb.*  Your Grace of York, in God's name then set forward.
*Arch.*  Before! and greet his Grace.—My lord, we come.

[*They go forward.*]

[SCENE II.] *Enter* PRINCE JOHN [*of* LANCASTER] *and his army.*

*Lanc.*  You are well encounter'd here, my cousin Mowbray;
Good day to you, gentle Lord Archbishop;
And so to you, Lord Hastings, and to all.
My Lord of York, it better show'd with you
When that your flock, assembled by the bell,                5
Encircled you to hear with reverence
Your exposition on the holy text
Than now to see you here an iron man,
Cheering a rout of rebels with your drum,

---

223–4. Be . . . Westmoreland.] *F*; [*one line*] *Q*.      226. armies.] *Q*; Armies? *F*.
227. God's] *Q*; heauen's *F*.      set] *Q*; *not in F*.      228. Grace.—My lord, we]
*Johnson*; grace (my lord) we *QF, subst.*; Grace; my lord, we *Theobald*; grace, my
lord: we *Collier*.      228. S.D.] *Wilson (N.C.S.)* ; *Exeunt. Capell* ; *not in QF*.

*Scene* II

SCENE II] *Capell* ; *not in QF*.       S.D.] *Q* (*Enter Prince Iohn and his Armie.*) [*after IV. i.*
*226*] ; *Enter Prince Iohn. F*.       *1. Lanc.*] *QF* (*Iohn*), *Rowe*.       *4. show'd*] *F*; shewed
*Q*.       8. Than] *F*; That *Q*.       man] *F*; man talking *Q*.

---

225. *Pleaseth*] Let it please; a corruption of 'please it' (*OED*, Please *v.* 3).

226. *just distance*] half-way; 'iust in
the midwaie betwixt both the armies'
(Hol. iii. 38).

228.] QF envisage no break between
this line and the next, and mark no
*Exeunt*. Prince John enters in Q after
l. 226, in F after l. 228. The place
changes to 'just distance 'tween our
armies' with no more ado than that the
army present and the army entering
take up positions on the stage. To

mark an *Exeunt* and change of place is
misleading.

*Scene* II

1. *cousin*] A mode of address common
among the nobility, regardless of
family relationship.

2. *gentle*] Cf. I. i. 189–91, note.

8. *iron*] (*a*) armoured; (*b*) merciless;
cf. *1H4*, II. iii. 51—'iron wars'. Q reads
'iron man talking'—perhaps Shakespeare's first thought, replaced by
'Cheering'.

Turning the word to sword, and life to death.　　10
That man that sits within a monarch's heart,
And ripens in the sunshine of his favour,
Would he abuse the countenance of the king,
Alack, what mischiefs might he set abroach
In shadow of such greatness! With you, Lord Bishop,　15
It is even so. Who hath not heard it spoken
How deep you were within the books of God,
To us the speaker in his parliament,
To us th'imagin'd voice of God himself,
The very opener and intelligencer　　20
Between the grace, the sanctities of heaven,
And our dull workings? O, who shall believe
But you misuse the reverence of your place,
Employ the countenance and grace of heav'n
As a false favourite doth his prince's name,　　25
In deeds dishonourable? You have ta'en up,
Under the counterfeited zeal of God,
The subjects of his substitute, my father,
And both against the peace of heaven and him

---

17. God] *Q;* Heauen *F.*　19. imagin'd] *Rowe 3;* imagine *QF;* image and *Rann, conj. Malone* [*Suppl. 1780*].　God himself] *Q;* Heauen it selfe *F.*　24. Employ] *F;* Imply *Q.*　heav'n] *Q;* Heauen *F.*　25–6. name, / In . . . dishonourable? You] *F;* name: / In . . . dishonourable you *Q.*　26. ta'en] *Q;* taken *F.*　27. God] *Q;* Heauen *F.*　28. his] *Q;* Heauens *F.*

---

10. *word . . . sword*] A word-play lost through sound change; cf. *Wiv.*, III. i. 44–5—'the sword and the word! Do you study them both, Master Parson?'

12.] Seemingly one of the many echoes of Nashe in the *Henry IV*s— 'assemble the famous men of all ages, and let me which of them all sate in the sun-shine of his soueraignes grace' (*Pierce Penilesse*; McKerrow, i. 186).

13. *countenance*] support, favour.

17. *within . . . God*] Both (*a*) in works of divinity (Holinshed describes him as of 'incomparable learning'; iii. 37), and (*b*) in God's good graces.

18.] i.e. the one who conveyed to us the counsels of God. The Speaker acted, and still acts, as intermediary between the monarch and the Commons.

20. *opener and intelligencer*] interpreter and messenger.

21. *grace . . . sanctities*] Since the Archbishop is thought of as Speaker of a celestial parliament, the image is probably, as Wilson (N.C.S.) suggests, 'the Divine Prince and the celestial hierarchy [*sanctities* = saints]. Shakespeare is thinking of monarch and court'. Cf. Milton, *P.L.*, iii. 60— 'About him all the Sanctities of Heaven / Stood thick as Starrs'.

22. *workings*] workings of mind, perceptions.

26. *ta'en up*] levied.

27. *zeal*] Apparently playing on 'seal'. The phrase echoes *Romans*, x. 2 —'they haue a zeale of God'.

28. *substitute*] deputy.

29. *peace . . . him*] A technical

Have here up-swarm'd them.

*Arch.*                              Good my Lord of Lancaster,
     I am not here against your father's peace;          31
     But, as I told my Lord of Westmoreland,
     The time misorder'd doth, in common sense,
     Crowd us and crush us to this monstrous form
     To hold our safety up. I sent your Grace          35
     The parcels and particulars of our grief,
     The which hath been with scorn shov'd from the court,
     Whereon this Hydra son of war is born,
     Whose dangerous eyes may well be charm'd asleep
     With grant of our most just and right desires,          40
     And true obedience, of this madness cur'd,
     Stoop tamely to the foot of majesty.

*Mowb.*  If not, we ready are to try our fortunes
     To the last man.

*Hast.*                              And though we here fall down,
     We have supplies to second our attempt:          45
     If they miscarry, theirs shall second them;
     And so success of mischief shall be born,

---

30. up-swarm'd] *Q ;* vp-swarmed *F.*        *Arch.] Q (Bishop), F (Bish.) [so throughout*
*scene].*     37. shov'd] *F ;* shoued *Q.*          *scene].*     38. Hydra son] *F (Hydra*-Sonne*), Han-*
*mer 2 ;* Hidra, sonne *Q.*     41. cur'd] *F ; mer 2 ;* Hidra, sonne *Q.*     41. cur'd] *F ;*
cured *Q.*

phrase; cf. Sir Thomas Smith, *De Republica Anglorum*, 1583, III. iii—'The Prince . . . must see iustice executed against all . . . offenders against the peace, which is called Gods and his'.

33. *in common sense*] as all can see.

34. *monstrous form*] distorted shape, abnormal course.

36. *parcels . . . grief*] details of our grievances.

37. *hath*] On the grammatical agreement, see IV. i. 80-4, note.

38. *Hydra . . . war*] i.e. Hydra-like offspring, war. Probably an echo of Daniel, *C.W.* iii. 86—'And yet new *Hydraes*, lo, new heades appeare / T'afflict that peace reputed then so sure'. The Hydra with its many heads was proverbial (Tilley, H278); it was the fabulous snake of the Lernæan marshes, whose heads grew again as fast as they were cut off, finally killed

by Hercules—cf. Ovid, *Metam.,* ix. 70-4. *OED*'s definition of the figurative senses suggests the comprehensive relevance of this image to the situation —'A thing, person, or body of persons compared to the Lernæan hydra in its baneful or destructive character, its multifarious aspects, or the difficulty of its extirpation'.

39.] The image changes from the many- (or hundred-) headed Hydra to Juno's hundred-eyed watchman Argus, charmed asleep by Mercury's music; Ovid, *Metam.,* i. 622-721. Shortly before dealing with the Archbishop of York's rebellion, Holinshed calls the Archbishop of Canterbury 'an other Argus, hauing his eie on each side' (Hol., iii. 31).

45-9.] A development of the Hydra metaphor of l. 38.

47. *success*] succession.

And heir from heir shall hold this quarrel up
Whiles England shall have generation.

*Lanc.* You are too shallow, Hastings, much too shallow,   50
To sound the bottom of the after-times.

*West.* Pleaseth your Grace to answer them directly
How far forth you do like their articles.

*Lanc.* I like them all, and do allow them well,
And swear here, by the honour of my blood,   55
My father's purposes have been mistook,
And some about him have too lavishly
Wrested his meaning and authority.
My lord, these griefs shall be with speed redress'd;
Upon my soul they shall. If this may please you,   60
Discharge your powers unto their several counties,
As we will ours; and here between the armies
Let's drink together friendly and embrace,
That all their eyes may bear those tokens home
Of our restored love and amity.   65

*Arch.* I take your princely word for these redresses.

*Lanc.* I give it you, and will maintain my word;
And thereupon I drink unto your Grace.

*Hast.* Go, captain, and deliver to the army
This news of peace. Let them have pay, and part.   70
I know it will well please them. Hie thee, captain.

                            *Exit [Officer].*

*Arch.* To you, my noble Lord of Westmoreland.

*West.* I pledge your Grace; and if you knew what pains
I have bestow'd to breed this present peace
You would drink freely; but my love to ye   75
Shall show itself more openly hereafter.

*Arch.* I do not doubt you.

*West.*               I am glad of it.

---

48. this] *F*; his *Q.*     50. *Lanc.*] *Q* (*Prince*), *F* (*Iohn*) [*so subst. through rest of scene*].
60. soul] *Q*; Life *F.*    shall. If] *F*; shal, if *Q.*    67. *Lanc.*] *F* (*Iohn*), *Rowe*; *not in*
*Q.*    69. *Hast.*] *F*; *Prince Q.*    71. S.D.] *F* (*Exit.*), *Capell*; *not in Q.*    73–4.]
*As Q*; I . . . Grace: / And . . . bestow'd, / To . . . Peace, / *F.*    74. bestow'd] *F*;
bestowed *Q.*

49. *generation*] offspring.
52. *Pleaseth*] Cf. IV. i. 225, note.
54–65.] Stow and Holinshed give this negotiation to Westmoreland (Prince John being only 16 years old).

Health to my lord and gentle cousin, Mowbray.

*Mowb.* You wish me health in very happy season,
For I am on the sudden something ill.                    80

*Arch.* Against ill chances men are ever merry,
But heaviness foreruns the good event.

*West.* Therefore be merry, coz, since sudden sorrow
Serves to say thus, 'Some good thing comes tomorrow'.

*Arch.* Believe me, I am passing light in spirit.          85

*Mowb.* So much the worse, if your own rule be true.

                                        *Shouts* [*within*].

*Lanc.* The word of peace is render'd. Hark how they shout!

*Mowb.* This had been cheerful after victory.

*Arch.* A peace is of the nature of a conquest,
For then both parties nobly are subdu'd,                90
And neither party loser.

*Lanc.*                    Go, my lord,
And let our army be discharged too. *Exit* [*Westmoreland*].
And, good my lord, so please you, let our trains
March by us, that we may peruse the men
We should have cop'd withal.

*Arch.*                        Go, good Lord Hastings,
And, ere they be dismiss'd, let them march by.          96

                                        *Exit* [*Hastings*].

*Lanc.* I trust, lords, we shall lie tonight together.


                *Enter* WESTMORELAND.


Now, cousin, wherefore stands our army still?

*West.* The leaders, having charge from you to stand,
Will not go off until they hear you speak.              100

*Lanc.* They know their duties.


                *Enter* HASTINGS.


86. S.D.] *Q* (*shout.*), *Capell; not in F.*     90. subdu'd] *F;* subdued *Q.*     92. S.D.]
*F* (*Exit.*) [*after l. 94*], *Rowe; not in Q.*     93. our] *QF;* your *Capell.*     96. S.D.] *F*
(*Exit.*), *Rowe 2; not in Q.*     97. S.D.] *Q; [after l. 96*], *F.*


79. *happy*] opportune.
81–2.] Parallels to this quasi-
proverbial sentiment occur in *Rom.*,
IV. ii. 46–7, v. i. 2–5, v. iii. 88–90, and
*Troil.*, I. i. 39–40; also in Webster

*White Devil*, I. ii. 259 (Lucas, i. 119)—
'Woe to light hearts!—they still fore-
run our fall'. Tilley, L277, gives many
instances under 'A lightening (light-
ning) before death'.

*Hast.*  My lord, our army is dispers'd already.

Like youthful steers unyok'd they take their courses

East, west, north, south; or, like a school broke up,

Each hurries toward his home and sporting-place.          105

*West.*  Good tidings, my Lord Hastings; for the which

I do arrest thee, traitor, of high treason;

And you, Lord Archbishop, and you, Lord Mowbray,

Of capital treason I attach you both.

*Mowb.*  Is this proceeding just and honourable?          110

*West.*  Is your assembly so?

*Arch.*  Will you thus break your faith?

*Lanc.*                              I pawn'd thee none.

I promis'd you redress of these same grievances

Whereof you did complain; which, by mine honour,

I will perform with a most Christian care.          115

But, for you rebels, look to taste the due

Meet for rebellion and such acts as yours.

Most shallowly did you these arms commence,

Fondly brought here, and foolishly sent hence.

Strike up our drums, pursue the scatter'd stray:          120

God, and not we, hath safely fought today.

Some guard these traitors to the block of death,

Treason's true bed and yielder-up of breath.          *Exeunt.*

---

102.] *Q; Our Army is dispers'd: F.*     103. take their courses] *Q;* tooke their
course *F.*     105. toward] *Q;* towards *F.*     116. you rebels,] *Q;* you (Rebels) *F.*
117. and ... yours] *F; not in Q.*     121. God ... hath] *Q;* Heauen ... haue *F.*
122. these traitors] *F;* this traitour *Q.*     123. S.D.] *F; not in Q.*

104–5. *like ... place*] 'This delight in
boy nature is evident ... in the many
images Shakespeare draws from it; and
the little vignettes he gives ... of the
boy in his daily life and play are of
great interest' (Spurgeon, p. 140).

109. *attach*] arrest.

111. *assembly*] The word is probably
used in its legal sense with reference
to the offence known as unlawful
assembly. 'Vnlawfull assemblie is
where people assemble themselves together to do some vnlawfull thing
against the peace' (*An exposition of cer-*

*taine ... Termes of the Lawes*, 1598, f.
120[r]).

120. *stray*] stragglers.

122. *these traitors*] Q's 'this traitour',
though it might mark the Archbishop's dominating role, is doubtless
wrong, since several rebels are executed, as Stow, Holinshed, and the
play equally make clear.

123. S.D.] Neither Q nor F marks
any break of scene, though F supplies
the *Exeunt*, which is not in Q. Falstaff's incursion at what is now IV. iii. I
is merely one of a series of episodes.

## [SCENE III.—*The same.*]

*Alarum. Excursions. Enter* FALSTAFF *and*
COLEVILE[, *meeting*].

*Fal.* What's your name, sir? Of what condition are you,
and of what place?

*Cole.* I am a knight, sir, and my name is Colevile of the
Dale.

*Fal.* Well then, Colevile is your name, a knight is your        5
degree, and your place the Dale. Colevile shall be
still your name, a traitor your degree, and the dungeon your place—a place deep enough; so shall you
be still Colevile of the Dale.

*Cole.* Are not you Sir John Falstaff?        10

*Fal.* As good a man as he, sir, whoe'er I am. Do ye yield,
sir, or shall I sweat for you? If I do sweat, they are
the drops of thy lovers, and they weep for thy death;
therefore rouse up fear and trembling, and do obser-
vance to my mercy.        15

*Cole.* [*Kneels*] I think you are Sir John Falstaff, and in
that thought yield me.

*Scene* III

SCENE III] *Capell; not in QF.        Location.*] *Capell, subst.        S.D. Alarum . . .
Falstaff*] Q (*Alarum Enter Falstaffe excursions*); *Enter Falstaffe F.        and Colevile*] F;
*not in* Q.        *meeting*] *Capell; not in QF.        2. place?*] Q; *place, I pray? F.        3–4.*]
*As* Q; I . . . Sir: / And . . . Dale. F.        6–7. be still*] Q; *still be F.        16. S.D.*]
*Wilson* (*N.C.S.*); *not in QF.*

S.D.] F gives Colevile an entry here
though it had already brought him on
at the beginning of this act.

1–68.] The episode is a farcical
counterpart of Falstaff's bogus valour
in 'killing' Hotspur in *1H4*, v. iv, and
is plausible only (if at all) in the light
of the reputation for prowess acquired
then. As Shaaber remarks, 'An
important motive [for the scene] was
certainly to give Falstaff his only
appearance in the longest act of the
play and to relieve the otherwise un-
relieved seriousness of its episodes'.

1. *condition*] rank.

3–4. *Colevile . . . Dale*] A 'sir Iohn
Colleuill of the Dale' is passingly men-

tioned among rebels executed for conspiracy at Durham, not York (Hol.,
iii. 38).

7–9. *the dungeon . . . Dale*] 'A *dale* is a
deep place; a *dungeon* is a deep place:
he that is in a *dungeon* may therefore be
said to be in a *dale*' (Johnson, *Var. '73*).
This seems all the interpretation needed, though Wilson (N.C.S.) and P. G.
Phialas ('Colevile of the Dale', *Sh. Q.*,
ix. 86–8) argue that the *dale/dungeon*
idea is of the pit (of hell).

12–13. *they . . . drops*] the sweat-
drops are the tears.

*lovers*] friends ('now rare'; *OED*).

16–17.] The result of Falstaff's
Shrewsbury renown.

*Fal.* I have a whole school of tongues in this belly of mine,
and not a tongue of them all speaks any other word
but my name. And I had but a belly of any indif-    20
ferency, I were simply the most active fellow in
Europe: my womb, my womb, my womb undoes
me. Here comes our general.

*Retreat [sounded]. Enter* PRINCE JOHN, WESTMORELAND,
[BLUNT,] *and others.*

*Lanc.*  The heat is past; follow no further now.
Call in the powers, good cousin Westmoreland.    25
                              [*Exit Westmoreland.*]
Now Falstaff, where have you been all this while?
When everything is ended, then you come.
These tardy tricks of yours will, on my life,
One time or other break some gallows' back.

*Fal.*  I would be sorry, my lord, but it should be thus. I    30
never knew yet but rebuke and check was the reward
of valour. Do you think me a swallow, an arrow, or a
bullet? Have I in my poor and old motion the expedition of thought? I have speeded hither with the
very extremest inch of possibility; I have foundered    35
nine score and odd posts; and here, travel-tainted as
I am, have in my pure and immaculate valour taken
Sir John Colevile of the Dale, a most furious knight
and valorous enemy. But what of that? He saw me,
and yielded; that I may justly say, with the hook-    40

23. S.D. *Retreat sounded*] Q (*Retraite*), *Staunton; not in F.*    *Enter . . . others.*] *Cambridge, subst.; Enter Iohn Westmerland, and the rest. Q; Enter Prince Iohn, and Westmerland. F.*    24. *Lanc.*] QF (*Iohn*) [*so also at l. 43*].    *further*] *Q; farther F.*
25. S.D. *Rowe; not in QF.*

18–20. *I have . . . name*] My paunch
proclaims me in all languages to the
world.

20–1. *indifferency*] ordinary kind.

22. *womb*] belly; cf. Scots 'wame'.

30. *but . . . thus*] if it should be otherwise.

33–4. *expedition*] speed, urgency.

36. *posts*] post-horses. 'Post-horses
are established at every ten miles or
thereabouts, which they ride a false

gallop after some ten miles an hower
sometimes' (Fynes Moryson, *Itinerary*,
1907, iii. 479). 'Falstaff claims to
have traversed at least 1800 miles, but
perhaps he "foundered" several
posts at each stage; cf. "horseback
breaker" (*1H4*, II. iv. 268)' (Wilson,
N.C.S.).

40–1. *hook-nosed*] This imperial
feature has been tracked down to the
medallion portrait of Caesar in

nosed fellow of Rome, three words, 'I came, saw, and overcame'.

*Lanc.* It was more of his courtesy than your deserving.

*Fal.* I know not: here he is, and here I yield him; and I beseech your Gràce, let it be booked with the rest of 45 this day's deeds, or by the Lord I will have it in a particular ballad else, with mine own picture on the top on't, Colevile kissing my foot: to the which course if I be enforced, if you do not all show like gilt twopences to me, and I in the clear sky of fame o'er- 50 shine you as much as the full moon doth the cinders of the element, which show like pins' heads to her,

---

41. Rome, three words,] *This edn;* Rome, there cosin, [*catchword Sig. G4ᶜ* their] *Q;* Rome, *F;* Rome there, *Cæsar,—Theobald;* Rome, their Cæsar, *Sisson;* Rome, your cousin,— *conj. Capell (Notes);* Rome, their first Cæsar,— *conj. Herr;* Rome, their true consul,— *or* Rome, thrice there consul, *conj. Vaughan;* Rome, thrasonic, *conj. Ridley.*          46. by the Lord] *Q;* I sweare *F.*          47. else] *Q; not in F.*          48. on't] *Q;* of it *F.*

---

North's *Plutarch*, showing it in profile (H. N. Paul, *apud* Shaaber).

41. *Rome, three words*] Q reads, 'Rome, there cosin'. The 'there' is the first word on G4ᵛ; the catchword on G4ʳ is 'their'. This makes little sense; Falstaff may be impudent, but he will hardly dare or indeed wish to call Prince John, whom he dislikes, 'cosin'. Emendations abound (cf. collation) but they sound unlikely. Plutarch's *Life of Caesar*, however, seems to furnish a clue for the solution. Against the marginal annotation, 'Caesar wryteth three wordes to certifie his victory', it reports that after King Pharnaces of Pontus was defeated Caesar 'onely wrote three words vnto Anitius at Rome, *Veni, Vidi, Vici*; to wit, I came, I saw, I ouercame' (Tudor Trans., 1895, p. 787). The writing in Q's copy-text was evidently not clear, and Q's compositor, trying to make something of it, might well misread 'three wordes' (or 'wdes') as 'their [?there] cosin' ('w' misread as 'co' and an illegible scribble as 'sin'). The proposed reading suits Falstaff's lofty self-approval and his flair,

especially in this scene, for literary style.

43.] A common formula; Tilley, G337, lists as proverbial, 'It is more of your goodness than my desert'.

46–7. *a particular ballad*] a ballad about me personally. Ballads were written on all kinds of news topics, and hawked among the crowds by ballad-singers, as by Autolycus (*Wint.*, IV. iv. 262 ff.); they were printed as broadsides and illustrated with rough wood-cuts. One could write, or have professionally written, accounts lauding one's exploits; in Webster's *Devil's Law Case*, v. iv. 192 (Lucas, ii. 316) Julio regrets that 'I made not mine owne Ballad'. One could also have them to lampoon one's enemies, as in Jonson, *Bart. Fair*, II. ii. 15–17 (H. & S., vi. 41)— 'and thou wrong'st me, . . . I'll finde a friend shall right me, and make a ballad of thee'.

49–50. *gilt . . . me*] counterfeits compared with me. Silver twopences (half-groats) were sometimes gilded and passed off as half-crowns, the two coins being the same size.

    believe not the word of the noble. Therefore let me
    have right, and let desert mount.

*Lanc.* Thine's too heavy to mount. 55

*Fal.* Let it shine, then.

*Lanc.* Thine's too thick to shine.

*Fal.* Let it do something, my good lord, that may do me
    good, and call it what you will.

*Lanc.* Is thy name Colevile?

*Cole.*                  It is, my lord. 60

*Lanc.* A famous rebel art thou, Colevile.

*Fal.* And a famous true subject took him.

*Cole.* I am, my lord, but as my betters are
    That led me hither. Had they been rul'd by me,
    You should have won them dearer than you have. 65

*Fal.* I know not how they sold themselves, but thou like a
    kind fellow gavest thyself away gratis, and I thank
    thee for thee.

*Enter* WESTMORELAND.

*Lanc.* Now, have you left pursuit?

*West.* Retreat is made and execution stay'd. 70

*Lanc.* Send Colevile with his confederates

---

55. *Lanc.*] Q (*Prince*), F [*Iohn*] [*so also through rest of scene*].    60.] *As verse, Steevens;
prose, QF.*    67. gratis] *Q; not in F.*    69. Now] *Q; not in F.*

---

53–4. *believe . . . mount*] Part of Falstaff's flair for literary elegance and
allusion. It sounds like parody of some
highflown style, and perhaps takes off
the grandiloquence of Basilisco in
*Soliman and Perseda.* Shakespeare jests
at Basilisco in *John,* i. i. 244, and
seemingly parodies him in Falstaff's
soliloquy on honour (*1 Henry IV,* New
Arden, p. xxxviii). The last words here
recall Basilisco's boast, 'I repute myself no coward; / For humilitie shall
mount' (*Soliman,* i. iii. 81–2). He brags
absurdly and cultivates a formal style,
e.g. 'Princes, what would you? / I haue
seen much, heard more, but done
most. / To be briefe, hee that will try
me, let him waft me with his arme', &c.
(*ibid.,* i. iii. 114–16).

55. *heavy*] A quibble on Falstaff's

weight, and on *heavy* as heinous.

57. *thick*] Another quibble, on the
opacity of Falstaff's carcase, and on
*thick* as dim; cf. *Ant.,* ii. iii. 27—'thy
lustre thickens'.

58–9. *do me good*] Though not
recorded in *OED,* 'certainly almost a
technical expression for promoting
someone's fortunes' (Shaaber, quoting
*R3,* iv. iii. 33—'think how I may do
thee good'; *Ado,* i. i. 292—'your highness now may do me good'; and *Hist.
MSS Comm., Hatfield MSS,* v. 189—
'Her Majesty . . . showing a gracious
disposition to do him [a Mr Buck]
good, and think him fit . . . for one of
the two offices').

60, 61, 71. *Colevile*] The name being
trisyllabic (cf. l. 71), ll. 60–1 appear
to be verses.

To York, to present execution.
Blunt, lead him hence, and see you guard him sure.

               *Exit [Blunt] with Colevile[, guarded].*

And now dispatch we toward the court, my lords;
I hear the King my father is sore sick.         75
Our news shall go before us to his Majesty,
Which, cousin, you shall bear to comfort him,
And we with sober speed will follow you.

*Fal.* My lord, I beseech you give me leave to go
    Through Gloucestershire, and when you come to court
    Stand my good lord, pray, in your good report.    81

*Lanc.* Fare you well, Falstaff. I, in my condition,
    Shall better speak of you than you deserve.

               *Exit[, with all but Falstaff ].*

*Fal.* I would you had but the wit, 'twere better than your
dukedom. Good faith, this same young sober-  85
blooded boy doth not love me, nor a man cannot
make him laugh; but that's no marvel, he drinks no
wine. There's never none of these demure boys come
to any proof; for thin drink doth so over-cool their
blood, and making many fish meals, that they fall  90
into a kind of male green-sickness; and then when

---

73. S.D.] F (*Exit with Colleuile.*), *Cambridge, subst.; not in* Q.    79–81.] *As verse,*
*Dyce; prose,* QF.    81. pray] F; *not in* Q.    82–3.] *As verse,* F; *prose,* Q.    83.
S.D.] F (*Exit.*), *Capell, subst.; not in* Q.    84. but] F; *not in* Q.    88. none]
Q; any F.

---

73. *Blunt*] Blunt's part could not be
less onerous; he says nothing, and this
is the only time he does anything.

79–81.] Prose in Q, which, not
having *pra* (l. 81), sounds less like
verse than F. Prose apparently also in
F (no capitals to *Through, Stand*),
though the line-lengths coincide with
verse-lines (accidentally, it would
seem), and the inclusion of *pray* makes
decasyllabic rhythm. The feeling is of
verse, and the *report/court* couplet is
the kind of rhyming tag Falstaff speaks
also at *1H4*, III. iii. 229–30 and IV. ii.
85–6.

82. *condition*] nature, disposition.

85–94. *Good faith . . . inflammation*]
'Falstaff speaks here like a veteran in

life. The young prince did not love
him, and he despaired to gain his
affection for he could not make him
laugh. Men only become friends by
community of pleasures. He who cannot be softened into gayety cannot
easily be melted into sadness' (Johnson).

88–9. *come . . . proof*] turn out well.

89–91. *for . . . green-sickness*] Perhaps
echoing Nashe—'I beseech the gods
of good fellowship thou maist fall into
a consumption with drinking smal
beere! Every day maist thou eate fish
. . . venison to thee' (*Sum-*
*mer's Last Will*, ll. 1094–8, McKerrow,
iii. 268). *Green-sickness*, anaemia incident to unmarried girls.

they marry they get wenches. They are generally
fools and cowards—which some of us should be too,
but for inflammation. A good sherris-sack hath a
twofold operation in it. It ascends me into the brain,    95
dries me there all the foolish and dull and crudy
vapours which environ it, makes it apprehensive,
quick, forgetive, full of nimble, fiery, and delectable
shapes, which delivered o'er to the voice, the tongue,
which is the birth, becomes excellent wit. The second    100
property of your excellent sherris is the warming of

92. *get wenches*] Hard drinking
rather than fish-eating was the usual
explanation for the begetting of girl
children; cf. Tilley, B195—'Who goes
drunk to bed begets but a girl'; also
Middleton, *Phoenix*, II. iii. 68–71
(Bullen, i. 155–6); Marston, *Fawn*, II.
i. 166 (Wood, ii. 163); May, *Heir*, I. i
(Hazlitt's *Dodsley*, xi. 524). But Falstaff, who lives in a context of meat-
eating, is doubtless disparaging lighter
diets in any way he can.

94. *inflammation*] excitement with
drink.

*sherris-sack*] sherry; i.e. a white wine
from Xeres (*OED*, Sack. *sb.*³). The
16th–17th c. form 'sherris' or 'sher-
ries' shows the derivation better than
the false singular 'sherry'.

94–100. *A good . . . wit*] This may
be part of Falstaff's Biblical facility,
from *Ecclesiasticus*, xxxi. 28—'wine
measurably drunken, is a reioy-
cing of the soule and body; a measur-
able drinking, is health to soule and
body'. But, as with his military doctrine, he is refurbishing accepted
authorities, as, for instance, Timothy
Bright's *Treatise of Melancholy*, 1586,
pp. 93–9—'Of all partes of the body,
in ech perturbation [reaction], two
are cheifly affected: first the brayne,
that both apprehendeth the . . . object
. . . and communicateth it with the
harte, which is the second part affected . . . . these carie with them all the
rest of the partes into a simpathy [p.
93]. . . This [an internal stimulus]
chiefly falleth to our bodies, when that

which giueth this occasion [the stimu-
lus] carieth force of gentle and light
spirits: as wine, and strong drinke, and
all aromaticall spices, which haue a
power to comfort the braine, and hart,
and affect all our bodie throughout
with celeritie and quicknesse, before
their spirits be spent . . .: then the
braine giueth merie report, & the hart
glad for it selfe, and all the fellow
members, as it were, daunceth for ioy,
and good liking, which it receaueth of
such internall prouocations [pp. 98–9].
Bloud thus tempered and replenished
with these aromaticall and merie
spirits, giueth occasion only of [i.e.
merely facilitates] this pleasantnesse,
and is no cause thereof, the hart
making iust claime to these affections as . . . vnder the soule, chiefe
author of these vnruly companions'
(p. 99).

96–7. *crudy vapours*] curdy, thick,
spirits. Timothy Bright describes
melancholy as 'of qualitie, grosse, dull,
and of fewe comfortable spirits; and
plentifully replenished with such as
darken all the clernesse of those san-
guineous, and ingrosse their subtil-
nesse, defile their purenesse with the
fogge of that slime' (*Treatise of Melancholy*, 1586, p. 100).

97. *apprehensive*] quickly responsive.

98. *forgetive*] creative, inventive (as
in 'the quick forge and working-house
of thought', *H5*, v. Chorus 23).

*fiery*] ardent, spirited (opposite to
the 'fogge' of melancholy.)

101–2. *warming of the blood*] 'Good

the blood, which before, cold and settled, left the
liver white and pale, which is the badge of pusillan-
imity and cowardice; but the sherris warms it, and
makes it course from the inwards to the parts' ex-    105
tremes. It illumineth the face, which, as a beacon,
gives warning to all the rest of this little kingdom,
man, to arm; and then the vital commoners, and
inland petty spirits, muster me all to their captain,
the heart; who, great and puffed up with this retinue,    110
doth any deed of courage; and this valour comes of
sherris. So that skill in the weapon is nothing without
sack, for that sets it a-work, and learning a mere
hoard of gold kept by a devil, till sack commences it
and sets it in act and use. Hereof comes it that Prince    115
Harry is valiant; for the cold blood he did naturally
inherit of his father he hath like lean, sterile, and
bare land manured, husbanded, and tilled, with
excellent endeavour of drinking good and good

105–6. parts' extremes] *Q* (partes extreames), *F1* (parts extremes), *Wilson*
(*N.C.S.*); parts extreme *F3;* parts extremes *Neilson.*          106. illumineth] *Q;*
illuminateth *F.*          110.] this *Q;* his *F.*

wine makes good blood' was proverbial; Tilley, W461.

103. *liver*] The supposed seat of the
passions; cf. I. ii. 174.

105–6. *extremes*] extremities.

107–8. *this . . . man*] Man is often
likened to a little kingdom or microcosm; e.g. *Caes.*, II. i. 67–9 ('the state of
man, / Like to a little kingdom');
*John,* IV. ii. 246; *Troil.,* II. iii. 185;
*Mac.,* I. iii. 139; *Lr,* III. i. 10–11; *Cor.,*
I. i. 99 ff. Falstaff's account of the little
kingdom in operation is based on the
physiological knowledge of the time.

108–9. *vital . . . spirits*] 'Certain
subtle highly-refined substances or
fluids (distinguished as *natural, animal,*
and *vital*) . . . supposed to permeate the
blood and chief regions of the body'
(*OED,* Spirit. *sb.* 16).

112–15. *weapon . . . use*] For both the
military and scholastic parts of this,
Wilson (N.C.S.) points out a Nashe
parallel—'So, I tell thee, giue a soldier
wine before he goes to battaile . . . it

makes him forget all scarres and
wounds, and fight in the thickest of his
enemies, as though hee were but at
foyles amongst his fellows. Giue a
scholler wine, going to his booke, or
being about to inuent, it sets a new
poynt on his wit, it glazeth it, it
scowres it, it giues him *acumen*' (*Summer's Last Will,* ll. 948–90; McKerrow,
iii. 265).

114. *hoard . . . devil*] Alluding to the
superstition that buried treasure was
guarded by evil spirits or dragons.

114–15. *commences . . . act*] Quibbles
on the Cambridge 'Commencement'
and the Oxford 'Act', i.e. the con-
ferring of the degree which authorizes
the student to set his hoard of learning
in act and use; cf. William Harrison,
*Description of England* (Hol., i. 251)—
'In Oxford this solemnitee is called an
Act, but in Cambridge they vse the
French word Commensement'.

118. *manured*] worked upon, tilled.
*husbanded*] cultivated.

store of fertile sherris, that he is become very hot and 120
valiant. If I had a thousand sons, the first human
principle I would teach them should be to forswear
thin potations, and to addict themselves to sack.

*Enter* BARDOLPH.

How now, Bardolph?
*Bard.* The army is discharged all and gone.              125
*Fal.* Let them go. I'll through Gloucestershire, and
there will I visit Master Robert Shallow, Esquire.
I have him already tempering between my finger
and my thumb, and shortly will I seal with him.
Come away.                              *Exeunt.*   130

SCENE IV.—[*Westminster. The Jerusalem Chamber.*]

*Enter the* KING, [*carried in a chair,*] WARWICK, THOMAS *Duke of*
CLARENCE, HUMPHREY [*Duke*] *of* GLOUCESTER[, *and others*].

*King.* Now, lords, if God doth give successful end

121. human] Q (humane), *Johnson; not in* F.          123. S.D.] Q [*after l. 124*], F.
130. S.D.] F; *not in* Q.

*Scene* IV

SCENE IV] *Capell; Scena Secunda.* F; *not in* Q.          *Location.*] *Cambridge; The Palace
at* Westminster. *Theobald.*          S.D.] F, *subst.* (*Enter King, Warwicke, Clarence,
Gloucester.*); *Enter the King, Warwike, Kent, Thomas duke of Clarence, Humphrey of
Gloucester.* Q.          *carried in a chair*] *Sisson; not in* QF.          *and others*] *Capell; not in* QF.
1. God] Q; Heauen F.

121. *human*] Q's 'humane' (accented
on the first syllable—as it is whenever
Shakespeare uses it in verse) was the
spelling of 'human' until the early 18th
c. (cf. Pope, *Ess. Crit.*, l. 527—'To err
is humane, to forgive divine'). Then
'human' (rare in the 17th c.) and
'humane' began to be differentiated in
the modern senses. Falstaff means
'secular' as opposed to 'divine'. Drinking is the first *human* principle he would
inculcate. The quality of the *divine*
principles may be deduced from his
way with Biblical texts.

129. *seal with him*] (*a*) have him

entirely softened for my purposes; (*b*)
come to a conclusion with him.

*Scene* IV

Location.] The 'chamber of the
abbats of Westminster called Ierusalem' (Hol., iii. 57; cf. IV. v. 232–40)
is in Westminster Abbey. That Shakespeare treats it as part of the Palace
need bother no one.

S.D.] That the King should be
brought in in a chair is probably the
most suitable way of introducing him
and allowing for his swoon (l. 110). In
the corresponding scene of *F.V.* he is

To this debate that bleedeth at our doors,
We will our youth lead on to higher fields,
And draw no swords but what are sanctified.
Our navy is address'd, our power collected,                    5
Our substitutes in absence well invested,
And every thing lies level to our wish;
Only we want a little personal strength,
And pause us till these rebels now afoot
Come underneath the yoke of government.                         10
*War.*  Both which we doubt not but your Majesty
    Shall soon enjoy.
*King.*                              Humphrey, my son of Gloucester,
    Where is the Prince your brother?
*Glou.*  I think he's gone to hunt, my lord, at Windsor.
*King.*  And how accompanied?
*Glou.*                              I do not know, my lord.    15
*King.*  Is not his brother Thomas of Clarence with him?
*Glou.*  No, my good lord, he is in presence here.
*Clar.*  What would my lord and father?
*King.*  Nothing but well to thee, Thomas of Clarence.
    How chance thou art not with the Prince thy brother?
    He loves thee, and thou dost neglect him, Thomas.    21
    Thou hast a better place in his affection

---

5. address'd] *Q;* addressed *F.*    12–13. Humphrey . . . brother?] *As verse, Pope;*
*prose, QF.*

from the outset apparently too ill to
walk, and refers to his chair (viii. 29).
Q's *Kent* (cf. collation) is another character whom Shakespeare, finding him
mentioned from time to time in
Holinshed, jotted down but never
used. F omits him.

1–10.] 'Sh. in these scenes welds together events which in reality are
separated by intervals of five and
eight years. The suppression of the
Archbishop's revolt is immediately
followed by the defeat of old Percy,
and the King's death happens shortly
after these events, whereas the historical dates are: 1405 for the first
event, 1408 for the battle of Bramham
Moor, and 1413 for the decease of
Henry IV' (Ax, p. 84).

2. *debate*] struggle.
3–4.] An allusion to the Crusade
which the King had proposed at the
beginning of his reign; cf. *R2*, v. vi.
49–50, *1H4*, I. i. 18 ff. On the King's
motives, see Appendix VIII, p. 242.
5. *address'd*] in readiness.
6. *substitutes*] deputies.
*invested*] i.e. with power.
7. *level*] prepared.
19–48.] Probably indebted to Stow
(cf. Appendix I, p. 215), though in
Stow the King warns Hal against
possible trouble from Thomas rather
than the other way round, while Hal
promises to cherish his brothers unless
they conspire against him. The gist is
similar, but the bearing of it is reversed.

Than all thy brothers: cherish it, my boy,
And noble offices thou mayst effect
Of mediation, after I am dead,                                    25
Between his greatness and thy other brethren.
Therefore omit him not, blunt not his love,
Nor lose the good advantage of his grace
By seeming cold, or careless of his will;
For he is gracious, if he be observ'd,                            30
He hath a tear for pity, and a hand
Open as day for melting charity:
Yet notwithstanding, being incens'd, he's flint,
As humorous as winter, and as sudden
As flaws congealed in the spring of day.                          35
His temper therefore must be well observ'd.
Chide him for faults, and do it reverently,
When you perceive his blood inclin'd to mirth;
But being moody, give him time and scope,
Till that his passions, like a whale on ground,                   40
Confound themselves with working. Learn this, Thomas,
And thou shalt prove a shelter to thy friends,
A hoop of gold to bind thy brothers in,
That the united vessel of their blood,
Mingled with venom of suggestion—                                 45
As force perforce the age will pour it in—

---

32. melting] *F;* meeting *Q.*     33. notwithstanding, being] *F;* notwithstanding
being *Q.*     he's] *F;* he is *Q.*     39. time] *Q;* Line *F.*

27. *omit*] neglect, disregard.

30. *observ'd*] paid due respect.

33. *flint*] i.e. hard, implacable.

34. *humorous*] capricious.

35. *flaws . . . day*] 'icy squalls at day-break' (Wilson, N.C.S.). *Flaws* can mean gusts of wind or flakes of ice; *sudden* (l. 34) implies the former.

36. *temper*] disposition.

39. *time*] Most editors follow F's 'Line', induced no doubt by the idea of fishing. But, as Sisson observes, 'it is not suggested that Thomas of Clarence should "play" his brother like a fish'. The image being one not of fishing but of a powerful, unmanageable creature threshing about until exhausted, *time*

*and scope* are just what the circumstances require.

40. *a whale on ground*] No particular instance is needed of this, but see Appendix I, p. 204.

43–8.] Wilson (N.C.S.) calls attention to the 'interesting amalgam of diverse images'. The meaning is conveyed by swift imagistic allusion to the golden hoop, the hoop binding a barrel, the union of brothers symbolized by the vial of blood, the virulent liquid working in the container, and the explosive substance striving to rend apart that which is united.

45. *suggestion*] instigation (to evil).

Shall never leak, though it do work as strong
    As aconitum or rash gunpowder.
*Clar.* I shall observe him with all care and love.
*King.* Why art thou not at Windsor with him, Thomas?          50
*Clar.* He is not there today, he dines in London.
*King.* And how accompanied? Canst thou tell that?
*Clar.* With Poins, and other his continual followers.
*King.* Most subject is the fattest soil to weeds,
    And he, the noble image of my youth,                       55
    Is overspread with them; therefore my grief
    Stretches itself beyond the hour of death.
    The blood weeps from my heart when I do shape
    In forms imaginary th'unguided days
    And rotten times that you shall look upon                  60
    When I am sleeping with my ancestors.
    For when his headstrong riot hath no curb,
    When rage and hot blood are his counsellors,
    When means and lavish manners meet together,
    O, with what wings shall his affections fly                65
    Towards fronting peril and oppos'd decay!
*War.* My gracious lord, you look beyond him quite.
    The Prince but studies his companions
    Like a strange tongue, wherein, to gain the language,
    'Tis needful that the most immodest word                  70
    Be look'd upon and learnt; which once attain'd,
    Your Highness knows, comes to no further use

51. *Clar.*] *Q (Tho.), F [so also at l. 53]*.     52. Canst . . . that?] *F; not in Q*.     69.
tongue, wherein, . . . language,] *F, subst., Cambridge;* tongue wherein . . . language:
*Q*.     72. further] *Q;* farther *F*.

48. *aconitum*] aconite or wolf's bane,
a poisonous plant of great potency.
  *rash*] sudden, violent.
  54.] Proverbial; cf. Tilley, W241—
'Weeds come forth on the fattest soil if
it is untilled'; and Lyly, *Euphues* (Bond,
i. 251, ll. 13–15)—'The fattest grounde
bringeth foorth nothing but weedes if
it be not well tilled'.
  54–66.] The chronicles have nothing as impassioned as this speech, or
that at IV. v. 92–137, which would
seem to owe the tone of despair to
*F.V.*, where the King reportedly thinks

of disinheriting the Prince (ii. 20),
whose wildness he fears 'will end his
fathers dayes' (iii. 45, vi. 113–14), so
that 'ruine and decaie' will destroy
'this noble Realme of England' (vi.
84–5).
  58. *blood . . . heart*] Each sigh was
thought to drain a drop of blood from
the heart.
  65. *affections*] inclinations.
  66. *fronting . . . decay*] the danger and
downfall that confront him.
  67. *look beyond him*] go too far in
judging him thus.

But to be known and hated. So, like gross terms,
The Prince will, in the perfectness of time,
Cast off his followers, and their memory          75
Shall as a pattern or a measure live
By which his Grace must mete the lives of other,
Turning past evils to advantages.

*King.* 'Tis seldom when the bee doth leave her comb
In the dead carrion.

*Enter* WESTMORELAND.

                  Who's here? Westmoreland?          80

*West.* Health to my sovereign, and new happiness
Added to that that I am to deliver!
Prince John your son doth kiss your Grace's hand:
Mowbray, the Bishop Scroop, Hastings and all
Are brought to the correction of your law.          85
There is not now a rebel's sword unsheath'd,
But Peace puts forth her olive everywhere.
The manner how this action hath been borne
Here at more leisure may your Highness read,
With every course in his particular.          90

*King.* O Westmoreland, thou art a summer bird,
Which ever in the haunch of winter sings
The lifting up of day.

*Enter* HARCOURT.

                  Look, here's more news.

*Har.* From enemies heaven keep your Majesty;
And when they stand against you, may they fall          95
As those that I am come to tell you of!

---

77. other] *Q*; others *F.*    80. S.D.] *Q* [*after l. 80*], *F.*    84. Bishop Scroop]
*Theobald*; Bishop, Scroope *QF.*    93. S.D.] *Q* [*after l. 93*], *F.*    94. heaven]
*F*; heauens *Q.*

77. *other*] others.

79–80. *'Tis . . . carrion*] i.e. He will
hardly forgo his pleasures, however
corrupt. The image may echo *Judges*,
xiv. 8—'he [Samson] turned out of the
way to see the carkeise of the Lion: and
beholde, there was a swarme of Bees
and hony in the carkeise of the Lion'.

90. *course*] proceeding.

92. *haunch of winter*] Shakespeare's
comparable expressions elsewhere are
only humorous—*LLL.,* v. i. 94,
'the posteriors of this day'; *Cor.,* ii.
i. 56, 'the buttock of the night'. This
line is *OED*'s only example of *haunch* as
'hinder part, latter end'.

The Earl Northumberland, and the Lord Bardolph,
With a great power of English and of Scots,
Are by the shrieve of Yorkshire overthrown.
The manner and true order of the fight        100
This packet, please it you, contains at large.
*King.*  And wherefore should these good news make me sick?
Will Fortune never come with both hands full,
But write her fair words still in foulest letters?
She either gives a stomach, and no food—        105
Such are the poor, in health; or else a feast
And takes away the stomach—such are the rich
That have abundance and enjoy it not.
I should rejoice now at this happy news,
And now my sight fails, and my brain is giddy.        110
O me! come near me, now I am much ill.
*Glou.*  Comfort, your Majesty!
*Clar.*                    O my royal father!
*West.*  My sovereign lord, cheer up yourself, look up.
*War.*  Be patient, Princes; you do know these fits
Are with his Highness very ordinary.        115
Stand from him, give him air; he'll straight be well.
*Clar.*  No, no, he cannot long hold out these pangs.
Th'incessant care and labour of his mind
Hath wrought the mure that should confine it in

99. shrieve] *Q;* Sherife *F.*    104. write . . . letters] *F;* wet . . . termes *Q.*    112.
*Glou.*] *Q (Hum.), F (Glo.)* [*so ll. 121, 130*].    Comfort . . . father] *As verse,*
*Steevens; prose, QF.*    117. out these] *Q;* out: these *F.*

97–9.] This brief and colourless
reference is the last mention of
Northumberland, whose role in the
play is singularly ignominious. In
Holinshed he ends his life with great
valour—see Appendix I, pp. 196–7.

102. *these . . . news*] Cf. i. i. 27, note.

104.] F's reading is perhaps as good
as any alternative, though it seems a
little glib and may indicate botching.
Alice Walker would retain Q's reading, except for emending 'wet' to
'mete' (*Textual Problems of the First
Folio*, p. 117). But *meting fair words* in
*foulest terms* hardly makes sense, in
either logic or imagery. Hilda Hulme,

*Explorations in Sh.'s Language*, p. 295,
offers etymological reasons for taking
Q's *wet* as a variant of 'wit' (in a 16th
c. sense of 'bequeath'), *words* as 'that
which is granted', and *terms* as 'conditions', the sense being that Fortune
delivers over what she grants in harsh
conditions. This is ingenious but requires three specialized interpretations in nine words.

105–8.] A proverbial sentiment; cf.
Tilley, M366—'The rich man walks to
get a stomach to his meat, the poor
man to get meat for his stomach'.

118–20.] A clear echo of Daniel,
*C.W.*, iii. 116; see Appendix I, p. 209.

So thin that life looks through and will break out.  120
*Glou.* The people fear me, for they do observe
    Unfather'd heirs and loathly births of nature.
    The seasons change their manners, as the year
    Had found some months asleep and leap'd them over.
*Clar.* The river hath thrice flow'd, no ebb between,  125
    And the old folk, time's doting chronicles,
    Say it did so a little time before
    That our great-grandsire Edward sick'd and died.
*War.* Speak lower, Princes, for the King recovers.
*Glou.* This apoplexy will certain be his end.  130
*King.* I pray you take me up, and bear me hence
    Into some other chamber: softly, pray.
[SCENE V.]     [*They take the King up and lay him on a bed.*]
    Let there be no noise made, my gentle friends,
    Unless some dull and favourable hand
    Will whisper music to my weary spirit.

120. and . . . out] *F; not in Q.*    125. flow'd] *F;* flowed *Q.*    132. softly, pray]
*F; not in Q.*    132. S.D.] *Capell, subst.; not in QF.*

*Scene* v

SCENE V] *Cambridge; not in QF.*

121. *fear*] alarm.
122. *Unfather'd heirs*] Offspring un-
naturally begotten. The old belief in
the existence of 'unfather'd' children
is reflected in Spenser, *F.Q.*, III. iii. 13,
where Merlin is 'not the sonne / Of
mortall Syre, or other liuing wight, /
But wondrously begotten, and be-
gonne / By false illusion of a guilefull
Spright / On a faire Ladie Nonne'.
Montaigne observes that 'in Mahomet's religion, by the easie beleefe of
that people, are many merlins found;
That is to say fatherles children:
Spirituall children, conceiued and
borne divinely in the wombs of vir-
gins' (*Essayes: Apology for Raymond
Sebonde*, Tudor Trans., 1893, ii. 243).
It is not clear, however, that such
births were portentous; and the reference may be to malformed infants (cf.
'loathly births', note below), sometimes thought the result of intercourse
between a witch and an incubus

(Shaaber, citing Gregory Zilboorg,
*The Medical Man and the Witch During
the Renaissance*, 1935, p. 124).
    *loathly births*] Probably an echo of
Daniel, *C.W.*, i. 115—'The wofull
mother, her owne birth affrights, /
Seeing a wrong deformed infant
borne, / Grieues in her paines,
deceiu'd in shame doth morn'.
123–4.] *MND.*, II. i. 111 ff., treats
the same theme of disturbed seasons
resulting from disturbed rule—'the
spring, the summer, / The child-
ing autumn, angry winter change /
Their wonted liveries'.
125–8.] Cf. Appendix I, p. 200.
None of the chronicles seems to con-
nect such an occurrence with Edward
III's death.

*Scene* v
Location.] See Appendix VI.
2. *dull*] producing drowsiness.
3. *music*] Cf. *F.V.*, viii. 10–11—

*War.*  Call for the music in the other room.
*King.*  Set me the crown upon my pillow here.                    5
*Clar.*  His eye is hollow, and he changes much.
*War.*  Less noise, less noise!

### *Enter* PRINCE HENRY.

*Prince.*                    Who saw the Duke of Clarence?
*Clar.*  I am here, brother, full of heaviness.
*Prince.*  How now, rain within doors, and none abroad?
    How doth the King?                                        10
*Glou.*  Exceeding ill.
*Prince.*                    Heard he the good news yet?
    Tell it him.
*Glou.*  He alter'd much upon the hearing it.
*Prince.*  If he be sick with joy, he'll recover without physic.
*War.*  Not so much noise, my lords. Sweet Prince, speak low;
    The King your father is dispos'd to sleep.              16
*Clar.*  Let us withdraw into the other room.
*War.*  Will't please your Grace to go along with us?
*Prince.*  No, I will sit and watch here by the King.
                          *[Exeunt all but the Prince.]*
    Why doth the crown lie there upon his pillow,           20
    Being so troublesome a bedfellow?
    O polish'd perturbation! golden care!
    That keep'st the ports of slumber open wide
    To many a watchful night! Sleep with it now:
    Yet not so sound, and half so deeply sweet,             25
    As he whose brow with homely biggen bound

7. S.D.] *Q (Enter Harry), F.*    9–10. How ... King] *As verse, Pope; verse (or prose?),
Q; prose, F.*    11. *Glou.*] *Q (Hum.), F (Glo.) [so throughout scene].*    11–12.] *As F;
prose, Q.*    13. alter'd] *Q corr.* (altred), *F;* vttred *Q uncorr.*    14.] *As Q; If ...
Ioy, / Hee'le ... Physicke. F.*    15–16.] *As verse, F; prose, Q.*    18. Will't] *Q
(Wilt), F (Wil't).*    19. S.D.] *Rowe 1, subst. [after l. 20], Rowe 3; not in QF.*
24. night! ... now:] *F (Night: ... now,), This edn; night, ... now! Q; night!—
... now!— Capell; night! ... now? Wilson (N.C.S.).*

'Draw the Curtaines and depart my
chamber a while, / And cause some
Musicke to rocke me asleepe'. Music
was played to soothe the ailing,
especially those ailing in spirit; e.g. it
tranquillizes Lear's 'untun'd and
jarring senses' (*Lr*, IV. vii. 1–25).

13. *alter'd*] sc. 'for the worse'.
20–30. *Why . . . safety*] This recalls
III. i. 4–31. For a comparable reflection
in Hoccleve's *Regement of Princes* cf.
Appendix VII.
23. *ports*] gates.
26–7. *whose . . . Snores*] The con-

Snores out the watch of night. O majesty!
When thou dost pinch thy bearer, thou dost sit
Like a rich armour worn in heat of day,
That scald'st with safety. By his gates of breath          30
There lies a downy feather which stirs not:
Did he suspire, that light and weightless down
Perforce must move. My gracious lord! My father!
This sleep is sound indeed; this is a sleep
That from this golden rigol hath divorc'd               35
So many English kings. Thy due from me
Is tears and heavy sorrows of the blood,
Which nature, love, and filial tenderness
Shall, O dear father, pay thee plenteously.
My due from thee is this imperial crown,               40
Which, as immediate from thy place and blood,
Derives itself to me. [*Putting it on his head*] Lo where it
      sits,
Which God shall guard; and put the world's whole
      strength
Into one giant arm, it shall not force
This lineal honour from me. This from thee             45
Will I to mine leave, as 'tis left to me.              *Exit.*

*King.*  Warwick! Gloucester! Clarence!

---

30. scald'st] *QF;* scalds *Theobald.*       safety. By . . . breath] *F* (safetie: by . . .
breath,), *Pope;* safty (by . . . breath) *Q.*       31. downy] *Q* (dowlny), *F1* (dowlney), *F4.*       32. down] *QF1* (dowlne), *F4.*       33. move. My] *F;* moue my *Q.*
42. S.D.] *Johnson* [*after* sits,]; *not in QF.*       where] *Q;* heere *F.*       43–6.] *As Q;
lines ending* . . . guard: / . . . Arme, / . . . me. / . . . leaue, / . . . me. *F.*       43. God] *Q;*
Heauen *F.*

---

struction takes a short cut but the
sense is clear. *Biggen* = coarse nightcap.

30. *scald'st*] Many editions read
'scalds', but QF's 'scaldst' is justi-
fiable by (*a*) grammatical attraction
from 'dost' (l. 28), and (*b*) logical
attraction, the scalding belonging to
the apostrophized 'majesty' as much
as do the pinching and sitting (l. 28).

31, 32. *downy, down*] Q's 'dowlny',
F's 'dowlney', and QF's 'dowlne', as
Wilson (N.C.S.) observes, 'as good as
prove this to be a Shakespearean

spelling, though it is not found elsewhere'. It is not found elsewhere in
Shakespeare, but it occurs in George
Wilkins's *Painefull Adventures of Pericles,*
1608 (ed. K. Muir, 1953, p. 25, l. 1—
'in steade of dowlny beds'). The word
seems to combine 'down' (soft plum-
age) and 'dowle' (soft fine feather, as in
*Tp.,* III. iii. 65—'One dowle that's in
my plume').

35. *rigol*] circle—the 'golden round'
of *Mac.,* I. v. 29.

43–6.] A clear echo of *F.V.,* viii. 74–
7; cf. Appendix I, p. 227.

*Enter* WARWICK, GLOUCESTER, CLARENCE[, *and the rest*].

*Clar.* Doth the King call?
*War.* What would your Majesty? How fares your Grace?
*King.* Why did you leave me here alone, my lords?        50
*Clar.* We left the Prince my brother here, my liege,
   Who undertook to sit and watch by you.
*King.* The Prince of Wales? Where is he? Let me see him.
   He is not here.
*War.* This door is open, he is gone this way.        55
*Glou.* He came not through the chamber where we
      stay'd.
*King.* Where is the crown? Who took it from my pillow?
*War.* When we withdrew, my liege, we left it here.
*King.* The Prince hath ta'en it hence. Go seek him out.
   Is he so hasty that he doth suppose        60
   My sleep my death?
   Find him, my Lord of Warwick, chide him hither.
                                    [*Exit Warwick.*]
   This part of his conjoins with my disease,
   And helps to end me. See, sons, what things you are,
   How quickly nature falls into revolt        65
   When gold becomes her object!
   For this the foolish over-careful fathers
   Have broke their sleep with thoughts,
   Their brains with care, their bones with industry;
   For this they have engrossed and pil'd up        70

---

47. S.D. *Enter . . . Clarence*] *QF* [*after l. 46*], *Capell, subst.*    *and the rest*] *Capell;*
*not in QF.*        49. How . . . Grace?] *F; not in Q.*        51–3.] *As verse, F; prose,*
*Q.*        54.] *As verse, Capell; prose, Q; not in F.*        59.] *As Q;* The . . . hence: / Go
. . . out. *F.*        60–4.] *As Q, subst.* [*ll. 60–1 one line in Q*] ; *lines ending . . . suppose* /
. . . Warwick) / . . . conioynes / . . . me. / . . . are: *F.*        62. S.D.] *Capell; not in QF.*
68–9.] *As QF;* Have . . . care, / Their . . . industry; *Capell.*        68. sleep] *Q;*
sleepes *F.*        70. pil'd] *F;* pilld *Q.*

60–6.] Mislined in F (and, as re-          70. *pil'd*] Q's 'pilld', though per-
gards ll. 60–1, in Q also). The manage-   haps less consonant with 'engrossed'
ment of the whole speech to l. 79, with   than F's 'pyl'd', and though it would
its half-lines, and with F's different    be unusual with 'up', may be right. It
readings in ll. 74, 75, and different     would give a vigorous meaning ('plun-
arrangement of ll. 75–9 (see collation),  dered') with 'strange-achieved gold';
suggests starts, restarts, cancellations  cf. *Timon,* IV. i. 11–12—'Large-handed
and additions, on Shakespeare's part.     robbers your grave masters are, / And
   63. *part*] action, piece of conduct.  pill by law'.

The canker'd heaps of strange-achieved gold;
For this they have been thoughtful to invest
Their sons with arts and martial exercises;
When, like the bee, tolling from every flower
The virtuous sweets,                                          75
Our thighs pack'd with wax, our mouths with honey,
We bring it to the hive; and like the bees
Are murder'd for our pains. This bitter taste
Yields his engrossments to the ending father.

*Enter* WARWICK.

Now where is he that will not stay so long          80
Till his friend sickness have determin'd me?
*War.* My lord, I found the Prince in the next room,

74. tolling] Q (toling); culling F.    75.] F; not in Q.    76.] As Q, subst., F,
subst. [F has our . . . Wax, concluding l. 75, Our . . . Honey, starting l. 76]; Our
thighs are packt . . . honey, Pope; Our thighs all packt . . . honey, Hanmer;
Packing our thighs . . . honey, Capell; Our thighs with wax, our mouths with
honey pack'd, Dyce 2.    thighs] F; thigh, Q.    76–9.] As Q; lines ending . . .
Wax, / . . . Hiue; / . . . paines. / . . . engrossements, / . . . Father. F.    78. murder'd] Q (murdred), Pope; murthered F.    79. S.D.] Q [after l. 81], F.    81.
have] Ridley; hands Q; hath F.

71. *strange-achieved*] Perhaps 'by
curious means', or 'in distant lands'.
No precise meaning is needed.

73. *arts . . . exercises*] The two
branches of a polite education in the
16th c.; cf. Massinger, *Great Duke of
Florence*, I. i. (*Works*, Mermaid ed., i.
211)—'For training up my youth in
arts and arms'; Middleton, *World Tost
at Tennis*, ll. 161–3 (Bullen, vii. 160)—
'Pallas . . . goddess of arts and arms, /
Of arms and arts, for neither have precedence, / For he's the complete man
partakes of both'.

74–9.] This is Q's lineation (with the
addition of 'The virtuous sweets' from
F); F's is markedly different.

75. *virtuous*] having natural virtue,
good qualities.

76.] Both Q and F are in difficulties
hereabouts (see collation, and ll. 60–6,
note). Perhaps *pack'd* should come at
the end of the line.

78. *murder'd*] It is in fact the drones,

not the workers, whom the bees kill off
when swarming is over.

78–9. *This . . . father*] i.e. The
treasures he has amassed yield this
bitter taste to the dying father, a
severe reversal of the proverb, 'The
Bee sucks honey out of the bitterest
flowers' (Tilley, B205). This line is
*OED*'s only instance of *ending* as an
adjective for 'dying': as a noun for
'death' it is frequent, e.g. *Lucrece*, l.
1612—'the sad dirge of her certain
ending'.

*Yields*] The singular form may be by
association with *taste* (the object)
instead of *engrossments* (the subject). Or
it may be the not infrequent Northern
plural; cf. Abbott, §§333, 335.

81. *have*] I follow Ridley in taking
Q's 'hands' as a misreading of 'haue'
(typical *n/u* and *d/e* errors), and
F's 'hath', though feasible, as an
error.

*determin'd*] put an end to.

Washing with kindly tears his gentle cheeks,
With such a deep demeanour in great sorrow,
That tyranny, which never quaff'd but blood,          85
Would, by beholding him, have wash'd his knife
With gentle eye-drops. He is coming hither.
*King.* But wherefore did he take away the crown?

*Enter* PRINCE HENRY.

Lo where he comes. Come hither to me, Harry.
Depart the chamber, leave us here alone.
                                        *Exeunt* [*Warwick and the rest*].          90
*Prince.* I never thought to hear you speak again.
*King.* Thy wish was father, Harry, to that thought;
I stay too long by thee, I weary thee.
Dost thou so hunger for mine empty chair
That thou wilt needs invest thee with my honours          95
Before thy hour be ripe? O foolish youth!
Thou seek'st the greatness that will overwhelm thee.
Stay but a little, for my cloud of dignity

87. drops. He] *F;* drops, he *Q.*     88. S.D.] *Q* (*Enter Harry.*) [*after l. 87*], *F.*
90. S.D.] *Q* (*exeunt.*), *Capell; Exit. F.*     91. *Prince*] *Q* (*Harry*), *F* (*P. Hen.*).
94. mine] *Q;* my *F.*     95. my] *Q;* mine *F.*

83. *kindly*] natural, filial.
85. *tyranny*] cruelty.
85–7.] The reference is probably to
Plutarch's *Life of Pelopides* (*Lives*,
Tudor Trans., ii. 324–5). This tells
how the blood-thirsty tyrant Alexander of Pherae was so moved by the
*Troades* of Euripides that he left the
theatre for shame at being seen to
weep. Sidney's *Defense of Poesie* relates
Plutarch's story also (*Works*, ed.
Feuillerat, iii. 23–4). Cowl and
Shaaber cite other similar stories.
92.] Proverbial; cf. Tilley, B269—
'We soon believe what we desire'.
92–137.] *F.V.*, viii, provides an
interesting parallel to this interview;
on its relationship to the tone of this
speech, see IV. iv. 54–66, note. 'The
bitter speech culminates in a picture
of the future of England almost as
terrible as that which Ulysses draws in
*Troilus & Cressida* of a world in which

"Degree" has been overthrown. . . .
Shakespeare penned these words with
a double purpose: first to give Hal an
occasion for his loyal and large-
hearted reply, completely satisfying to
his father and still further exalting him
in our estimation; and secondly to
show us what would have followed had
the Prince chosen Vanity instead of
Government, Falstaff and not the
Lord Chief Justice' (Wilson, *Fortunes*,
pp. 79–80).
98–100. *my cloud . . . dim*] Commenting on the metaphorical assimilation of
concrete and abstract in Shakespeare's
mature style, Clemen remarks on this
passage, '*Cloud of dignity* is the result of
such a wedding of the abstract element
with the concrete. . . *So weak a wind*,
too, suggests two things at the same
time: first, the expiring breath of the
dying man, and then—in keeping
with the concrete image—the real

Is held from falling with so weak a wind
That it will quickly drop; my day is dim.                    100
Thou hast stol'n that which after some few hours
Were thine without offence, and at my death
Thou hast seal'd up my expectation.
Thy life did manifest thou lov'dst me not,
And thou wilt have me die assur'd of it.                     105
Thou hid'st a thousand daggers in thy thoughts,
Which thou hast whetted on thy stony heart,
To stab at half an hour of my life.
What, canst thou not forbear me half an hour?
Then get thee gone, and dig my grave thyself,               110
And bid the merry bells ring to thine ear
That thou art crowned, not that I am dead.
Let all the tears that should bedew my hearse
Be drops of balm to sanctify thy head,
Only compound me with forgotten dust.                       115
Give that which gave thee life unto the worms;
Pluck down my officers; break my decrees;
For now a time is come to mock at form—
Harry the fifth is crown'd! Up, vanity!
Down, royal state! All you sage counsellors, hence!         120
And to the English court assemble now
From every region, apes of idleness!

107. Which] *F;* Whom *Q.*     108, 109. hour] *Q* (hower); howre *F.*     111.
thine] *Q;* thy *F.*     119. Harry] *Q;* Henry *F.*     122. every] *Q;* eu'ry *F.*

wind which keeps the cloud from
falling down. Thus ambiguity has
gradually become an important factor
in the creation of the imagery. *My day
is dim* is called forth by association by
the first (half-concealed) image (of
the rain-cloud). . . . Summing up, we
observe as characteristic features of
this passage the following: mingling of
the concrete and the abstract, concentration of content, ambiguity, connection of the parts by association and
suggestiveness' (*Devel. of Sh.'s Imagery,*
1951, p. 80).

103. *seal'd . . . expectation*] confirmed
my fears.

106-8.] In *F.V.,* vi. 108-20, the

Prince enters with a dagger, and the
King reproaches him for intending
him harm. In the *Henry IV*s Hal never
wishes for his father's death, but popular rumours that he did are echoed
both here and at *1H4,* v. iv. 51-7,
where, after rescuing the King from
Douglas, Hal rejects as slanders the reports that 'I hearken'd for your death'.

108. *hour*] *Q*'s 'hower' is disyllabic
(perhaps in l. 109 also).

114. *balm*] consecrated oil for anoint-
ing the king at his coronation.

118. *form*] law and order. Wilson
(N.C.S.) quotes the 'Shakespearean'
Addition to *Sir Thomas More,* l. 146—
'gyue vp yo* self to forme'.

Now, neighbour confines, purge you of your scum!
Have you a ruffian that will swear, drink, dance,
Revel the night, rob, murder, and commit          125
The oldest sins the newest kind of ways?
Be happy, he will trouble you no more.
England shall double gild his treble guilt,
England shall give him office, honour, might:
For the fifth Harry from curb'd licence plucks          130
The muzzle of restraint, and the wild dog
Shall flesh his tooth on every innocent.
O my poor kingdom, sick with civil blows!
When that my care could not withhold thy riots,
What wilt thou do when riot is thy care?          135
O, thou wilt be a wilderness again,
Peopled with wolves, thy old inhabitants!

*Prince.* [*Kneels*]  O, pardon me, my liege! But for my tears,
The moist impediments unto my speech,
I had forestall'd this dear and deep rebuke,          140
Ere you with grief had spoke and I had heard
The course of it so far. There is your crown;
And He that wears the crown immortally
Long guard it yours! If I affect it more
Than as your honour and as your renown,          145
Let me no more from this obedience rise,

---

124. will] *Q; swill F.*     132. on] *Q; in F.*     138. S.D.] *Rowe [after liege!]; not in QF.*     139. moist] *Q; most F.*

---

124. *dance*] The dramatists often include dancing (doubtless the wilder sort) with drinking, swearing, and other vices; e.g. Jonson, *E.M.I.*, i. iv. 56–8 (H. & S., iii. 214–15)—'He and his wild associates . . . / Sweare, leape, and dance, and revell night by night'.

128.] A common quibble; cf. *H5*, ii. Chorus 26—'the gilt of France—O guilt indeed', and *Mac.*, ii. ii. 56–7.

132. *flesh*] plunge into flesh, as an initiation in bloodshed.

134, 135. *riots, riot*] Somewhat of a word-play: *thy riots* = your own wild living; *riot is thy care* = the kingdom's uproar is what you have to govern.

The word had some Morality associations; e.g. in the interlude *Youth* (c. 1550, often reprinted), Ryot is the Vice, who tempts Youth to wine and women.

138–76.] This repeatedly echoes *F.V.*; e.g. Hal's tears (ll. 138–9; *F.V.*, viii. 21–3, 50–1); his return of the crown and prayer for the King (ll. 142–4; *F.V.*, viii. 55–7); his appeal to God's witness (l. 149; *F.V.*, viii. 50); his feelings on entering (ll. 149–51; *F.V.*, viii. 46–9); his reluctance to have the crown (ll. 171–6; *F.V.*, viii. 54–7). See Appendix I, p. 226.

140. *dear*] dire, grievous; perhaps also, heart-felt.

Which my most inward true and duteous spirit
Teacheth this prostrate and exterior bending.
God witness with me, when I here came in,
And found no course of breath within your Majesty,   150
How cold it struck my heart! If I do feign,
O, let me in my present wildness die,
And never live to show th'incredulous world
The noble change that I have purposed!
Coming to look on you, thinking you dead,          155
And dead almost, my liege, to think you were,
I spake unto this crown as having sense,
And thus upbraided it: 'The care on thee depending
Hath fed upon the body of my father;
Therefore thou best of gold art worst of gold.       160
Other, less fine in carat, is more precious,
Preserving life in med'cine potable;
But thou, most fine, most honour'd, most renown'd,
Hast eat thy bearer up'. Thus, my most royal liege,
Accusing it, I put it on my head,               165
To try with it, as with an enemy
That had before my face murder'd my father,
The quarrel of a true inheritor.
But if it did infect my blood with joy,
Or swell my thoughts to any strain of pride,       170
If any rebel or vain spirit of mine
Did with the least affection of a welcome
Give entertainment to the might of it,

147. inward . . . and] *Q*; true, and inward *F*.     148. Teacheth] *QF*; Teacheth,
*Capell.*     148–9. bending. . . . me,] *F*; bending, . . . me. *Q*.     149. God] *Q*;
Heauen *F*.     157. this] *Q*; the *F*.     160. worst of] *F*; worse then *Q*.     161.
fine . . . is] *F* (fine in Charract, is); fine, in karrat *Q*.     164. thy] *Q*; the *F*.
up'. Thus . . . liege,] *As Q*; vp. / Thus . . . Liege) / *F*.     most] *Q*; *not in F.*
167. murder'd] *F* (murdred); murdered *Q*.

161. *carat*] purity, quality.

162. *med'cine potable*] i.e. 'aurum
potabile', a drug supposed to contain
gold and be highly efficacious; cf.
Chaucer, *Prol. Cant. T.*, l. 443—'For
gold in phisik is a cordial'. William
Ward's translation of *The Secretes of
Alexis*, ed. 1568, Pt I, sig. A6ᵛ, gives a
recipe 'To dissolue and reduce gold

into a potable licour, which con-
serueth the youth and health of a man,
. . . and wil heale euery disease that is
thought vncurable, in the space of
seuen dayes at the furthest'. Cowl
gives further references.

170. *strain*] pitch (of emotion; perhaps with musical connotation too).

172. *affection of*] disposition towards.

Let God for ever keep it from my head,
And make me as the poorest vassal is,                    175
That doth with awe and terror kneel to it!
*King.* O my son,
God put it in thy mind to take it hence,
That thou mightst win the more thy father's love,
Pleading so wisely in excuse of it!                      180
Come hither, Harry, sit thou by my bed,
And hear, I think, the very latest counsel
That ever I shall breathe. God knows, my son,
By what by-paths and indirect crook'd ways
I met this crown, and I myself know well               185
How troublesome it sat upon my head.
To thee it shall descend with better quiet,
Better opinion, better confirmation,
For all the soil of the achievement goes
With me into the earth. It seem'd in me                190
But as an honour snatch'd with boist'rous hand,
And I had many living to upbraid
My gain of it by their assistances,
Which daily grew to quarrel and to bloodshed,
Wounding supposed peace. All these bold fears          195
Thou seest with peril I have answered;
For all my reign hath been but as a scene
Acting that argument. And now my death
Changes the mood, for what in me was purchas'd

---

174. God] *Q;* heauen *F.*      177.] *F; not in Q.*      178. God] *Q;* Heauen *F.*
put it] *F;* put *Q.*      179. win] *Q;* ioyne *F.*      183. God] *Q;* Heauen *F.*      195.]
*As Q;* Wounding . . . Peace. / All . . . Feares, / *F.*      196. answered] *F;* answerd *Q.*
199. mood] *QFf1–2;* Mode *F3.*

179. *win*] On F's reading 'ioyne' see
Intro., p. lxxviii.

181–219.] Stow and Daniel (not
Holinshed) give the King long death-
bed exhortations. Daniel presumably
derives from Stow, who cites as his
authority the early 16th c. MS additions to Tito Livio's *Vita Henrici
Quinti* (Stow, *Chron.,* p. 578; *Annales*
does not mention the source).

181–6.] This is close to *F.V.,* viii. 62,
70–1—'But come neare my sonne . . . /

For God knowes my sonne, how hardly
I came by it, / And how hardly I haue
maintained it'. It is slightly less close to
Holinshed—'Well, faire sonne (said
the king with a great sigh) what right
I had to it God knoweth' (iii. 57).

195. *fears*] objects of fear.

199. *mood*] OED (Mood. *sb.*[2] 3d),
quoting this line, takes the word primarily in the sense of a musical scale
(mode), the character of which alters
according to the note on which it

Falls upon thee in a more fairer sort;                    200
So thou the garland wear'st successively.
Yet though thou stand'st more sure than I could do,
Thou art not firm enough, since griefs are green;
And all my friends, which thou must make thy friends,
Have but their stings and teeth newly ta'en out;         205
By whose fell working I was first advanc'd,
And by whose power I well might lodge a fear
To be again displac'd; which to avoid,
I cut them off, and had a purpose now
To lead out many to the Holy Land,                       210
Lest rest and lying still might make them look
Too near unto my state. Therefore, my Harry,
Be it thy course to busy giddy minds
With foreign quarrels, that action hence borne out
May waste the memory of the former days.                 215
More would I, but my lungs are wasted so
That strength of speech is utterly denied me.
How I came by the crown, O God forgive,
And grant it may with thee in true peace live!
*Prince.*  My gracious liege,                            220

204. my friends] *Rann, conj. Tyrwhitt;* thy friends *QF, Sisson;* the foes *Keightley;*
my foes *Dyce 2, conj. Lettsom;* thy foes *conj. Walker.*        205. ta'en] *Q;* tak'n *F.*
212.] *As Q;* Too . . . State. / Therefore . . . *Harrie) | F.*        218. God] *Q;* heauen *F.*
220.] *F; not in Q.*

begins; but secondarily in that of emotional mood, citing *Lycidas,* l. 87—
'That strain I heard was of a higher
mood'.

*purchas'd*] 'acquire[d] otherwise
than by inheritance or descent'
(Onions)—a legal sense.

201. *garland*] crown; cf. Holinshed,
iii. 57—'Well (said the prince) if you
die king, I will haue the garland'.

*successively*] by right of succession.
'Every usurper snatches a claim or
hereditary right as soon as he can'
(Johnson).

204. *my friends . . . thy friends*] In both
places QF read 'thy', which Clarke
(ed. 1865) defends—'By the first *thy
friends* the king means those who are
friendly inclined to the prince and
who . . . must be made securely

friends'; but if Shakespeare meant this
he would surely have conveyed it
differently.

207. *lodge*] harbour.

208–12. *which . . . state*] Close to
Holinshed but closer to Daniel. After
describing Anglo-French wars in 1413,
Holinshed says that Henry planned a
crusade to divert 'the great malice of
christian princes' (i.e. the opposed
English and French leaders) from each
other to the infidel (iii. 56–7). Daniel
gives the somewhat ambiguous version which Shakespeare adopts (*C.W.,*
iii. 127); cf. Appendix VIII.

214. *hence borne out*] undertaken
abroad.

215. *waste*] efface.

220–4.] Cf. *F.V.,* viii. 72–6; Appendix I, p. 227.

You won it, wore it, kept it, gave it me;
Then plain and right must my possession be,
Which I with more than with a common pain
'Gainst all the world will rightfully maintain.

*Enter* PRINCE JOHN *of* LANCASTER, WARWICK[, *and others*].

*King.* Look, look, here comes my John of Lancaster.          225
*Lanc.* Health, peace, and happiness to my royal father!
*King.* Thou bring'st me happiness and peace, son John,
     But health, alack, with youthful wings is flown
     From this bare wither'd trunk. Upon thy sight
     My worldly business makes a period.          230
     Where is my Lord of Warwick?
*Prince.*                    My Lord of Warwick!
*King.* Doth any name particular belong
     Unto the lodging where I first did swoon?
*War.* 'Tis call'd Jerusalem, my noble lord.
*King.* Laud be to God! Even there my life must end.          235
     It hath been prophesied to me, many years,
     I should not die but in Jerusalem,
     Which vainly I suppos'd the Holy Land.
     But bear me to that chamber; there I'll lie;
     In that Jerusalem shall Harry die.          *Exeunt.*     240

224. S.D.] *F* (*Enter Lord Iohn of Lancaster, and Warwicke.*), *Capell, subst.; enter Lancaster. Q.*     226. *Lanc.*] *Q; Iohn. F.*     233. swoon] *Q* (swound), *F1* (swoon'd),
*F4.*     235. God] *Q; heauen F.*     240. S.D.] *F; not in Q.*

221. *You . . . wore it*] 'Win it and
wear it' was proverbial; Tilley, W408.
     232–40.] Closely from Holinshed;
cf. Appendix I, p. 202. This prophecy
(of which there seems no historical
record) is paralleled in the case of
other potentates. Pope Sylvester II
(d. 1003) reportedly deemed himself
safe on hearing the Devil's message
that he would die in Jerusalem, and
then was stricken down in Rome in the
church of The-Holy-Cross-in-Jeru-
salem; see Andrew of Wyntoun, *Original Chronicle* (STS, ed. Amours, 1906,
iv. 210), and Lodge, *Divel Coniur'd*,
1596, sig. Iii⁽ᵛ⁾. Barbour's *Bruce* tells
how Edward I, expecting to die in the

'burgh' of Jerusalem, in fact met his
end at Burgh-on-the-sands near Carlisle in 1307 (Bk IV, ll. 207–10, EETS,
1870, Extra ser., xi. 84). Shaaber
records similar legends about other
persons and places.
     234. *Jerusalem*] The Jerusalem
Chamber, 'which has so many historical associations that it is almost a
national shrine' (*Sh.'s Engl.*, ii. 163) is
a hall in Westminster Abbey, originally the Abbot's private drawing-
room but after the dissolution of the
Abbey the meeting-place of the Dean
and Chapter. The name comes from
the mention of Jerusalem in inscrip-
tions round the fireplace.

# ACT V

## SCENE I.—[*Gloucestershire. Shallow's house.*]

*Enter* SHALLOW, FALSTAFF, BARDOLPH, *and* PAGE.

*Shal.* By cock and pie, sir, you shall not away tonight.
 What, Davy, I say!
*Fal.* You must excuse me, Master Robert Shallow.
*Shal.* I will not excuse you, you shall not be excused,
 excuses shall not be admitted, there is no excuse          5
 shall serve, you shall not be excused. Why, Davy!

### [*Enter* DAVY.]

*Davy.* Here, sir.
*Shal.* Davy, Davy, Davy, Davy; let me see, Davy; let me
 see, Davy; let me see—yea, marry, William cook, bid
 him come hither. Sir John, you shall not be excused.     10
*Davy.* Marry, sir, thus: those precepts cannot be served;

---

### ACT V

#### *Scene* I

ACT V SCENE I] F (*Actus Quintus. Scæna Prima.*); *not in* Q.     *Location.*] *Theobald,
subst.*     S.D.] *Capell, subst.; Enter Shallow, Falstaffe, and Bardolfe* Q [*against IV. v.
239–40*]; *Enter Shallow, Silence, Falstaffe, Bardolfe, Page, and Dauie.* F.     1. sir] Q;
*not in* F.     6. Why, Davy] *As* Q; [*separate line*] F.     6. S.D.] *Theobald; not in QF.*
8. Davy; let me see, Davy] Q; *not in* F.     9. yea, marry] Q; *not in* F.

---

S.D.] F brings on Davy (who should
not enter until called a second time, at
l. 6) and also Silence. It doubtless supposes that where Shallow is, there
Silence must be also.

 1. *By . . . pie*] A trifling oath, 'By God
and pie', *pie* being the Roman Catholic
rule-book for the ordering of church
offices. Henry Porter's *Two Angry
Women of Abington* (Mal. Soc., l. 862)
includes it with other harmless ex-

pressions which 'th'ancient of the
parish' utter over their cups.

 9. *William cook*] Instances abound in
the drama of this naming by occupation; e.g. 'Robin Ostler' (*1H4*, II. i.
12), 'Robin Brewer, Ned Butler, Rafe
Horssekeeper, Gyles Porter' (*Sir Thos
More*, Mal. Soc., ll. 1675–8), 'Jeremy
butler' (Jonson, *Alch.*, v. i. 27; H. & S.,
v. 388).

 11. *precepts*] writs, warrants.

and again, sir—shall we sow the hade land with
wheat?

*Shal.* With red wheat, Davy. But for William cook—are
there no young pigeons?                                    15

*Davy.* Yes, sir. Here is now the smith's note for shoeing
and plough-irons.

*Shal.* Let it be cast and paid. Sir John, you shall not be
excused.

*Davy.* Now, sir, a new link to the bucket must needs be    20
had; and sir, do you mean to stop any of William's
wages, about the sack he lost the other day at Hinckley fair?

*Shal.* A shall answer it. Some pigeons, Davy, a couple of
short-legged hens, a joint of mutton, and any pretty    25
little tiny kickshaws, tell William cook.

---

12. hade land] *Q;* head-land *F.*        16–17.] *As Q, prose;* Yes Sir. / Heere . . .
Shooing, / And Plough-Irons. / *F* [*irregular lines*].        20. Now] *Q; not in F.*
22. the other day] *F; not in Q.*        22–3. Hinckley] *F;* Hunkly *Q.*        24. A] *Q;*
He *F.*        it. Some] *Q;* it: / Some *F.*        26. tiny] *Q;* tine *F.*

---

12. *hade land*] A strip at the side of an
arable field upon which the plough
turns, and so plantable only when the
rest is finished (Wright, *Engl. Dial.
Dict.*, Hade, *sb.*). Q's form is more
countrified than F's.

14. *red wheat*] A reddish variety
sown in Gloucestershire in August–
September, known locally as 'red
Lammas', Lammas being 1 August
(Madden, p. 381).

18. *cast*] reckoned up.

20. *link*] According to *OED* this may
be (*a*) rope, (*b*) chain, (*c*) section (of a
rope or chain). Which is meant here is
hard to say.

*bucket*] The sense of 'pail' is probably
more frequent than that of 'yoke', but
either would suit.

22–3. *Hinckley*] A market-town near
Coventry, 30 miles N.E. of Stratford,
with a famous fair on Whit Mondays
and an August Fair also. Q reads
'Hunkley' ('inc' probably read as
'un').

25. *short-legged hens*] Still recognized
in the trade as better table-birds than
long-legged ones, having heavier

bodies and more flesh. Beaumont &
Fletcher's *Love's Pilgrimage*, 1. i (Glover
& Waller, vi. 237), calls for 'a short-
leg'd Hen / Daintily carbonado'd'
(grilled).

26. *little tiny*] F's 'tine' (and 'tyne' at
v. iii. 55) may be what Shakespeare
wrote, rather than Q's 'tinie' and 'tiny'
respectively, of which no other instances occur in Shakespearean Qq
during his lifetime, or in F. *OED*
records several instances from 1400 to
1605 of 'tine' following 'little', as at v.
iii. 55 and in both other occurrences of
'tine' in Shakespeare, *Tw.N.*, v. i. 398
(F; there is no Q) and *Lr*, III. ii. 74
(both Qq and F also). Probably 'little
tine' was a (?provincial, ?playful)
formula; *OED*'s Shakespearean examples are from Shallow and the
fools in *Twelfth Night* and *Lear* (with
a folk-song air, e.g. *Tw.N.*, v. i.
398—'He that has and a little-tyne
wit').

*kickshaws*] fancy extras (Fr. *quelques
choses*). Cotgrave has, 'Fricandeaux
. . . short skinlesse, and daintie pud-
dings, or Quelkchoses'.

*Davy.* Doth the man of war stay all night, sir?

*Shal.* Yea, Davy, I will use him well: a friend i'th'court is
better than a penny in purse. Use his men well,
Davy, for they are arrant knaves, and will backbite.     30

*Davy.* No worse than they are backbitten, sir, for they
have marvellous foul linen.

*Shal.* Well conceited, Davy—about thy business, Davy.

*Davy.* I beseech you, sir, to countenance William Visor of
Woncot against Clement Perkes a'th'Hill.     35

*Shal.* There is many complaints, Davy, against that
Visor; that Visor is an arrant knave, on my knowledge.

*Davy.* I grant your worship that he is a knave, sir: but yet
God forbid, sir, but a knave should have some coun-     40
tenance at his friend's request. An honest man, sir, is
able to speak for himself, when a knave is not. I have
served your worship truly, sir, this eight years; and if

---

28. Yea] *Q;* Yes *F.*     Davy, I] *Q; Dauy:* / I *F.*     31. backbitten] *Q;* bitten *F.*
34. sir, to] *Q;* sir, / To *F.*     35. Woncot] *Q* (Woncote), *F;* Wincot *Rann.*
a'th'] *Q* (a'th); *of the F.*     36. is] *Q;* are *F.*     40. God] *Q;* heauen *F.*     43.
this] *Q;* these *F.*     if] *F; not in Q.*

---

28-9. *a friend . . . purse*] Proverbial;
Tilley, F687.

33. *Well conceited*] Very witty.

33-48.] Commenting on Davy as a
model of rustic fidelity, Tillyard
observes (p. 303), 'The upset in
Shallow's house caused by Falstaff's
visit must have been great. But Davy is
undefeated. Through all the turmoil
of unusual hospitality he insists on seeing to the details of his job: the bucket
must have a new link; and his friend
William Visor of Woncot (though a
knave) must not be allowed to suffer at
the plea of Clement Perkes'.

34-5.] Shaaber lays out fully the
competing claims of places and per-
sons for the honour of these references.
The best case seems to be that made by
R. Webster Huntley (*Gloss. of the
Cotsw. Dial.*, 1868, p. 22) and by
Madden (pp. 84-5), for a family
named Visor or Vizard, recorded
from at least 1612 to the later 19th c. at
Woodmancote (locally pronounced

Woncot), adjoining Dursley in Gloucestershire, and for a family named
Purchase or Perkis, with a house on
nearby Stinchcombe Hill (locally
known as 'The Hill'). That Shakespeare knew the district seems evident
from *R2*, II. iii, when Bolingbroke and
Northumberland, travelling south-
west through the 'high wild hills' of
Gloucestershire, and asking how far
away Berkeley is, are told, 'There
stands the castle by yon tuft of trees'.
Berkeley is, in fact, easily visible in a
woody copse less than four miles west
of Stinchcombe Hill (cf. Spurgeon,
pp. 374-7). This makes a strong case
for these identifications. One would
give much to know what prompted
Shakespeare to make Shallow call
William Visor 'an arrant knave, on
my knowledge' (ll. 37-8). Wilm-
cote near Stratford ('Wincot' in *Shr.*,
Induc., ii. 23) has been suggested
for *Woncot*, but the other details do
not fit.

I cannot once or twice in a quarter bear out a knave
against an honest man, I have but a very little credit          45
with your worship. The knave is mine honest friend,
sir, therefore I beseech your worship let him be
countenanced.

*Shal.* Go to; I say he shall have no wrong. Look about,
Davy. [*Exit Davy.*] Where are you, Sir John? Come,          50
come, come, off with your boots. Give me your hand,
Master Bardolph.

*Bard.* I am glad to see your worship.

*Shal.* I thank thee with all my heart, kind Master
Bardolph; and [*To the Page*] welcome, my tall          55
fellow. Come, Sir John.

*Fal.* I'll follow you, good Master Robert Shallow. [*Exit
Shallow.*] Bardolph, look to our horses. [*Exeunt Bardolph and Page.*] If I were sawed into quantities, I
should make four dozen of such bearded hermits'          60
staves as Master Shallow. It is a wonderful thing to
see the semblable coherence of his men's spirits and
his. They, by observing of him, do bear themselves
like foolish justices; he, by conversing with them, is
turned into a justice-like servingman. Their spirits          65
are so married in conjunction, with the participation
of society, that they flock together in consent, like so
many wild geese. If I had a suit to Master Shallow, I

45. but a very] *F; not in Q.*     47. your worship] *F;* you *Q.*     49–52.] *As Q,
prose;* Go too, / I . . . *Davy.* / Where . . . Boots. / Giue . . . *Bardolfe.* / *F [irregular
lines].*     49. Go to; I say] *F, subst.;* Go to I say, *Q.*     50. S.D.] *Capell; not in QF.*
50–1. Come, come, come,] *Q;* Come, *F.*     54. all] *F; not in Q.*     55. S.D.]
*Rowe [after* fellow.]*; not in QF.*     55–6.] *As Q;* Bardolfe . . . Fellow: / Come . . .
Iohn. / *F [irregular lines].*     57–8, 58–9. S.D.s] *Capell; not in QF.*     63. of] *F;
not in Q.*

46. *honest*] A vague epithet of appreciation; cf. II. iv. 326.

55–6. *tall fellow*] This might be intended for Bardolph but it seems
addressed to someone else, and the
Page is likeliest. Q gives him no entry
in this scene, but F brings him on at the
beginning. Since he is tiny (cf. I. ii. 11–
15, v. iii. 30, 55) *tall* (= both 'lofty'
and 'valiant') is the same genial irony
as Falstaff's 'you giant' at I. ii. 1.

57–8, 58–9. S.D.s] QF have no
directions for departure, but clearly
Falstaff is alone during ll. 59–82.

59. *quantities*] little bits; cf. *Shr.*, IV.
iii. 112—'thou rag, thou quantity,
thou remnant'.

62. *semblable coherence*] close correspondence.

64. *conversing*] associating.

66. *so . . . conjunction*] joined in so
intimate a union.

would humour his men with the imputation of being
near their master: if to his men, I would curry with    70
Master Shallow that no man could better command
his servants. It is certain that either wise bearing or
ignorant carriage is caught, as men take diseases, one
of another; therefore let men take heed of their company. I will devise matter enough out of this Shallow    75
to keep Prince Harry in continual laughter the wearing out of six fashions, which is four terms, or two
actions, and a shall laugh without intervallums. O,
it is much that a lie with a slight oath, and a jest with
a sad brow, will do with a fellow that never had the    80
ache in his shoulders! O, you shall see him laugh till
his face be like a wet cloak ill laid up!

*Shal.* [*Within*] Sir John!
*Fal.* I come, Master Shallow, I come, Master Shallow.　　*Exit.*

78. a] *Q; he F.*　　without] *Q; with F.*　　83. S.D.] *Theobald; not in QF.*
84. S.D.] *F* [*Exeunt*], *Theobald, subst.; not in Q.*

69–70. *with . . . near*] by implying
that I am intimate with.

70. *curry with*] flatter. The metaphor
is from currying, smoothing down a
horse.

73. *carriage*] behaviour.

74–5. *let . . . company*] Proverbial;
Tilley, M536.

76–7. *the wearing . . . fashions*] The
changeableness of fashions was often
satirized, as it still is; e.g. Lyly,
*Euphues, Anat. of Wyt*, Preface (Bond,
i. 182, l. 20)—'a fashion is but a dayes
wearing'; Jasper Mayne, *City Match*,
II. iv (Hazlitt's *Dodsley*, xiii. 237)—'to
wear a gown / Out a whole fashion, or
the same jewels twice?'

77. *four terms*] i.e. a legal year,
Michaelmas, Hilary, Easter, and
Trinity terms.

78. *actions*] Falstaff was acquainted

with these; cf. II. i. I. 'There is something humorous in making a spend-
thrift compute time by the operation of
an action for debt' (Johnson). As
Wilson (N.C.S.) notes, these jests
seem intended for Inns-of-Court
students.

*intervallums*] Perhaps more Inns-of-
Court humour; Delius, ed. 1857,
glosses, 'intervals between the various
terms and actions. . . . Hence the
Latin expression'.

80. *sad*] serious.

82. *like . . . up*] i.e. wrinkled with
innumerable creases; *ill laid up* =
packed carelessly away. Face-wrink-
ling seems to have prompted Shakespeare's wit; cf. *Tw.N.*, III. ii. 84–5—
'He does smile his face into more lines
than is in the new map with the augmentation of the Indies'.

## SCENE II.—[*Westminster. The palace.*]

*Enter* WARWICK *and the* LORD CHIEF JUSTICE[*, meeting*].

*War.* How now, my Lord Chief Justice, whither away?
*Ch. Just.* How doth the King?
*War.* Exceeding well: his cares are now all ended.
*Ch. Just.* I hope, not dead.
*War.*            He's walk'd the way of nature,
   And to our purposes he lives no more.             5
*Ch. Just.* I would his Majesty had call'd me with him.
   The service that I truly did his life
   Hath left me open to all injuries.
*War.* Indeed I think the young King loves you not.
*Ch. Just.* I know he doth not, and do arm myself      10
   To welcome the condition of the time,
   Which cannot look more hideously upon me
   Than I have drawn it in my fantasy.

*Enter* [PRINCE] JOHN *of* LANCASTER, CLARENCE, GLOUCESTER,
[*and others*].

*War.* Here come the heavy issue of dead Harry.
   O that the living Harry had the temper             15
   Of he, the worst of these three gentlemen!

*Scene* II

SCENE II] *F (Scena Secunda.)* ; *not in* Q.     *Location.*] *Capell, subst.*     S.D.] *F (Enter the Earle of Warwicke, and the Lord Chiefe Iustice.), Capell, subst.; Enter Warwike, duke Humphrey, L. chiefe Iustice, Thomas Clarence, Prince Iohn, Westmerland. Q corr.; Enter . . . Prince, Iohn Westmerland. Q uncorr.*    1. whither] *Q ;* whether *F.*    2. Ch. Just.] *Q (Iust.), F [so throughout scene].*    3.] *As Q ;* Exceeding . . . Cares / Are . . . ended. / *F.*    13. S.D. *Enter . . . Gloucester*] *Q, subst. (Enter Iohn, Thomas, and Humphrey.); Enter Iohn of Lancaster, Gloucester, and Clarence. F.*    *and others*] *Capell; not in QF.*    16. he] *Q ;* him *F.*

S.D.] Q's S.D. may reflect Shakespeare's initial intention to bring on at once the whole group most nearly affected by the King's death, an intention presumably changed as soon as he began writing, since Q brings on *Iohn, Thomas,* and *Humphrey* at l. 13 also.

3. *well*] To speak of the dead as 'well' was proverbial; Tilley, H347,

'He's well since he is in Heaven'.

6–41.] These forebodings derive from the Wild-Prince legends. In *F.V.*, on the accession, the Lord Chief Justice releases the thief for whose imprisonment he has been boxed on the ear, 'For feare of my Lord the yong Prince' (ix. 1–5). Holinshed's comment is of quite contrary tone; cf. Appendix I, p. 203.

How many nobles then should hold their places
That must strike sail to spirits of vile sort!

*Ch. Just.* O God, I fear all will be overturn'd.

*Lanc.* Good morrow, cousin Warwick, good morrow.	20

*Glou.* ⎫
*Clar.* ⎭ Good morrow, cousin.

*Lanc.* We meet like men that had forgot to speak.

*War.* We do remember, but our argument
Is all too heavy to admit much talk.

*Lanc.* Well, peace be with him that hath made us heavy!	25

*Ch. Just.* Peace be with us, lest we be heavier!

*Glou.* O good my lord, you have lost a friend indeed;
And I dare swear you borrow not that face
Of seeming sorrow—it is sure your own.

*Lanc.* Though no man be assur'd what grace to find,	30
You stand in coldest expectation.
I am the sorrier; would 'twere otherwise.

*Clar.* Well, you must now speak Sir John Falstaff fair,
Which swims against your stream of quality.

*Ch. Just.* Sweet Princes, what I did I did in honour,	35
Led by th'impartial conduct of my soul.
And never shall you see that I will beg
A ragged and forestall'd remission.

---

19. O God] *Q ;* Alas *F.*	20. *Lanc.*] *QF (Iohn) [so throughout scene].*	21. *Glou. Clar.*] *Q (Prin. ambo),F.*	27. *Glou.*] *Q (Humph.),F.*	36. impartial] *Q ;* Imperiall *F.*	38. forestall'd] *Q (forestald),F (fore-stall'd) ;* forestaled *Wilson (N.C.S.),* conj. *McIlwraith.*	38–9. remission. . . . me,] *F ;* remission, . . . me. *Q.*

34. *swims . . . quality*] goes against the current of your nature and position.

38.] Probably, (a) a beggarly pardon 'that it is pre-determined shall not be granted' (Mason, 1785), or (b) 'a pardon begged by a voluntary confession and *anticipation* of the charge' (Johnson). Massinger seems to be echoing Shakespeare—(a) *Duke of Milan,* 1623, III. i. 152 (*Works,* Mermaid ed., i. 48)—'Nor come I as a Slaue, / . . . / Falling before thy Feet, kneeling and howling, / For a forestal'd remission'; (b) *Bondman,* 1624, III. iii. 169 (*Works,* ed. Gifford, ii. 68)— 'better expose / Our naked breasts to their keen Swords, . . . / . . . then to

trust / In a forestal'd remission'. For 'forstald' (Q), 'forestal'd' (i.e. 'forestaled') has been proposed rather than 'forestall'd', as a Shakespearean coinage (*OED* does not record 'Forestale'). The line would mean 'rendered stale [or distasteful], before it is received, by the ignominy of begging it' (A. K. McIlwraith, in *TLS,* 19 Jan. 1933, p. 40). But the word seems to mean not a *distasteful* pardon but one 'forestalled', rendered void in advance, broken already. And Q's 'forestald' at *2H4,* IV. v. 140 ('I had forestald this deere and deep rebuke'), certainly means 'forestall'd'. F reads 'forestall'd' in both places. The Lord Chief

     If truth and upright innocency fail me,
     I'll to the King my master that is dead,        40
     And tell him who hath sent me after him.
*War.* Here comes the Prince.

        *Enter* KING HENRY THE FIFTH, *attended.*

*Ch. Just.* Good morrow, and God save your Majesty!
*King.* This new and gorgeous garment, majesty,
     Sits not so easy on me as you think.        45
     Brothers, you mix your sadness with some fear.
     This is the English, not the Turkish court;
     Not Amurath an Amurath succeeds,
     But Harry Harry. Yet be sad, good brothers,
     For by my faith it very well becomes you.       50
     Sorrow so royally in you appears
     That I will deeply put the fashion on,
     And wear it in my heart. Why then, be sad;
     But entertain no more of it, good brothers,
     Than a joint burden laid upon us all.       55
     For me, by heaven, I bid you be assur'd,
     I'll be your father and your brother too;
     Let me but bear your love, I'll bear your cares.
     Yet weep that Harry's dead, and so will I;
     But Harry lives, that shall convert those tears       60
     By number into hours of happiness.
*Princes.* We hope no otherwise from your Majesty.
*King.* You all look strangely on me—and you most;
     You are, I think, assur'd I love you not.

---

39. truth] *Q; Troth F.*    42. S.D.] *Capell, subst.; Enter the Prince and Blunt Q*
[*against ll. 41–2*]; *Enter Prince Henrie. F.*    43. God] *Q;* heauen *F.*    44. *King*]
*QF* (*Prince*), *Theobald 2, subst.* [*so subst. throughout scene*].    46. mix] *F;* mixt *Q.*
48. Amurath . . . Amurath] *Q; Amurah . . . Amurah F.*    50. by my faith] *Q;* to
speake truth *F.*    59. Yet] *Q;* But *F.*    62. *Princes.*] *Q* (*Bro.*), *F* (*Iohn, &c.*),
*Staunton.*    otherwise] *Q;* other *F.*

Justice, in short, is refusing to plead for a beggarly boon sure to be denied.

    42. S.D.] Q brings on Blunt as Hal's attendant, mute as ever.

    48. *Amurath*] Upon succeeding his father, Selim II, in 1574, Sultan Murad (Amurath) III had his brothers killed; his successor, Muhammad III, did likewise in January 1596. The name became a byword for tyranny; cf. Jonson, *The Case is Altered*, IV. x. 30–1 (H. & S., iii. 166)—
'I tell thee, if *Amurath*, the great Turke, were here, I would speake, and he should here [sic] me'.

*Ch. Just.* I am assur'd, if I be measur'd rightly,          65
    Your Majesty hath no just cause to hate me.
*King.* No?
    How might a prince of my great hopes forget
    So great indignities you laid upon me?
    What! rate, rebuke, and roughly send to prison          70
    Th'immediate heir of England? Was this easy?
    May this be wash'd in Lethe and forgotten?
*Ch. Just.* I then did use the person of your father;
    The image of his power lay then in me;
    And in th'administration of his law,          75
    Whiles I was busy for the commonwealth,
    Your Highness pleased to forget my place,
    The majesty and power of law and justice,
    The image of the King whom I presented,
    And struck me in my very seat of judgment;          80
    Whereon, as an offender to your father,
    I gave bold way to my authority
    And did commit you. If the deed were ill,
    Be you contented, wearing now the garland,
    To have a son set your decrees at naught?          85
    To pluck down justice from your aweful bench?
    To trip the course of law, and blunt the sword
    That guards the peace and safety of your person?
    Nay more, to spurn at your most royal image,
    And mock your workings in a second body?          90

67–8. No? / How ... forget] *Steevens;* No? how ... forget *QF [one line].*

72. *Lethe*] The river in Hades, the
waters of which produced oblivion.

73. *use the person*] personate, represent. 'All the King's courts were, and
indeed still are, supposed to be emana-
tions of the King himself as the foun-
tain of justice, the judges being merely
his delegates' (*Sh.'s Engl.*, i. 383–4).
Shakespeare's phrase is closely paralleled in John Case's *Sphæra Ciuitatis*,
1588, p. 179—'Locus, quo nunc
abuteris, tribunal tui patris est, iudex
que[m] inuadis *personam tui patris gerit*
. . . iudex in tribunale *personam gerit
principis*' (editor's italics). This may be
because both use the same technical

term; but for another possible echo of
Case see ll. 108–12, note.

74. *image*] counterpart.

76–80.] The Lord Chief Justice presided in the Court of King's Bench.

84. *garland*] Cf. iv. v. 201, note.

85–90.] Most editors change QF's
question-marks, which Elizabethan
printers often use for exclamations;
but 'Question your royal thoughts'
(l. 91) suggests the trend of Shakespeare's feeling.

86. *aweful*] Cf. iv. i. 176, note.

90.] 'treat with contempt your acts
exercised by a representative' (Johnson).

Question your royal thoughts, make the case yours,
Be now the father, and propose a son,
Hear your own dignity so much profan'd,
See your most dreadful laws so loosely slighted,
Behold yourself so by a son disdain'd:                                    95
And then imagine me taking your part,
And in your power soft silencing your son.
After this cold considerance sentence me;
And, as you are a king, speak in your state
What I have done that misbecame my place,                            100
My person, or my liege's sovereignty.
*King.*  You are right, Justice, and you weigh this well.
Therefore still bear the balance and the sword;
And I do wish your honours may increase
Till you do live to see a son of mine                                      105
Offend you and obey you, as I did.
So shall I live to speak my father's words:
'Happy am I, that have a man so bold
That dares do justice on my proper son;
And not less happy, having such a son                                    110

---

95. disdain'd] *Rowe;* disdained *QF.*     96. your] *Q;* you *F.*     102. right,
Justice] *Hanmer;* right Iustice *QF.*     110. not] *Q;* no *F.*

92. *propose*] imagine.

97. *soft*] gently.

99. *in your state*] 'in your regal character and office . . . with the impartiality of a legislator' (Johnson).

102. *right, Justice*] Following QF, Ridley and Wilson (N.C.S.) read 'right justice', i.e. 'justice itself', which is not impossible but sounds the less natural of the two, as the King's opening words.

103.] Cf. *F.V.,* ix. 193 ff.; Appendix I, p. 229. Following Elyot, Stow makes much of Hal's submission when the offence is originally committed, but he mentions no later meeting with the Lord Chief Justice. Holinshed describes the new King as electing 'the best learned men in the lawes of the realme, to the offices of iustice' (iii. 62) but says nothing about the confirmation of the Lord Chief Justice.

108–12. *Happy . . . justice*] On Stow's and Shakespeare's closeness here to Elyot's *Gouernour,* see Intro., p. xxxvi, and Appendix I, pp. 218–21. The play's words also resemble John Case's *Sphæra Ciuitatis,* 1588, p. 179—'O me beatum (inquit) qui tam iustum & sincerum iudicem, qui tam pium & obedientem filium ante sepulchrum video' (D. T. Starnes, 'More about the Prince Hal Legend', *PQ,* xv. 358–66). Case's book would be well known, since in 1590 the University of Oxford decreed that every bachelor should, on 'determining', take a copy of it (*Dict. Nat. Biog.,* John Case). Shakespeare may have seen it, though except for 'O me beatum'/'Happy am I' he is nearer to Elyot and Stow. For another possible echo of Case, cf. above, l. 73, note.

109. *proper*] own.

That would deliver up his greatness so
Into the hands of justice.' You did commit me:
For which I do commit into your hand
Th'unstained sword that you have us'd to bear,
With this remembrance—that you use the same        115
With the like bold, just, and impartial spirit
As you have done 'gainst me. There is my hand.
You shall be as a father to my youth,
My voice shall sound as you do prompt mine ear,
And I will stoop and humble my intents        120
To your well-practis'd wise directions.
And Princes all, believe me, I beseech you,
My father is gone wild into his grave,
For in his tomb lie my affections;
And with his spirits sadly I survive        125
To mock the expectation of the world,
To frustrate prophecies, and to raze out
Rotten opinion, who hath writ me down
After my seeming. The tide of blood in me
Hath proudly flow'd in vanity till now.        130
Now doth it turn, and ebb back to the sea,
Where it shall mingle with the state of floods,
And flow henceforth in formal majesty.
Now call we our high court of parliament,
And let us choose such limbs of noble counsel        135
That the great body of our state may go
In equal rank with the best-govern'd nation;

---

112. justice.' You] *F* (Iustice. You); Iustice you *Q*.        125. spirits] *QFf1–2*;
spirit *F3*.        127. raze] *QF* (race), *Theobald*.

117–21. *There . . . directions*] 'The
whole movement is to bring the Lord
Chief Justice up to the throne, away
from the role of defendant in his own
case to that of the King's Adviser. Law
has ceased to be on trial: thus natural
order is restored' (John Lawlor, *The
Tragic Sense in Sh.*, 1960, p. 25).

123–4.] 'My wildness is buried with
my father, for in his tomb my passions
lie' (Monro, ed. 1957).

125. *spirits*] sentiments, feelings.
*sadly*] soberly, gravely.

126. *mock*] prove wrong.

130. *proudly flow'd*] A rich Shakespearean suggestiveness is felt here,
combining the senses of 'imperiously',
'flauntingly', 'overbearingly', and
'swollenly'; cf. *MND.*, ii. i. 90–2—
'contagious fogs . . . / Have every pelt-
ing river made so proud / That they
have overborne their continents'.

132. *state of floods*] majesty of the
sea.

135. *limbs*] members; the state is a
'body' politic in the next line.

That war, or peace, or both at once, may be
As things acquainted and familiar to us;
In which you, father, shall have foremost hand.          140
Our coronation done, we will accite,
As I before remember'd, all our state:
And, God consigning to my good intents,
No prince nor peer shall have just cause to say,
God shorten Harry's happy life one day!          *Exeunt.*          145


SCENE III.—[*Gloucestershire. Shallow's orchard.*]

*Enter* FALSTAFF, SHALLOW, SILENCE, DAVY, BARDOLPH,
[*and*] PAGE.

*Shal.*  Nay, you shall see my orchard, where, in an arbour,
we will eat a last year's pippin of mine own graffing,

140. you] *Q corr., F;* your *Q uncorr.*     143. God] *Q;* heauen *F.*     145. God] *Q;*
Heauen *F.*     145. S.D.] *Q (exit.), F.*

*Scene* III

SCENE III] *F (Scena Tertia.); not in Q.          Location.] Capell, subst.          S.D.]
Q (Enter sir Iohn, Shallow, Scilens, Dauy, Bardolfe, page.); Enter Falstaffe, Shallow,
Silence, Bardolfe, Page, and Pistoll. F.*          1. my] *Q;* mine *F.*          2. mine] *Q;*
my *F.*

141. *accite*] summon; cf. II. ii. 56,
note.

142. *remember'd*] mentioned, made
known.

*state*] men of rank.

143. *consigning to*] endorsing, re-
inforcing.

*Scene* III

Tillyard (p. 302) well observes that
this scene of country life, representing
the heart of England, occurs 'precisely as the Prince becomes Henry V',
the King most intimate with his
people. See also his comment quoted
in the first note to III. ii.

2–3. *we . . . pippin . . . carawayes*] List-
ing 'pepins' among 'the best Apples
that we haue in England', Thomas
Cogan's *Haven of Health*, 1584, declares

that apples 'may be eaten with least
detriment, if they be gathered ull ripe,
and well kept untill the next winter, or
the yeare following'. It continues, 'We
are woont to eate Carawayes [i.e.
caraway seeds, or cakes containing
these] or Biskettes, or some other kinde
of Comfittes, or seedes together with
Apples, thereby to breake winde en-
gendred by them' (p. 89). Apples,
Andrew Boorde recommends in his
*Dyetary of Helth*, 1542, 'shuld be eaten
with suger or comfettes or with fenell-
sede, or anys-sede, bycause of theyr
ventosyte' (EET'S, Extra ser., x, 1870,
p. 284). *Caraway* is, however, also an
obsolete Somerset word for a kind
of apple (Wright, *Engl. Dial. Dict.*),
and that might be Shallow's meaning.

with a dish of caraways, and so forth—come, cousin
Silence—and then to bed.

*Fal.* Fore God, you have here a goodly dwelling, and a    5
rich.

*Shal.* Barren, barren, barren; beggars all, beggars all,
Sir John—marry, good air. Spread, Davy, spread,
Davy, well said, Davy.

*Fal.* This Davy serves you for good uses; he is your    10
serving-man, and your husband.

*Shal.* A good varlet, a good varlet, a very good varlet, Sir
John—by the mass, I have drunk too much sack at
supper—a good varlet. Now sit down, now sit down
—come, cousin.    15

*Sil.* Ah, sirrah! quoth-a, we shall
[*Sings*]    Do nothing but eat, and make good cheer,
And praise God for the merry year,
When flesh is cheap and females dear,
And lusty lads roam here and there,    20
So merrily,
And ever among so merrily.

---

4. Silence] Q (Scilens), F [*so also at ll. 36, 47, 50, 125; and see collation at l. 16*].
5. Fore God] Q; *not in* F.    here a . . . and a] F; here . . . and Q.    13. by the
mass] Q; *not in* F.    16. Sil.] Q (*Scilens*), F [*so also at ll. 32, 38, 44, 48, 51, 100; and
see collation at l. 4*].    Ah] Q (A), F.    17. S.D.] Rowe, subst.; *not in* QF.    17–
22.] *As verse*, Rowe, subst.; *prose*, QF.    18. God] Q; heauen F.

---

3. *and so forth*] A phrase used repeatedly as a meaningless gag by Josselin, a fussy citizen, in Thomas Heywood's *1 Edward IV* (Shepherd, i. 12 ff.).

9. *well said*] Cf. III. ii. 270, note.

11. *husband*] husbandman, steward.

16. *Ah, sirrah*] An ejaculation sometimes addressed to nobody in particular, like the American 'Yes sir!', 'Yes sir*ree*!'; cf. Gabriel Harvey, *Letters* (Grosart, i. 22)—'Ah Syrrha, and Iesu Lord, thought I'; and *Rom.*, I. v. 31, 128; *AYL.*, IV. iii. 166.

17–22.] Prose in QF (continuous with l. 16), like all the songs and snatches in this scene except F's at ll.

32–6—an instance, Shaaber suggests, of the difficulty of distinguishing prose and verse in the MS of a scene where they alternate frequently. This snatch looks like a traditional song but no original has been found. As H. N. Hudson agreeably observes, 'in this vocal flow of Silence we catch the right spirit and style of old English mirth. For he must have passed his life in an atmosphere of song, since it was only by dint of long custom and endless repetition that so passive a memory as his could get stored with such matter' (*Sh., His Life, Art, and Character*, 1872, ii. 103).

22. *ever among*] all the while.

*Fal.* There's a merry heart, good Master Silence! I'll give
    you a health for that anon.

*Shal.* Give Master Bardolph some wine, Davy.                    25

*Davy.* Sweet sir, sit—I'll be with you anon—Most sweet
    sir, sit; master page, good master page, sit. Proface!
    What you want in meat, we'll have in drink; but you
    must bear; the heart's all.                    [*Exit.*]

*Shal.* Be merry, Master Bardolph, and my little soldier    30
    there, be merry.

*Sil.* [*Sings*] Be merry, be merry, my wife has all,
        For women are shrews, both short and tall.
        'Tis merry in hall, when beards wags all,
        And welcome merry Shrove-tide! Be merry,
          be merry.                    35

*Fal.* I did not think Master Silence had been a man of
    this mettle.

*Sil.* Who, I? I have been merry twice and once ere now.

*Enter* DAVY.

23. *Fal.*] Q (*sir Iohn*), F.    25. Give . . . Bardolph] Q; Good M. *Bardolfe:* F.
29. must] Q; *not in* F.    29. S.D.] *Theobald; not in* QF.    32. S.D.] *Rowe,
subst.; not in* QF.    32–5.] *As verse,* F; *prose,* Q.    32. wife has] Q; wife ha's F;
wife's as *Rann, conj. Farmer.*    34. wags] Q; wagge F.    37. mettle] Q (mettall),
F.    38. S.D.] Q; *not in* F.

26–7. *Sweet . . . Proface*] Davy takes it
on himself to play the host.

*Proface*] Welcome to it!—a formula
before a meal, frequent in the 16th–
17th cs., from obsolete Fr. 'prou fasse'
(i.e. 'bon prou vous fasse!'—May it do
you good!). Thomas Heywood's *Wise-
Woman of Hogsden*, IV. i (Shepherd, v.
335), has, 'The dinner's halfe done
before I say Grace, / And bid the old
knight and his guest proface'.

28. *What . . . drink*] An echo of the
proverb, 'What they want in meat let
them take in drink' (Tilley, M845).

32–5.] Prose in Q, verse in F. Like
ll. 17–22, this looks like a popular song,
but no original is known save for l. 34
which was proverbial (Tilley, H55)
and is found as early as *Kyng Alisaunder*
(1312)—'Mery swithe it is in halle, /
whan that berdes waweth alle' (EETS,
Orig. ser., 227, p. 67, ll. 1163–4).

34. *wags*] Survivals of the old
northern verb plural in -s are common; cf. Abbott, §333.

35. *Shrove-tide*] A season of festivities comprising the Sunday and two
following days (Shrove Monday and
Tuesday) preceding Ash Wednesday
and Lent.

38. *twice and once*] This formula, with
different numbers, occurs humorously
as an expression of frequency; e.g.
*Merry Devil of Edmonton* (Hazlitt's
*Dodsley*, x. 245)—'Mine host, my
bully, . . . I haue been drunk in thy
house twenty times and ten'; and *Contention between Liberality and Prodigality*,
I. iv (Hazlitt's *Dodsley*, viii. 338). Cowl
gives other examples. Considering
that Silence has lived a long time, his
merry-making has been of the lowest
degree of frequency. The spectator is
privileged to be present at one of the

*Davy.* [*To Bardolph*] There's a dish of leather-coats for
  you.                                                    40

*Shal.* Davy!

*Davy.* Your worship? I'll be with you straight. [*To Bardolph*] A cup of wine, sir?

*Sil.* [*Sings*]    A cup of wine that's brisk and fine,
                   And drink unto thee, leman mine,        45
                   And a merry heart lives long-a.

*Fal.* Well said, Master Silence.

*Sil.* And we shall be merry, now comes in the sweet o'th'
  night.

*Fal.* Health and long life to you, Master Silence.        50

*Sil.* [*Sings*]    Fill the cup, and let it come,
                   I'll pledge you a mile to th'bottom.

*Shal.* Honest Bardolph, welcome! If thou want'st anything, and wilt not call, beshrew thy heart. [*To the
  Page*] Welcome, my little tiny thief, and welcome       55
  indeed, too! I'll drink to Master Bardolph, and to all
  the cabileros about London.

---

39. S.D.] *Cambridge; not in QF.*    There's] *Q; There is F.*    42–3. S.D.]
*Capell; not in QF.*    44. S.D.] *Rowe, subst.; not in QF.*    44–6.] *As verse, Rowe,
subst.; prose, QF.*    45. thee,] *Wilson (N.C.S.);* the *QF.*    48. And] *Q; If F.*
o'th'] *Q* (a'th), *White 2;* of the *F.*    51. S.D.] *Capell, subst.; not in QF.*    51–2.]
*As verse, Capell; prose, QF.*    52. to th'] *Q* (too th); to the *F.*    54–5. S.D.]
*Capell [after thief, l. 55], Dyce 2; not in QF.*    55. tiny] *Q;* tyne *F.*    57. cabileros]
*Q;* Cauileroes *F.*

rare occurrences of this striking phe-
nomenon.

39. *leather-coats*] russet apples (from
their rough skin).

45. *thee, leman*] QF's 'the leman'
makes better sense if rendered thus, as
it is by Wilson (N.C.S.); 'the' is a frequent Elizabethan spelling of 'thee'.
*Leman* = sweetheart.

46.] Proverbial; Tilley, H320a.

48–9. *the sweet o'th' night*] Silence's
sentiment resembles Falstaff's own at
II. iv. 364.

51. *let it come*] Pass it round! a
drinking cry; cf. *2H6*, II. iii. 66—'Let
it come, i'faith, and I'll pledge you all'.
Cowl gives further examples.

52. *a mile . . . bottom*] i.e. the whole
cupful, were it a mile deep. 'One that

will drink deep, though it be a mile to
the bottom' is given as a tavern-phrase
in *The Eighth Liberal Science: or a new-
found Art and Order of Drinking* (cited E.
Partridge, *Dict. of Slang*, 3rd edn,
1949). Many such sayings were current; e.g. Jonson, *E.M.I.*, v. iii. 153
(H. & S., 280)—'I pledge M.
Doctor and't were a sea to the bot-
tome'. Tilley, A207, lists as proverbial
'To set all agoing if it were a mile to the
bottom'.

55. *tiny*] Cf. v. i. 26, note.

57. *cabileros*] A jocular term for
'gallant', 'fine fellow'; usually 'cava-
liero' (cf. F's 'Cauileroes'). Either
'Shallow uses the Spanish form' (Wilson, N.C.S.), or Q's compositor made
the easy *v/b* misreading.

*Davy.* I hope to see London once ere I die.

*Bard.* And I might see you there, Davy,—

*Shal.* By the mass, you'll crack a quart together—ha!     60
 will you not, Master Bardolph?

*Bard.* Yea, sir, in a pottle-pot.

*Shal.* By God's liggens, I thank thee; the knave will stick
 by thee, I can assure thee that. A will not out, a; 'tis
 true bred!                                                65

*Bard.* And I'll stick by him, sir.

*Shal.* Why, there spoke a king. Lack nothing! Be merry!
 (*One knocks at door.*) Look who's at door there, ho!
 Who knocks?                                   [*Exit Davy.*]

*Fal.* [*To Silence, seeing him take off a bumper*] Why, now     70
 you have done me right.

*Sil.* [*Sings*]          Do me right,
                         And dub me knight:
                         Samingo.

---

59. And] *Q; If F.*     60. By the mass] *Q; not in F.*     62. Yea] *Q; Yes F.*
63. By . . . liggens] *Q; not in F.*     64. that. A] *F* (that. He); *that a Q.*     A
. . . out, a; 'tis] *Q* (a wil not out, a tis); He will not out, he is *F.*     68. S.D.]
*Q* [*against l. 66*], *Capell, subst.; not in F.*     68. Look who's] *Q; Looke, who's F.*
69, 70. S.D.s] *Capell; not in QF.*     72. S.D.] *Rowe, subst.; not in QF.*     72-4.] *As
verse, Malone; prose, QF.*

---

58. *once*] one day.

60 *crack*] drink, empty.

62. *pottle-pot*] two-quart tankard.
Bardolph doubles Shallow's estimate.

63. *By God's liggens*] F omits. An
oath unknown elsewhere and un-
explained: *liggens* may represent a
diminutive, 'lidkins', from 'lid' (i.e.
eye-lid), as in *Troil.*, I. ii. 228—'By
God's lid, it does one's heart good'.
'God's lid' occurs frequently in Jonson,
*E.M.I.* Cf. 'bodikins' from 'God's
body', and the many oaths on the body
of God.

64. *A . . . out*] He won't drop out.
*Stick by thee* and *true bred* suggest a hunting term for sticking to the pack, or to
the scent (Madden, p. 53); but the
phrase occurs in convivial contexts
where the sticking is rather to the
wine-cups—e.g. *Ant.*, II. vii. 33-4—
'Pompey. . . . A health to Lepidus!

*Lepidus.* I am not so well as I should be,
but I'll ne'er out'.

71. *done me right*] done the right thing
by me (by matching drink for drink).
'Do me right' was a drinking formula
used in challenging a person to pledge;
e.g. Jonson, *E.M.O.*, v. iv. 79–81 (H.
& S., iii. 578)—'*2 Cup.* Nay, doe me
right, sir. *1 Cup.* So I doe, in good
faith'; and Dekker, *1 Honest Whore*, I.
iv. 167 (Bowers, ii. 40). Cowl cites
other examples.

72-4.] The lines are from a drinking-
song, *Monsieur Mingo*, translated from
a French version, which Orlando di
Lasso set to music. 'From 1592 to 1604
several Elizabethan playwrights quote
fragments of the English version. . .
The concluding phrase [i.e. Silence's
bit] seems to have been the best-known
part of the song, and became, in fact, a
popular refrain' (F. W. Sternfeld, *Sh.*

Is't not so?	75

*Fal.* 'Tis so.

*Sil.* Is't so? Why then, say an old man can do somewhat.

[*Enter* DAVY.]

*Davy.* And't please your worship, there's one Pistol come
from the court with news.

*Fal.* From the court? Let him come in.	80

*Enter* PISTOL.

How now, Pistol?

*Pist.* Sir John, God save you!

*Fal.* What wind blew you hither, Pistol?

*Pist.* Not the ill wind which blows no man to good. Sweet
knight, thou art now one of the greatest men in this	85
realm.

*Sil.* By'r lady, I think a be, but goodman Puff of Barson.

*Pist.* Puff?

Puff i'thy teeth, most recreant coward base!

Sir John, I am thy Pistol and thy friend,	90

77. S.D.] *Capell; not in* QF.	78. And't] *Q;* If it *F.*	80. S.D.] *Q* [*against l.* 79],
*F.*	82. God save you] *Q;* 'saue you sir *F.*	84. no man] *Q;* none *F.*	84–5.
good. Sweet knight,] *Q, subst.;* good, sweet Knight: *F.*	85. this] *Q;* the *F.*
87. By'r lady] *Q;* Indeed *F.*	a] *Q;* he *F.*	89–93.] *As verse, Pope; prose,* QF.
89. i'thy] *Neilson;* ith thy *Q;* in thy *F.*

*Q.,* ix. 105–15); cf. Nashe, *Summer's
Last Will,* ll. 968–71 (McKerrow, iii.
264)—'Mounsieur Mingo for quaffing
doth surpasse, / In Cuppe, in Canne,
or glasse. / God Bacchus, doe mee
right, / And dubbe me Knight
Domingo'; Marston, *Antonio & Mellida,* v (Wood, i. 55)—'Doe me right,
and dub me knight *Balurdo'.* Scraps of
it occur also, e.g. in Jonson, *E.M.O.,* v.
iv. 75–9 (H. & S., iii. 578) and Chapman, *All Fools,* v. ii. 95 (*Comedies,* ed.
Parrott, ii. 156). Of Domingo (? Don
Mingo) or Samingo (? Sir Mingo),
Sisson observes (*New Readings*), 'The
derivation from the Latin verb *mingo*
[make water] is lamentably clear, and
the mock-title could be applied to any
toper, Sir John Falstaff for instance, as

indicated in this present play at II.
iv. 33'.

73. *dub me knight*] An allusion to
the custom of 'knighting' whoever in
the company had shown special prowess in drinking healths.

83.] Proverbial; Tilley, W441.

84.] Proverbial; Tilley, W421.

87.] As *Puff* implies, Silence takes
'greatest' to refer to Falstaff's girth.

*goodman*] A title given to yeomen
and others below the rank of gentleman.

*Barson*] Identified, though not very
firmly, with either Barston between
Coventry and Solihull, or Barcheston
(locally pronounced Barston) ten
miles S. of Stratford. Both are in
Warwickshire.

And helter-skelter have I rode to thee,
And tidings do I bring, and lucky joys,
And golden times, and happy news of price.

*Fal.* I pray thee now, deliver them like a man of this
world.                                                                        95

*Pist.* A foutre for the world and worldlings base!
I speak of Africa and golden joys.

*Fal.* O base Assyrian knight, what is thy news?
Let King Cophetua know the truth thereof.

*Sil.* [*Sings*]    And Robin Hood, Scarlet, and John.        100

*Pist.* Shall dunghill curs confront the Helicons?
And shall good news be baffled?
Then, Pistol, lay thy head in Furies' lap.

*Shal.* Honest gentleman, I know not your breeding.

*Pist.* Why then, lament therefor.                              105

91. And] *Q; not in F.*    94. *Fal.*] *Q* (*Iohn*), F [*so also at l. 98*].    pray thee] *Q;*
prethee *F.*    96–9.] *As verse, F; prose, Q.*    99. Cophetua] *Q* (Couetua), *Pope;*
*Couitha F.*    100. S.D.] *Johnson, subst.; not in QF.*    101–3.] *As verse, F; prose, Q.*
103. Furies'] *QF* (Furies), *Capell;* Fury's *Rowe.*    104.] *As Q;* Honest Gentleman, / I . . . breeding. / *F.*    105. therefor] *QF* (therefore), *Bullen 1904.*

94–5. *man . . . world*] ordinary
mortal.

96. *A foutre*] A ruder version of 'A
fig'.

97. *Africa*] The land of fabulous
wealth.

98. *Assyrian*] Why *Assyrian* is uncertain, except for the appropriate
highflown Orientalism. Noble (p. 262)
citing *Isaiah*, x. 6 and 13, suggests that
the Assyrians were associated with
robbery and pillage, and so akin to
Pistol. But the term occurs elsewhere.
In Dekker's *Shoemaker's Holiday*, Simon
Eyre, along with other playful Biblical designations such as 'Meso-
potamians' (II. iii. 71; Bowers, i. 42),
'Philistines' (II. iii. 97; Bowers, i. 43),
and 'Babylonian' (III. ii. 141; Bowers,
i. 54), salutes 'my fine dapper Assyrian lads' (v. i. 48; Bowers, i. 74).

99. *King Cophetua*] The ballad of *A
Beggar and a King* (known first in
Richard Johnson's *Crowne Garland of
Goulden Roses*, 1612, and thence re-
printed in Percy's *Reliques*, 1765)
begins, 'I read that once in Affrica, / A

Prince that there did raine: / Who had
to name Cophetua, / As Poets they did
faine'. Shakespeare refers to it in
*LLL.*, I. ii. 115, IV. i. 66; *Rom.*, II. i. 14;
*R2*, v. iii. 80; and Jonson in *E.M.I.*,
III. iv. 56 (H. & S., iii. 352)—'as rich as
King COPHETVA'.

100.] A scrap from the ballad of
*Robin Hood and the Jolly Pinder of Wake-
field* (Child, *Popular Ballads*, iii. 131,
st. 3).

101. *Helicons*] 'i.e. the Muses (or true
poets like himself). Pistol had given
much thought to the delivery of his
news' (Wilson, N.C.S.).

102. *baffled*] treated with contume-
ly.

105.] A histrionic tag, found also in
Jonson, *Poetaster*, III. iv. 256 (H. & S.,
iv. 253), and Ford, *Love's Sacrifice*, IV. i
(Dyce, ii. 78). Similar phrases are
common; e.g. Pistol's 'Why then,
rejoice therefore', and 'We must
yearn therefore' (*H5*, III. vi. 51 and II.
iii. 6); 'The Guise is slain, and I
rejoice therefore', Marlowe, *Massacre
at Paris*, xviii. 150.

*Shal.* Give me pardon, sir; if, sir, you come with news
    from the court, I take it there's but two ways, either
    to utter them or conceal them. I am, sir, under the
    King, in some authority.

*Pist.* Under which king, Besonian? Speak, or die.     110

*Shal.* Under King Harry.

*Pist.*               Harry the Fourth, or Fifth?

*Shal.* Harry the Fourth.

*Pist.*              A foutre for thine office!
    Sir John, thy tender lambkin now is King;
    Harry the Fifth's the man: I speak the truth.
    When Pistol lies, do this, and fig me, like     115
    The bragging Spaniard.

*Fal.*             What, is the old King dead?

*Pist.* As nail in door! The things I speak are just.

*Fal.* Away, Bardolph, saddle my horse. Master Robert
    Shallow, choose what office thou wilt in the land,
    'tis thine. Pistol, I will double-charge thee with     120
    dignities.

*Bard.* O joyful day!
    I would not take a knighthood for my fortune.

*Pist.* What, I do bring good news?

*Fal.* Carry Master Silence to bed. Master Shallow, my     125

---

106. sir; if] *Q ;* Sir. / If *F.*    107. there's] *Q ;* there is *F.*    108. or] *Q ;* or to *F.*
110.] *As Q ;* Vnder . . . King? / *Bezonian, . . . dye.* / *F.*    113–16.] *As verse, F ; prose,*
*Q.*    117.] *As Q ;* As . . . doore. / The . . . iust. / *F.*    118–21.] *As prose, Q ;* Away
. . . Horse, / Master . . . wilt / In . . . thee / With Dignities. / *F [irregular lines].*
122–3.] *As verse, F ; prose, Q.*    123. knighthood] *F ;* Knight *Q.*

---

108. *them . . . them*] Cf. i. i. 27, note.

110. *Besonian*] ignoramus; lit. a raw
recruit (Span. 'bisoño' or Ital.
'bisogno', need). Robert Barret, *Theo-*
*rike and Practike of Moderne Warres*, 1598,
re ers repeatedly to Besonians as lacking in skill; e.g. 'the *Bisognios* are rawe
men' (p. 16), 'a *Bisognio* or *Bisonnio*, a
raw souldier, vnexpert in his weapon,
and other Military points' (sig. Y4ʳ).
One would give much to have had
Pistol present during III. ii. 273–81.

112. *A foutre . . . office*] 'On the death
of a king a J.P.'s office terminated'
(Wilson, N.C.S.).

115. *do . . . me*] i.e. insult me, by

sticking the thumb between two
fingers, so making 'the fig of Spain'—
which Pistol uses to Fluellen (*H5*, III.
vi. 62); Span. 'higos dar', 'give the
fig'.

120. *double-charge*] A play on Pistol's
name.

125–34. *Master Shallow . . . Justice*]
'[Falstaff's] opulent fancy and large
nature take pleasure in ideas of lavish
gifts as well as ample gain. He bids
Shallow 'be what thou wilt', Pistol 'devise something to do thyself good'; and
while denouncing 'woe to my lord
chief justice', exclaims, '[Blessed] are
they [that] have been my friends!'

Lord Shallow—be what thou wilt; I am Fortune's
steward! Get on thy boots, we'll ride all night. O
sweet Pistol! Away, Bardolph! [*Exit Bardolph.*]
Come, Pistol, utter more to me; and withal devise
something to do thyself good. Boot, boot, Master          130
Shallow! I know the young King is sick for me. Let
us take any man's horses—the laws of England are
at my commandment. Blessed are they that have
been my friends, and woe to my Lord Chief Justice!

*Pist.* Let vultures vile seize on his lungs also!          135
'Where is the life that late I led?' say they:
Why, here it is; welcome these pleasant days!          *Exeunt.*

128. S.D.] *Capell; not in QF.*          133. Blessed . . . that] *Q;* Happie . . . which *F.*
134. to] *Q;* vnto *F.*          135–7.] *As verse, F; prose, Q.*          137. these] *Q;* those *F.*
137. S.D.] *Q (exit.), F.*

Falstaff's luxuriant composition has a
quality of generosity; he has abundance to bestow as well as to possess'
(Clarke, 1865). This is pleasantly said,
but it looks too uncritically on Falstaff's *hubris*. His 'abundance to bestow' is not his own, and in the upshot
Shallow is £1,000 the poorer.

132. *take . . . horses*] press them in the
King's name (at a nominal price, and
so avoid the expense of hiring). Falstaff is not actually stealing them.

132–3. *the laws . . . commandment*] Dr
Harold Brooks writes to me, 'It is not
easy to exaggerate the enormity of this
for an Elizabethan audience. I am
inclined to think that Sh. would have
in mind an article (among those reported by Holinshed) which helped to
give grounds for the deposition of
Richard II, charging him with having
said that "the laws of England were in
his head, and sometimes in his breast".
. . . Falstaff, the would-be "overmighty

subject", arrogates a power which had
been thought matter for deposition
when claimed even by the legitimate
sovereign'.

134. *woe . . . Justice*] This outburst
even Maurice Morgann finds damning
—'After this we ought not to complain
if we see Poetic Justice duly executed
upon him, and that he is finally given
up to shame and dishonour' (*Dramatic
Character of . . . Falstaff*, 1777, p. 179).

135. *Let . . . lungs*] Pistol alludes, as
he does also in *Wiv.,* i. iii. 94 ('Let
vultures gripe thy guts'), to the story
either of Prometheus or of Tityos the
Titan (Virgil, *Aen.,* vi. 595–600;
Ovid, *Metam.,* iv. 457–8); both were
chained to the ground and had their
vitals gnawed by vultures.

136. '*Where . . . led?*'] A surviving
scrap of a poem (quoted also in *Shr.,*
iv. i. 143), in which, apparently, a
doting lover yearned for his former
freedom (Anders, p. 181).

## SCENE IV.—[*London. A street.*]

*Enter* BEADLES, [*dragging in*] HOSTESS QUICKLY *and*
DOLL TEARSHEET.

*Host.* No, thou arrant knave! I would to God that I
might die, that I might have thee hanged. Thou hast
drawn my shoulder out of joint.

*First Bead.* The constables have delivered her over to me,
and she shall have whipping-cheer enough, I war-        5
rant her; there hath been a man or two lately killed
about her.

*Doll.* Nut-hook, nut-hook, you lie! Come on, I'll tell thee
what, thou damned tripe-visaged rascal, and the
child I go with do miscarry, thou wert better thou        10
hadst struck thy mother, thou paper-faced villain.

*Scene* IV

SCENE IV] F (*Scena Quarta.*); *not in* Q.        *Location.*] *Theobald, subst.*        S.D.] *F*
(*Enter Hostesse Quickly, Dol Teare-sheete, and Beadles.*), *Malone; Enter Sincklo and
three or foure officers.* Q.        1. to God that] Q; *not in* F.        4. *First Bead.*] Q (*Sincklo*),
*F* (*Off.*), *Rowe* (*Bead.*), *Malone* [*so subst. throughout scene*].        5. enough] *F; not in Q-*
6. lately] *F; not in* Q.        8. *Doll*] Q (*Whoore*), F (*Dol.*) [*so throughout scene*].
9. and] Q; *if* F.        10. I] Q; I *now* F.        wert] Q; had'st F.

S.D.] Q's S.D. looks thoroughly
authorial, with its indeterminate numbers, omission of essential characters,
and naming of the actor. John Sincklo
is named also in F *3H6*, III. i (in S.D.s
and speech-prefixes throughout), F
*Shr.*, Induc., i. 88, the 'plot' of *2 Seven
Deadly Sins*, c. 1590–1, and the Induction to Marston's *Malcontent*, 1604. He
is thought to have been pale and
strikingly thin (on this see Shaaber,
pp. 433–4), and so to have qualified
for Doll's and the Hostess's abuse in
ll. 8–30; he may also have played
Shadow since the company would
scarcely have *two* skeletons on its
strength.

Beadles] Minor parish officers who
punished petty offences.

3. *drawn . . . joint*] References
abound to officers and their shoulder-
seizing; e.g. Chapman, *May Day*, IV. i.
25–6 (*Comedies*, ed. Parrott, p. 210),
calls        sergeants        'pewter-buttoned

shoulder-clappers'. Cowl gives many
examples.

4. *delivered her over*] Constables hand-
ed minor offenders over to the beadles
for punishment.

5. *whipping-cheer*] a bellyful of whip-
ping—the recognized punishment in
Bridewell for whores.

7. *about her*] Either 'over her' or 'in
her company' (cf. ll. 17–18). Tavern-
killings were not unusual; cf. Dekker,
*1 Honest Whore*, III. iii. 77–80 (Bowers,
ii. 70)—'O how many thus . . . haue
let out / Their soules in Brothell houses
. . . and dyed / Iust at their Harlots
foot'.

8. *Nut-hook*] lit. a hooked stick for
pulling branches down; hence, beadle,
constable, catchpole.

9. *tripe-visaged*] flabby, sallow.

9–10. *the child . . . with*] To plead
pregnancy was a recognized means of
avoiding or postponing the death-
penalty.

*Host.* O the Lord, that Sir John were come! He would
make this a bloody day to somebody. But I pray God
the fruit of her womb miscarry!

*First Bead.* If it do, you shall have a dozen of cushions    15
again; you have but eleven now. Come, I charge
you both, go with me, for the man is dead that you
and Pistol beat amongst you.

*Doll.* I'll tell you what, you thin man in a censer, I will
have you as soundly swinged for this—you blue-    20
bottle rogue, you filthy famished correctioner, if you
be not swinged I'll forswear half-kirtles.

*First Bead.* Come, come, you she knight-errant, come!

*Host.* O God, that right should thus overcome might!
Well, of sufferance comes ease.    25

*Doll.* Come, you rogue, come, bring me to a justice.

12. the Lord] *Q; not in F.*    He] *F; I Q.*    13. pray God] *Q; would F.*    14.
miscarry] *Q;* might miscarry *F.*    18. amongst] *Q;* among *F.*    19. you . . .
you] *Q;* thee . . . thou *F.*    21. bottle] *Q;* Bottel'd *F.*    24. God] *Q; not in
F.*    overcome] *Q;* o'recome *F.*    26.] *As Q;* Come . . . come: / Bring . . . Iustice. / *F.*

13. *make . . . somebody*] A proverbial
tag; Tilley, D88.

13–14. *I pray . . . miscarry*] Some
commentators have thought that (*a*)
Doll is in fact with child; (*b*) Falstaff is
the father; and (*c*) the Hostess means
what she says (i.e. she hopes the child
will die so that the Beadle will be
charged with murder). But (*a*) Doll is
not with child (cf. l. 16); (*b*) Falstaff is
therefore not the father; and (*c*) the
Hostess means the opposite of what she
says (as in l. 24 also).

15. *cushions*] As in Chapman &
Shirley, *Chabot*, III. ii. 114 (Chapman,
*Tragedies*, ed. Parrott, p. 305)—'She
. . . will wear a cushion to seem with
child'.

19. *man in a censer*] figure on a per-
fuming-pan. Censers had figures thinly
embossed on them. Shakespeare often
likens thin men to low-relief carved or
hammered figures; e.g. III. ii. 259–60,
note; New Arden *1H4*, I. iii. 206, note;
*LLL.*, v. ii. 617–20, where Holofernes
is compared to 'the face of an old

Roman coin, scarce seen', 'The carv'd-
bone face on a flask', and 'St. George's
half-cheek in a brooch'; and *John*, I. i.
143, where Robert Faulconbridge's
face is as thin as the profile on a
coin.

20–1. *bluebottle*] Beadles, like modern
policemen, wore blue coats (Linthicum, p. 27).

21. *correctioner*] one from the 'House
of Correction', as Bridewell was
called; the word is apparently Doll's
coinage.

22. *forswear half-kirtles*] give up
wearing skirts. A kirtle comprised
bodice and skirt, a half-kirtle the skirt
portion (Linthicum, p. 186).

23. *knight-errant*] 'A quibble on
night-errant (sinner by night)' (Wilson, N.C.S.); cf. the 'knight-night'
pun in New Arden *1H4*, I. ii. 24–5,
note.

24.] The Hostess characteristically
garbles the proverb, 'Might overcomes
right'; Tilley, M922.

25.] Proverbial; Tilley, S955.

*Host.* Ay, come, you starved bloodhound.
*Doll.* Goodman death, goodman bones!
*Host.* Thou atomy, thou!
*Doll.* Come, you thin thing, come, you rascal!	30
*First Bead.* Very well.	*Exeunt.*


SCENE V.—[*Westminster. Near the Abbey.*]

*Enter three* GROOMS, *strewers of rushes.*

*First Groom.* More rushes, more rushes!
*Second Groom.* The trumpets have sounded twice.
*Third Groom.* 'Twill be two o'clock ere they come from
the coronation. Dispatch, dispatch.	*Exeunt.*

*Trumpets sound, and the* KING *and his train pass over the stage:
after them enter* FALSTAFF, SHALLOW, PISTOL, BARDOLPH,
*and the* PAGE.

27. Ay, come] *Q* (I come); Yes, come *F.*	29. atomy] *Q*; Anatomy *F.*	30.]
*As Q*; Come ... Thing: / Come ... Rascall. / *F.*	31. S.D.] *F*; *not in Q.*

*Scene* v

SCENE V] *F* (*Scena Quinta.*); *not in Q.*	Location.] Theobald, *subst., Capell.*	S.D.
three Grooms] *Dyce 2*; two Groomes. *F*; *not in Q.*	strewers of rushes] *Q*; *not in F.*
1. *First Groom*] *Q* (1), *F* (1. *Groo.*).	2. *Second Groom*] *Q* (2), *F* (2. *Groo.*).	3.
*Third Groom*] *Q* (3); 1. *Groo. F.*	'Twill] *Q*; It will *F.*	o'] *Q* (a), *Capell*; of the
*F.*	4. Dispatch, dispatch] *Q*; *not in F.*	4. S.D. *Exeunt*] *F1* (*Exit Groo.*), *F3*
(*Exeunt Grooms.*); *not in Q.*	Trumpets ... Bardolph, and the] *Q*; Enter Falstaffe,
Shallow, Pistoll, Bardolfe, and *F.*	Page] *Q* (Boy), *F.*

29. *atomy*] An Elizabethan form of
'atom', but here a blunder for 'anatomy' (skeleton), which indeed is F's
reading.

30. *rascal*] An allusion to the First
Beadle's thinness, *rascal* being the term
for a lean deer.

*Scene* v

S.D.] For the difference between Q
and F see Intro., p. lxxv.

3. Third Groom] F gives this to the
first groom, saving an acting part.

3–4.] This speech is a little curious.
If, following Q, one brings the King in

after l. 4, going *to* the Abbey, the third
groom should presumably refer to his
approach to (rather than return from)
the coronation. If, following F, one
brings the King in only after l. 40,
coming *from* the Abbey, haste here is
unnecessary (perhaps this is why F
omits *Dispatch, dispatch*) and 'The
trumpets have sounded twice' (l. 2) is
inappropriate. Precision should not be
expected in such fleeting exchanges.

4. S.D.] Q's entry here seems better
than F's postponement of it to l. 40.
The two trumpet-calls of l. 2 receive
here the expected third.

*Fal.* Stand here by me, Master Robert Shallow, I will    5
make the King do you grace. I will leer upon him as
a comes by, and do but mark the countenance that
he will give me.

*Pist.* God bless thy lungs, good knight!

*Fal.* Come here, Pistol, stand behind me. [*To Shallow*] O,    10
if I had had time to have made new liveries, I would
have bestowed the thousand pound I borrowed of
you. But 'tis no matter, this poor show doth better,
this doth infer the zeal I had to see him.

*Shal.* It doth so.    15

*Fal.* It shows my earnestness of affection—

*Shal.* It doth so.

*Fal.* My devotion—

*Shal.* It doth, it doth, it doth.

*Fal.* As it were, to ride day and night, and not to deliber-    20
ate, not to remember, not to have patience to shift
me—

*Shal.* It is best, certain.

*Fal.* But to stand stained with travel, and sweating with
desire to see him, thinking of nothing else, putting all    25
affairs else in oblivion, as if there were nothing else to
be done but to see him.

5. Robert] *F; not in Q.*    7. a] *Q; he F.*    9. God] *Q; not in F.*    10. S.D.]
*Collier; not in QF.*    13. 'tis] *Q; it is F.*    no] *Q, F corr.; bo F uncorr.*    15.
Shal.] *F; Pist. Q.*    16. of] *Q; in F.*    affection—] *Dyce; affection. QF.*
17. Shal.] *Hanmer; Pist. QF [so also at l. 19].*    18. devotion—] *Dyce; deuotion.*
*QF.*    20–2.] *As Q; As ... night, / And ... remember, / Not ... me. / F [irregular*
*lines].*    22. me—] *Dyce; me. QF.*    23. best,] *Q (best), Cambridge; most*
*F.*    23–4. certain. / Fal. But] *F; certain: but Q.*    26. affairs else] *Q;*
affayres *F.*

6. *leer*] look invitingly (without the
modern sense of slyness). Wilson
(N.C.S.) quotes *The Brut,* c. 1479—
'whan they [the revellers] were come
before hym [after the coronation],
some of them wynkyd on hym, & some
smylyd, & thus they made nyse
semblaunte vnto hym ... But for al
that the Prynce kept his countynaunce
ful sadly vnto them' (ed. Brie, EETS,
Orig. ser., 136, p. 594).

11. *liveries*] uniforms of the royal
service.

14. *infer*] imply, demonstrate.

15. Shal.] Q gives this to Pistol. But
Falstaff's main remarks (ll. 10–14)
are to Shallow, who surely should
reply.

17, 19. Shal.] QF give both speeches
to Pistol. But they are so unlike the
Pistolian rant of ll. 9, 28 ff., and so
like Shallow's reiterative habit (and
eagerness here to accord with Falstaff), that Hanmer's switch seems
right.

21–2. *shift me*] change my shirt.

*Pist.* 'Tis *semper idem*, for *obsque hoc nihil est*; 'tis all in every
    part.
*Shal.* 'Tis so, indeed.                                     30
*Pist.* My knight, I will inflame thy noble liver,
    And make thee rage.
    Thy Doll, and Helen of thy noble thoughts,
    Is in base durance and contagious prison,
    Hal'd thither                                        35
    By most mechanical and dirty hand.
    Rouse up Revenge from ebon den with fell Alecto's
      snake,
    For Doll is in. Pistol speaks naught but truth.
*Fal.* I will deliver her.        [*Shouts within.*]  *The trumpets sound.*
*Pist.* There roar'd the sea, and trumpet-clangor sounds.    40

    *Enter the* KING *and his train,* [*the*] LORD CHIEF JUSTICE
                      [*among them*].

*Fal.* God save thy Grace, King Hal, my royal Hal!

28. all] *F; not in Q.*    31–2.] *As verse, Johnson; prose, QF.*    33–8.] *As verse, Pope*
[*lines ending . . . thoughts / . . . prison; / . . . hands. / . . . snake, / . . . truth.*], *Capell;*
*prose, QF.*    35. Hal'd] *Q* (halde), *F4;* Hall'd *F1;* Hauld *Pope.*    38. truth] *Q;*
troth *F.*    39. S.D. *Shouts within*] *Steevens; not in QF.*    *The . . . sound*] *F* [*after l. 40*],
*Malone; not in Q.*    40. roar'd] *F;* roared *Q.*    40. S.D. *Enter . . . train*] *Q; The*
*Trumpets sound. Enter King Henrie the Fift, Brothers,* F.    *Lord Chief Justice*] *F; not in*
*Q.*    *among them*] *Capell; not in QF.*    41. God] *Q; not in F.*

28. *semper idem*] ever the same.

    *obsque . . . est*] apart from this there
is nothing. Whether *obsque* (for *absque*)
is Pistol's blunder, or Shakespeare's,
or misreading of 'a' for 'o', cannot be
decided. *Semper idem* was a motto; this
may be another, or a legal tag.

    28–9. *'tis . . . part*] Apparently meant
as a rough rendering of the quoted
Latin tags. 'All in all and all in every
part' was proverbial (Tilley, A133),
expressing absolute perfection or
identity.

    31. *liver*] Supposedly the seat of the
passions, here of anger.

    33. *Helen*] The name of Helen of
Troy was often applied jocularly to a
wife or mistress. Cowl gives many
examples.

    35. *Hal'd*] Q's 'Halde' might mean

'haul'd' ('haul' was spelt 'hall' until
the 17th c.), as F's 'Hall'd' does. Pope
and some other editors have taken it
so.

    37. *Rouse up Revenge*] No precise
identification is needed for Pistol's
tags, but this sounds like Kyd, *Span.*
*Trag.*, III. xv (Boas, pp. 80–1), where
the Ghost repeatedly cries out,
'Awake, *Revenge*'.

    *Alecto*] One of the Furies, represent-
ed with serpents twined in their hair
and blood dripping from their eyes;
cf. *Ant.*, II. v. 40—'Thou shouldst come
like a Fury crown'd with snakes'. They
punished the guilty both before and
after death; cf. Virgil, *Aen.*, vii. 346.

    38. *in*] *OED* cites this as its earliest
instance of *in* as equivalent to 'in
prison'.

*Pist.* The heavens thee guard and keep, most royal imp of
    fame!
*Fal.* God save thee, my sweet boy!
*King.* My Lord Chief Justice, speak to that vain man.
*Ch. Just.* Have you your wits? Know you what 'tis you
    speak?         45
*Fal.* My King! My Jove! I speak to thee, my heart!
*King.* I know thee not, old man. Fall to thy prayers.
    How ill white hairs becomes a fool and jester!
    I have long dreamt of such a kind of man,
    So surfeit-swell'd, so old, and so profane;     50
    But being awak'd I do despise my dream.
    Make less thy body hence, and more thy grace;
    Leave gormandizing; know the grave doth gape

---

43. God save] *Q;* 'Saue *F.*    45. *Ch. Just.*] *Q* (*Iust.*), *F* [*so subst. throughout scene*].
48. becomes] *Q;* become *F.*    51. awak'd] *Q;* awake *F.*

---

42. *imp*] scion (of a noble house);
now obsolete in this sense. Cf. Peele,
*Battle of Alcazar*, II. i. 46 (Bullen, i. 245)
—'the imp of royal race'.

44. *vain*] foolish.

46. *My . . . Jove*] Doubtless another
Daniel echo, from *The Complaint of
Rosamond*, 1594, ll. 239–40—'Doost
thou not see, how that thy King (thy
*Ioue*) / Lightens forth glory on thy
darke estate . . . ?'

47–71.] 'If . . . the speech sounds
formal and homiletic, that is because
Hal is learning to speak, not as Bradley
complains "like a clergyman", but
like the Chief Justice, to whom he had
just promised that his voice should
sound as he did prompt his ear. The
adoption of the Justice as his father
and the consecration at the Abbey had
completed the process of separation
[from Falstaff]. . . Not that he relishes
the task or finds it easy. When Falstaff
first confronts him, and that great red
face breaks in upon his "white celestial
thought", he tries to avoid the encounter, begging the Lord Chief
Justice to say for him what must be
said. But Falstaff, on fire with anticipation, brushes the old judge aside, so

that there is nothing for it: the King
must speak the unpleasant words himself. . . . King Henry V is a new man;
he had buried his "wildness" in his
father's grave; he speaks as the representative and embodiment of "The
majesty and power of law and justice".
I cannot believe that members of an
Elizabethan audience would have felt
the "sermon" anything but fine and
appropriate' (Wilson, *Fortunes*, pp.
121–2).

48. *becomes*] Q's 'becomes' may be
the old northern plural; cf. v. iii. 34,
note. Or *white hairs* may be thought of
collectively (= a white head).

52. *Make . . . grace*] Falstaff's gesture
towards self-control and repentance in
his last speech in Part 1 has been
strikingly unfulfilled (*1H4*, v. iv. 167–9
—'If I do grow great, I'll grow less,
for I'll purge and leave sack, and
live cleanly, as a nobleman should
do').

53–5. *know . . . jest*] Warburton
apud) Theobald, 1733) notes it as 'one
of Shakespeare's grand Touches of
Nature' that Hal lapses momentarily
into familiar jesting, but at once pulls
himself, and Falstaff, up short.

For thee thrice wider than for other men.
Reply not to me with a fool-born jest;                    55
Presume not that I am the thing I was;
For God doth know, so shall the world perceive,
That I have turn'd away my former self;
So will I those that kept me company.
When thou dost hear I am as I have been,              60
Approach me, and thou shalt be as thou wast,
The tutor and the feeder of my riots.
Till then I banish thee, on pain of death,
As I have done the rest of my misleaders,
Not to come near our person by ten mile.             65
For competence of life I will allow you,
That lack of means enforce you not to evils;
And as we hear you do reform yourselves,
We will, according to your strengths and qualities,
Give you advancement. [*To the Lord Chief Justice*] Be
     it your charge, my lord,                                  70
To see perform'd the tenor of my word.
Set on.                              *Exit King [with his train].*

*Fal.* Master Shallow, I owe you a thousand pound.

*Shal.* Yea, marry, Sir John, which I beseech you to let me
     have home with me.                                        75

*Fal.* That can hardly be, Master Shallow. Do not you
     grieve at this; I shall be sent for in private to him.
     Look you, he must seem thus to the world. Fear not
     your advancements; I will be the man yet that shall
     make you great.                                           80

---

57. God] *Q*; heauen *F.*     67. evils] *Q*; euill *F.*     69. strengths] *Q*; strength *F.*
70. S.D.] *Capell; not in QF.*     71–2.] *As Pope;* [*one line*] *QF.*     71. my] *Q*; our *F.*
72. S.D. *Exit King] F; not in Q.     with his train] Capell, subst.; not in QF.*     73.
*Fal.*] *Q* (*Iohn*), *F* [*so also at ll. 76, 85, 88*].     74. Yea] *Q*; I *F.*     79. advance-
ments] *Q*; aduancement *F.*

---

73.] Critics have argued much as to
Falstaff's manner when saying this—
businesslike, regretful, humiliated,
frank, stoical, broken-hearted, humorous, and so on. It seems best to assume
that, digesting his astonishment as
quickly as possible, he seeks to
take command of the situation and

shows a resilience (or a returning
hubris?) only to be quashed at
ll. 91–5.

76. *That . . . Shallow*] A masterly
touch of Falstaffian impudence. Shallow is not to have his money even
though (cf. ll. 10–13) it is not yet
spent.

*Shal.* I cannot perceive how, unless you give me your
 doublet, and stuff me out with straw. I beseech you,
 good Sir John, let me have five hundred of my
 thousand.

*Fal.* Sir, I will be as good as my word. This that you heard   85
 was but a colour.

*Shal.* A colour that I fear you will die in, Sir John.

*Fal.* Fear no colours. Go with me to dinner. Come, Lieutenant Pistol; come, Bardolph. I shall be sent for
 soon at night.                90

*Enter [the* LORD CHIEF] JUSTICE *and* PRINCE JOHN[, *with Officers.*]

*Ch. Just.* Go carry Sir John Falstaff to the Fleet;
 Take all his company along with him.

*Fal.* My lord, my lord,—

*Ch. Just.* I cannot now speak: I will hear you soon.
 Take them away.              95

81. cannot] *Q;* cannot well *F.*    give] *Q;* should give *F.*    87. that I fear] *Q;*
I feare, that *F.*    88–90.] *As prose, Pope;* Fear . . . dinner: / Come . . . Bardolfe, /
I . . . night. / *QF* [*irregular lines*].    90. S.D. Enter . . . *John*] *Q (Enter Iustice and
prince Iohn); not in F.*    with *Officers*] Capell, *subst.; not in QF.*    91. *Ch. Just.*] *Q
(Iust.), F [so ll. 94, 102, 104].*    94–5.] *As verse, F; prose, Q.*

86. *colour*] pretence.

87. *colour . . . die in*] Puns on 'colour—
collar' (noose), and 'dye—die'. Q's
'collour' (l. 86), 'collor' (l. 87), suggests the pronunciation. Shallow's jest,
even if lugubrious, does him credit in
the circumstances.

88. *Fear no colours*] Fear no enemy,
fear naught. Proverbial; Tilley, C520.

88–9. *Lieutenant*] Pistol's sudden
promotion, which Dyce, edn 2, was the
first to notice, may be Shakespeare's
inattention or, Shaaber suggests, one
of the 'dignities' Falstaff has promised
(v. iii. 121). If the latter, it would need
special emphasis on the stage.

90. *at night*] at the old revelling time,
presumably, when such as the Lord
Chief Justice are out of the way.

91. *the Fleet*] This, the famous prison
east of Fleet Ditch, just north of where
Fleet Street and Ludgate Hill join, had
not then the bad reputation it acquired

between 1641 and 1846, when used as
a debtors' prison. In *F.V.*, iv. 103, it is
the prison to which the Prince is committed for striking the Lord Chief
Justice. 'Falstaff's ultimate disgrace
and punishment have gained for him
much undeserved commiseration; the
punishment . . . temporary imprisonment in the Fleet and banishment from
Court—was not exceptionally severe.
Queen Elizabeth inflicted similar sentences upon favourite courtiers and
court ladies who incurred her displeasure. To Shakespeare's contemporaries, the King's treatment of Falstaff would not appear harsh' (Cowl,
pp. xxix–xxx). The incarceration is
merely an interim measure; the ten-
mile banishment is inconsistent with
long detention in London.

92. *all his company*] Including, it
appears, Shallow, whose state of mind
is left to the imagination.

*Pist.* *Si fortuna me tormenta, spero me contenta.*
　　　　　　*Exeunt all but Prince John and [the] Chief Justice.*
*Lanc.* I like this fair proceeding of the King's.
　　　He hath intent his wonted followers
　　　Shall all be very well provided for,
　　　But all are banish'd till their conversations　　　　　　100
　　　Appear more wise and modest to the world.
*Ch. Just.* And so they are.
*Lanc.* The King hath call'd his parliament, my lord.
*Ch. Just.* He hath.
*Lanc.* I will lay odds that, ere this year expire,　　　　　　105
　　　We bear our civil swords and native fire
　　　As far as France. I heard a bird so sing,
　　　Whose music, to my thinking, pleas'd the King.
　　　Come, will you hence?　　　　　　　　　　　*Exeunt.*

96. *tormenta, spero*] Q; *tormento, spera* F.　　*me*] F; *not in* Q.　　*contenta*] Q;
*contento* F.　　96. S.D.] F (*Exit. Manet Lancaster and Chiefe Iustice.*), *Cambridge;
exeunt.* Q [*after l. 95*].　　97. *Lanc.*] QF (*Iohn*) [*so also at ll. 103, 105*].　　107.
*heard*] Q; *heare* F.　　109. S.D.] F; *not in* Q.

96.] Cf. II. iv. 177, note.

97–101.] Mr Dipak Nandy writes to
me, 'I cannot really accept Prince
John's summing-up. The forcing of the
note in [these lines] I find unpleasant.
This is a *manipulation* of one's response,
not a direction of judgment. Furthermore, what does it mean to say [ll.
100–1]? Throughout, Falstaff and
Eastcheap have acted as a centre for
subverting and parodying the world of
high politics. . . They have given us
both an escape from (therefore irre-
sponsible) and a critique of (therefore
responsible) the world of Necessity
where "musts" perennially over-rule

"oughts". To demand of *this* Falstaff
that he reform his conversation in
order to appear more "wise" and
"modest" to unsmiling men like Prince
John is to demand that he should
cease to exist'. It is true that the King's
conditions are unlikely to be complied
with, and that nothing Prince John
says is likely to be heard with pleasure:
but these lines should be taken as a
clear reminder that the Falstaffians
are to be 'very well provided for'. The
schoolmasterly tone may grate, but the
message is satisfactory.

107. *I . . . sing*] Proverbial; Tilley
B374.

# EPILOGUE.

First, my fear; then, my curtsy; last, my speech.

My fear, is your displeasure; my curtsy, my duty;
and my speech, to beg your pardons. If you look for a
good speech now, you undo me, for what I have to
say is of mine own making; and what indeed I should    5
say will, I doubt, prove mine own marring. But to
the purpose, and so to the venture. Be it known to
you, as it is very well, I was lately here in the end of a
displeasing play, to pray your patience for it, and to
promise you a better. I meant indeed to pay you      10
with this; which if like an ill venture it come un-
luckily home, I break, and you, my gentle creditors,
lose. Here I promised you I would be, and here I
commit my body to your mercies. Bate me some, and

*Epilogue*

10. meant] *Q ; did meane F.*

'Applause was often invited in the closing speech or in a formal epilogue. . . . This might also lead up to or perhaps represent the prayer for the sovereign' (Chambers, *El. St.*, ii. 550). Q has the prayer at the end of the first paragraph: F transfers it to the very end. Not all three paragraphs would be delivered at any one time; if they were, they would be over-long, and awkward too. The first is spoken by its author, presumably Shakespeare: the assumption sometimes made, that he had nothing to do with it, is unwarranted by style or matter. It would soon be out-of-date through its reference to a recent 'displeasing play'. The second and third paragraphs need a dancer (a role in which one hardly sees Shakespeare), and they make the Oldcastle apology; they must belong to

another occasion, and in use they would need prefacing with some introductory matter. Pope and many editors mark the whole Epilogue as '*Spoken by a Dancer*', but this suits only the latter parts.

1. *curtsy*] bow (by either sex; cf. II. i. 123).

5–6. *making . . . marring*] A frequent antithesis; the vowels sounded alike.

6. *doubt*] fear.

6–7. *But . . . venture*] But to the matter in hand—and so I'll chance it.

9. *displeasing play*] This remains unidentified.

11. *ill venture*] unsuccessful trading voyage.

12. *break*] (*a*) break my promise; (*b*) go bankrupt.

14. *Bate me*] Let me off.

I will pay you some, and, as most debtors do, pro-   15
mise you infinitely: and so I kneel down before you
—but, indeed, to pray for the Queen.

If my tongue cannot entreat you to acquit me, will
you command me to use my legs? And yet that were
but light payment, to dance out of your debt. But a   20
good conscience will make any possible satisfaction,
and so would I. All the gentlewomen here have forgiven me: if the gentlemen will not, then the gentlemen do not agree with the gentlewomen, which was
never seen before in such an assembly.   25

One word more, I beseech you. If you be not too
much cloyed with fat meat, our humble author will
continue the story, with Sir John in it, and make you
merry with fair Katharine of France; where, for
anything I know, Falstaff shall die of a sweat, unless   30
already a be killed with your hard opinions; for Old-

16–17. and . . . Queen] Q; [after l. 34] F [omitting I].   22. would] Q; will F.
25. before] F; not in Q.   31. a] Q; he F.

16–17. and . . . Queen] 'The speaker kneels, ostensibly to beg pardon of the audience, and then, waggishly, pro-tests it is to pray for the Queen' (Wilson, N.C.S.).

22–5. All . . . assembly] Cf. AYL., Epil. 11–18, for similar coaxing of the gentlewomen and gentlemen. 'This suggests a Court audience, and that the speaker had already won popularity with the ladies. Had he played the little page?' (Wilson, N.C.S.).

28. with . . . it] Why Shakespeare broke this promise, or whether he kept it and then revised Henry V to exclude Falstaff, is a problem fortunately more relevant to that play than this. Here it is enough (a) to note that at this point Shakespeare considers Falstaff any-thing but down and out; and (b) to quote Johnson's advice—'Let meaner authours learn from this example, that it is dangerous to sell the bear which is yet not hunted, to promise to the publick what they have not written'

(note on Falstaff's death, H5, II. iii).

30. die . . . sweat] The man who at Gad's Hill 'sweats to death, / And lards the lean earth as he walks along' (1H4, II. ii. 115–16) may be expected to do likewise in France. But also, 'the English sweat', or sweating-sickness, was a term both for the plague and for venereal disease, brought on by 'excesse and superfluitie, especially in eating and drinking . . . and women' (Thomas Cogan, Haven of Health, 1584, p. 265). So Falstaff's prophesied fate is in character (A. A. Mendilow, 'Fal.'s Death of a Sweat', Sh. Q., ix. 479–83).

31–2. Oldcastle . . . martyr] Editors follow F, but Q can claim the support of Marston, 2 Antonio & Mellida (Mal. Soc., l. 1952)—'Let him die slaue'—and Field, Amends for Ladies, II. iv. 47–8 (Peery, p. 191)—'I haue euer liu'd Gentlewoman' (J. C. Maxwell, '2H4, Epilogue [32]', in NQ, vol. 195, p. 314).

castle died martyr, and this is not the man. My
tongue is weary; when my legs are too, I will bid you
good night.

## FINIS.

32. martyr] *Q; a Martyr F.*    34. good night. / Finis.] *Q; good night; and so
kneele downe before you: But (indeed) to pray for the Queene. F.*

# Appendix I

## SOURCE MATERIAL

1. *Raphael Holinshed: 'The Chronicles of England, Scotlande, and Irelande'* (2nd edition, 1587). The references are to the 6-volume reprint of 1807–8.

### KING HENRY'S UNQUIET REIGN

Anno Reg. 3.
Owen Glendouer.
The danger of the king to haue beene destroied.

[1401] About the same time, Owen Glendouer and his Welshmen did much hurt to the kings subiects. One night as the king was going to bed, he was in danger to haue beene destroied; for some naughtie traitorous persons had conueied into his bed a certeine iron made with smiths craft, like a caltrop, with three long prickes, sharpe and small, standing vpright, in such sort, that when he had laid him downe, & that the weight of his bodie should come vpon the bed, he should haue beene thrust in with those pricks, and peradventure slaine: but as God would, the king not thinking of any such thing, chanced yet to feele and perceiue the instrument before he laid him downe, and so escaped the danger. Howbeit he was not so soone deliuered from feare; for he might well haue his life in suspicion, & prouide for the preseruation of the same; sith perils of death crept into his secret chamber, and laie lurking in the bed of downe where his bodie was to be reposed and to take rest. Oh what a suspected state therefore is that of a king holding his regiment with the hatred of his people, the hartgrudgings of his courtiers, and the peremptorie practises of both togither? Could he confidentlie compose or setle himselfe to sleepe for feare of strangling? Durst he boldly eat and drinke without dread of poisoning? Might he aduenture to shew himselfe in great meetings or solemne assemblies without mistrust or mischeefe against his person intended? What pleasure or what felicitie could he take in his princelie pompe, which he knew by manifest and fearefull experience, to be enuied and maligned to the verie death? The state of such a king is noted by the poet in Dionysius, as in a mirror, concerning whome it is said,

> Districtus ensis cui super impia    Hor. lib.ca.3
> Ceruice pendet, non Siculæ dapes    Ode 1.
> Dulcem elaborabunt saporem,
> Non auium cytharæque cantus.[1]    (iii. 18–19)

### ATTACKS BY THE WELSH AND THE FRENCH

**The Welshmen molest the English subiects.**

[1403] The king returning foorth of Yorkeshire, determined to go into Northwales, to chastise the presumptuous dooings of the vnrulie Welshmen, who (after his comming from Shrewesburie, and the marches there) had doone much harme to the English subiects. (iii. 27)

**The Frenchmens demand of the Ile of Wight.**

[1404] The Frenchmen about the same time came before the Ile of Wight with a great nauie, and sent certeine of their men to the shore, to demand in name of king Richard, and of his wife queene Isabell, a tribute or speciall subsidie in monie, of the inhabitants of that Ile. (iii. 28)

**Owen Glendouer wasted the English marches.**

All this summer, Owen Glendouer and his adherents, robbed, burned, and destroied the countries adioining neere to the places where he hanted, and one while by sleight & guilefull policie, an other while by open force, he tooke and slue manie Englishmen, brake downe certeine castels which he wan, and some he fortified and kept for his owne defense. (iii. 29)

The fifteenth of March at a place in Wales called Huske, in a conflict fought betwixt the Welshmen and certeine of the princes companie, the sonne of Owen Glendouer was taken, and fifteene hundred Welshmen taken and slaine. Also in Maie about the feast of S. Dunstane, was the Chancellor of the said Owen taken prisoner, and a great number of other taken and slaine. (iii. 33–4)

---

1. Creizenach, *The Engl. Drama in the Age of Sh.*, 1916, p. 172, suggests this passage as a source of the King's apostrophe to sleep, III. i. 5 ff. Except for the first two sentences, it does not appear in the 1577 edition of Holinshed.

After relating several other warlike operations by the French, Holinshed continues:

[1405] The king of England in deed hearing of the preparation made for warre by the Frenchmen, leuied foure thousand men which he sent vnto Calis, and to the sea, of the which 3000 were vnder the conduct of the kings sonne. The lord Thomas of Lancaster, and the earle of Kent, the two and twentith daie of Maie (as some write) came vpon the coast of Flanders, and entring the hauen of Sluis, burnt foure great ships which they found there lieng at anchor.
(iii. 35)

*An armie sent to Calis and to the sea.*

*Chr. Fland. Ia. Meir.*

Whilest such dooings were in hand betwixt the English and French, as the besieging of Marke castell by the earle of saint Paule, and the sending foorth of the English fleet, vnder the gouernance of the lord Thomas of Lancaster, and the earle of Kent, the king was minded to haue gone into Wales against the Welsh rebels, that vnder their cheefteine Owen Glendouer, ceassed not to doo much mischeefe still against the English subiects. (iii. 36)

### THE NORTHERN REBELLION

*A new cōspiracie against king Henrie by the earle of Northumberland & others.*

[1405] But at the same time, to his further disquieting, there was a conspiracie put in practise against him at home by the earle of Northumberland, who had conspired with Richard Scroope archbishop of Yorke Thomas Mowbraie earle marshall sonne to Thomas duke of Norfolke, who for the quarrell betwixt him and king Henrie had beene banished (as ye haue heard) the lords Hastings, Fauconbridge, Berdolfe, and diuerse others. It was appointed that they should meet altogither with their whole power, vpon Yorkeswold, at a daie assigned, and that the earle of Northumberland should be cheefteine, promising to bring with him a great number of Scots. The archbishop accompanied with the earle marshall, deuised certeine articles of such matters, as it was supposed that not onelie the commonaltie of the Realme, but also the nobilitie found themselues greeued with: which articles they shewed first vnto such of their adherents as were neere about them & after sent them abroad to their freends further off, assuring them that for redresse of such oppressions, they would shed the last drop of blood in their bodies, if need were.

The archbishop of Yorke one of the cheefe conspirators.

The archbishop not meaning to staie after he saw himselfe accompanied with a great number of men, that came flocking to Yorke to take his part in this quarrell, foorthwith discouered his enterprise, causing the articles aforsaid to be set vp in the publike streets of the citie of Yorke, and vpon the gates of the monasteries, that ech man might vnderstand the cause that mooued him to rise in armes against the king, the reforming whereof did not yet apperteine vnto him. Herevpon knights, esquiers, gentlemen, yeomen, and other of the commons, as well of the citie, townes and countries about, being allured either for desire of change, or else for desire to see a reformation in such things as were mentioned in the articles, assembled togither in great numbers; and

The archbishop in armor.

the archbishop comming foorth amongst them clad in armor, incouraged, exhorted, and (by all meanes he could) pricked them foorth to take the enterprise in hand, and manfullie to continue in their begun purpose, promising forgiuenesse of sinnes to all them, whose hap it was to die in the quarrell: and thus not onelie all the citizens of Yorke, but all other in the countries about, that were able to beare weapon, came to the archbishop, and the earle marshall. In deed the respect that men had to the archbishop, caused them to like the better of the cause, since the

The estimation which men had of the arch-bishop of Yorke.

grauitie of his age, his integritie of life, and incomparable learning, with the reuerend aspect of his amiable personage, mooued all men to haue him in no small estimation.

The king aduertised of these matters, meaning to preuent them, left his iournie into Wales, and marched with all speed towards the north parts.

The earle of Westmerland and the lord Iohn of Lancaster the kings sonne prepare themselues to resist the kings enimies.

Also Rafe Neuill earle of Westmerland, that was not farre off, togither with the lord Iohn of Lancaster the kings sonne, being informed of this rebellious attempt, assembled togither such power as they might make, and togither with those which were appointed to attend on the said lord Iohn to defend the borders against the Scots, as the lord Henrie Fitzhugh, the

lord Rafe Eeuers, the lord Robert Umfreuill, &
others, made forward against the rebels, and comming into a plaine within the forrest of Galtree,
caused their standards to be pitched downe in like
sort as the archbishop had pitched his, ouer against

The forest of
Galtree.

them, being farre stronger in number of people than
the other, for (as some write) there were of the rebels
at the least twentie thousand men.

The subtill
policie of the
earle of
Westmerland.

When the earle of Westmerland perceiued the
force of the aduersaries, and that they laie still and
attempted not to come forward vpon him, he sub-
tillie deuised how to quaile their purpose, and
foorthwith dispatched messengers vnto the archbishop to vnderstand the cause as it were of that
great assemblie, and for what cause (contrarie to the
kings peace) they came so in a[r]mour. The arch-

The archbishops
protestation
why he had on
him armes.

bishop answered, that he tooke nothing in hand
against the kings peace, but that whatsoeuer he did,
tended rather to aduance the peace and quiet of the
commonwealth, than otherwise; and where he and
his companie were in armes, it was for feare of the
king, to whom he could haue no free accesse, by
reason of such a multitude of flatterers as were about
him; and therefore he mainteined that his purpose
to be good & profitable, as well for the king himselfe, as for the realme, if men were willing to vnderstand a truth: & herewith he shewed foorth a scroll,
in which the articles were written wherof before ye
haue heard.

The messengers returning to the earle of Westmerland, shewed him what they had heard &
brought from the archbishop. When he had read the
articles, he shewed in word and countenance out-
wardly that he liked of the archbishops holie and
vertuous intent and purpose, promising that he and
his would prosecute the same in assisting the archbishop, who reioising hereat, gaue credit to the earle,
and persuaded the earle marshall (against his will as
it were) to go with him to a place appointed for them
to commune togither. Here when they were met
with like number on either part, the articles were
read ouer, and without anie more adoo, the earle of
Westmerland and those that were with him agreed

to doo their best, to see that a reformation might be had, according to the same.

The earle of Westmerland vsing more policie than the rest: Well (said he) then our trauell is come to the wished end: and where our people haue beene long in armour, let them depart home to their woonted trades and occupations: in the meane time let vs drinke togither in signe of agreement, that the people on both sides maie see it, and know that it is true, that we be light at a point. They had no sooner shaken hands togither, but that a knight was sent streight waies from the archbishop, to bring word to the people that there was peace concluded, commanding ech man to laie aside his armes, and to resort home to their houses. The people beholding such tokens of peace, as shaking of hands, and drinking togither of the lords in louing manner, they being alreadie wearied with the vnaccustomed trauell of warre, brake vp their field and returned homewards: but in the meane time, whilest the people of the archbishops side withdrew awaie, the number of the contrarie part increased, according to order giuen by the earle of Westmerland; and yet the archbishop perceiued not that he was deceiued, vntill the earle of Westmerland arrested both him and the earle marshall, with diuerse other. Thus saith Walsingham.

But others write somewhat otherwise of this matter, affirming that the earle of Westmerland in deed, and the lord Rafe Eeuers, procured the archbishop & the earle marshall, to come to a communication with them, vpon a ground iust in the midwaie betwixt both the armies, where the earle of Westmerland in talke declared to them how perilous an enterprise they had taken in hand, so to raise the people, and to mooue warre against the king, aduising them therefore to submit themselues without further delaie vnto the kings mercie, and his sonne the lord Iohn, who was present there in the field with banners spred, redie to trie the matter by dint of sword, if they refused this counsell: and therefore he willed them to remember themselues well; & if they would not yeeld and craue the kings pardon, he bad them doo their best to defend themselues.

Herevpon as well the archbishop as the earle marshall submitted themselues vnto the king, and to his sonne the lord Iohn that was there present, and returned not to their armie. Wherevpon their troops scaled and fled their waies: but being pursued, manie were taken, manie slaine, and manie spoiled of that that they had about them, & so permitted to go their waies. Howsoeuer the matter was handled, true it is that the archbishop, and the earle marshall were brought to Pomfret to the king, who in this meane while was aduanced thither with his power, and from thence he went to Yorke, whither the pri-soners were also brought, and there beheaded the morrow after Whitsundaie [8 June 1405] in a place without the citie, that is to vnderstand, the arch-bishop himselfe, the earle marshall, sir Iohn Lamp-leie, and sir Robert Plumpton. Vnto all which per-sons though indemnitie were promised, yet was the same to none of them at anie hand performed. . . .

The archbishop of Yorke, the earle marshall, & others put to death. Abr. Fl. out of Thom. Walsin. Hypod. pag. 168

After the king, accordinglie as seemed to him good, had ransomed and punished by greeuous fines the citizens of Yorke (which had borne armour on their archbishops side against him) he departed frō Yorke with an armie of thirtie and seuen thousand fighting men, furnished with all prouision neces-sarie, marching northwards against the earle of Northumberland. At his cōming to Durham, the lord Hastings, the lord Fauconbridge, sir Iohn Colleuill of the Dale, and sir Iohn Griffith, being conuicted of the conspiracie, were there beheaded. The earle of Northumberland, hearing that his counsell was bewraied, and his confederats brought to confusion, through too much hast of the arch-bishop of Yorke, with three hundred horsse got him to Berwike. The king comming forward quickelie, wan the castell of Warkewoorth. Wherevpon the earle of Northumberland, not thinking himselfe in suertie at Berwike, fled with the lord Berdolfe into Scotland.   (iii. 36–8)

The lords executed.

The earle of Northumberland.

## THE RISING OF NORTHUMBERLAND
## AND LORD BARDOLPH

[1408]  The earle of Northumberland, and the lord
Bardolfe, after they had beene in Wales, in France
and Flanders, to purchase aid against king Henrie,
were returned backe into Scotland, and had remained there now for the space of a whole yeare: and
as their euill fortune would, whilest the king held a
councell of the nobilitie at London, the said earle of
Northumberland and lord Bardolfe, in a dismall
houre, with a great power of Scots returned into
England, recouering diuerse of the earles castels and
seigniories, for the people in great numbers resorted
vnto them. Heereupon incouraged with hope of
good successe, they entred into Yorkeshire, & there
began to destroie the countrie. At their cõming to
Threske, they published a proclamation, signifieing
that they were come in comfort of the English nation,
as to releeue the common-wealth, willing all such as
loued the libertie of their countrie, to repaire vnto
them, with their armor on their backes, and in
defensible wise to assist them.

The king aduertised hereof, caused a great armie
to be assembled, and came forward with the same
towards his enimies: but yer the king came to Not-
ingham, sir Thomas, or (as other copies haue) Rafe
Rokesbie shiriffe of Yorkeshire, assembled the
forces of the countrie to resist the earle and his power,
comming to Grimbaut brigs, beside Knaresbourgh,
there to stop them the passage; but they returning
aside, got to Weatherbie, and so to Tadcaster, and
finallie came forward vnto Bramham more, neere to
Haizelwood, where they chose their ground meet
to fight vpon. The shiriffe was as readie to giue battell as the earle to receiue it, and so with a standard
of S. George spred, set fiercelie vpon the earle, who
vnder a standard of his owne armes incountred his
aduersaries with great manhood. There was a sore
incounter and cruell conflict betwixt the parties but
in the end the victorie fell to the shiriffe. The lord
Bardolfe was taken, but sore wounded, so that he
shortlie after died of the hurts. As for the earle of

The earle of
Northumberland
slaine.

Northumberland, he was slaine outright: so that
now the prophesie was fulfilled, which gaue an ink-
ling of this his heauie hap long before; namelie,

Abr. Fl. out of
Tho. Walsin.
Hypod. pag. 172

   Stirps Persitina periet confusa ruina.
For this earle was the stocke and maine root of all
that were left aliue called by the name of Persie; and
of manie more by diuerse slaughters dispatched. For
whose misfortune the people were not a little sorrie,
making report of the gentlemans valiantnesse, re-
nowme, and honour. . . This battell was fought the
nineteenth day of Februarie.   (iii. 44–5)

### THE DEATH OF GLENDOWER

Owen Glendouer
endeth his life
in great miserie.

[1409]  The Welsh rebell Owen Glendouer made an
end of his wretched life in this tenth yeare of king
Henrie his reigne, being driuen now in his latter time
(as we find recorded) to such miserie, that in manner
despairing of all comfort, he fled into desert places
and solitarie caues, where being destitute of all
releefe and succour, dreading to shew his face to anie
creature, and finallie lacking meat to susteine
nature, for meere hunger and lacke of food, miser-
ablie pined awaie and died.   (iii. 48)

### THE KING AND PRINCE RECONCILED

[1412]  Whilest these things were a dooing in
France, the lord Henrie prince of Wales, eldest

The prince of
Wales accused
to his father.

sonne to king Henrie, got knowledge that certeine of
his fathers seruants were busie to giue informations
against him, whereby discord might arise betwixt
him and his father: for they put into the kings head,

Iohn Stow.

not onelie what euill rule (according to the course of
youth) the prince kept to the offense of manie: but
also what great resort of people came to his house, so
that the court was nothing furnished with such a

The suspicious
gelousie of the
king toward his
son.

traine as dailie followed the prince. These tales
brought no small suspicion into the kings head,
least his sonne would presume to vsurpe the crowne,
he being yet aliue, through which suspicious
gelousie, it was perceiued that he fauoured not his
sonne, as in times past he had doone.

  The Prince sore offended with such persons, as by
slanderous reports, sought not onelie to spot his good

name abrode in the realme, but to sowe discord also betwixt him and his father, wrote his letters into euerie part of the realme, to reprooue all such slanderous deuises of those that sought his discredit. And to cleare himselfe the better, that the world might vnderstand what wrong he had to be slandered in such wise: about the feast of Peter and Paule, to wit, the nine and twentith daie of Iune, he came to the court with such a number of noble men and other his freends that wished him well, as the like traine had beene sildome seene repairing to the court at any one time in those daies. He was apparelled in a gowne of blew satten, full of small oilet holes, at euerie hole the needle hanging by a silke thred with which it was sewed. About his arme he ware a hounds collar set full of SS of gold, and the tirets likewise being of the same metall.

*The prince goeth to the court with a great traine. His strange apparell.*

The court was then at Westminster, where he being entred into the hall, not one of his companie durst once aduance himselfe further than the fire in the same hall, notwithstanding they were earnestlie requested by the lords to come higher; but they regarding what they had in commandement of the prince would not presume to doo in any thing contrarie therevnto. He himselfe onelie accompanied with those of the kings house, was streight admitted to the presence of the king his father, who being at that time greeuouslie diseased, yet caused himselfe in his chaire to be borne into his priuie chamber, where in the presence of three or foure persons, in whome he had most confidence, he commanded the prince to shew what he had to saie concerning the cause of his comming.

*The prince cōmeth to the kings presēce.*

The prince kneeling downe before his father said: Most redoubted and souereigne lord and father, I am at this time come to your presence as your liege man, and as your naturall sonne, in all things to be at your commandement. And where I vnderstand you haue in suspicion my demeanour against your grace, you know verie well, that if I knew any man within this realme, of whome you should stand in feare, my duetie were to punish that person, thereby to remooue that greefe from your heart. Then how

*His words to his father.*

much more ought I to suffer death, to ease your grace of that greefe which you haue of me, being your naturall sonne and liege man: and to that end I haue this daie made my selfe readie by confession and receiuing of the sacrament. And therefore I beseech you most redoubted lord and deare father, for the honour of God, to ease your heart of all such suspicion as you haue of me, and to dispatch me heere before your knees, with this same dagger (and withall he deliuered vnto the king his dagger, in all humble reuerence; adding further, that his life was not so deare to him, that he wished to liue one daie with his displeasure) and therefore in thus ridding me out of life, and your selfe from all suspicion, here in presence of these lords, and before God at the daie of the generall iudgement, I faithfullie protest clearlie to forgiue you.

The kings words to the prince his son.

The king mooued herewith, cast from him the dagger, and imbracing the prince kissed him, and with shedding teares confessed, that in deed he had him partlie in suspicion, though now (as he perceiued) not with iust cause, and therefore from thenceforth no misreport should cause him to haue him in mistrust, and this he promised of his honour. . . .

Abr. Fl. out of Angl. præliis.

Thus were the father and the sonne reconciled, betwixt whom the said pickthanks had sowne diuision, insomuch that the sonne vpon a vehement conceit of vnkindnesse sproong in the father, was in the waie to be worne out of fauour. Which was the more likelie to come to passe, by their informations that priuilie charged him with riot and other vnciuill demeanor vnseemelie for a prince. Indeed he was youthfullie giuen, growne to audacitie, and had chosen him companions agreeable to his age; with whome he spent the time in such recreations, exercises, and delights as he fansied. But yet (it should seeme by the report of some writers) that his behauiour was not offensiue or at least tending to the damage of anie bodie; sith he had a care to auoid dooing of wrong, and to tedder his affections within the tract of vertue, whereby he opened vnto himselfe a redie passage of good liking among the pru-

200                    THE SECOND PART OF

his disposition, which was in no degree so excessiue,
as that he deserued in such vehement maner to be
suspected. In whose dispraise I find little, but to his
praise verie much.    (iii. 53–5)

*Abr. Fl. out of Fabian pag. 388*

### THREE FLOOD TIDES IN THE THAMES

[1412]  In this yeare, and vpon the twelfth day of
October, were three flouds in the Thames, the one
following vpon the other, & no ebbing betweene:
which thing no man then liuing could remember the
like to be seene.    (iii. 55)

*Three floods without ebbing between.*

### A CRUSADE PREPARED

[1412]  In this fourteenth and last yeare of king
Henries reigne, a councell was holden in the white
friers in London, at the which, among other things,
order was taken for ships and gallies to be builded
and made readie, and all other things necessarie to
be prouided for a voiage which he meant to make
into the holie land, there to recouer the citie of Ierusalem from the Infidels. For it greeued him to consider the great malice of christian princes, that were
bent vpon a mischeefous purpose to destroie one
another, to the perill of their owne soules, rather
than to make war against the enimies of the christian
faith, as in conscience (it seemed to him) they were
bound. He held his Christmas this yeare at Eltham,
being sore vexed with sicknesse, so that it was
thought sometime, that he had beene dead: notwithstanding it pleased God that he somwhat recouered his strength againe, and so passed that
Christmasse with as much ioy as he might. (iii. 57)

*Fabian. The K. meant to haue made a iournie against the Infidels.*

*The king is vexed with sicknesse.*

### THE KING'S LAST ILLNESS

[1413]  The morrow after Candlemas daie began a
parlement, which he had called at London, but he
departed this life before the same parlement was
ended: for now that his prouisions were readie . . .
for such a roiall iournie as he pretended to take into
the holie land, he was eftsoones taken with a sore
sicknesse, which was not a leprosie, striken by the
hand of God (saith maister Hall) as foolish friers

*A parlement.*

*The K. sick of an apoplexie. Hall.*

imagined; but a verie apoplexie, of the which he languished till his appointed houre, and had none other greefe nor maladie; . . . During this his last sicknesse, he caused his crowne (as some write) to be set on a pillow at his beds head, and suddenlie his pangs so sore troubled him that he laie as though all his vitall spirits had beene from him departed. Such as were about him, thinking verelie that he had beene departed, couered his face with a linnen cloth.

The prince his sonne being hereof aduertised, entered into the chamber, tooke awaie the crowne, and departed. The father being suddenlie reuiued out of that trance, quicklie perceiued the lacke of his crowne; and hauing knowledge that the prince his sonne had taken it awaie, caused him to come before his presence, requiring of him what he meant so to misuse himselfe. The prince with a good audacitie answered; Sir, to mine and all mens iudgements you seemed dead in this world, wherefore I as your next heire apparent tooke that as mine owne, and not as yours. Well faire sonne (said the king with a great sigh) what right I had to it, God knoweth. Well (said the prince) if you die king, I will haue the garland, and trust to keepe it with the sword against all mine enimies, as you haue doone. Then said the king, I commit all to God, and remember you to doo well. With that he turned himselfe in his bed, and shortlie after departed to God in a chamber of the abbats of Westminster called Ierusalem, the twentith daie of March, in the yeare 1413, in the yeare of his age 46, when he had reigned thirteene yeares, fiue moneths and od daies, in great perplexitie and little pleasure. . .

We find, that he was taken with his last sicknesse, while he was making his praiers at saint Edwards shrine, there as it were to take his leaue, and so to proceed foorth on his iournie: he was so suddenlie and greeuouslie taken, that such as were about him, feared least he would haue died presentlie, wherfore to releeue him (if it were possible) they bare him into a chamber that was next at hand, belonging to the abbat of Westminster, where they laid him on a pallet before the fire, and vsed all remedies to re-

*Marginal notes:*

Hall.

The prince taketh awaie the crowne before his father was dead.

He is blamed of the king.

His answer.

A guiltie conscience in extremitie of sicknesse pincheth sore.

The death of Henrie the fourth.

Fabian.

uiue him. At length, he recouered his speech, and vnderstanding and perceiuing himselfe in a strange place which he knew not, he willed to know if the chamber had anie particular name, wherevnto answer was made, that it was called Ierusalem. Then said the king; 'Lauds be giuen to the father of heauen, for now I know that I shall die heere in this chamber, according to the prophesie of me declared, that I should depart this life in Ierusalem'.

(iii. 57–8)

### KING HENRY DESCRIBED

His stature.

This king was of a meane stature, well proportioned, and formallie compact, quicke and liuelie, and of a stout courage. In his latter daies he shewed himselfe so gentle, that he gat more loue amongst the nobles and people of this realme, than he had purchased malice and euill will in the beginning.

But yet to speake a truth, by his proceedings, after he had atteined to the crowne, what with such taxes, tallages, subsidies, and exactions as he was constreined to charge the people with; and what by punishing such as mooued with disdeine to see him vsurpe the crowne (contrarie to the oth taken at his entring into this land, vpon his returne from exile) did at sundrie times rebell against him, he wan himselfe more hatred, than in all his life time (if it had beene longer by manie yeares than it was) had beene possible for him to haue weeded out & remooued. And yet doubtlesse, woorthie were his subiects to tast of that bitter cup, sithens they were so readie to ioine and clappe hands with him, for the deposing of their rightfull and naturall prince king Richard, whose cheefe fault rested onlie in that, that he was too bountifull to his freends, and too mercifull to his foes; speciallie if he had not beene drawne by others, to seeke reuenge of those that abused his good and courteous nature.   (iii. 58)

### KING HENRY THE FIFTH

Anno Reg. I.

Henrie prince of Wales, son and heire to K. Henrie the fourth, borne in Wales at Monmouth on the riuer of Wie, after his father was departed tooke vpon him the regiment of this realme of England, the twentith of March, the morrow after proclamed king, by the name of Henrie the fift, in the yeare ... 1413 ...

Such great hope, and good expectation was had of this mans fortunate successe to follow, that within three daies after his fathers deceasse, diuerse noble men and honorable personages did to him homage, and sware to him due obedience, which had not beene seene doone to any of his predecessors kings of this realme, till they had beene possessed of the crowne. He was crowned the ninth of Aprill being Passion sundaie, which was a sore, ruggie, and tempestuous day, with wind, snow and sleet, that men greatlie maruelled thereat, making diuerse interpretations what the same might signifie. But this king euen at first appointing with himselfe, to shew that in his person princelie honors should change publike manners, he determined to put on him the shape of a new man. For whereas aforetime he had made himselfe a companion vnto misrulie mates of dissolute order and life, he now banished them all from his presence (but not vnrewarded, or else vnpreferred) inhibiting them vpon a great paine, not once to approch, lodge, or soiourne within ten miles of his court or presence: and in their places he chose men of grauitie, wit, and high policie, by whose wise counsell he might at all times rule to his honour and dignitie;[1] calling to mind how once to hie offense of the king his father, he had with his fist striken the cheefe iustice for sending one of his minions (vpon desert) to prison, when the iustice stoutlie commanded himselfe also streict to ward, & he (then prince) obeied. The king after expelled him out of his priuie councell, banisht him the court, and made the duke of Clarence ... president of councell in his steed. ... Beside this, he elected the best learned men in the lawes of the realme, to the offices of iustice;

*Homage doone to K. Henrie before his coronation.*

*The day of king Henries coronation a verie tempestuous day.*

*A notable example of a woorthie prince.*

---

1. The 1577 edn adds the following, which the revised version of 1587 omits: 'wheras if he should haue reteined the other lustie companions aboute him, he doubted least they might haue allured him vnto suche lewde and lighte partes, as with them before tyme he had youthfully vsed, not alwayes to his owne commendation, nor yet to the cōtentation of his father.'

A parlement.

and men of good liuing, he preferred to high degrees and authoritie. Immediatlie after Easter he called a parlement.  (iii. 60–2)

## A WHALE ON GROUND

A monstrous fish (but not so monstrous as some reported) for his eies being great, were in his head and not in his backe.

[1574] The ninth of Iulie at six of the clocke at night, in the Ile of Thanet besides Ramesgate, in the parish of saint Peter vnder the cliffe, a monstrous fish or whale of the sea did shoot himselfe on shore, where for want of water, beating himselfe on the sands, he died about six of the clocke on the next morning, before which time he roared, and was heard more than a mile on the land.  (iv. 325)

2. *Samuel Daniel:* '*The First Fowre Bookes of the Ciuile Wars Between the Two Houses of Lancaster and Yorke*' (*1595*)

### Book I

#### THE COMMON PEOPLE LAMENT BOLINGBROKE'S EXILING

70     Ah must we leaue him here: that here were fit
       We should retain the pillar of our state;
       Whose vertues well deserue to gouerne it,
       And not this wanton young effeminate?
       Why should not he in regal honour sit,
       That best knowes how a realm to ordinate?
       Yet one daie ô we hope thou shalt bring backe
       Deare *Bullingbrooke* the iustice that we lacke.

71       Thus muttred lo the malecontented sort
       That loue kings best before they haue them still,
       And neuer can the present state comport,
       But would as oft change as they change their will:
       For this good Duke had wonne them in this sort
       By suckring them and pittying of their ill,
       That they supposed straight it was one thing,
       To be both a good man, and a good king.

85       And all this[1] makes for thee, ô *Bullingbrooke*,
       To worke a waie vnto thy soueraintie;

1. i.e. Richard's absence on the Irish campaign, and his misgovernment, luxury, and exactions at home.

This care the heauens, fate and fortune tooke
To bring thee to thy scepter easily:
Vpon the[e] fals that hap which him forsooke
Who crownd a King, a King yet must not die,
Thou wert ordained by prouidence to raise
A quarrell lasting longer then thy daies.

### BOLINGBROKE'S MOTIVES DISCUSSED

92      This this pretence saith shee,[1] th'ambitious finde
To smooth iniustice, and to flatter wrong:
Thou dost not know what then will be thy mind
When thou shalt see thy selfe aduanc'd and strong:
When thou hast shak'd off that which others binde
Thou soone forgettest what thou learnedst long:
Men doe not know what they themselues will be
When as more then themselues, themselues they see.

93      And herewithall turning about he wakes,
Lab'ring in sprite, troubled with this strange sight:
And musd a while, waking aduisement takes
Of what had past in sleepe and silent night.
Yet hereof no important reck'ning makes
But as a dreame that vanisht with the light:
The day designes, and what he had in hand
Left it to his diuerted thoughts vnskand.

94      Doubtfull at first, he warie doth proceed
Seemes not t'affect, that which he did effect,
Or els perhaps seemes as he ment indeed,
Sought but his owne, and did no more expect:
Then fortune thou art guilty of his deed,
That didst his state aboue his hopes erect,
And thou must beare some blame of his great sin
That left'st him worse then when he did begin.

95      Thou didst conspire with pride, and with the time
To make so easie an assent to wrong,
That he that had no thought so hie to clime,
(With fauoring comfort still allur'd along)
Was with occasion thrust into the crime,
Seeing others weakenes and his part so strong:

1. A vision of Britain which appears to Bolingbroke as he purposes to invade England.

And ô in such a case who is it will
Do good, and feare that maie liue free with ill.


96        We will not say nor thinke O *Lancaster*,
But that thou then didst meane as thou didst swere
Vpon th'Euangelists at *Doncaster*,
In th'eie of heauen, and that assembly there
That thou but as an vpright orderer
Sought'st to reforme th'abused kingdome here,
And get thy right, and what was thine before,
And this was all, thou would'st attempt no more.


97        Though we might say & thinke that this pretence
Was but a shadow to th'intended act,
Because th'euent doth argue the offence
And plainely seemes to manifest the fact:
For that hereby thou mightst win confidence
With those whom els thy course might hap distract,
And all suspition of thy drift remoue,
Since easily men credit whom they loue.


98        But God forbid we should so nerely pry
Into the low deepe buried sinnes long past
T'examine and conferre iniquity,
Whereof faith would no memory should last:
That our times might not haue t'exemplifie
With aged staines, but with our owne shame cast,
Might thinke our blot the first not done before,
That new-made sins might make vs blush the more.


99        And let vnwresting charity beleeue
That then thy oth with thy intent agreed,
And others saith, thy faith did first deceiue,
Thy after fortune forc'd thee to this deed:
And let no man this idle censure giue
Because th'euent proues so, twas so decreed:
For ô what counsels sort to other end
Then that which frailty did at first intend?


100       Whilst those that are but outward lookers on,
That cannot sound these misteries of state,
Deemes things were so contriu'd as they are done,
Holding that policie, that was but fate:

Wondring how strange twas wrought, how close begun,
And thinke all actions else did tend to that
When ô how short they come, or cast too fare
Making the happy wiser then they are.

### PORTENTS DURING BOLINGBROKE'S INVASION

114     Thus[1] they in zeale whose humbled thoughts were good:
Whil'st in this wide spread volume of the skies,
The booke of prouidence disclosed stood,
Warnings of wrath, foregoing miseries;
In lines of fire and caracters of blood,
There fearefull formes in dreadfull flames arise,
Amazing Comets, threatning Monarches might
And new-seene starres, vnknowne vnto the night.

115     Red fiery dragons in the aire doe flie,
And burning Meteors, poynted-streaming lights,
Bright starres in midst of day appeare in skie,
Prodigious monsters, gastly fearefull sights:
Straunge Ghosts, and apparitions terrifie,
The wofull mother her owne birth affrights,
Seeing a wrong deformed infant borne
Grieues in her paines, deceiu'd in shame doth morn.

116     The Earth as if afeard of bloud and woundes
Trembles in terror of these falling bloes:
The hollow concaues giue out groning sounds
And sighing, murmurs to lament our woes:
The Ocean all at discord with his boundes,
Reiterates his strange vntimely floes:
Nature all out of course to checke our course,
Neglects her worke to worke in vs remorse.

## Book II

### BOLINGBROKE STARTS A TRAIN OF EVENTS BEYOND HIS CONTROL

9     So often things which seeme at first in shew
Without the compasse of accomplishment,
Once ventred on to that successe do grow,
That euen the Authors do admire th'euent:

---

1. I.e. offering up prayers for peace.

So manie meanes which they did neuer know
Doe second their designes, and doe present
Straunge vnexpected helpes, and chiefly then
When th'Actors are reputed worthy men.

RICHARD IN WALES LAMENTS THE
CHANGEABLENESS OF HIS PEOPLE

13      Which seeing this[1]: thus to himselfe complaines:
O why do you fond false deceiued so
Run headlong to that change that nothing gaines
But gaine of sorrow, onlie change of wo?
Which is all one if he be like that raignes:
Why will you buy with bloud what you forgoe?
Tis nought but shewes that ignorance esteemes,
The thing possest is not the thing it seemes.

14      And when the sinnes of *Bullingbrooke* shall be
As great as mine, and you vnanswered
In these your hopes; then may you wish for me
Your lawfull Sou'raigne from whose faith you fled,
And grieued in your soules the error see
That shining promises had shadowed:
As th'humorous sicke remouing finde no ease,
When changed Chambers change not the disease.

15      Then shall you finde this name of liberty
(The watchword of rebellion euer vsd
The idle eccho of vncertainty,
That euermore the simple hath abusd)
But new-turnd seruitude and miserie,
And euen the same and worse before refusd,
Th'aspirer once attaind vnto the top
Cuts off those meanes by which himselfe got vp.

16      And with a harder hand and streighter raine
Doth curbe that loosenes he did finde before,
Doubting th'occasion like might serue againe,
His owne example makes him feare the more:
Then ô iniurious land what dost thou gaine
To aggrauate thine owne afflictions store?
Since thou must needs obay to gouernement,
And no rule euer yet could all content.

1. The defection of his supporters.

## Book III

HENRY'S STATE OF MIND AFTER INSTIGATING
EXTON TO THE MURDER OF RICHARD

58      So foule a thing ô thou iniustice art
        That tortrest both the doer and distrest,
        For when a man hath done a wicked part,
        O how he striues t'excuse to make the best,
        To shift the fault, t'vnburthen his charg'd hart
        And glad to finde the least surmise of rest:
        And if he could make his seeme others sin,
        O what repose, what ease he findes therein?

HENRY'S SICKNESS AND REMORSE

115     But now the king retires him to his peace,
        A peace much like a feeble sicke mans sleepe,
        (Wherein his waking paines do neuer cease
        Though seeming rest his closed eyes doth keepe)
        For ô no peace could euer so release
        His intricate turmoiles, and sorrowes deepe,
        But that his cares kept waking all his life
        Continue on till death conclude the strife.

116     Whose harald sicknes, being sent before
        With full commission to denounce his end,
        And paine, and griefe, enforcing more and more,
        Besiegd the hold that could not long defend,
        And so consum'd all that imboldning store
        Of hote gaine-striuing bloud that did contend,
        Wearing the wall so thin that now the mind
        Might well looke thorow, and his frailty find.

117     When lo, as if the vapours vanisht were,
        Which heate of boyling bloud & health did breed,
        (To cloude the sence that nothing might appeare
        Vnto the thought, that which it was indeed)
        The lightned soule began to see more cleere
        How much it was abusd, & notes with heed
        The plaine discouered falsehood open laid
        Of ill perswading flesh that so betraid.

118     And lying on his last afflicted bed
        Where death & conscience both before him stand,

Th'one holding out a booke wherein he red
In bloudie lines the deedes of his owne hand;
The other shewes a glasse, which figured
An ougly forme of fowle corrupted sand:
Both bringing horror in the hyest degree
With what he was, and what he straight should bee.

119　　Which seeing all confused trembling with feare
He lay a while, as ouerthrowne in sprite,
At last commaunds some that attending were
To fetch the crowne and set it in his sight,
On which with fixed eye and heauy cheere
Casting a looke, O God (saith he) what right
I had to thee my soule doth now conceiue;
Thee, which with bloud I gote, with horror leaue.

120　　Wert thou the cause my climing care was such
To passe those boundes, nature, and law ordaind?
Is this that good which promised so much,
And seemd so glorious ere it was attaind?
Wherein was neuer ioye but gaue a touch
To checke my soule to thinke, how thou wert gaind,
And now how do I leaue thee vnto mine,
Which it is dread to keepe, death to resigne.

121　　With this the soule rapt wholy with the thought
Of such distresse, did so attentiue weigh
Her present horror, whilst as if forgote
The dull consumed body senceles lay,
And now as breathles quite, quite dead is thought,
When lo his sonne comes in, and takes awaie
The fatall crowne from thence, and out he goes
As if vnwilling longer time to lose.

122　　And whilst that sad confused soule doth cast
Those great accounts of terror and distresse,
Vppon this counsell it doth light at last
How she might make the charge of horror lesse,
And finding no way to acquit thats past
But onely this, to vse some quicke redresse
Of acted wrong, with giuing vp againe
The crowne to whom it seem'd to appertaine.

123    Which found, lightned with some small ioy shee hyes,
       Rouses her seruants that dead sleeping lay,
       (The members of hir house,) to exercise
       One feeble dutie more, during her stay:
       And opening those darke windowes he espies
       The crowne for which he lookt was borne awaie,
       And all-agrieu'd with the vnkind offence
       He causd him bring it backe that tooke it thence.

124    To whom (excusing his presumteous deed
       By the supposing him departed quite)
       He said: ô Sonne what needes thee make such speed
       Vnto that care, where feare exceeds thy right,
       And where his sinne whom thou shalt now succeed
       Shall still vpbraid thy inheritance of might,
       And if thou canst liue, and liue great from wo
       Without this carefull trauaile; let it go.

125    Nay father since your fortune did attaine
       So hye a stand: I meane not to descend,
       Replyes the Prince; as if what you did gaine
       I were of spirit vnable to defend:
       Time will appease them well that now complaine,
       And ratefie our interest in the end;
       What wrong hath not continuance quite outworne?
       Yeares makes that right which neuer was so borne.

126    If so, God worke his pleasure (said the king)
       And ô do thou contend with all thy might
       Such euidence of vertuous deeds to bring,
       That well may proue our wrong to be our right:
       And let the goodnes of the managing
       Race out the blot of foule attayning quite:
       That discontent may all aduantage misse
       To wish it otherwise then now it is.

127    And since my death my purpose doth preuent
       Touching this sacred warre I tooke in hand,
       (An action wherewithall my soule had ment
       T'appease my God, and reconcile my land)
       To thee is left to finish my intent,
       Who to be safe must neuer idly stand;

But some great actions entertaine thou still
To hold their mindes who else will practise ill.

128        Thou hast not that aduantage by my raigne
To riot it (as they whom long descent
Hath purchasd loue by custome) but with payne
Thou must contend to buy the worlds content:
What their birth gaue them, thou hast yet to gaine
By thine owne vertues, and good gouernment,
And that vnles thy worth confirme the thing
Thou canst not be the father to a king.

129        Nor art thou born in those calme daies, where rest
Hath brought a sleepe sluggish securitie;
But in tumultuous times, where mindes adrest
To factions are inurd to mutinie,
A mischiefe not by force to be supprest
Where rigor still begets more enmitie,
Hatred must be beguild with some new course
Where states are strong, & princes doubt their force.

130        This and much more affliction would haue said
Out of th'experience of a troublous raigne,
For which his high desires had dearly paide
Th'interest of an euer-toyling paine:
But that this all-subduing powre here staid
His faultring tongue and paine r'inforc'd againe,
And cut off all the passages of breath
To bring him quite vnder the state of death.

*3. John Stow: 'The Annales of England'* (*1592*)

THE NORTHERN REBELLION

[1405] *Henry Percy* earle of Northumberland, *Richard Scroope* Archbishop of Yorke, *Thomas Mowbray* earle Marshall, *Thomas* lord *Bardolph* and other, conspiring against king *Henry*, assembled togither the Citizens of Yorke, & many other, to stand with them for the commodity of the realme. And to animate the commons to be the readier vnto this businesse, they set articles vpon the doores of the monasteries and churches of the same citie, written in English against

Conspiracy against king Henry by the archbishop of Yorke and other.

the king, because he had put downe k. *Richard*, offer,
ing themselues for those articles to liue and die-
which caused great number of people to resort to
them: but *Ralph Neuill* Earle of Westmerland that
was not far off, together with *Iohn* duke of Lancaster,
the kings sonne, being enformed of these things,
gathered an armie with speed to go against the Archbishops company, but al was in vaine, for the Archbishops power was farre greater than theirs, wherevpon the Earle of Westmerland sent messengers, to
enquire of the Archbishop the cause of so great an
assembly in armor, contrary to the Kings peace:
wherevnto the archbishop answered, that he took
nothing in hand against the kings peace, and he was
in armor, & munited with men, only for fear of the
K. whom he could not safly come vnto to speake, but
his purpose (he said) was good and commodious
both for the king and realme, if happily they would
know it: and then hee shewed a scedule, in which the
Articles were contained, which when the earle of
Westmerland had read, he with word and coun-
tenaunce praysed the bishops holy and vertuous
intent, and promised, that he and his would prosecute the same with the Archbishop.

The Archbishop being glad of this, beleeued the
Earles wordes, and perswaded the earle Marshall,
being vnwilling thereunto, to go with him to a place
appointed to talk togither, to whom they with like
number came, and the writing with the articles was
read ouer: straightway the earle and they that were
with him gaue their assent to these articles: then
sayd the earle being subtiller than the rest, behold
the labor that we haue taken in hand is come to such
end as we would haue it, and the people hath now
bin long in armor, let some of your men beare word
vnto the people to go their way home, and to lay
downe their armor, and euery man to fall to his
occupation and accustomed labor: in the meane
season, we, in token of concord will drinke togither,
that the people on both sides shall see it, and without
delay, after they had taken ech other by the hands, a
knight was sent on the archbishops behalf, to beare

word to the people that it was peace, and to command euery man to lay down their armor, & to go to their owne home.

The people beholding signes of peace, and the lords drinking togither, being wearied with the vnaccustomed trauell of war, turned the reines of their bridles homewards, and so it came to passe, that when the people of the archbishops side went away, the number of the aduersaries increased, as before it was appointed, and the archbishop did not perceiue that he was betrayed, vntill such time as the earle arrested him: hee arrested the Marshall also, and many other with him, to all which it was promised that they should haue no harme, but that promise was not kept, for both the archbishop and the earle Marshal were brought to Pontfract to the king, who in the meane while was aduanced thither with his power, and from thence he went to Yorke, whither the prisoners were also brought... [The Archbishop was taken to the place of execution] where with fiue strokes his head was smitten off on the morrow after Whitsonday: with him were condemned and executed the erle Marshal, sir *Iohn Lampley*, and sir *Robert Plimpton*. . . . At his comming to Durham the L. *Hastings*, the L. *Fawconbridge*, sir *Iohn Coluile* of the Dale, and sir *Iohn Griffith*, being conuicted of the conspiracie, were beheaded. (pp. 529–30)

## THE RISING OF NORTHUMBERLAND AND LORD BARDOLPH

[1408] Whiles the king held a great Councell at London with the nobles of the realme, *Henrie* Earle of Northumberlande, and *Thomas* Lord *Bardolfe* came againe into England, who after long iourneying, when they came to the towne of Thriske, they caused to bee proclaimed, that who so would haue libertie, should take vp armour and weapon and followe them, whereupon much people resorted to them: but sir *Thomas Rockley* Sherife of Yorkeshire, with other knights of that countrie went against them, and at Bramham Moore neere to Hasewold, fought with them a great battell, and slue the Earle, whose head was streight waies cut off. The Lord

Bardolfe was sore wounded and taken aliue, but died shortly after. (p. 535)

Owen Glē-
douerdew
died mise-
rably.

[1409] Owen Glendouerdew, though he was pardoned by the K. at the request of Dauid Holbech esquire: yet being now driuē to such misery, that in maner despairing of all comfort, he fled into desert places, and solitary caues, where being destitute of al releefe and succor, dreading to shew his face to any creature, and finally, lacking to sustaine nature, for pure hunger miserably pined away and died. (p. 539)

## THE KING'S DEATH-BED COUNSEL

[1413] In the time of whose languishing the king gaue to the prince his sonne diuers notable doctrines and insignements, that not onely of him, but of euery prince are to be holden and followed: among the which eruditions one is this: The king lieng greeuously diseased, called before him the prince his sonne, and said vnto him: My sonne, I feare me sore, after my departure from this life, some discord shall grow and arise betweene thee and thy brother Thomas duke of Clarence, whereby the realme may be brought to destruction and misery, for I know you both to be of great stomacke and courage. Wherefore I feare, that he through his high mind wil make some enterprise against thee, intending to vsurp vpon thee, which I know thy stomacke may not abide easily. And for dread hereof, as oft as it is in my remembrance, I sore repent me, that euer I charged my selfe with the crowne of this realme. To these words of the king the prince answered thus: Right redoubted lord and father, to the pleasure of God your grace shall long continue with vs, and rule vs both: but if God haue so prouided that euer I shal succeed you in this realme, I shall honor & loue my brethren aboue al men, as long as they be to me true, faithfull and obedient, as to their soueraigne lord, but if any of them fortune to conspire or rebell against me, I assure you, I shall as soone execute iustice vpon one of them, as I shall vpon the worst and most simplest person within this your realme.

The king hearing this answere, was therewith

King Henry his
counsell to his
sonne Henry.

maruellously reioyced in his mind, and said: My deere and welbeloued sonne, with this answere thou hast deliuered me of a great and ponderous agony: and I beseech thee, and vpon my blessing charge thee, that like as thou hast said, so thou minister iustice equally, and in no wise suffer not them that be oppressed long to call vpon thee for iustice, but redresse oppressions, and indifferently and without delay, for no perswasion of flatterers, or of them that be partiall, or such as do haue their hands replenished with gifts, deferre not iustice till tomorrow, if that thou mayest do iustice this day, lest (peraduenture) God do iustice on thee in the meane time, and take from thee thine authority: remember that the wealth of thy body, and thy soule, and of thy realm, resteth in the execution of iustice, and do not thy iustice so, that thou be called a tirant, but vse thy selfe meanely betwixt iustice and mercy in those things that belong to thee. And betweene parties do iustice truely and extremely, to the consolation of thy poore subiects that suffer iniuries, and to the punition of them that be extortioners and doers of oppressions, that other thereby may take example: and in thus doing, thou shalt obtaine the fauour of God, and the loue and feare of thy subiects, and therefore also thou shalt haue thy realme more in tranquillitie and rest, which shal be occasion of great prosperitie within thy realme, which Englishmen naturally doo desire: for so long as they haue wealth and riches, so long shalt thou haue obeysance: and when they be poore, then they be alwaies ready at euery motion to make insurrections, and it causeth them to rebell against their soueraigne lord: for the nature of them is such, rather to feare loosing of their goodes and worldly substance, than the ieoperding of their liues. And if thou thus keepe them in subiection mixed with loue and feare, thou shalt haue the most peaceable and fertile countrey, and the most louing, faithfull, and manly people of the world, which shall be cause of no small feare to thine aduersaries. My sonne, when it shall please God to call me to the way decreede for euery worldly creature, to thee (as my sonne and heire) I must leaue my crowne and my realme, which I aduise thee not to take vainely, and as a man elate in pride, and reioyced in worldly honour, but thinke that thou art more oppressed with charge, to purueie for euery person within the realme, than exalted in vaine honour of the world. . . Thou shalt bee exalted vnto the crowne, for the wealth and conseruation of the realme, and not for thy singular commoditie and auaile.

## THE KING'S RESPONSIBILITIES
## AS HEART OF THE BODY POLITIC

. . . My sonne, thou shalt be a minister to thy realme to keepe it in tranquillitie and defend it. Like as the hart in the middest of the body is principall and chiefe thing in the body, and serueth to couet and desire that thing that is most necessarie to euery of thy members, so (my sonne) thou shalt be amongst thy people as chiefe and principall of them to minister, imagine and acquire those things that may be most beneficiall for them. And then thy people shall be obedient to thee, to ayde and succour thee, and in all things to accomplish thy commandements, like as thy members labour, euery one of them in their office, to acquire and get that thing that the heart desireth, and as thy heart is of no force and impotent without the aide of thy members, so without thy people, thy raigne is nothing. My sonne, thou shalt feare and dread God aboue all things, and thou shalt loue, honour, and worship him with all thy heart, thou shalt attribute and ascribe to him al things wherein thou seest thy selfe to be well fortunate, be it victorie of thine enemies, loue of thy friends, obedience of thy subiects, strength and actiueness of body, honor, riches, or fruitfull generations, or any other thing what so euer it be that chanceth to thy pleasure. Thou shalt not imagine that any such thing should fortune to thee, by thine acte, nor by thy desert, but thou shalt thinke that all commeth onely of the goodnesse of the Lord. Thus thou shalt with all thine heart, prayse, honour, and thanke God for all his benefites that he giueth vnto thee. And in thy selfe eschew all vaineglorie and elation of heart, following the wholesome counsell of the Psalmist, which saieth, *Non nobis Domine, non nobis sed nomini tuo da gloriam,* which is to say, *Not vnto us Lord, not vnto us, but to thy holy name be giuen laud and praise.* These and many other admonishments and doctrines this victorious king gaue vnto this noble prince his sonne, who with effect followed the same, after the death of his father: whereby hee obtained grace of our Lorde to attaine to great victories and many glorious and incredible conquests, through the helpe and succour of our Lorde, whereof he was neuer destitute. The king his father drawing to his end, after due thankes giuen, and supplications made to God, gaue his benediction to the prince his son, and so yeelded to God his spirit, the xx. of March, *Anno* 1412 [i.e. 1413, New Style]. (pp. 545–6)

### THE COMMITTAL OF PRINCE HENRY

Sir Thomas Eliot writeth thus. The renowmed prince king Henry the fift, during the life of his father, was noted to be fierce, & of wanton courage. It hapned that one of his seruants, whom he fauored, was for felony by him committed, arraigned at the kings bench, whereof the prince being aduertised, and incensed by light persons about him, in furious rage came hastily to the bar, where his seruant stood as prisoner, and commanded him to be vngiued and set at libertie, whereat all men were abashed, reserued the chiefe Iustice, who humbly exhorted the prince to be ordered according to the ancient laws of the realme, or if he would have him saued from the rigor of the lawes, that he should obtaine if he might of the king his father, his gracious pardon, whereby no law or iustice should be derogate. With the which answere the prince nothing appeased, but rather more inflamed, indeuoured himselfe to take away his seruant. The Judge, considering the perillous example and inconueniencie that might thereby ensue, with a valiant spirit & courage commanded the prince vpon his allegiance to leaue the prisoner, and to depart his way: with which commandement the prince being set all in a fury, all chafed, and in a terrible maner came up to the place of iudgement, men thinking that he would haue slaine the Judge, or haue done to him some domage, but the Judge sitting still, without moouing, declaring the maiestie of the kings place of iudgement, and with an assured bold countenance, had to the prynce these words following: Sir, remember your selfe, I keep here the place of your soueraigne lord and father, to whom you owe double obeisance, wherefore eftsoones in his name I charge you desist off your wilfulnes and vnlawfull enterprise, & from hencefoorth giue good example to those which hereafter shall be your proper subiects: and now for your contempt and disobedience, go you to the prison of the kings bench, wherevnto I commit you, and remain you there prisoner vntil the pleasure of the king your father be further known. With which words, being abashed, and also wondering at the maruellous grauitie of that worshipfull Justice, the prince layeng his weapon apart, doing reuerence, departed, and went to the kings bench as he was commanded. Whereat his seruants disdaining, came & shewed the king all the whole affaire. Whereat he a while studieng, after, as a man all rauished with gladnes, holding his hands and eies towards heauen, abraid with a loude voice: O mercifull God! how much am I bound to thy infinit goodnes, especially for that thou hast giuen me a Judge, who feareth not to minister iustice, and also a sonne, who can suffer semblably and obey iustice. Now (saith Thomas Eliot) here a man may behold three persons worthy memory: first a Judge, who being a subiect feared not to execute iustice on the eldest sonne of his soueraigne lord, and by the order of nature his successour. Also a prince, and sonne and heire of the K. in the middest of his folly, more considered his euill example, and the Judges conscience in iustice, than his owne estate or wilfull appetite. Thirdly, a noble king and wise father, who contrary to the custome of parents, reioyced to see his sonne, and the heire of his crowne, to be for his disobedience by his subiect corrected: wherefore I co[n]clude, that nothing is more honorable or to be desired in a prince, or noble man, than placability, as contrariwise nothing is so detestable,

or to be feared in such a one as wrath & cruel
malignitee. (pp. 547–8)

## THE ACCESSION OF HENRY THE FIFTH

To this noble prince (by assent of parliament) all
the estates of the realme, after three daies, offered to
do fealtie before he was crowned, or had solemnized
his oth, well and iustly to gouerne the common
weale, which offer, before was neuer found to be
made to any prince of England.

The king gaue them al generally thanks, for their
good mindes towards him, and therewith exhorted
them to the zeale of the publike prosperitie &
honour of the Realme. If any man had offended him,
he pardoned their trespas, and desired hartily of
God that if he should rule and do all things well to
the honour of God and the prosperous commoditie
of the realme, that then God would suffer him to be
crowned. But if his fortune should be to do otherwise,
that then God should take him to his mercy, and
suffer him rather to be buried than to enterprise the
charge of the realme. (p. 549)

## DISMISSAL OF THE SCAPEGRACES

After which coronation, he called vnto him all
those yoong lords and gentlemen that were the
folowers of his yoong actes, to euery one of whom he
gaue rich and bounteous gifts, and then commanded
that as many as would change their maners as he
intended to do, should abide with him in his court,
and to all that would perseuer in their former light
conuersation, he gaue expresse commandement
vpon paine of their heads, neuer after that day to
come in his presence. (p. 549)

## 4. Sir Thomas Elyot: 'The Boke named the Gouernour' (1531)

The most renomed prince, kynge Henry the fifte, late kynge of
Englande, durynge the life of his father was noted to be fierce and
of wanton courage: it hapned that one of his seruantes, whom he
well fauored, for felony by hym committed, was arrayned at the
kynges benche: wherof he being aduertised, and incensed by light
persones aboute hym, in furious rage came hastily to the barre,

where his seruant stode as a prisoner: and commaunded hym to be vngyued and sette at libertie: where at all men were abasshed, reserued the chiefe iustice, who humbly exhorted the prince to be contented, that his seruaunt mought be ordred accordyng to the auncient lawes of this realme: or if he wolde haue hym saued from the rigour of the lawes, that he shuld optaine, if he moughte of the kynge his father his gracious pardone: wherby no lawe or iustice shulde be derogate. with which answere the prince nothynge appeased, but rather more inflamed, endeuored hym selfe to take away his seruaunt. The iuge consideringe the perilous example and inconuenience that moughte therby ensue: with a valiant spirite and courage, commaunded the prince vpon his alegeance, to leaue the prisoner, and departe his way. with whiche commandment the prince being set all in a fury, all chafed & in a terrible maner, came vp to the place of iugement, men thinkyng that he wolde haue slayne the iuge, or haue done to hym some damage: but the iuge sittyng styll without mouynge, declarynge the maiestie of the kynges place of iugement, And with an assured and bolde countenance, hadde to the prince these wordes folowyng. Sir remembre your selfe: I kepe here the place of the king your soueraigne lorde and father, to whom ye owe double obedience, wherfore eftsones in his name, I charge you desiste of your wilfulness, and vnlaufull entreprise: & from hensforth gyue good example to those, whiche hereafter shall be your propre subiectes: And nowe for your contempt and disobedience, go you to the prisone of the kynges benche, where vnto I committe you: and remayne ye there prisoner, vntill the pleasure of the kyng your father be further knowen. with whiche wordes beinge abasshed, and also wondrynge at the meruailous grauitie of that worshipful Iustice, the noble prince layinge his waipon aparte, doinge reuerence departed, and wente to the kynges benche, as he was commaunded. wherat his seruantes disdainyng, came and shewed to the kynge all the hole affaire. wherat he a whiles studienge, after as a man all rauisshed with gladnesse, holdyng his eien and handes vp towarde heauen, abrayded sayinge with a loude voice: O mercifull god, howe moche am I aboue all other men bounde to your infinite goodnes: specially for that ye haue gyuen me a iuge, who feareth nat to ministre iustice, And also a sonne who can suffre semblably and obey iustice?

(Sig. P. vii$^r$—P. viii$^v$)

5. *Anon.*: '*The Famous Victories of Henry the Fifth: Containing the Honourable Battell of Agin-court*' (*1598*)—passages utilized for the second part of *Henry IV*.[1]

BRAWLING IN EASTCHEAP

[Sc. ii]

*Enter the Vintners boy.*

*Boy.* How now good man Cobler?

*Cob.* How now Robin, what makes thou abroad
At this time of night? [92]

*Boy.* Marrie I haue beene at the Counter,
I can tell such newes as neuer you haue heard the like.

*Cobler.* What is that Robin, what is the matter?

*Boy.* Why this night about two houres ago, there came [96] the young Prince, and three or foure more of his companions, and called for wine good store, and then they sent for a noyse of Musitians, and were very merry for the space of an houre, then whether their Musicke liked them not, or [100] whether they had drunke too much Wine or no, I cannot tell, but our pots flue against the wals, and then they drew their swordes, and went into the streete and fought, and some tooke one part, & some tooke another, but for the space [104] of halfe an houre, there was such a bloodie fray as passeth, and none coulde part them vntill such time as the Maior and Sheriffe were sent for, and then at the last with much adoo, they tooke them, and so the yong Prince was carried [108] to the Counter, and then about one houre after, there came a Messenger from the Court in all haste from the King, for my Lord Maior and the Sheriffe, but for what cause I know not.... [112]

THE ASSAULT ON THE LORD CHIEF JUSTICE

[Sc. iv]

*Enter Lord chiefe Iustice, Clarke of the Office, Iayler, Iohn Cobler, Dericke, and the Theefe.*

*Iudge.* Iayler bring the prisoner to the barre.

*Der.* Heare you my Lord, I pray you bring the bar to the prisoner.

*Iudge.* Hold thy hand vp at the barre. [4]

*Theefe.* Here it is my Lord.

*Iudge.* Clearke of the Office, reade his inditement.

*Cleark.* What is thy name?

---

1. The original (1598) is in black letter. Scene- and line-divisions here are from the Praetorius-Daniel facsimile, 1887.

*Theefe.* My name was knowne before I came here, [8]
    And shall be when I am gone, I warrant you.

*Iudge.* I, I thinke so, but we will know it better before thou go.

*Der.* Sownes and you do but send to the next Iaile, [12]
    We are sure to know his name,
    For this is not the first prison he hath bene in, ile warrant you.

*Clearke.* What is thy name?

*Theef.* What need you to aske, and haue it in writing. [16]

*Clearke.* Is not thy name Cutbert Cutter?

*Theefe.* What the Diuell need you ask, and know it so well.

*Clearke.* Why then Cutbert Cutter, I indite thee by the name of
    [20] Cutbert Cutter, for robbing a poore carrier the 20 day of
    May last past, in the fourteen yeare of the raigne of our
    soueraigne Lord King Henry the fourth, for setting vpon a
    poore Carrier vpon Gads hill in Kent, and hauing [24] beaten
    and wounded the said Carrier, and taken his goods from him.

*Der.* Oh maisters stay there, nay lets neuer belie the man, for he
    hath not beaten and wounded me also, but hee [28] hath
    beaten and wounded my packe, and hath taken the great rase
    of Ginger, that bouncing Besse with the iolly buttocks should
    haue had, that greeues me most.

*Iudge.* Well, what sayest thou, art thou guiltie, or not [32] guiltie?

*Theefe.* Not guiltie, my Lord.

*Iudge.* By whom wilt thou be tride?

*Theefe.* By my Lord the young Prince, or by my selfe [36] whether
    you will.

        *Enter the young Prince, with Ned and Tom.*

*Hen. 5.* Come away my lads, Gogs wounds ye villain, what make
    you heere? I must goe about my businesse my selfe, and you
    must stand loytering here. [40]

*Theefe.* Why my Lord, they haue bound me, and will not let me
    goe.

*Hen. 5.* Haue they bound thee villain, why how now my Lord?
                                      [44]

*Iudge.* I am glad to see your grace in good health.

*Hen. 5.* Why my Lord, this is my man,
    Tis maruell you knew him not long before this,
    I tell you he is a man of his hands. [48]

*Theefe.* I Gogs wounds that I am, try me who dare.

*Iudge.* Your Grace shal finde small credit by acknowledging him to
    be your man.

*Hen. 5.* Why my Lord, what hath he done? [52]

*Iud.* And it please your Maiestie, he hath robbed a poore Carrier.

*Der.* Heare you sir, marry it was one Dericke,
  Goodman Hoblings man of Kent.

*Hen. 5.* What wast you butten-breech?                    [56]
  Of my word my Lord, he did it but in iest.

*Der.* Heare you sir, is it your mans qualitie to rob folks in iest? In
  faith, he shall be hangd in earnest.

*Hen. 5.* Well my Lord, what do you meane to do with [60] my
  man?

*Iudg.* And please your grace, the law must passe on him,
  According to iustice, then he must be executed.

*Der.* Heare you sir, I pray you, is it your mans quality [64] to rob
  folkes in iest? In faith he shall be hangd in iest.

*Hen. 5.* Well my Lord, what meane you to do with my man?

*Iudg.* And please your grace the law must passe on him    [68]
  According to iustice, then he must be executed.

*Hen. 5.* Why then belike you meane to hang my man?

*Iudge.* I am sorrie that it falles out so.

*Hen. 5.* Why my Lord, I pray ye who am I?                 [72]

*Iud.* And please your Grace, you are my Lord the yong Prince, our
  King that shall be after the decease of our soueraigne Lord,
  King Henry the fourth, whom God graunt long to raigne. [76]

*Hen. 5.* You say true my Lord:
  And you will hang my man.

*Iudge.* And like your grace, I must needs do iustice.

*Hen. 5.* Tell me my Lord, shall I haue my man?            [80]

*Iudge.* I cannot my Lord.

*Hen. 5.* But will you not let him go?

*Iud.* I am sorie that his case is so ill.

*Hen. 5.* Tush, case me no casings, shal I haue my man?    [84]

*Iudge.* I cannot, nor I may not my Lord.

*Hen. 5.* Nay, and I shal not say, & then I am answered?

*Iudge.* No.

*Hen. 5.* No: then I will haue him.                       [88
          *He giueth him a boxe on the eare.*

*Ned.* Gogs wounds my Lord, shal I cut off his head?

*Hen. 5.* No, I charge you draw not your swords,
  But get you hence, prouide a noyse of Musitians,
  Away, be gone.                        *Exeunt the Theefe.* [92]

*Iudge.* Well my Lord, I am content to take it at your hands.

*Hen. 5.* Nay and you be not, you shall haue more.

*Iudge.* Why I pray you my Lord, who am I?                 [96]

*Hen. 5.* You, who knowes not you?
  Why man, you are Lord chiefe Iustice of England.

*Iudge.* Your Grace hath said truth, therfore in striking me in this
place, you greatly abuse me, and not me onely, [100] but also
your father: whose liuely person here in this place I doo represent. And therefore to teach you what prerogatiues meane, I
commit you to the Fleete, vntill we haue spoken with your
father.                                                                                    [104]

*Hen. 5.* Why then belike you meane to send me to the Fleete?

*Iudge.* I indeed, and therefore carry him away.

*Exeunt Hen. 5. with the Officers.*

*Iudge.* Iayler, carry the prisoner to Newgate againe, [108] vntil the
next Sises.

*Iay.* At your commandement my Lord, it shalbe done.

THE TAKING OF THE CROWN
[Sc. viii]

*Enter the King with his Lords.*

*Hen. 4.* Come my Lords, I see it bootes me not to take any phisick,
for all the Phisitians in the world cannot cure me, no not one.
But good my Lords, remember my last wil and Testament
concerning my sonne, for truly my [4] Lordes, I doo not thinke
but he will proue as valiant and victorious a King, as euer
raigned in England.

*Both.* Let heauen and earth be witnesse betweene vs, if we accomplish not thy wil to the vttermost.                                       [8]

*Hen. 4.* I giue you most vnfained thāks, good my lords,
Draw the Curtaines and depart my chamber a while,
And cause some Musicke to rocke me a sleepe.

*He sleepeth.*                                                                *(Exeunt Lords.*

*Enter the Prince.*

*Hen. 5.* Ah Harry, thrice vnhappie, that hath neglect so [12] long
from visiting of thy sicke father, I wil goe, nay but why doo I
not go to the Chamber of my sick father, to comfort the melancholy soule of his bodie, his soule said I, here is his bodie indeed, but his soule is, whereas it needs no bo[16]die. Now
thrice accursed Harry, that hath offended thy father so much,
and could not I craue pardon for all. Oh my dying father,
curst be the day wherin I was borne, and accursed be the
houre wherin I was begotten, buṭ what shal [20] I do? if
weeping teares which come too late, may suffice the negligence
neglected to some, I wil weepe day and night vntil the foun-
taine be drie with weeping.                                             *Exit.*

*Enter Lord of Exeter and Oxford.*

*Exe.* Come easily my Lord, for waking of the King.          [24]

*Hen. 4.*  Now my Lords.

*Oxf.*  How doth your Grace feele your selfe?

*Hen. 4.*  Somewhat better after my sleepe,
  But good my Lords take off my Crowne,    [28]
  Remoue my chaire a litle backe, and set me right.

*Ambo.*  And please your grace, the crown is takē away.

*Hen. 4.*  The Crowne taken away,
  Good my Lord of Oxford, go see who hath done this
   deed:    [32]
  No doubt tis some vilde traitor that hath done it,
  To depriue my sonne, they that would do it now,
  Would seeke to scrape and scrawle for it after my death.
    *Enter Lord of Oxford with the Prince.*

*Oxf.*  Here and please your Grace,    [36]
  Is my Lord the yong Prince with the Crowne.

*Hen. 4.*  Why how now my sonne?
  I had thought the last time I had you in schooling,
  I had giuen you a lesson for all,    [40]
  And do you now begin againe?
  Why tel me my sonne,
  Doest thou thinke the time so long,
  That thou wouldest haue it before the    [44]
  Breath be out of my mouth?

*Hen. 5.*  Most soueraign Lord, and welbeloued father,
  I came into your Chamber to comfort the melancholy
  Soule of your bodie, and finding you at that time  [48]
  Past all recouerie, and dead to my thinking,
  God is my witnesse: and what should I doo,
  But with weeping tears lament ẙ death of you my father,
  And after that, seeing the Crowne, I tooke it:  [52]
  And tel me my father, who might better take it then I,
  After your death? but seeing you liue,
  I most humbly render it into your Maiesties hands,
  And the happiest man aliue, that my father liue:  [56]
  And liue my Lord and Father, for euer.

*Hen. 4.*  Stand vp my sonne,
  Thine answere hath sounded wel in mine eares,
  For I must need confesse that I was in a very sound sleep, [60]
  And altogither vnmindful of thy comming:
  But come neare my sonne,
  And let me put thee in possession whilst I liue,
  That none depriue thee of it after my death.  [64]

*Hen. 5.*  Well may I take it at your maiesties hands,

But it shal neuer touch my head, so lōg as my father liues.
*He taketh the Crowne.*

*Hen. 4.*  God giue thee ioy my sonne,
 God blesse thee and make thee his seruant,   [68]
 And send thee a prosperous raigne.
 For God knowes my sonne, how hardly I came by it,
 And how hardly I haue maintained it.

*Hen. 5.*  Howsoeuer you came by it, I know not,   [72]
 But now I haue it from you, and from you I wil keepe it:
 And he that seekes to take the Crowne from my head,
 Let him looke that his armour be thicker then mine,
 Or I will pearce him to the heart,   [76]
 Were it harder then brasse or bollion.

*Hen. 4.*  Nobly spoken, and like a King.
 Now trust me my Lords, I feare not but my sonne
 Will be as warlike and victorious a Prince,   [80]
 As euer raigned in England.

*L. Ambo.*  His former life shewes no lesse.

*Hen. 4.*  wel my lords, I know not whether it be for sleep,
 Or drawing neare of drowsie summer of death,   [84]
 But I am verie much giuen to sleepe,
 Therefore good my Lords and my sonne,
 Draw the Curtaines, depart my Chamber,
 And cause some Musicke to rocke me a sleepe.   [88]
    *Exeunt omnes.*

         *The King dieth.*


EXPECTATIONS OF ANARCHY
[Sc. ix]
    *Enter the Theefe.*

*Theefe.*  Ah God, I am now much like to a Bird
 Which hath escaped out of the Cage,
 For so soone as my Lord chiefe stustice [sic] heard
 That the old King was dead, he was glad to let me go, [4]
 For feare of my Lord the yong Prince:
 But here comes some of his companions,
 I wil see and I can get any thing of them,
 For old acquaintance.   [8]
    *Enter Knights raunging.*

*Tom.*  Gogs wounds, the King is dead.

*Ioc.*  Dead, then gogs blood, we shall be all kings.

*Ned.*  Gogs wounds, I shall be Lord chiefe Iustice
 Of England.   [12]

*Tom.* Why how, are you broken out of prison?
*Ned.* Gogs wounds, how the villaine stinkes.
*Ioc.* Why what wil become of thee now?
  Fie vpon him, how the rascall stinkes. [16]
*Theef.* Marry I wil go and serue my maister againe.
*Tom.* Gogs blood, doost think that he wil haue any such
  Scab'd knaue as thou art? what man he is a king now.
*Ned.* Hold thee, heres a couple of Angels for thee, [20]
  And get thee gone, for the King wil not be long
  Before he come this way:
  And hereafter I wil tel the king of thee. *Exit Theefe.*
*Ioc.* Oh how it did me good, to see the king [24]
  When he was crowned:
  Me thought his seate was like the figure of heauen,
  And his person like vnto a God.
*Ned.* But who would haue thought, [28]
  That the king would haue changde his countenance so?
*Ioc.* Did you not see with what grace
  He sent his embassage into France? to tel the French king
  That Harry of England hath sent for the Crowne, [32]
  And Harry of England wil haue it.
*Tom.* But twas but a litle to make the people beeleeue,
  That he was sorie for his fathers death.

THE REJECTION
[Sc. ix]
                    *The Trumpet sounds.*
*Ned.* Gogs wounds, the king comes, [36]
  Lets all stand aside.
            *Enter the King with the Archbishop, and*
                *the Lord of Oxford.*
*Ioc.* How do you my Lord?
*Ned.* How now Harry? [40]
  Tut my Lord, put away these dumpes,
  You are a king, and all the realme is yours:
  What man, do you not remember the old sayings,
  You know I must be Lord chiefe Iustice of England,
  Trust me my lord, me thinks you are very much
    changed, [44]
  And tis but with a litle sorrowing, to make folkes beleeue
  The death of your father greeues you,
  And tis nothing so.
*Hen. 5.* I prethee Ned, mend thy maners, [48]

And be more modester in thy tearmes,
For my vnfeined greefe is not to be ruled by thy flattering
And dissembling talke, thou saist I am changed,
So I am indeed, and so must thou be, and that quickly,     [52]
Or else I must cause thee to be chaunged.

*Ioc.*  Gogs wounds how like you this?
Sownds tis not so sweete as Musicke.

*Tom.*  I trust we haue not offended your grace no way.     [56]

*Hen. 5.*  Ah Tom, your former life greeues me,
And makes me to abandō & abolish your company for euer
And therfore not vpō pain of death to approch my presence
By ten miles space, then if I heare wel of you,     [60]
It may be I wil do somewhat for you,
Otherwise looke for no more fauour at my hands,
Then at any other mans: And therefore be gone,
We haue other matters to talke on.     [64]

*Exeunt Knights.*

CONFIRMATION OF THE LORD CHIEF JUSTICE

[Sc. ix]

*Enters Lord chiefe Iustice of England.*     [184]

*Exe.*  Here is the King my Lord.

*Iustice.*  God preserue your Maiestie.

*Hen. 5.*  Why how now my lord, what is the matter?

*Iustice.*  I would it were vnknowne to your Maiestie.

*Hen. 5.*  Why what aile you?     [188]

*Iust.*  Your Maiestie knoweth my griefe well.

*Hen. 5.*  Oh my Lord, you remember you sent me to the Fleete, did
you not?

*Iust.*  I trust your grace haue forgotten that.     [192]

*Hen. 5.*  I truly my Lord, and for reuengement,
I haue chosen you to be my Protector ouer my Realme,
Vntil it shall please God to giue me speedie returne
Out of France.     [196]

*Iust.*  And if it please your Maiestie, I am far vnworthie
Of so high a dignitie.

*Hen. 5.*  Tut my Lord, you are not vnworthie,
Because I thinke you worthie:     [200]
For you that would not spare me,
I thinke wil not spare another,
It must needs be so, and therefore come,
Let vs be gone, and get our men in a readinesse.     [204]

*Exeunt omnes.*

RECRUITING METHODS

[Sc. x]

*Enter a Captaine, Iohn Cobler and his wife.*

*Cap.* Come, come, there's no remedie,
    Thou must needs serue the King.
*Iohn.* Good maister Captaine let me go,
    I am not able to go so farre. [4]
*Wife.* I pray you good maister Captaine,
    Be good to my husband.
*Cap.* Why I am sure he is not too good to serue ẙ king?
*Iohn.* Alasse no: but a great deale too bad, [8]
    Therefore I pray you let me go.
*Cap.* No, no, thou shalt go.
*Iohn.* Oh sir, I haue a great many shooes at home to Cobble. [12]
*Wife.* I pray you let him go home againe.
*Cap.* Tush I care not, thou shalt go.
*Iohn.* Oh wife, and you had beene a louing wife to me,
    This had not bene, for I haue said many times, [16]
    That I would go away, and now I must go
    Against my will.         *He weepeth.*

*Enters Dericke.*

*Der.* How now ho, *Basillus Manus*, for an old codpeece,
    Maister Captaine shall we away? [20]
    Sownds how now Iohn, what a crying?
    What make you and my dame there?
    I maruell whose head you will throw the stooles at,
    Now we are gone. [24]
*Wife.* Ile tell you, come ye cloghead,
    What do you with my potlid? heare you
    Will you haue it rapt about your pate?
        *She beateth him with her potlid.*
*Der.* Oh good dame, here he shakes her, [28]
    And I had my dagger here, I wold worie you al to peeces
    That I would.
*Wife.* Would you so, Ile trie that.

        *She beateth him.*
*Der.* Maister Captaine will ye suffer her? [32]
    Go too dame, I will go backe as far as I can,
    But and you come againe,
    Ile clap the law on your backe thats flat:
    Ile tell you maister Captaine what you shall do? [36]
    Presse her for a souldier, I warrant you,
    She will do as much good as her husband and I too.

*Enters the Theefe.*

Sownes, who comes yonder?

*Cap.* How now good fellow, doest thou want a maister?          [40]

*Theefe.* I truly sir.

*Cap.* Hold thee then, I presse thee for a souldier,
          To serue the king in France.

*Der.* How now Gads, what doest knowes thinkest?          [44]

*Theefe.* I, I knew thee long ago.

*Der.* Heare you maister Captaine?

*Cap.* What saist thou?

*Der.* I pray you let me go home againe.          [48]

*Cap.* Why what wouldst thou do at home?

*Der.* Marry I haue brought two shirts with me,
          And I would carry one of them home againe,
          For I am sure heele steale it from me,          [52]
          He is such a filching fellow.

*Cap.* I warrant thee he wil not steale it from thee,
          Come lets away.

*Der.* Come maister Captaine lets away,          [56]
          Come follow me.

*Iohn.* Come wife, lets part louingly.

*Wife.* Farewell good husband.

*Der.* Fie what a kissing and crying is here?          [60]
          Sownes, do ye thinke he wil neuer come againe?
          Why Iohn come away, doest thinke that we are so base
          Minded to die among French men?
          Sownes, we know not whether they will laie          [64]
          Vs in their Church or no: Come M. Captain, lets
              away.

*Cap.* I cannot staie no longer, therefore come away.

                                        *Exeunt omnes.*


## 6. John Eliot: 'Ortho-epia Gallica' (*1593*)

In an important article, 'Shakespeare's French Fruits', in the *Shakespeare Survey*, 6, 1953, pp. 79–90, Professor J. W. Lever points out a likely, indeed virtually certain, original in *Ortho-epia Gallica* for Pistol's classical learning; cf. II. iv. 163–4. Eliot is presenting the person of the Braggart and, as Lever remarks, 'the authentic Ur-Pistol may be heard at the top of his form':

Ho Caetzo great Diuel of hell, awake thy sleepie Cyclopes: Thou Vulcan who limpest with thy cosins Asteropes, Brontes, Steropes, Polyphemus and Pyracmon, I will set you a worke. I giue my selfe to an hundred pipes of old Diuels, in case that if you will not fight, I do not make you eat the two egges of Proserpina. . .

Where is this so furious Hercules? I would fight with him for a litle quarter of an houre. . .

Where is Hector that Troian Lad? I haue a great desire to breake a Lance against his Cuirace.

Where is Alexander, the great drunkard of Greece? I will make him drinke a carouse. To marciall men we must not spare good wine.

Where is Achilles the Grig, Captaine of the Mirmidons, I would send his soule by and by into hell.

Where is this pettie companion Ulysses? He should do me a message unto Pluto.

Where is this quaking-quiuering coward Julius Caesar? . . .

I feare death no more then a butterflie, or the tickling of a flea in mine eare: and as for me, I feare not to fight with a whole Army, if it be not of these mescreant Tartarians, Canniballes, Indians and Moscouites.

'Pistol's meaning may at last be expounded', Lever comments. 'What for him are the triumphs of Tamburlaine that he has heard Alleyn declaiming? Nothing to compare with the fustian boasts of his prototype in *Ortho-epia*. Single combats with all the Trojan Greeks, and the quavering-quivering coward Julius Caesar, are as nothing to him. But for that matter, why draw the line at Tartarians, Cannibals, and the like? He will take on Cannibals too! It is a worthy utterance: yet generation after generation of commentators has attributed to Pistol a certain confusion, to be expected only from such uninformed persons as the Hostess, between cannibals and Hannibal.'

# Appendix II

## HALL PROBABLY NOT A SOURCE

*Edward Hall: 'The Vnion of the two noble and illustrate famelies of Lancastre and Yorke' (1548, 1550).* The page references are to the 1809 reprint.

How far, if at all, Hall's chronicle contributed directly to Shakespeare's history plays has been much discussed. *2 Henry IV*, like *1 Henry IV*, gives no apparent sign of direct relationship.[1] Much of

1. For *1 Henry IV*, see New Arden edition, pp. 195–7.

Hall, admittedly, was transcribed into Holinshed and so contributed indirectly, and his general sense that from Richard II to Henry VIII English history had a providential shape and a moral bearing was widely influential in Tudor historiography.[1] But Shakespeare's version of the historical events in *2 Henry IV* appears to owe nothing to Hall at first hand. In one particular he differs radically. Hall explicitly attributes the suppression of the Archbishop's revolt to the King's vigour of movement in gathering his forces and marching northwards so fast as to take the rebels by surprise and seize the leaders. There is no word of Prince John of Lancaster or of Westmoreland, or, consequently, of the trick so disagreeably effective in Holinshed and Shakespeare.

One or two points may at first suggest Hall's influence. At the end of *1 Henry IV* and the beginning of *2 Henry IV* Hal accompanies his father against the Welsh. Holinshed has nothing of this, but Hall, while not mentioning the King's participation, does say that immediately after Shrewsbury the King 'sent into Wales with a great army prince Henry his eldest sonne against the said Owen' (Hall, p. 31). As a result the Welsh are dispersed and Owen dies miserably. But before one concludes Hall to be the source two things may be noted: one, that the Prince's leadership may have come from the *Myrroure for Magistrates* (cf. p. xxxvi, above), and secondly, that Shakespeare's pairing of the King and Prince is the natural step to balance the other joint leadership, that of Westmoreland and Prince John against the northern rebels. Were Hal left out, he would compare badly with the others of his family at the very moment he has redeemed himself to chivalry. Further, instead of making capital of Glendower's death immediately after Shrewsbury, Shakespeare tosses it in casually half-way through *2 Henry IV* (III. i. 103). He may have been misled by Holinshed's account of the slaughter of the Welsh and the capture of Owen's son in 1405; it is on this occasion that the Welshwomen's atrocities, merely alluded to earlier (Hol., iii. 20 and *1H4*, I. i. 43–6), are set forth in full (Hol., iii. 34); and there can be no doubt that the passage in Holinshed caught Shakespeare's eye. So the other point thought to indicate a contribution from Hall (for instance, by Professor Shaaber, New Var., 549)—that is, the bringing forward of Glendower's death from 1409 (as in Holinshed) to 1405, the time of the Archbishop's rebellion—is unsubstantial; the transfer is more likely to come from Holinshed's reference to Owen's loss of his son, or from Stow, who relates this loss immediately before the northern conspiracy is described (*Annales*, p. 529).

1. Cf. Tillyard, pp. 40 ff.

# Appendix III

## II. i. 88: THE SINGING-MAN OF WINDSOR

The discussion occasioned by this mysterious person is set forth by E. Brennecke, 'Shakespeare's Singing-Man of Windsor' (*PMLA*, lxvi, 1951, pp. 1189–92). Singing-men were professional musicians in royal and university chapels and in cathedrals. They were in general well-reputed, but some Puritans, as Fuller says of one Dr Cornelius Burges, 'heauily aggravated the debauchednesse of Singingmen, not only uselesse, but hurtfull by their vicious conversations' (*Church History*, 1655; Cent. XVII, Bk xi. 179). Some non-Puritans derided them; Nashe has, 'he nodded with his nose like an olde singing man teaching a yong querister to keepe time', and 'coapes and costly vestments decke the hoarsest and beggerly-est singing-man' (*Unfortunate Traveller*; McKerrow, ii. 250, 317: this latter comment relates to a Roman festival). Best known is Earle's satire: 'The Common Singing-men in Cathedral Churches are a bad Society, and yet a Company of Good Fellowes, that roare deep in the Quire, deeper in the Tauerne. . . Their pastime or recreation is prayers, their exercise drinking, yet herein so religiously addicted that they serve God oftest when they are drunke' (*Microcosmographie*, 1628, no. 69). But why should a comparison to a singing-man, especially one of Windsor, be offensive? The clue may lie in Sir Philip Sidney's *Discourse to the Queen's Majesty* (1580), warning her against pretenders to the throne and against foreign connections (the Anjou marriage). He writes: 'Lett the singing man in Henry the IV[ths] time, Perkin Warbeck in your grand-fathers . . . be sufficient to prove that occasions geve mindes scope to stranger thinges then ever would haue ben imagined' (*Works*, ed. Feuillerat, iii. 53). In *Memoirs of . . . Sir Philip Sidney* (1808, p. 126), Thomas Zouch suggested that this false-pretender singing-man was John Magdalen, the priest used as Richard II's double in the Abbot of Westminster's conspiracy during Henry IV's first year (Hol., iii. 9–13; Stow, *Annales*, pp. 515–16). Though he is not said to sing, he was 'a Chaplaine of K. Richard' (Stow, p. 515), 'one of king Richards chappell' (Hol., iii. 10). He is not said to belong to Windsor, but the whole plot was directed towards that town, where the King was holding Christmas; it is repeatedly mentioned, and the plotters, with Magdalen dressed as Richard, tried to seize the King there. Shakespeare might associate Magdalen with St George's Chapel. Or some undiscovered source may have provided the links missing for the final identification. Any reference to

Henry IV as a pretender involved in a dethronement of the true king would certainly qualify Falstaff for a broken head.

## APPENDIX IV

### JUSTICE SHALLOW AND GLOUCESTERSHIRE

The conscientious insertion of locations by editors has concealed the fact, evident in the Quarto and Folio, that Shakespeare makes no mention of Gloucestershire as Justice Shallow's habitat until *2 Henry IV*, IV. iii. 80, 126–7. Shallow is 'a poor esquire of this county' in III. ii, but no county is named. Various places are mentioned in this scene, but only one suggests any clue as to Shallow's whereabouts. That one is his inquiry, 'How a good yoke of bullocks at Stamford fair?' (III. ii. 38). Even this, unfortunately, is confused by the fact that the Quarto reads 'Samforth'. Perceiving that Stamford is unconvincingly related to Gloucestershire, Arthur Gray suggested that 'Samforth' was meant for Tamworth (cited *2 Henry IV*, New Var., p. 241), but there seems no reason why Tamworth should be a claimant. The Folio provides a good number of authentic corrections, so Stamford is in all probability correct here, since its fair was a notable one. Elizabethan fairs were certainly matters of more than local concern. Yet if, in III. ii, Shallow really is thought of as in Gloucestershire, an inquiry after Stamford prices is hardly what one would expect. Were it not for the information provided later (in IV. iii and V. i), one would assume that he lived not far from the Great North Road, somewhere in Lincolnshire perhaps, where prices ruling at Stamford would be of immediate interest.

Arthur Gray's remark—'Falstaff comes to Gloucestershire, of all unlikely places, to raise soldiers for the war in Yorkshire'[1]—represents much critical comment. A characteristic observation is C. H. Herford's:

> The scene of Falstaff's 'recruiting' is laid in Gloucestershire, which is as far off the route to the north as were his recruits from being serviceable soldiers. His former recruiting, for Shrewsbury, (described in *1 Henry IV*, IV. ii), had been duly carried out on the line of march . . .; but it was clearly more 'Falstaffian' to make a jest of 'honour' in his choice of a route as well as in his choice of men.[2]

1. A. Gray, *A Chapter in the Early Life of Sh.*, 1926, p. 75.
2. Warwick Shakespeare, *2 Henry IV*, head-note to III. ii.

Dover Wilson comments similarly:

> The scene is far from the road to the north; but if Prince John
> and the 'dozen captains' are in a hurry, Falstaff is not, and the
> route he takes enables Shakespeare to give us a glimpse of life in
> his own district.[1]

But if, at this point of the play, Shakespeare in fact thought of him
as in Lincolnshire, Falstaff's supposed irresponsibility in going to
York *via* the west country is dispelled. It is true that he is a slow
starter. At i. ii. 62–4 he is 'going with some charge to the Lord John
of Lancaster, . . . to York', but at ii. i. 63–5, 181–2, the Lord Chief
Justice chides him for loitering, since he should be impressing
soldiers *en route*, and at ii. iv. 355–7, 368–9, a dozen captains are
urgently seeking him. Yet once he has started, he *is* in a hurry, *pace*
Dover Wilson. He will drink with Shallow but, surprisingly, 'cannot stay dinner' (iii. ii. 186–7); he 'must a dozen mile tonight' (*ibid.*,
285). Having delayed in leaving London (yet not more than Prince
Hal) he still reaches Gaultree in time to round up an important,
if absurd, captive, before the pursuit has yet ended. Shakespeare
sometimes uses dramatic time and place elastically, it is true; but
in this instance we may well conclude, with Maurice Morgann,
that 'it appears then manifestly that *Shakespeare* meant to shew
*Falstaff* as really using the utmost speed in his power; he arrives [at
Gaultree] almost literally *within the extremest inch of possibility*' (*On
The Dramatic Character of Sir John Falstaff*, 1777, p. 88). When Gaultree is over and he is due to return, it transpires that his second visit
to Shallow is to take place in Gloucestershire, and thereafter the
place-names relate to that county. But up to the arrival at Gaultree
it would seem that Shakespeare thought of Falstaff as setting off
northwards, calling on Shallow not far from Stamford, and continuing without delay to York; only afterwards did he send him
back on a long digression. He either did not think it necessary or
did not bother to harmonize the two journeys, and indeed the discrepancy has escaped notice. Why he apparently shifted the location thus can hardly be ascertained. But Falstaff, as it seems, should
be relieved of one slur at least on his military reputation.

---

1. New Cambridge Shakespeare, *2 Henry IV*, head-note to iii. ii.

## APPENDIX V

### GAULTREE

A scholarly discussion of Prince John's stratagem is to be found in an article by Paul A. Jorgensen entitled 'The "Dastardly Treachery" of Prince John of Lancaster'.[1] Dr Jorgensen assembles a battery of critical protests, from Johnson onwards, against Prince John's trick; he points out not only that Shakespeare exceeds his sources in attributing it to John rather than to Westmoreland but also that, had he so wished, Shakespeare could have shown the royal cause as triumphing rather in the heroic battle of Bramham than in the subterfuge of Gaultree. In Elizabethan drama, and in early accounts of military tactics, cunning and perfidy are normally reprobated, as they are in Thomas Heywood's *1 King Edward IV*—

> We have no trickes nor policies of warre,
> But by the antient custom of our fathers
> We'll soundly lay it on.[2]

Thomas Proctor's *Of the Knowledge and Conducte of Warres* (1578) is equally unambiguous:

> The Captayne [General] ought to flye from the faulte of infi-delitie and untrothe, as from a rocke. For there is no regarde to bee hadde of the man that is not iust and honest, and firme of his woorde, but fycle and variable of promise, which ought alwaies to bee perfourmed towardes souldiours, frende, & enemie.[3]

Most relevant to Prince John's case is a citation from Bertrand De Loque's *Discourse of Warre and Single Combat* (trans. J. Eliot, 1591): De Loque (p. 33) holds up as a horrifying case of treachery the action of Cleomenes,

> who having confirmed a truce with the Argians for 7. dayes, the third night after set upon them whilest they were all sleeping, and so slewe and ouerthrew them all, alledging for his reason, that the truce he concluded, was made for the daies, and not for the nightes.

1. *PMLA*, lxxvi, Dec. 1961, pp. 488–92.    2. *Works* (Shepherd), i. 17.
3. *Op. cit.*, fol. 17. Other evidence is cited from Marlowe, *2 Tamburlaine*, Shakespeare, *1 Henry VI* and *Antony and Cleopatra*, Barnaby Rich, *Allarme to England* (1578), and Thomas Rogers, *The Anatomie of the Minde* (1576); Jorgensen, *op. cit.*, p. 489. One might add Elyot's *Gouernour* (1531) which asserts that even towards enemies 'consideration aught to be had of iustyce and honestie' (Bk iii, ch. v).

But during the 1590's the growing stress and wearisomeness of military campaigns produced, it seems, a mood in which the end appeared to justify the means. (To say this is not to blink the recurrent alliance, at all times and in all places, of politics and perfidy.) Again relevant to Prince John's case is the assertion in Lodowick Lloyd's *Stratagems of Jerusalem* (1602) that 'all stratagems, victories, & good counsell cometh from the Lord' (sig. A2ᵛ), a point of view with which, as Dr Jorgensen observes, John would be in full accord. In particular, the long struggle against the elusive enemy in Ireland was reducing the English government to desperation and unscrupulousness. Tyrone hoodwinked the English forces so often that Camden comments:

> I am weary of running over the particular clokes of his dissimulation. In a word, when any danger threatned him from the English, hee then both in countenance and words bare such a feigned shew of submission, and pretended such penitency for his faults, that he deluded them till the opportunity of prosecuting him was lost.[1]

The Irish were equally bitter about perfidious Albion, and indeed Elizabeth and her Privy Council ordered every means to be used, honourable or not, to reduce the enemy. *Raison d'état* was, naturally, improved by piety. Celebrating a victory of Sir John Norris over rebels in Brittany, an anonymous writer comments:

> Whereby we may see how God rebateth the edge of rebels harts, daunteth their courages and ranverseth their actions with his byblows or unlooked-for counterbuffs.[2]

Elizabethan audiences, then, Dr Jorgensen argues, would probably accept John's unlooked-for counterbuff without enthusiasm but with a sense that war requires it, and that commanders are by nature speciously pious. The kind of victory Shakespeare chooses to show reflects the tenor of the time, a tenor which owed something of its 'realism' to the influence of Machiavelli but more to political desperation.[3]

1. William Camden, *The Historie of . . . Princess Elizabeth*, 1630, iv. 88.
2. Anon., *The True Reporte of the Service in Britanie Performed lately by the Honourable Knight Sir Iohn Norreys . . . before Guingand*, 1591, sig. A3.
3. One need not, however, divide the sixteenth century into an early honourable era and a late dishonourable. Long before Machiavelli or the Irish campaigns made themselves felt, Sir Thomas Elyot has a splendidly sardonic remark in *The Gouernour* (1531)—'That maner of injurie, which is done with fraude and deceyte, is at this present tyme so communely practised, that if it be but a litle, it is called policie, and if it be moche and with a visage of grauitie, it is then named and accounted for wisedome' (III. iv).

Dr Jorgensen, then, helpfully puts Gaultree into a contemporary context. He does not make it palatable nor does he claim to. If the rebels, having superior numbers, can be beaten only by deceit, Shakespeare seems not only to swallow the trickery as a historical fact but to make less of a gulp than the chroniclers.[1] What now sticks in the throat is the combination of trickery with gratitude to God. It is one thing to hold, as Carlisle does to the wavering Richard II, that 'The means that Heaven yields must be embrac'd'; it is another to behave as John and Westmoreland do, and one would welcome some more serious sign that Shakespeare found John disagreeable than Falstaff's satire on 'demure boys' in IV. iii. At the same time it should be recognized how powerful was the doctrine that rebellion itself was sacrilege. A characteristic position is that of Archbishop Sandys, who, basing himself on St Paul's injunction, 'Be thou subject to the higher powers', exhorts his hearers to obey rulers and magistrates, in the following words:

God hath placed him [the magistrate] and ordained him to be thy governor; in respect whereof thou art bound for thy conscience sake towards God for to obey him. Another reason why every soul should live in subjection to the higher powers is, because *whosoever resisteth the ordinance of God, provoketh the judgment of God against himself.* . . *Resisters and rebels receive to themselves condemnation; they never have, neither ever shall, escape the heavy hand of God's wrath.* . . Withdraw not thyself from obedience . . . for if the bad were not bridled more by the authority of the magistrate, than by any moderation in themselves, they would eat up the good; and a wonderful confusion would soon follow. . . It is not a strange, or a new custom, to pay custom [sic] to princes: all nations, all people, have ever used it and yielded it; and magistrates well deserve it. For their office is both painful and chargeable. . . These magistrates must be supported. . . Pay unto the magistrate obedience, fear, honour, tribute, custom; all this is due unto him, all this is thy debt. . . *God is still the same God: he hateth iniquity, and will not suffer conspiracy, rebellion, or treason against lawful magistrates either unrevealed or unrevenged.*[2]

1. In the play the numbers of the opposing sides are uncertain; the King thinks the rebels to be 'fifty thousand strong' but Westmoreland rejoins that rumour has doubled their numbers (III. i. 95–8). The King's army, the rebels are informed, is thirty thousand, and this, Mowbray comments, is the number expected (IV. i. 21–3). But there is no clear evidence. In Holinshed, however, the rebels, with 'at the least twentie thousand men', are reported 'farre stronger in number of people than the other' (Hol., iii. 37), and Westmoreland, who 'perceiued the force of the aduersaries', has reason to resort to deceit.

2. 11th Sermon of *The Sermons of Edwin Sandys*, ed. J. Ayres, Parker Soc., 1841, pp. 198–200. This sermon was delivered c. 1580–5, published in 1585. Italics not in the original.

With this in mind, the following considerations may explain
Shakespeare's treatment of Gaultree. First, Northumberland's
outburst (I. i. 150–60) is so nihilistic that even his adherents protest and, though he abandons the rebels, an invitation to total
chaos has been issued. Lord Bardolph speaks of the rebellion as the
whole subversion of the realm—'almost to pluck a kingdom down /
And set another up' (I. iii. 49–50). Second, by using the persuasions
of the Church, the Archbishop sacrilegiously 'turns insurrection to
religion' (I. i. 200–6); in Holinshed he makes the most questionable
use of his spiritual office, 'promising forgiueness of sinnes to all
them, whose hap it was to die in the quarrell' (Hol., iii. 36). How
heinous this behaviour was can be gauged by reference to Sandys's
condemnation. And third, even if the Archbishop avoided the sin
of sacrilege, his office should have kept him from sharing in, still
more from leading, a rebellion over grievances 'the reforming
whereof', says Holinshed, 'did not yet apperteine vnto him'. This is
a point which Westmoreland and Prince John take up (IV. i. 30–52;
IV. ii. 4–30). Revering the established order, Shakespeare may have
held too uncritically the maxim *salus populi suprema lex*. But one
must not overlook the fact that into the play he wrote the strongest
possible indications that the rebellion was ill-conceived, sacrilegious, destructive, hastily raised on flimsy pretexts and, whatever
good intentions may have gone into it, promising nothing but
chaos.[1]

# Appendix VI

## THE CONTINUITY OF SCENES IN ACT IV,
### i–ii, and iv–v

The action is unbroken in QF between Act IV, scenes i and ii; cf.
IV. i. 228, note. To think of the scenes as separate entities, calling
for changes of place, is misleading. More important, the action
is also unbroken in QF in Act IV between scenes iv and v, even
though it envisages a change of place from the Jerusalem chamber
(where the King swoons), to some other, and back again. To carry
the King out and in again, interrupting his speech, is wrong. A

1. A recent comment is interesting—'Modern critics have regarded [Gaul-
tree] as a proof of moral turpitude, but wrongly. Almost any trickery was justified
in dealing with rebels, and John of Lancaster's verbal quibble . . . was a per-
missible if unheroic device. He must not be made heroic lest he overshadow his
brother, but he is brought to our notice as a clever and promising prince';
Geoffrey Bullough, *Narrative and Dramatic Sources of Sh.*, 1962, iv. 258–9.

modern producer will manage by changing stage-position, lighting, curtains, and so on, while the King is on-stage. How the scene was arranged originally is not clear. The essential movements are (*a*) entrance (or disclosure) of the King at IV. iv. 1 (whether on inner or outer stage); (*b*) transport without break of action at IV. iv. 132 (from one part of the stage to another); and (*c*) re-transport at IV. v. 239–40 to the spot where the King swooned. *The Famous Victories*, sc. viii, offers tantalizing hints merely. Here the King is very ill from the beginning, and reclines in a chair. Having addressed the lords he says, 'Draw the Curtaines and depart my chamber a while, / And cause some Musicke to rocke me a sleepe' (ll. 10–11). This sounds as if he is on the inner stage, the curtains of which are to be closed, but he cannot be, for the Prince enters, sees his 'dead' father, takes the crown (which the King seems to be wearing; l. 28) and leaves. The King revives, asks for his crown to be removed and his chair shifted, and notices the loss. After reconciliation with the Prince he again says, 'Draw the Curtaines, depart my Chamber, / And cause some Musicke to rocke me a sleepe' (ll. 87–8). Apart from indicating business with curtains this does not throw much light, and the duplication of ll. 10–11 at ll. 87–8 is suspicious.

# Appendix VII

## IV. v. 20–30: 'WHY DOTH THE CROWN LIE THERE...'

Though no Shakespearean debt is implied, Dr Harold Brooks suggests the following as a parallel in Hoccleve to the Prince's address to his father's crown. The tradition of the king who addressed his crown and lamented his lost safety and ease is interesting.

> Onës þer was a Kyng, as I haue rad,
> When his coronë was vn-to hym broght,
> Or he it tok, in thoght he stood al sad;
> And þus he seidë, after he had thoght:
> "O þou coronë, noble and faire y-wroght,
> What man þat þe receyueth or admittith,
> More esë þan he weneth from hym flittith.
>
> Who-so þe peril know, and charge and fere
> That is in the, thogh þou at therthe lay

He woldë noght the vp areyse or rere
But lat þe lyë stille, and go his way.

> (Hoccleve, *Regement of Princes*, *Works*, III, st. 311,
> ll. 2171–81, EETS, Extra ser., lxxii, 1897)

# APPENDIX VIII

## HENRY AND THE CRUSADE

The Machiavellian strain in Daniel's deathbed advice (see above, pp. 211–12) produces in Shakespeare an effect of curious ambiguity. In *Richard II*, v. vi. 49–50, Henry's motives for a crusade are purely penitential. In *2 Henry IV*, iv. v. 208–15, they seem purely Machiavellian. The intervening references to the subject are teasing, but were it not for what the King says on his deathbed one would not take them as based on duplicity. In Part 1, i. i. 9–27, Henry seems genuine in proposing, now that the *Richard II* risings are over, to carry out his penitential scheme of warring for the Holy Places; only by using the light of hindsight to read other intentions into the lines would one cavil at his motives. At Part 2, III. i. 107–8, his mournful ruminations lead to a renewed proposal for a crusade which again seems, in its context, to spring from a desire to make atonement to God rather than to work a shrewd political trick. The same can be said of his address at iv. iv. 1–10. In view of the 'policy' shown at Gaultree, it is of course natural to think that on his deathbed Henry is being practical-cynical, and that the Machiavellianism is his leading, indeed his only, motive. But unless, under Daniel's influence, Shakespeare has had a late change of mind, the tenor of the three preceding passages on the subject would suggest not that he here meant the King to be cynical but that in the press of composition he has taken Daniel over automatically and without adequate amendment.